POSITIVE APPROACHES TO PEACEBUILDING

POSITIVE APPROACHES TO PEACEBUILDING

A RESOURCE FOR INNOVATORS

EDITED BY

Cynthia Sampson

Mohammed Abu-Nimer

Claudia Liebler

Diana Whitney

PACT PUBLICATIONS ⁊ WASHINGTON, D.C.
2003

POSITIVE APPROACHES TO PEACEBUILDING:
A RESOURCE FOR INNOVATORS

First Printing.

PACT PUBLICATIONS
1200 18th Street, NW, Suite 350
Washington, D.C. 20036

www.pactpublications.com

Printed by
Kirby Lithographic Company, Inc.

Text set in ITC Berkeley Oldstyle

Library of Congress Catalog Card Number: 2003108625
ISBN 1-888753-25-0

TABLE OF CONTENTS

You are not here merely to make a living.
You are here to enable the world to live
more amply, with greater vision, and with
a finer spirit of hope and achievement.
You are here to enrich the world.
You impoverish yourself if you forget this errand.

WOODROW WILSON

ACKNOWLEDGEMENTS

*T*his volume is an outgrowth of a pioneering conference, "Positive Approaches to Peacebuilding: A Practitioners' Exploration," held at American University in Washington, D.C., September 28–29, 2001. We extend special appreciation to the Center for Global Peace, which hosted the conference, and in particular, to Center Director Dr. Abdul-Aziz Said and Associate Director Betty Sitka. We warmly acknowledge Jud Potter and Heather Woodman of Peace Discovery Initiatives for their abundant attention to conference management and the needs of participants, and our conference facilitators, David Cooperrider, Diana Whitney, Claudia Liebler, and Mohammed Abu-Nimer for leading us in a lively exploration and experience of new ideas. We also extend appreciation to the many peacebuilding organizations that served as co-conveners of the conference and Appreciative Inquiry practitioner groups that partnered with us in delivering the conference, all of which contributed in one form or another to ensure its success. Their names are listed below.

We extend our deep gratitude to the past and present members of the board of directors of Peace Discovery Initiatives (PDI)—John Cochran, Libby Hoffman, Bruce Jeffrey, Susan Macfarlane, Amy Potter, Cynthia Sampson, and Heather Woodman—who have had a vision for advancing the development of positive approaches to peacebuilding since the organization's founding in 1999. PDI initiated and staffed this project and has served as its secretariat throughout.

We wish to acknowledge three organizations that have provided special accompaniment and support for this work and the development of these ideas over a number of years: the United Religions Initiative, with special thanks to our colleagues, Barbara Hartford and Charles Gibbs; the Conflict Transformation Program of Eastern Mennonite University, whose faculty and staff have contributed to advancing these ideas through their courses, providing opportunities for us to share them, and by contributing to this book in various ways; and the instructors and staff of the former GEM Initiative of Case Western Reserve University, who welcomed a sole peacebuilder into their training course on Appreciative Inquiry for development practitioners and encouraged her many steps along the way. We're grateful for the opportunities we've had to share these ideas in learning environments in recent months, through training courses on Appreciative Inquiry for peacebuilders at American University, Eastern Mennonite University's Summer Peacebuilding Institute, with support from the United Religions Initiative

(URI), and the Caux Scholars Program in Switzerland, as well as at the URI Global Assembly in Rio de Janeiro. The participants in these events all enlivened our exploration and deepened our understanding of positive approaches to peacebuilding. We wish to acknowledge those individuals who offered chapters for the book but for whatever reason were unable to bring them to fruition. They, too, contributed their best thinking, and this book is the richer for them.

We are so grateful to our publisher, Pact Publications, and in particular, to Evan Bloom, who immediately embraced this book as significant, as well as to Sabrina Atwater, Christopher Bennett, Sarah Newhall, and Crystal Woods for their enthusiasm and tangible support in bringing this book to print. Extra special thanks go to Jeannie Ferber, who created the initial design for the book; Michelle Peña, who carried the graphic and typographical aspects of the book through to completion; and to Bill and Janet Todd, who provided the index.

Finally, we extend our deep appreciation to our funders, without whom none of the above would have been possible. The United States Institute of Peace provided a generous grant, although all opinions, findings, conclusions, and recommendations expressed herein are solely those of the authors. Major funding has come from Peace Discovery Initiatives and its generous contributors.

CO-CONVENING ORGANIZATIONS

Catholic Relief Services
Center for Global Peace, American University
Conflict Transformation Across Cultures (CONTACT), School for
    International Training
Conflict Transformation Program, Eastern Mennonite University
General Board of Church and Society and JUSTPEACE Center for Mediation
    and Conflict Resolution, The United Methodist Church
Institute for Conflict Analysis and Resolution, George Mason University
Institute for Multi-Track Diplomacy
International Alert
International Conflict Resolution Program, Columbia University
Peace Discovery Initiatives
Preventive Diplomacy Program, Center for Strategic and International
    Studies
Search for Common Ground
United Religions Initiative
West Africa Network for Peacebuilding
    Women Waging Peace

PARTNER ORGANIZATIONS

Appreciative Inquiry Resource eCentre

Corporation for Positive Change

Global Excellence in Management (GEM) Initiative, Case Western Reserve University

SIGMA Program for Human Cooperation and Global Action, Case Western Reserve University

Taos Institute

If you would sing the song of this land, you
must listen to the dreams of its inhabitants.
Only those who can feel the hope of the future
have the courage to undo the knots of the past.
If you are to sing free of fear, sing free of suffering,
then you must catch the dreams of your people and
dissolve them, liberating their future.

DAVID LA CHAPELLE

POSITIVE APPROACHES TO PEACEBUILDING:

A RESOURCE FOR INNOVATORS

We must form perfect models in thought and look at them continually, or we shall never carve them out in grand and noble lives.

MARY BAKER EDDY

INTRODUCTION

Cynthia Sampson

This book was born in the immediate aftermath of the terrorist attacks on the United States of September 11, 2001.
Seventeen days later, seventy-five people met for a working conference at American University, "Positive Approaches to Peacebuilding: A Practitioners' Exploration." In spite of the great turmoil in the country and world at that time, only one participant canceled her registration due to recent events, not she said, out of a fear of flying, but because if there was a war, she did not want to be so far away from home.

A year and a half later, as we readied this manuscript for publication, war clouds carrying American bombers were indeed darkening the skies, over Iraq.

What does this volume add to the global landscape of war making and peacebuilding? The draw for many who attended our conference was a yearning for "something new." This book attempts to feed that yearning.

It does not offer a peacemaking panacea, though. Panaceas are hard to come by in a world made jittery by terrorist destruction taken to new heights and a world whose superpower clings to the geopolitics of military might. Nor does the book offer a whole new way of doing things—a prescription for abandoning the old. Nothing could be more reckless, counterproductive, and disrespectful of our peacemaking forbearers.

But the "something new" here is different enough to stand apart and bring a distinctive new element to the peacebuilding mix. It is embryonic enough to be dismissed by many and discarded as fanciful by others; but may yet catch the eye of some—those given, perhaps, to adventuring and a certain amount of daring or "divine naiveté."[1]

Just days before U.S. and British troops were to invade Iraq, a former assistant secretary general of the United Nations and visionary of peace, Robert Muller, was seeing something quite remarkable on the global scene: "As unhappy as I am that war is upon us," he said, "I'm taking great comfort in what's going on in our world today. The world community is waging peace." History will record, he continued, that the twenty-first century began with the global community "in an unprecedented public conversation" about the legitimacy of the impending war. "It is tense, it is tough, it is challenging, but this kind of global conversation has not happened before on this scale. . . . This is a stunning new era of global listening, speaking, and responsibility. . . . This is what waging peace looks like. . . ." (2003).

3

This speech gave heart to many who were deeply concerned over the Middle East action. Even though this war would surely happen, Muller's vision implied that the world would not be the same on the other side of the war as it had been after all previous wars. This implication gave hope and flight to imagination on the part of some: "*How* will the postwar world be different in light of this new global conversation, and what can *I* do to help realize the promise of this new era of possibility?"

Although as we go to press it is too soon to know just how the world might be different in this now-postwar period, this story provides a timely illustration of the starting premise of this book. That is, without positive vision and an image of a better future that can draw our sights toward a new horizon, stir our energies, and give impulse to our actions, it is hard to know where we are headed and even harder to get there! It is in the writing of new narratives and the envisioning of new vistas that we can keep hope alive and chart a clearer and more sure path to a future of our choosing.

This book is about finding concrete ways for accomplishing these high goals and realizing new possibilities in peacebuilding. It asks no small amount from each of us, as readers. It asks us, first, to join together in valuing the best of our peacebuilding practice to date, some fine examples of which appear on these pages. It asks us, singly and together, to bring our own best imagining to how some new methods and approaches might be introduced or might enrich current practice in fresh new ways. It then invites us to courageously innovate in our own peacebuilding practice—or perhaps extend a supportive hand to others venturing to do so. It invites us into the conviction that a new world order is being born and that we are the co-creators of it. And for some of us, simply getting started—and reading on—may require a certain act of faith, the suspending of disbelief, or a healthy measure of divine naiveté.

Whatever the case, let's get started!

WHAT DO WE MEAN BY *POSITIVE APPROACHES?*

Positive approaches are a group of concepts, theories, and activities for working toward change in relationships, organizations, communities, and other human systems.[2] Developed predominantly in the organizational development, education and training, psychotherapy, and counseling sectors, positive approaches are distinguished from more traditional, problem-focused approaches by the assumptions they hold and the characteristics they share. A primary assumption of most positive approaches is that in all human systems there are things that work well, or have in the past, and that these can be identified, analyzed, and built upon as the foundation for envisioning, designing, and implementing system change. Positive approaches often rely on interviewing for data collection and pay particular attention to how questions are framed, whenever possible seeking to discover when and how things are working at their best.

A basic tenet of social constructionist thought, which informs much of the thinking about positive approaches, is that there is a direct link between image and action and between positive image and positive action. Positive approaches, therefore, have a forward-looking orientation to producing change, rather than focusing on analyzing the ills of the past, and they place emphasis on visioning and creating a positive image of a preferred future.

Rooted in the experiences and lives or histories of individuals and groups in the system, positive approaches are culturally relevant and contextualized to each new situation. They value diversity as a source of creativity and innovation and seek the participation of diverse stakeholders so that the full system is represented in any change initiative affecting them. Positive approaches offer tools for bringing people together to discover shared values and purposes and for helping a diverse group plan and act together on a common future. They promote the distribution of power across the entire system, giving opportunities for any stakeholder to step into a leadership role as the situation dictates. The traditional concept of centralized control and coordination gives way to the idea of multiple centers of control and many points of coordination.

Common Characteristics of Positive Approaches

A number of characteristics are common to most or all positive approaches to social change[3]:

- They share an orientation to the positive power and potential of human beings, and they draw the analytical focus to that positive potential for the purpose of more effectively mobilizing it.

- There is an emphasis on the importance of meaning-making, which is usually done together, in relationship with others in the system.

- There is an emphasis on eliciting and telling stories as a means of conveying holistic wisdom, knowledge, and meaning.

- Focused attention is given to indigenous resources for change—those strengths, capacities, practices, and experiences that are inherent in any system.

- Attention is given to that which inspires and gives hope in the human experience.

- There is an emphasis on generating visual images and exhibiting positive examples.

- The intent is to motivate and mobilize for action.

These common characteristics find expression in a broad variety of forms. Positive approaches to peacebuilding may take the form of a specific technique, method, or practice; a phased methodology or group process; a full-fledged strategy for producing systemic change, involving multiple interventions, phases, techniques, and/or processes; an art form such as music or drama; or as a philosophy of living. In this volume we shall meet examples of each of these forms.

Positive Approaches to Peacebuilding

In this volume we give particular attention to potential applications in peacebuilding of *Appreciative Inquiry,* a positive-change methodology that involves a system's stakeholders in moving through a four-phased process of Discovery, Dream, Design, and Delivery (or Destiny), known as the *4-D Cycle,* to connect to the capacities, strengths, and lived experience within the system, create a shared vision of the future, and mobilize creative action toward its realization. Appreciative Inquiry (AI) originated in the organizational development field in the mid-1980s and is in wide use around the world today in businesses, communities, international development, and social-change organizations of many kinds.

Peacebuilders experimenting with Appreciative Inquiry have at times used the entire 4-D Cycle and at times parts of it, most typically appreciative interviewing from AI's Discovery Phase. *Appreciative interviewing* is the practice of using affirmative questions to carry out inquiry among stakeholders into the positive-core elements in the life of the system. *Positive-core elements* are the essential life-giving—and peace-promoting—resources, capacities, and experiences in the conflict system that can be built upon as foundations for peacebuilding. They include living values and virtues; collective wisdom and knowledge; traditions and rituals; indigenous, cultural, and religious teachings and practices that promote tolerance, pluralism, justice, and peace; and the lived experience of the people and groups embodied in their stories of courage, strength, resilience, compassion, and cooperation in living with differences, as well as their hopes, dreams, and visions for a better future. It is these forces for goodness that positive-change methodologies tap to inspire vision and mobilize action.

Sometimes peacebuilders access these positive-core elements through other forms of *appreciative process* (in addition to or instead of interviewing), such as scholarly research, dialogue processes, rituals, and various forms of artistic expression. As with appreciative interviewing, these other appreciative processes may stand alone as an intervention, or they may be combined with other conflict resolution and peacebuilding methods, including problem-oriented approaches.

A PREVIEW OF WHAT IS TO COME

In this volume we explore positive approaches to peacebuilding in theory and practice. Part one, "Origins and Encounters," lays the groundwork for examining a wide array of applications in the remainder of the book. In the first chapter, Mohammed Abu-Nimer establishes the foundations of this exploration in the conflict resolution and peacebuilding field by giving an historical sketch of the development of the field, identifying core assumptions and principles of peacebuilding, and describing positive elements in existing peacebuilding practice. Next, Diana Whitney, Claudia Liebler, and David Cooperrider present the theory and practice of Appreciative Inquiry as it originated in organizational development and was expanded and adapted to international development. They conclude by proposing five areas in which Appreciative Inquiry might contribute to the practice of peacebuilding. In chapter three, Claudia Liebler and Cynthia Sampson relate the conceptual and theoretical underpinnings of Appreciative Inquiry to the practice of peacebuilding and show some of the ways in which the AI 4-D Cycle lends itself to experimentation and adaptation in peacebuilding contexts.

The sections that follow present five arenas of practice of positive approaches to peacebuilding. In part two, "Toward Cultures of Peace," Elise Boulding presents her methodology for imaging a nonviolent world and describes the findings from one imaging workshop. Mark Chupp describes the process for creating a Local Zone of Peace in a violence-prone region of postwar El Salvador. John Paul Lederach offers a short essay with a "non-theory" of how positive approaches operate as a prelude to a case study in which he and Herm Weaver show the power of music and storytelling in putting forward a positive vision of a how one high school could help bring peace to the world. Joseph Montville and Heidi Paulson Winder describe how a project documenting the long history of creative coexistence by Muslims, Jews, and Christians in Muslim Spain and the medieval Mediterranean is being used to promote a vision of coexistence for contemporary Israelis and Palestinians.

In part three, "Social Transformation," Sam Gbaydee Doe describes a strategic opportunities assessment of Guinea-Conakry, carried out by the West Africa Network for Peacebuilding, as part of a strategy for strengthening the peace-generating capacities in that country. Peter Delahaye and Bharat Krishnan tell how Appreciative Inquiry was used in the Indian state of Nagaland to involve diverse stakeholders, including children in large numbers, in developing a vision and concrete ideas for achieving progress toward socioeconomic development, peace, and good governance in that state. Mary Hope Schwoebel and Erin McCandless describe how appreciative process is used as part of a strategy for empowering marginalized communities in Zimbabwe and then consider the potential for use of Appreciative Inquiry in complex peacebuilding and development contexts.

In part four, "Conflict Resolution," Michael Henderson tells the story of the Initiatives of Change center for reconciliation in Caux, Switzerland, and how personal stories and stage productions are used there to convey universal truths and positive examples of inner personal change, moral courage, and forgiveness and reconciliation. Thomas Porter and Mark Mancao present a model for transforming conflict within The United Methodist Church in the United States that combines the use of circle practice, appreciative questioning, and the principles of restorative justice. Mauricio Rios and Scott Fisher propose a model for an Appreciative Dialogue Workshop to advance the peace process in a longstanding maritime conflict between Bolivia and Chile.

In part five, "Healing and Reconciliation," Peggy Green describes her experience with using appreciative questions in facilitating dialogue between gay and evangelical Christians. Anastasia White uses a social-constructionist lens to interpret the process whereby her relationship with a former adversary from the apartheid regime of South Africa was transformed through the rewriting of their respective conflict narratives. Nancy Good Sider explores the role of positive approaches in posttraumatic healing and growth, and presents findings derived from appreciative interviews conducted with peacebuilders who have suffered trauma. Paula Green and Tamra d'Estrée write about the practice of giving voice to the voiceless in conflict situations, and tell how the "infusion" of a dialogue group of second-generation Holocaust survivors into a dialogue group of Bosnian Serbs and Muslims provided the latter group with a model of healed relationship. Amela and Randy Puljek-Shank explore the question, "How does healing take place?" and examine the intersection of Appreciative Inquiry principles and methods with various approaches to healing in the aftermath of conflict.

In part six, "Designing Organizations for Peacebuilding," Charles Gibbs and Barbara Hartford describe how Appreciative Inquiry has contributed to the development of the organizational design, charter, organizational culture, and peacebuilding program of the global network, United Religions Initiative. Jaco Cilliers, Robin Gulick, and Meg Kinghorn tell how appreciative approaches, including Appreciative Inquiry, were used to advance the strategic visioning and design process for the peacebuilding program at Catholic Relief Services.

In the Conclusion, the editors highlight the major findings of the book, discuss appropriate contexts for the use of positive approaches in peacebuilding, as well as the major challenges to their use, and they propose an agenda for further research and experimentation with positive approaches to peacebuilding.

ENDNOTES

1. *Divine naiveté* is a term coined by John Paul Lederach, which he defines informally as "when you pursue things that along the way don't seem that important, or even advisable, but later turn out to be key and the most important" (2003).
2. This section is based on unpublished work (dated March 2003) by Andrea Strimling and Claudia Liebler in conceptualizing how positive approaches might be used in advancing interfield cooperation in complex conflicts.
3. This section is drawn from unpublished work (dated March 2002) by Claudia Liebler and Cynthia Sampson on a typology of positive approaches to peacebuilding.

REFERENCES

Lederach, John Paul. 2003. Email message to the author (April 24).
Muller, Robert. 2003. "Waging Peace: Taking Comfort from Footholds Gained." As reprinted at http://www.goodmorningworld.org/documents/030319.pdf.

PART I:

ORIGINS AND ENCOUNTERS

We inhabit a world that is always subjective and shaped by our interactions with it. Our world is impossible to pin down, constantly changing and infinitely more interesting than we ever imagined.

MARGARET WHEATLEY

CHAPTER ONE

TOWARD THE THEORY AND PRACTICE OF POSITIVE APPROACHES TO PEACEBUILDING

Mohammed Abu-Nimer

This chapter grounds the volume's exploration of positive approaches to peace-building by first providing a brief overview of the development of the conflict res-olution and peacebuilding field over the last four decades in North America and, more recently, worldwide—a history that brings us to this moment of new evolu-tionary possibility. Next it looks at the core assumptions and principles of peace-building, which set a framework for considering, throughout the book's explo-rations, the ways in which positive approaches are in affinity with the assumptions and values of peacebuilding and support key aspects of peacebuilding practice, as well as the ways in which positive approaches may fall short and possibly will need to stand aside or be developed further. The chapter concludes with a discus-sion of positive elements in existing peacebuilding practice as the first step toward the more systematic study and practice of positive approaches to peacebuilding to which this volume is committed.

❧

*T*he field of conflict resolution and peacebuilding[1] has devel-oped tremendously in the last three decades. Hundreds of aca-demic programs grant degrees in this field, and there is an ongoing process of professionalization, with thousands of nongovernmental organizations (NGOs) and independent practitioners engaged daily in work-ing to resolve interpersonal and intra- or inter-community conflicts.[2] In addition, hundreds of governmental, intergovernmental, and nongovernmen-tal agencies and initiatives attempt to address conflicts at the international level. The Institute for Multi-Track Diplomacy has identified nine different sectors or tracks of peacebuilding practice: government; religion; research, training, and education; business; funding; nongovernmental/professional (e.g., humanitarian relief and development); private citizens; activism; and media and communications (Diamond and McDonald 1996).

Several major social and political movements contributed to the emer-gence of the conflict resolution field in North America. In the 1940s and

1950s, the human relations studies field developed concepts and approaches for dealing with prejudice and stereotypes. The civil rights movement of the late 1950s and 1960s produced a new awareness of the possibilities for change through empowerment and activism of minority groups. New understandings of the function of conflict in the organizational relations field in the 1960s and 1970s led to cooperative approaches in business and labor-management relations. Also in that period, an overwhelmed American judicial system began to refer small-claims, divorce, and other types of suits to lawyers trained in mediation and arbitration, in what became known as "alternative dispute resolution" or "ADR." In the early 1970s, neighborhood justice centers or community mediation centers were created to address the grievances of individuals and groups.[3]

In the international arena, the late 1960s and early 1970s saw the first experiments with problem-solving workshops in an attempt to apply new conflict resolution concepts to international and interethnic conflicts.[4] Also at that time, the Quakers and then Mennonites became active in international peacemaking, leading the way in what today is a rapidly expanding sector of religious and interreligious peacebuilding.[5] The late 1980s and the 1990s saw increasing attention to the perceptual and psychological aspects of conflict behavior and conflict resolution; to indigenous, cultural, and religious/ spiritual resources for dispute resolution and peacemaking; to the processes of forgiveness, reconciliation, and trauma healing; and more recently still, to the role of narrative, ritual, metaphor, the arts, and other holistic ways of defining, knowing, and transforming conflicts.

Finally, the post–Cold War period of the 1990s also saw extensive development in peacebuilding beyond North America and Europe, and training workshops, peacebuilding centers, and NGOs working in peacebuilding can now be found across Africa, Asia, the Middle East, and Latin America. Today, it is safe to say that peacebuilding concepts and approaches are being applied and developed globally, and the field is expanding further by exploring its theoretical and practical connections with other fields, such as international development, human rights, environment, communications and the media, and business.

This book is itself an example of one such new-frontier exploration, in this case primarily at the interface with social constructionist thought and the Appreciative Inquiry methodology as it emerged in the field of organizational development and then in international development. Paralleling the emergence of positive-change methodologies in numerous other fields,[6] Appreciative Inquiry and other positive approaches to peacebuilding represent a new thrust toward methods that draw the focus of analysis, process design, and action to the peace-promoting capacities and positive potential for transformation that exist in all human systems.

We turn next to a discussion of some of the core assumptions and principles in conflict resolution and peacebuilding that will inform our examination of the theory and practice of positive-change methodologies, in general, and Appreciative Inquiry, in particular.

KEY ASSUMPTIONS AND PRINCIPLES OF PEACEBUILDING[7]

Although there are many processes of conflict resolution and peacebuilding applied by practitioners and analyzed and theorized by scholars, it is possible to identify a set of core assumptions and principles shared by the majority of peacebuilders. These, in turn, highlight the values that motivate practitioners and scholars to engage in this work.

Conflict as a Source of Change

One key assumption in this field is that conflict is not necessarily negative or evil. Most peacebuilders perceive conflict as often leading to needed change and therefore potentially a creative force that can generate new options for solving existing problems. Differences in opinions, incompatible goals, and competing interests are not inherently destructive forces, although they often lead parties to engage in violence or other exclusionary behavior toward the other side. When such behavior takes place, other aspects of the existing relationship between the disputing parties are marginalized or destroyed. Thus, though conflict itself is a natural process, it can lead to either constructive or destructive outcomes, depending on the ways in which parties approach the issues in contention and one another. The conflict resolver's mission, then, is to help the parties identify potential avenues for change that accommodate the interests and needs of all the parties.

Moral and Pragmatic Superiority of Nonviolence

It is assumed in the conflict resolution field that nonviolent methods are more effective in persuading the adversary to change their perceptions, resolve the issues, and agree to settle a conflict than the use of violent force. In the short and long term, violent approaches are more costly and harmful to the parties than nonviolent approaches. Nonviolent methods allow parties to grow and establish a more productive relationship than violent methods. While most conflict resolution and peacebuilding practitioners and scholars believe that nonviolent methods are morally superior to violent methods, not all are pacifists, and there are some who would not exclude the use of limited and conditioned force (violence) in resolving certain types of conflicts.

Cooperation to Resolve Differences

Another assumption is that differences in values, interests, and needs can be resolved jointly and cooperatively. Cooperative relations generate energy and possibilities for overcoming differences since parties are not pre-occupied with—and limited by—a win-lose outcome. Parties join their efforts to resolve problems with a willingness to negotiate differences, instead of separately competing to fulfill their interests and negate those of the other side. For cooperation to take place, however, parties need to have a basic understanding of the issues in contention and a willingness to acknowledge the other party's perspective. Much effort in conflict resolution processes is therefore dedicated to clearing up misperceptions, breaking down negative stereotypes, and rehumanizing images of the enemy. Once perceptions have shifted from animosity and hatred to trust and a willing-ness to cooperate, resolution of the substantive issues becomes much more feasible.[8]

People Are Not Problems

This classic assumption that people are not problems (Fisher and Ury 1981) underlies negotiation and mediation, as well as other conflict resolu-tion approaches. Practitioners focus on the problem (differences in values, interests, goals, needs) and respect the people as individuals. The problem is reframed as a shared and mutual concern for the parties to jointly address, while there is an inherent respect for the person and the rights of each indi-vidual involved. By protecting the person, the negotiator or mediator avoids insults and the need to deal with personal injuries. The practitioner assumes that the problem will be easy to resolve once parties redirect their attention and energy to the issues and leave out the personal or collective characters of the others involved. At its core, conflict resolution practice aims to enhance and protect human dignity and fulfill basic human needs (Burton 1990).

Perceptual Change Through Communication

Even if parties are disputing distribution or redistribution of tangible resources, a change in their perceptions and consequently their communica-tion patterns is essential to the resolution of the issues. Communication is a major channel by which negative feelings and perceptions are discovered and corrected or modified among the parties. To change perceptions, effec-tive communication (active listening, paraphrasing, empathy, etc.) is a neces-sary process, regardless of the nature and type of the conflict. Such a process requires the building of an environment of security, trust, and willingness to take risks in moving toward resolution.

When conflict resolution practitioners assume a stance of genuine and deep listening, without judgment, and allowing people to speak their stories and describe their grievances and pain, individuals and groups in conflict can change. Whether the change is deeply rooted (transformative) or temporary, a change in positions cannot take place without a change in perceptions through communication.

Collaborative and Creative Problem Solving

The primary basis of conflict resolution is a collaborative problem-solving process, which aspires to move parties with genuine or perceived substantive differences towards a shared and agreed-upon resolution. With or without the help of a third party, problem-solving processes assume that parties are capable of resolving their own conflicts and finding satisfactory solutions to the issues involved. The effective problem-solving process requires communication and a basic willingness on the part of the parties to meet the adversary or *the Other*, jointly address the problem, and creatively seek different ways to fulfill their needs, interests, or desires. Creativity in conflict resolution processes enables the parties to leave their comfortable, secure positions and move with their opponents to the exploration of new options.

Building Sustainable Relationship

Sustainable relationship can be achieved only when disputing parties have reconciled their past histories, recognized their present differences, and agreed upon a future vision for staying in relationship. The sustainability of conflict resolution settlements requires that they provide mechanisms for the parties to resolve future differences and conflicts peacefully through mutually negotiated agreements. The torn relationship is restored and a new type of relationship among the parties is established that is based upon respect for individual and collective rights and recognition of the interdependent relationship that binds them. This ensures that future disagreements will not escalate into violent conflict, but will be resolved in mutually satisfactory ways. To accomplish this requires attention to justice issues, as well as dealing effectively with actual or perceived historical injustices as crucial to the success of any peacebuilding process.

Creating Change Agents

Peacebuilding processes assume that change in people, relationships, and systems is possible and necessary to resolve conflicts, therefore preparing disputants to be change agents is a central principle in the field. Peacebuilding training and problem-solving workshops are aimed at producing change agents who can carry the message back to their home communities and be catalysts for change. The dominant discourse in peacebuilding frameworks regarding social and political change (especially in North American models) is one that envisions and prepares for gradual types of change, as opposed to sudden revolutionary changes in elite leadership or mass movements for change. Nonviolent resistance and other forms of social activism are often excluded from training and academic programs in conflict resolution and peacebuilding.

Transforming Power Relationships

Conflict resolution and peacebuilding processes are aimed at producing change in the existing power relationships in a society or among the conflicting parties by transforming destructive, dominant power dynamics into constructive relationships that are balanced through the empowerment of all parties (Curle 1971; Laue and Cormick 1978); and by transforming abusive power (via ideology, coercive use of force, control of resources, etc.) to the joint construction and utilization of power. Giving voice to the voiceless and empowering the marginalized is a central principle in peacebuilding. Empowerment and giving voice can produce tremendous energy for change and transformation on the part of individuals and societies and is essential to the sustainability of peace.

Action and Development

The importance of integrating concrete systemic change as an outcome of a conflict resolution process is gaining greater recognition in the peacebuilding field, especially in the context of international development. Concrete actions and changes in the reality of the parties ensure sustainability of the process and outcomes. In many settings, economic development and improvement of living conditions are essential and may require various forms of advocacy and social activism to be achieved. Such outcomes insure that conflict resolution processes are an integral part of larger processes of social, political, and economic change in the society, as opposed to becoming mechanisms for maintaining the status quo and existing power relations.

POSITIVE ELEMENTS IN CONFLICT RESOLUTION PRACTICES

While all of the above core assumptions and principles of peacebuilding are designed to bring positive, constructive change to systems in conflict, this section highlights aspects of peacebuilding practice that specifically build upon or create hopeful, empathetic, and cooperative dynamics in the interparty relationship and, in turn, give life to the peacebuilding process overall. One of the guiding principles in the practice of mediation, for example, is to *identify commonalities and build on the small agreements*

achieved by disputants in order to build up to larger agreements or settlements. This principle often requires the mediator to highlight even the smallest accomplishments in the process, for example, that the parties have been sitting together for the last hour in a spirit of cooperation, without exchanging insults, or that they have reached agreement on the time, place, and agenda for the next meeting.

Similarly, peacebuilders *seek defining moments of cooperation* in the broader arena of a conflictual relationship and magnify them to illustrate the potential for positive relationship among the conflicting parties and to instill hope and motivation for change. Celebrating moments of connectedness, even though these may be few in number and small in scale, can nevertheless be highly effective in generating positive energy among the parties and empowering the peacebuilding process. One such defining moment of cooperation that has given inspiration to others is the case of an Israeli woman, Dalia Landau, who inherited a house in Ramle that had originally been built by a Palestinian family. The family was then forcibly evacuated in the 1948 war. With her husband, Rabbi Yehezkel Landau, she joined with members of the al-Khairy family, the original owners, in dedicating the house to Arab-Jewish peace and educational activities, and they gave it the name "Open House" (Gentile 2002).

Practices for *(re)humanizing and developing empathy for the Other* are central to peacebuilding. This process entails not only recognition of the humanness of each individual, but also of the innate equality of all people and the potential contribution that different individuals and groups can make to enriching the human experience. It also fosters a sense of human connectedness and interdependency among former adversaries and confronts them with the prospect that there are harmful consequences to all from inflicting pain on another.

Storytelling to convey holistic meaning and nourish caring and connection among the parties is a primary peacebuilding tool for humanizing the Other and healing trauma. In training, mediation, facilitation, and problem-solving workshops, peacebuilders open space for the stories to be told, both painful as well as stories of hope and positive interaction (Duryea and Potts 1993). The stories, if told with honesty, compassion, and passion, may transform perceptions, instill hope that change is possible and worth working for, and inspire and motivate participants to take concrete actions to transform their conflict reality. We will also see in this volume how a storytelling project was able to dispel a sense of helplessness, unleash positive energy, and point the way to concrete actions that could be taken by American youths to reach out to the Arab world in the aftermath of the "9/11" terrorist attacks (see appendix to chapter six).

Peacebuilders often use *rituals that enact aspects of meaningful, compassionate interaction* to infuse meaning, life, and new forms of shared experience into a dysfunctional system of relationship. Rituals allow people to connect without words or ideologies through their spirituality and universal human connectedness and as such are powerful constructs for rehumanizing the Other and creating images of positive relationship. Even simple rituals such as joint meals, music, dancing, and sports are used by peacebuilders to significant effect in interethnic encounters (see Schirch [2001] on the use of rituals with Greek and Turkish Cypriot youths; and Abu-Nimer [1999] on Israeli and Palestinian dialogue rituals).

Most peacebuilding processes assume that "the cure is in the pain" and that disputants should be given the opportunity to recall their suffering and air their grievances and negative emotions together in a safe and secure environment, in order for the parties to understand and reprocess these memories differently. This experience is often exhausting and draining, however, and can overwhelm the participants with a sense of helplessness and the magnitude of the problem. Often the participants feel more apart and discouraged as a result of this phase of the process (see Abu-Nimer 2001). To counteract these effects, either following these experiences or concurrently with them, peacebuilders introduce activities for *building trust and forging new positive relationships through games, humor, art, music, and other fun and uplifting experiences.*

Peacebuilding processes also infuse hope and help the conflict parties *construct a new vision for future relationship.* Elise Boulding's methodology for visioning a nonviolent world (see chapter four) was used, for example, in the Usulutan province of El Salvador to help former adversaries in that country's civil war create a common vision for peaceful community in their region, complete with details related to the roles and functions of the state and civil society, police and courts, cultural rituals, and civil-sector mechanisms for promoting peace (see chapter five).

In interethnic dialogue and encounter, facilitators often design an intervention process with a *task or goal to be accomplished by the parties that does not relate directly to the issues in the conflict.* In Northern Ireland and in Israel-Palestine, for example, teachers and students from the two conflicting sides have cooperated in creating a curriculum for environmental studies that they use separately in teaching their students. The accomplishment of such a task gives the parties an opportunity to build trust and the experience of success in a joint effort.

CONCLUSION

Peacebuilding is about bringing change in human relationships and institutions. As we have seen from the above examples, many peacebuilding techniques and approaches cultivate the positive, life-giving forces that exist in every conflict system to enable people caught in the web of violence to see the potential for a different future. These approaches assume that there are sources of energy and capacities for innovation, passion, hope, imagination, and transformation within the human system—the people, relationships, groups, and communities—that if awakened can be a moving and powerful force for change. In fact, learning and practicing ways to identify and create these positive resources as a path to the future is one of the things that differentiates peacebuilders from other people who experience conflicts.

Yet typically, peacebuilders aim to empower communities primarily by devoting enormous energy to validating and acknowledging the pain and injustice, hoping to motivate people to see the potential for peaceful alternatives. Many of us in the field still overemphasize the pain and victimhood in our intervention processes and the need to show the participants the destructive consequences of violent conflict. Our assumption is that when people realize and acknowledge the horrible reality of war, as rationalistic human beings they will shun violence and prefer peaceful alternatives.

At the same time, most people living in a constant conflict situation lose any hope for a positive future, and more importantly, they lose confidence in their ability as individuals or as a collective to contribute to positive change. This calls upon us as peacebuilders to motivate people and groups and help them find the strength, courage, and confidence to change. These can be better cultivated if people share what it is they really yearn for and what their dream of peace would look like, and if they learn how to view themselves as positive change agents, rather than as helpless victims.

Finally, the fundamental desire that characterizes the gathering of groups and individuals for peacebuilding is to improve their individual lives and help their communities to move forward by reducing violence and resolving conflicts. This implicit link that binds people from opposing sides of the conflict to be together for a few days (even if it is only a temporary bond of but a few days) is a strong positive force, yet it is underestimated and underutilized in many peacebuilding processes. Constructively tapping into the deep desire for more fulfilling relationships and a better future is the main challenge of peacebuilding field.

This chapter and book assert that peacebuilders can be more effective in bringing change if they intentionally integrate positive elements, processes, and approaches into their current practices. It is in these types of approaches that parties can feel free and able to connect with one another and can acknowledge their potential role in changing the system. The challenge for peacebuilders is to become constantly attuned to the positive elements present in their contexts and processes and to access and activate them. And more, beyond this piecemeal approach, a framework for positive approaches to peacebuilding is needed. What remains to be developed are strategies and methods for more systematically and comprehensively integrating positive-change principles and practices in all aspects of peacebuilding, including training and education. It is to that purpose that this volume is committed.

ENDNOTES

1. The term *peacebuilding* is used here as an umbrella term that includes the full spectrum of conflict resolution and transformation frameworks and approaches, including negotiation, conciliation, mediation, facilitation, alternative dispute resolution, problem-solving workshops, education and training, advocacy, and nonviolent resistance, among others.
2. See, for example, the *Global Directory of Peace Studies and Conflict Resolution Programs* of the Consortium on Peace Research, Education, and Development (O'Leary 2000).
3. On the development of the conflict resolution field in the United States, see Scimecca (1991).
4. For a full review of the historical development of the conflict resolution field, including the problem-solving workshop, see Kriesberg (1997) and Fisher (1997).
5. On the development of the religious and interreligious sector of the peacebuilding field, see Sampson (1997), Appleby (2000), and Smock (2002).
6. For a brief survey of positive, strengths-based approaches in psychology, criminal justice, social work, and in the treatment of trauma survivors, see chapter sixteen.
7. Some of the assumptions discussed in this section were identified in Abu-Nimer (1999).
8. In various surveys of Israelis and Palestinians, for example, on the issue of Jerusalem, which is one of the most difficult obstacles for peace between these two groups, the majority of people agreed that there were many possible solutions. At least thirty-two options were identified by Jerome Segal (1989) to resolve the status of Jerusalem. None of these options could be pursued, however, without a minimal degree of trust and willingness to cooperate on the part of the parties.

REFERENCES

Abu-Nimer, Mohammed. 1999. *Dialogue, Conflict Resolution, and Change: Arab-Jewish Encounters in Israel.* Albany, N.Y.: State University of New York Press.

———. 2001. "Education for Coexistence in Israel: Potential and Challenges." In *Reconciliation, Justice, and Coexistence: Theory and Practice.* Mohammed Abu-Nimer, ed. Lanham, Md.: Lexington Books.

Appleby, R. Scott. 2000. *The Ambivalence of the Sacred.* Lanham, Md.: Rowman and Littlefield.

Burton, John. 1990. *Conflict Resolution and Provention.* New York: St. Martin's Press.

Curle, Adam. 1971. *Making Peace.* London: Tavistock Press.

Diamond, Louise, and John McDonald. 1996. *Multi-Track Diplomacy: A Systems Approach to Peace*. West Hartford, Conn.: Kumarian Press.

Duryea, Michelle LeBaron, and Jim Potts. 1993. "Story and Legend: Powerful Tools for Conflict Resolution." *Mediation Quarterly* 10:4, pp. 387–395.

Fisher, Roger, and William Ury. 1981. *Getting to Yes: Negotiating Agreement without Giving In*. New York: Penguin.

Fisher, Ronald J. 1997. *Interactive Conflict Resolution*. Syracuse, N.Y.: Syracuse University Press.

Gentile, Derek. 2002. "Jew, Arabs Working to Promote Peace." *Berkshire Eagle* (July 15), as reprinted at http://www.openhouse.org.il/article25.shtml.

Kriesberg, Louis. 1997. "The Development of the Conflict Resolution Field." In *Peacemaking in International Conflict: Methods & Techniques*. I. William Zartman and J. Lewis Rasmussen, eds. Washington, D.C.: U.S. Institute of Peace Press.

Laue, James, and Gerald Cormick. 1978. "The Ethics of Intervention in Community Disputes." In *The Ethics of Social Intervention*. Gordon Bermant, Herbert C. Kelman, and Donald P. Warwick, eds. Washington, D.C.: Halsted Press.

O'Leary, Daniel. 2000. *Global Directory of Peace Studies and Conflict Resolution Programs*. Fairfax, Va.: Consortium on Peace Research, Education, and Development.

Sampson, Cynthia. 1997. "Religion and Peacebuilding." In *Peacemaking in International Conflict: Methods & Techniques*. I. William Zartman and J. Lewis Rasmussen, eds. Washington, D.C.: U.S. Institute of Peace Press.

Schirch, Lisa. 2001. "Ritual Reconciliation: Transforming Identity/Reframing Conflict." In *Reconciliation, Justice, and Coexistence: Theory and Practice*. Mohammed Abu-Nimer, ed. Lanham, Md.: Lexington Books.

Scimecca, Joseph A. 1991. "Conflict Resolution in the United States: The Emergence of a Profession?" In *Conflict Resolution: Cross-Cultural Perspectives*. Kevin Avruch, Peter W. Black, and Joseph A. Scimecca, eds. Westport, Conn.: Greenwood Press.

Segal, Jerome M. 1989. *Creating the Palestinian State*. Chicago: Lawrence Hill Books.

Smock, David, ed. 2002. *Interfaith Dialogue and Peacebuilding*. Washington, D.C.: U.S. Institute of Peace Press.

Peace is a state of mind and a path of action. It is a concept, a goal, an experience, a path. Peace is an ideal. It is both intangible and concrete, complex and simple, exciting and calming. Peace is personal and political; it is spiritual and practical, local and global. It is a process and an outcome, and above all a way of being.

LOUISE DIAMOND

CHAPTER TWO

APPRECIATIVE INQUIRY IN ORGANIZATIONS AND INTERNATIONAL DEVELOPMENT:
AN INVITATION TO SHARE AND LEARN ACROSS FIELDS

Diana Whitney, Claudia Liebler, and David Cooperrider

This chapter provides an overview of the theory and practice of Appreciative Inquiry, a positive-change approach used for organizational innovation and capacity building, strategic planning, and partnership, network, or coalition building in businesses, international development agencies, and social-change organizations of all kinds. Powered by the principle of "wholeness," Appreciative Inquiry involves people from every stakeholder group in connecting to the positive core of a system's capacities, strengths, and assets to create a shared dream of the future and mobilize creative energies to work towards its realization. After defining Appreciative Inquiry, the chapter takes the reader on a journey through the 4-D Cycle of Discovery, Dream, Design, and Destiny, giving examples of the work that is done in each phase. The Appreciative Inquiry Summit, a high-participation, full-voice process is described; and the chapter concludes by proposing five areas in which Appreciative Inquiry might be put to the service of peacebuilding.

⚹

In our hearts and minds there is no more worthy endeavor than building peace. From the cultivation of inner peace, to the creation of peaceful communities, to the resolution of conflict among differing persons, groups, or nations, to the healing of wounds and the establishment of relationships after acts of violence, peacebuilding is a core competency in the creation of sustainable organizations, civil societies, and a viable global community.

All societies and organizations have means of resolving differences and maintaining harmony among members. Some approaches are peaceful, others are not; some means are life giving, others are life taking; some approaches are liberating, others are oppressive; some means are relationship enhancing, others are divisive; and some means serve the highest good of humanity, while others diminish human potential.

When we look at some conspicuous approaches to resolving differences today, we see many closed conversations—embedded in secret meetings, enmeshed in the many dimensions of the conflict, and not involving people who are impacted. This kind of top-level process has its strengths, but there are weaknesses as well, and these are being played out on the world stage in these times. This type of peace process rises and falls on *high-level leaders* and presumes that: (1) representative leaders *can* be identified, (2) they *will* articulate and advocate, from the perspective of those they represent, the concerns giving rise to the conflict, and (3) they *possess* the power, or at least the influence, to deliver the support of their respective communities for the implementation of any agreements reached (Lederach 1997). But what if people no longer follow monolithic power structures? What if high-level leaders such as Yasser Arafat and Ariel Sharon do not possess the power or influence to bring along parts of their constituencies (e.g., the Palestinian Hamas and Israeli extreme right-wing parties)? If the trickle-down approach to peacemaking can no longer carry the day, how do we build peace as well from the bottom up and middle out, engaging all sectors of society? That is the peacebuilding project of today.

The proposition we subscribe to in this chapter is that for there to be any chance of long-term success in any peacebuilding process, it must be open to everyone who has a serious stake in it—political leaders, religious communities, the business sector, educators, artists, youth, people from the world community, media, victims and offenders, the oppressed and the oppressors, and many others. With Lederach and others, we argue for a system-wide approach to peacebuilding, involving all concerned sectors of society. At the largest level, this proposition implies that the means and ends of peacebuilding must be better matched, even the same. If we want whole-system change, we need whole-systems methods. Likewise, if we want sustainable justpeace, we need positive approaches to peacebuilding.

The purpose of this chapter is to introduce the theory and practice of Appreciative Inquiry (AI) and to begin to build a bridge from the field of business management and leadership, where AI was born and has made tremendous impact, and from the world of international development, where it has been successfully used, among others, by the Global Excellence in Management (GEM) Initiative through its work with nongovernmental organizations (NGOs),[1] to the field of international conflict resolution and peacebuilding.

In the first section, we share a brief overview of Appreciative Inquiry, including what it is and where it has been successful in organizational development and strategic planning in business, international development, and other kinds of social-change organizations. In the second section, we take the reader through the four stages of the AI process or 4-D Cycle— Discovery, Dream, Design, and Destiny—giving examples of applications in each phase. In section three, we introduce one of the most powerful ways to use AI with a system, the Appreciative Inquiry Summit, a large-group methodology that involves all stakeholders in connecting the positive core of a system's past and present to a vision and design for system change. In the final section, we offer five ways that we believe the adaptation and application of Appreciative Inquiry can serve the peacebuilding field.

WHAT IS APPRECIATIVE INQUIRY?

> ### OUR DEFINITION
>
> **Ap-pre'ci-ate, v.,**
> 1. *Valuing; the act of recognizing the best in people or the world around us; affirming past and present strengths, successes, and potentials, to perceive those things that give life (health, vitality, excellence) to living systems.*
> 2. *To increase in value, e.g., the economy has appreciated in value.*
>
> *Synonyms: valuing, prizing, esteeming, honoring.*
>
> **In-quire', v.**
> 1. *The act of exploration and discovery.*
> 2. *To ask questions; to be open to seeing new potentials and possibilities.*
>
> *Synonyms: discovery, search, systematic exploration and study.*

AI is both a philosophy of positive change and a methodology for high-participation, collaborative transformation. At the heart of AI is the understanding that human systems move in the direction of what they continuously study, analyze, and discuss. Appreciative Inquiry is therefore a call to study "root causes of success," rather than "root causes of failure." It is a call to reframe the focus of attention from deficit discourse, a growing body of vocabularies produced by the critical and problem-oriented approaches to social scientific research, to positive discourse. It is a shift from investigation into problems, pain, suffering, failure, breakdown, and victimization to curiosity about living potential, key success factors, images of the ideal future, and hope.

As a philosophy of positive change, Appreciative Inquiry suggests that change occurs most readily when people engage together in inquiry into their strengths, resources, capacities, best practices, successes, hopes, dreams, and ideals—in other words the *positive core* of their shared or other life experiences. Positive change begins with inquiry and analysis into the positive core—the essential life-giving resources, capacities, and forces for goodness—at the center of any human system.

Thus, a more comprehensive description of Appreciative Inquiry is,

> the cooperative search for the best in people, their organizations, and the world around them. It involves systematic discovery of what gives a system "life" when it is most effective and capable in economic, ecological, and human terms. AI involves the art and practice of asking questions that strengthen a system's capacity to heighten positive potential. . . . In AI, intervention gives way to imagination and innovation; instead of negation, criticism, and spiraling diagnosis there is discovery, dream, and design. AI assumes that every living system has untapped, rich, and inspiring accounts of the positive. Link this "positive-change core" directly to any change agenda, and changes never thought possible are suddenly and democratically mobilized. (Cooperrider and Whitney 1999, 10)

But—What About Problems, Pain, and Suffering?[2]

This is one of the most frequently asked questions about Appreciative Inquiry. "Isn't it unrealistic to deny what's wrong?" people ask. "Aren't you asking us to ignore problems, or to act as if suffering and violence don't exist?" Let us be clear. We are not saying to deny or ignore problems, pain, or suffering. What we are saying is that if you want to transform a relationship, a situation, an organization, or community, focusing on strengths is more effective than focusing on problems. Throughout this chapter we offer stories about organizations and communities that have benefited by using AI to shift their attention from problems to possibilities.

We often work in situations fraught with anxiety, tension, and stress, be they union-management relations, cross-gender or intercultural relationships, or competing interests among diverse groups within a system. Time and again, when we turn people's attention from what is wrong to who we are when we are at our best, conflict turns to cooperation.

We do not dismiss accounts of problems, stress, or conflict. We simply do not use them as the basis of analysis or action. We listen when they arise, validate them as lived experience, and seek to reframe them. For example, in the corporate environment, the problem of high turnover becomes an inquiry into magnetic work environments or a question of retention, thereby redirecting the focus of analysis. The problem of low management credibility becomes an inquiry into moments of management credibility or inspired leadership. The problem of sexual harassment at work becomes a question of positive cross-gender working relationships. This simple shift in attention allows people and organizations to rise above or move beyond the conditions in which the problems originally existed.

From Problem Solving to Possibility

Historically, the field of community development has focused upon problem identification and resolution. Development initiatives have begun with the identification of problems and led to analysis and dialogue about "what needs to be changed." The central organizing focus of this work was the "root cause of failure." An example of this problem-oriented approach to development is illustrated by the "Problem-Solving Tree" (see Figure 1).

Figure 1
PROBLEM-SOLVING TREE

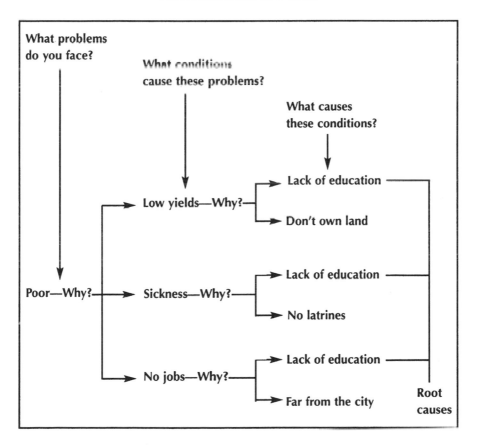

SOURCE: CRWRC (1997, 86). Reprinted by permission of the publisher.

This approach has contributed to some of the most successful community development around the world. Yet when a group of development workers in Africa was introduced to it, the members felt there might be a better way. Having been introduced to Appreciative Inquiry, they noted that a typical problem tree would take them in a circle and would not lead to understanding or a consensus on tangible actions to take. Their problem tree, for example, suggested that the lack of education is caused by poverty, which is caused by no jobs, which is caused by lack of education.

So instead, they created a "Possibility Tree" (see Figure 2), which shifted the focus from problem to possibility, changed both the information and ideas generated, and also pointed the way to specific actions to be taken.

Figure 2
POSSIBILITY TREE

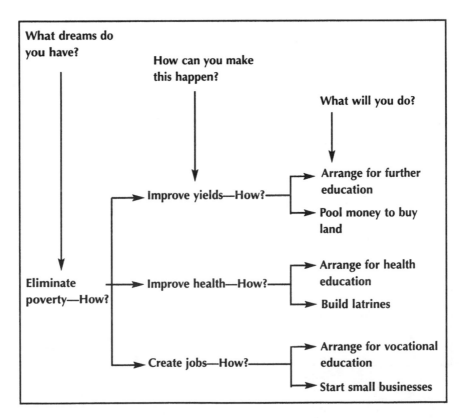

SOURCE: CRWRC (1997, 87). Reprinted by permission of the publisher.

APPRECIATIVE INQUIRY 4-D CYCLE

The Appreciative Inquiry methodology follows a process known as the 4-D Cycle (Cooperrider and Whitney 1999). The four phases in the process can occur as rapidly and informally as a conversation with a friend or colleague, or as formally as an organization- or community-wide process involving every stakeholder. Figure 3 shows the 4-D Cycle of Discovery, Dream, Design, and Destiny (or Delivery), a step-by-step process for building a vision informed by positive experiences and then working to realize the vision in action. What follows is a brief description and illustration of each phase, starting with an explanation of affirmative topic choice, at the center of the model.

Figure 3
APPRECIATIVE INQUIRY 4-D CYCLE

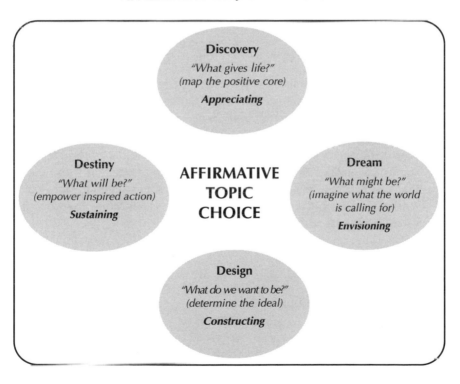

Affirmative Topic Choice: A Fateful Act

The starting point for an Appreciative Inquiry process is the determination of the focus of the process—the topics for consideration, inquiry, and dialogue. Human systems—relationships, organizations, identity groups, communities, societies—move in the direction of what they discuss, analyze, and reflect upon. As an inquiry into what gives life to the human system, AI begins with a clear discernment of what is desirable to the system involved, as captured in a set of affirmative topics.

Many hospitals around the world, for example, are adapting Appreciative Inquiry for building communication among doctors and nurses, to include the voice of the patient in strategic planning, and to build cultures of inclusion and respect. Our colleague, AI practitioner and consultant Susan Wood, shared with us the following example of topic choice from her work with one large urban hospital in applying Appreciative Inquiry as a means of enhancing nursing retention. At a time when nurses in many places are feeling overworked and under appreciated, these nurses selected the following affirmative topics for inquiry and conversation into how they might be strengthened.

- *The privilege of nursing.* We make our professional life count by caring, listening, and understanding, whatever the circumstance. It is a privilege to participate in another person's life. It is our privilege to share our passion for nursing to ignite the spark in you. Be part of the many, the proud, and the caring!

- *Humor—a vital sign.* Humor is an important sign of life—critical to our survival. It enables us to cope with absurdities, sad situations, and the insecurities of our lives. Laughter is contagious and makes the air sing. Humor is a prism that expands and amplifies. The intuitive knowing of when and how to use humor is priceless.

- *Appreciation.* We crave it and want more of it. We want it from each other, patients, leaders, and self. It sounds like kind words, it looks like nice letters, and it comes from the heart.

In many situations, the selection of topics for inquiry requires a reframing of some problem into an affirmative topic, as illustrated in Figure 4.

In the field of international development, the shift from problem to affirmative topic in one situation produced life-saving results.[3] When Save the Children sent Jerry Sternin and his wife to Vietnam in the 1990s to open an office, nearly half of the country's children were malnourished. The Vietnamese government gave him just six months to make a difference. Instead of diving into a study of the causes of malnutrition, Sternin turned to the theory of amplifying positive deviance: In every community or group, there are individuals whose exceptional behavior or practices

Figure 4
REFRAMING PROBLEMS INTO AFFIRMATIVE TOPICS

Authoritarian leadership	Participatory leadership
Discrimination	Diversity as a source of innovation
Ethnic conflict	Creative coexistence
Silenced voice	Full-voiced participation

enable them to get better results than their neighbors from the same set of resources. Without realizing it, these "positive deviants" have discovered the path to progress for the entire group if their methods can be isolated, analyzed, and shared with others.

Sternin knew little about Vietnam, but was certain that the only way to come up with a plan to fight malnutrition was to discover it within the Vietnamese village culture itself. The Sternins, together with Save the Children's Vietnamese staff and a volunteer, Nguyen Thanh Hien, enlisted village women to help identify the mothers within the villages whose children were not malnourished because they had discovered ways to feed and care for their children effectively. The lessons revealed by these positive deviants enabled everyone else in the village to learn to practice those survival skills on their own. Within a two-year period, the incidence of malnutrition dropped 65–85 percent throughout Vietnamese villages.

A CHALLENGE TO THE STATUS QUO. The process of topic choice often requires people to rethink the way they do what they do. It challenges the status quo by asking people to focus on what they want *more* of rather than what they don't want. The example of British Airways is illustrative.[4] In 1998, British Airways Customer Service NA selected topics for a system-wide inquiry. Forty people from twenty-two locations gathered to learn about Appreciative Inquiry and to identify three to five topics. Before long, a particularly nettlesome topic considered paramount to the well-being of their business surfaced—"baggage." Participants shared stories of the wedding dress that didn't make it to the wedding on time and had to be replaced at British Airways' expense; of camping gear that didn't get to the Grand Canyon until the vacation was over; of the daily disturbances of luggage not making the transfer from Heathrow to Gatwick airports in time for connecting flights.

The AI facilitators paraphrased the stories to demonstrate an understanding of the participants' concerns for the issue and then invited small groups to frame the baggage issue as a topic. The response came too quickly and unanimously to be anything but a habitual response to the situation: "better service recovery." "Let's see if we have this right," the facilitators replied. "It's okay to lose a customer's baggage, as long as you recover it promptly?" Clearly, the answer was *no*. "Given that organizations move in the direction of what they study," the facilitators coached, "what is it that you want more of. What affirmative topic would move this organization in the direction you want?"

After another twenty minutes' discussion, one group came out with an innovative and emphatic reply: "exceptional arrival experience." How much more it would be like British Airways at its best, one person pointed out, if customer service agents were focused on providing exceptional arrival experiences rather than worrying about lost baggage. This was the topic that would bring real progress, and the large group adopted it by consensus.

THE KEY TO SUCCESSFUL AFFIRMATIVE TOPICS. As the stories above illustrate, good AI topics are things that members of the organization, community, or other group sincerely want to learn about and create more of in their lives; and they may be problems or concerns reframed and stated as what is wanted. Affirmative topics elicit stories about people, the organization, or the community at its best. They are said to be "fateful" because they set the tone and direction for discovery, conversation, learning, and transformation.

The best AI topics are "home grown," that is, they are chosen by the people who are involved in the process. In our work with businesses, employees and executives together have decided the focus of their inquiry by selecting the topics. In medical facilities, patients, doctors, nurses, and administrators have joined in selecting the topics for their Appreciative Inquiry. In schools where AI has been adopted, students, teachers, parents, and administrators have selected topics they believed would help them learn and co-create the future they desired. From the start, Appreciative Inquiry is a democratic process that gives equal voice to all stakeholders.

Discovery Phase: Crafting Questions and Conducting Interviews

The primary Discovery Phase task is uncovering positive capacity. This occurs through the crafting of positive questions, about the topics selected, which serve as the basis for widespread appreciative interviews. What distinguishes Appreciative Inquiry at this phase is that every question is positive. In addition to being positive, good AI questions elicit stories. They generate rich accounts of the best of what is and has been, as well as images of what might be.[5]

WHO SHOULD BE INTERVIEWED? When asked how many people should be interviewed in the Discovery Phase or who should do the interviews, we increasingly say "everyone" because in the process, people reclaim their ability to value, be surprised, and be inspired. As people throughout a system connect to study qualities, examples, and analysis of the positive core—each one appreciating and everyone being appreciated—hope grows and community expands.

Consider the example of Leadshare, a major Canadian accounting firm that used Appreciative Inquiry to support the tough transition in executive succession of its "legendary" managing partner. Leadshare seized the moment as a leadership-development opportunity for all four hundred partners. An extensive two-hour interview protocol was designed focusing on affirmative topics like innovation, equality, partnership, speed to market, and valuing diversity. The firm's thirty junior partners were paired for interviews with the more seasoned senior partners. A powerful and instant intergenerational connection was made, and organizational history came alive in face-to-face storytelling. Like a good piece of poetry filled with endless interpretive meaning, people began to relate to their company's history as a reservoir of positive possibility. At the next annual partners' meeting, attended by all of the four hundred partners, the interview stories and data were coupled to the future through a strategic planning process. The stories instilled a strong sense of continuity and served as the foundation for bold new directions for the future. This strategic planning session turned out to be one of the "best" the partners could remember (Rainey 1996).

In the international development context, a less formal approach is often taken to interviewing. In Canada, the International Institute for Sustainable Development (IISD) carried out an Appreciative Inquiry in partnership with the Skownan First Nation to explore how to incorporate aboriginal values into land-use and resource-management programs in the province of Manitoba.[6] A project team composed of IISD and Skownan representatives conducted appreciative interviews with more than one hundred members of the Skownan community during three seasons. All age groups, family groups, and a rough gender balance were represented in the survey sample. The team's interviews with the Skownan people were informal and relaxed, usually taking place over a cup of tea in the home or while the person was working on the land. The interviewer would begin by asking the person to tell the story of a peak experience—an outstanding success in fishing or hunting, for example, or a particularly memorable family outing. The interviewer would then ask why the person valued that activity so highly and what it gave them in terms of economic benefit and spiritual fulfillment. Finally, the interviewer would ask the person for ideas for how to make experiences like this happen more frequently or readily. This response would lead into a discussion of the person's vision for the Skownan First Nation in the future.

Yet another approach to interviewing was developed by MYRA-DA, a south Indian development agency, in the Kamasamudram region. To get stories of peak moments and achievement, MYRADA staff would walk through the village with a group of villagers to look for examples of previous achievements. If a hill had been replanted with trees or a temple constructed, the staff asked how it happened, who did what, who else was present, and how they felt when it was completed. They tried to identify the strengths that the villagers drew upon to complete the task. Other questions related to what the villagers felt most proud of in the village and what achievements they would want to showcase if an important person were to visit. The goal was to find stories that evoked pride and fond memories from the villagers to create an atmosphere conducive to further storytelling (Ashford and Patkar 2001).

INTERVIEW PARTNERS: IMPROBABLE PAIRS. Appreciative interviews are an exceptional vehicle for bringing together people who might not otherwise talk with one another. Whenever people come together across a divide—whether of age, gender, race, ethnicity, religion, class, politics, or ideology—there is a need for a safe way to meet so that people may express themselves and be heard. The positive nature of Appreciative Inquiry fosters safety and facilitates relationship building. We have been surprised again and again by the deep connections created during appreciative interviews. As angry union leaders and corporate managers have interviewed one another, we've watched roles drop and human hearts connect. As members of warring religions have shared their stories, we've seen hurt and pain turn to tears of remorse and commitment to partner for peace. As youth have interviewed teachers and principals we've observed the adults recommit to making the world a better place.

As we do this work we ask ourselves, "Who are the people who need to get to know one another, person to person? Who are the people who haven't felt safe to share their stories, hopes, and dreams and really need to give voice to them? Who are all the people invested emotionally, financially, socially, or physically in the well-being of this organization or community? Who are all the people who need to be involved to make things better, safer, more life giving, just, or sustainable?"

And then we invite them to do appreciative interviews with one another . . . to share their stories . . . to listen to one another . . . and to imagine the future together. They focus on the positive core—of their lives, cultures, traditions, beliefs, and practices—and the most positive possibilities for their future together.

In 1998 Catholic Relief Services (CRS), with help from the GEM Initiative of Case Western Reserve University, began an initiative to improve the quality of its partnerships with local churches and NGOs in countries where the development agency was active. Through honest dialogue with indigenous partners who were unlike the huge global organization in many ways, and by gathering stories of partnership excellence, innovation, and best practices, there emerged a fresh way to view partnerships, moving from a model of resource-based dependence to one of mutual benefit and strength (Kinghorn 2001).

Dream Phase: Envisioning and Enacting What Might Be

Appreciation draws our eye toward life, stirs our feelings, triggers our curiosity, and inspires the envisioning mind. AI's Dream Phase asks people to actively envision and dramatically enact their ideal future—a time when things are just as they wish they could be; a time when they and their organization or community are contributing to a better world. As people share what they learned in their interviews and listen together to vital moments in the life of the system, the future becomes visible though ideals interwoven with actual experiences, and this energizes and moves people to action.

During a merger-integration summit for Child Welfare Services in Nevada, one young man, himself a foster child, took the microphone and said, "I do have a dream. I want to redesign the courtrooms so children are not afraid when they go to their foster care or adoption hearings. I want there to be round tables that everyone sits around—the kids, lawyers, social workers. Even the judges should come down from their high desks and sit at the round table. I want the judges to wear regular clothes instead of black robes. Maybe even there could be cookies on the table so the kids can feel at ease." The room was silent as the images portrayed in the young man's dream settled into the hearts and minds of the social workers, foster parents, lawyers, and judges in the room. And then a judge spoke, "I love your idea and I am willing to do it in my courtroom. Will you help me make it the way you believe will be good for the kids?" At that point the room was filled with the voices of volunteers offering to help rewrite policy, move furniture, and make this one dream a reality.

The more positive, hopeful, and life giving our images of the future, the more positive and affirming our actions are in the present. Powerful dreams and compelling images of the future can lead to dramatic results. Organizations are centers of human relatedness thriving when there is an appreciative eye—when people see the best in one another, when they can dialogue about their dreams and concerns in affirming ways, and when they are connected in full voice to create not just new worlds but better worlds.

Design Phase: Creating Statements of the Ideal

Once the dream is articulated—a vision of a better world, a powerful purpose, or a compelling statement of strategic intent—attention turns to creating the ideal organization or community, a design of the system in relation to its world. When inspired by a great dream, organizations, schools, teams, or communities feel compelled to design something very new and very necessary.

One aspect differentiating Appreciative Inquiry from other planning methodologies is that future images emerge through real examples from the positive past. Good-news stories are used to craft provocative propositions that bridge the best of "what is" with the collective aspiration of "what might be." People challenge the status quo, as well as common assumptions underlying the system's design. They explore: "What would our system look like if it were designed to maximize the positive core and accelerate realizing our dreams?"

CRAFTING PROVOCATIVE PROPOSITIONS. The Design Phase of Appreciative Inquiry comes forth in the form of provocative propositions (or possibility statements), statements of the ideal relationship, organization, or community written in the present tense, as if the ideal already exists. Provocative propositions stretch the system in new directions in relation to key elements of organizing, such as relationships, distribution of power and authority, leadership, communication, learning, financial rewards, and in the case of business, products, technology, and customer service.

Many organizations, for example, seek to reduce the incidence of sexual harassment in the workplace. They spend a great deal of time and money studying the problem, its causes, and its consequences. As a result, they become experts in sexual harassment yet often are unable to reduce its occurrences. One organization, however, was able to shift the focus of inquiry and analysis from sexual harassment to the affirmative topic, "positive cross-gender working relationships." At the Avon Company in Mexico, the many stories gathered in response to this topic provided positive images of healthy, strong, and productive cross-gender working relationships and generated the knowledge needed to create a safe work environment and foster positive relationships.

From the interviews it became clear that positive working relationships are not created in workshops. Rather, they come about as women and men work together as equals on committees, projects, and tasks of significance. Based on this finding, staff members wrote the following provocative proposition: "Every task force or committee at Avon, whenever possible, is co-chaired by a cross-gender pairing." The result? Within two years this company was awarded the 1997 Catalyst Award as the best place in Mexico for women to work (Schiller 2002).

Once a compelling dream is articulated, the need for new relationships, structures, systems, and decision-making processes becomes apparent. Redesigning the policies, organizations, and institutions that hold injustice, inequality, and abuse in place is not a simple task. It takes attention, time, resources, a favorable policy environment, the commitment of leaders, and consciousness to go from complaining about systems to redesigning them. It takes thoughtful consideration and dialogue among all stakeholders to design systems that reflect the values of human well-being, respect for differences, equality, and peaceful coexistence.

APPRECIATIVE INQUIRY AND ABORIGINAL VALUES. Returning to the story of the Skownan First Nation introduced above, the Discovery Phase was followed by six community workshops during which possibility statements on eight topics were formulated as "Values, Visions, and Action Plans,"[7] as follows:

- *Respecting the land.* Our people respect the lands and waters. We work to ensure that the land and water are clean and healthy for our children and the animals.

- *Community.* Our people work together to build a strong, safe, and united community for our children and future generations.

- *Family.* Our people spend time with our families to learn from our elders and to pass on our culture, language, and values to our children.

- *Recreation.* Our people build pride, unity, and strength in our bodies and minds through recreation and meditation.

- *Education.* Our people strive for higher education. We complete high school, excel at our jobs, achieve our goals, and bring meaningful employment requiring skills and education back to Skownan First Nation. Our children are educated in our traditional values, and we have the skills, knowledge, and respect needed to survive on the land. Our people speak Ojibway.

- *Spirituality.* Our people respect each other's spirituality or ways be they Roman Catholic, Pentecostal, Native culture, or atheist, and we are free to practice our own beliefs.

- *Livelihoods.* Our people provide for our families through productive works based on traditional activities on the land. Working individually, we support our community as a whole.

- *Health and nutrition.* Our people share food from the land gained through hunting, fishing, trapping and gardening, and learn the traditional medicines from our elders.

An initial action plan was developed to achieve some of the goals identified, such as planting trees, preserving aboriginal culture through the educational system, and maintaining access to and the health of Skownan's traditional lands.

The project concluded with a series of focus-group workshops that enabled the Skownan First Nation people to communicate their values and vision to decision makers, explore the benefits and opportunities of using Appreciative Inquiry, and discuss how to engage in collaborative processes when carrying the work forward with other aboriginal communities.

Destiny Phase: Empowering Inspired, Self-Organized Actions

Some call this phase Destiny, some call it Delivery. Either way, we've discovered that momentum for change and long-term sustainability in organizations increases the more we abandon traditional "delivery" ideas of action planning, building implementation strategies, and monitoring progress. Change in a human system should look more like an inspired movement than a neatly packaged plan or engineered product. The story of GTE (now Verizon), one of the largest telecommunications companies in the United States, is suggestive. Dan Young, the head of organization development at GTE, and his colleagues call it "organizing for change from the grassroots to the frontline." Or, it might be called the path of positive protest or a strategy for positive subversion.

Begun as a pilot at GTE to see what would happen if Appreciative Inquiry were given to frontline employees, things took off. Frontline employees launched interview studies into topics like "innovation," "inspired leadership," "revolutionary customer responsiveness," and "fun." One employee, newly trained in AI, did two hundred interviews into the positive core of a major call center, which handles a large volume of calls from customers. "I'm trying to learn about the best innovations. I see you as someone with insight into creating settings where innovation happens...," the interviews began. Soon these affirmative topics began to find their way into meetings, corridor conversations, and senior planning sessions. The ensuing conversations began to change corporate attention, language, agendas, and knowledge. Other employees started brainstorming AI applications, like surveying customers who were 100 percent *satisfied* with GTE service and changing call-center performance measures from measures of deficits to measures of effectiveness and success.

The pilot attracted requests from new people wanting to participate. Ten regional training sessions linked by satellite conferencing were held. Then the unions raised serious concerns about not having been consulted about this process early on. A meeting was called for the unions and GTE management. At the meeting the leaders of two major unions said they saw something fresh and unique about Appreciative Inquiry. They agreed to bring two hundred union leaders together for an evaluation and vote on AI, to see if it had any place in GTE's future. The outcome was an endorsement of the process, and eight months later, an in-house document announced an historic Statement of Partnership: "The company and the Unions realize that traditional adversarial labor-management relations must change to adapt to the new global telecommunications marketplace. . . . The company and the Unions have agreed to move in a new direction emphasizing partnership. . . ."8

THE 4-D CYCLE IN INTERNATIONAL DEVELOPMENT. The transformation of the SHARED Project, a ten-year project of the international NGO World Learning and funded by the U.S. Agency for International Development (USAID), into an indigenous, independently supported NGO was a complicated, frustrating, time-consuming, and joyful experience.9 Begun in 1990 through a USAID–World Learning cooperative agreement, the SHARED project was the single largest source of support for the development of an indigenous NGO sector in Malawi. It provided grants management and technical assistance to more than forty-five organizations in the burgeoning nongovernmental sector. Midway through the agreement, the parties began to realize how important it would be to the goals of sustainable devolvement for the work of SHARED to continue beyond the agreed ten-year framework. They settled on an innovative idea whereby the final outcome of the project would be the creation of an independent indigenous NGO. This new entity would be the means by which the expertise and resources of SHARED would continue as a primary agent of NGO capacity building in Malawi.

The GEM Initiative worked with the parties in designing and carrying out a multi-phased, iterative 4D-Cycle process, which initially involved the core staff of SHARED and later a larger group of stakeholders. One SHARED staff member recalled one workshop as a significant milestone in envisioning the pathway to transformation: "It was at that workshop that the origins of a clear vision, strategy, and process were first hatched. It is surely the clarity from that retreat that had carried us through a very busy, overwhelming, and sometimes frustrating transformation. The breakthrough for me was the involvement of all stakeholders in the process and the chance to make decisions that still guide our actions even today" (GEM Initiative n.d. [1998], 11).

THE APPRECIATIVE INQUIRY SUMMIT

Appreciative Inquiry has been applied in a wide variety of situations and ways.10 In this section we present one process for applying AI that we have found useful for businesses, nonprofits, and communities and believe holds promise for peacebuilding contexts—the Appreciative Inquiry Summit.11 We offer here a basic description of the summit process with the hope that readers will adapt it to meet the demands of their own situations.

The AI Summit is a large-group methodology for positive change. While each use of the summit is tailored to the unique situation of a given organization or community, all summits share four common characteristics: they include the whole system; they are focused on a common task; they

Ⓠ

are organized around the 4-D Cycle; and they foster dialogue that is affirmative and life giving.

Whether the system is a department, organization, multi-organizational alliance, community, or global social movement, AI summits allow everyone who has an important stake in a particular topic or future vision to join in a face-to-face "dialogue of equals" with others who also share in that stake. In a school summit, for example, students, parents, teachers, administrators, counselors, and community leaders all meet together to chart the course for the school's future. The summit is based on the simple idea that in any system, momentum for change requires large amounts of positive energy and social coordination—things like hope, enthusiasm, inspiration, cooperation, and a shared commitment to build the future together—and that the more engaged people are in the process, the more committed they will be to the change effort.

AI Summits are purposefully focused and are intended to generate dialogue and open up possibilities for action. The purpose may be a business objective (e.g., strategy formation, leadership development, merger and acquisition integration, process improvement, organization design, staffing and retention, customer satisfaction) or a social objective (e.g., economic development, community health, educational reform, environmental preservation, peacebuilding), in addition to being a learning objective (engaging the whole system in learning as much as it can about its history, identity, and modus operandi, including best practices and sources of excellence).

The 4-D Cycle serves as the framework for the summit agenda and supports the group in discovering and tapping into its strengths, envisioning the future its members want, designing the type of system that will enable the realization of their dreams, and then launching action teams to realize the future.

While still in its infancy as a large-group process, the AI Summit methodology has successfully advanced a number of major initiatives, including at medical centers, universities, corporations, international development NGOs, and with other kinds of social-change organizations. The summit was used to craft the innovative union-management partnership at GTE (described above) and to launch the global United Religions Initiative (described in chapter nineteen). Two Brazilian companies, Nutrimental and Dia, have used AI summits to gather all employees together with customers, vendors, distributors, and community leaders—mayors, city planners, educators, environmentalists, etc.—for strategic visioning and planning. The rewards for these two companies have been both qualitative and quantitative, with reduced rates of absenteeism and turnover and with revenues more than doubling.

When to Hold an AI Summit

An AI Summit is the intervention of choice when *the task requires high levels of participation and cooperation.* The ratio of monologue to dialogue during a summit is about 10 percent monologue to 90 percent dialogue among participants. There are no formal leadership presentations. Every person present participates with equal voice and stays the entire time. All stakeholders (or representatives of all stakeholder groups) are included and participate in discussions that span boundaries. The AI Summit is a high-participation, full-voice process.

The AI Summit works best when there is a need to *accelerate the process of change,* as in the case of the Brazilian company Nutrimental. The capacity to bring large numbers of people together in a participatory process builds consensus and momentum in a short period of time and therefore enables system change to occur rapidly and effectively.

Through *experience with highly diverse and at times conflicting groups,* we have discovered the AI Summit's capacity for building and nurturing relationships and cooperation among diverse groups of people involved in high-stakes, high-innovation work. Summit participation affords opportunities for relationship building across levels and functional sectors in the organization or community, as well as with constituencies and community-interest groups. The summit provides a rich field for informal conflict resolution and reconciliation as people work affirmatively together toward the task focus. Sharing stories, getting to know one another's hopes and dreams, and working affirmatively together builds relationships that endure. In addition to any formal mechanisms and structures that may result from visioning and designing at a summit, the informal relationships forged frequently lead to ad hoc cooperation for the good of the organization. Overall, enhanced cooperation is an outcome of the majority of AI summits.

The AI Summit also serves well as the umbrella process when there is a need for *integrating and making sense out of multiple change initiatives.* As a philosophy and methodology it provides a set of principles and practices that enhance participation and hence commitment to change. Change in an organization's internal operations and way of working in the world, for example, requires a phased process of weaving new ways of relating and working throughout the organizational system. When these changes occur via Appreciative Inquiry, the process has integrity and makes sense. The summit serves as an integrating event—a time for envisioning the system in the future and for putting order into all of the change initiatives underway and newly planned.

There is widespread recognition among leaders in many sectors of the benefits of whole-system positive change. When the financial manager of a family-medicine clinic was asked by the director if they could afford to close the clinic for two days to bring all personnel together, his answer was, "We cannot afford *not* to do it. We need to get everyone involved in crafting our future if we want them on board in making it happen." And so, for the first time in its thirty-year history, the clinic was closed and all one hundred personnel, along with a number of patients, patient advocates, and community members, gathered to chart the course of the clinic's future.

Appreciative Inquiry Summit Design

As a starting point, we present here an illustrative four-day process for an AI Summit for a business or other type of organizational context. This would need to be appropriately adapted for a peacebuilding setting. Each summit draws people together for a unique task, and each group of summit participants has a unique and diverse cultural and geographical mix; a unique set of relationships among stakeholders; and unique ways of expressing its most precious values, honoring relationships, making meaning, and taking decisions. Each type of uniqueness must be considered in designing the AI Summit process to ensure resonance, engagement, and collaboration among participants.

DAY 1–DISCOVERY. The first day's focus is on the discovery of many facets of the organization's positive core. Discovery includes questions such as: "Who are we, individually and collectively?" "What resources do we bring?" "What are our core competencies?" "What hopes and dreams do we have for the future?" "What are the most hopeful macro trends impacting us at this time?" And, "What ways can we imagine going forward together?"

Specific activities of the Discovery Phase include:

- *Setting the task focus*—a brief introduction to the context and purpose of the meeting.

- *Appreciative interviews*—all participants engage in one-on-one interviews organized around the topics of the meeting.

- *Who we are at our best*—small-group recollection of story highlights and best practices discovered during the interview process.

- *Positive-core map*—large-group process to illustrate the strengths, resources, capabilities, competencies, positive hopes and feelings, relationships, alliances, etc., of the organization.

- *Continuity search*—large-group process to create organization, industry (or other organizational context), and global time lines to identify factors that have sustained the organization over time and are desirable in the future.

DAY 2–DREAM. The second day is a day of envisioning the organization's greatest potential for positive influence and impact in the world. Dialogues are stimulated by questions such as: "We are in the year 2015 and have just awakened from a long sleep. As you wake and look around, you see that the organization is just as you have always wished and dreamed it might be. What is happening? How is the organization different?" Another way of asking the dream question is: "Imagine it is 2015 and your organization has just won an award for the outstanding socially responsible business of the year. What is the award for? What is said about your organization as the award is presented? What are customers saying? What are employees saying? What did it take to win the award?"

Specific activities of the Dream Phase include:

- *Sharing of dreams*—small groups discuss dreams collected during the interview process.
- *Enlivening the dreams*—small groups discuss specific, tangible examples of their dream and develop creative, metaphorical presentations.
- *Enacting the dreams*—group presentations of dramatic dream enactments to the large group.

DAY 3–DESIGN. During day three participants focus on designing an organization in which the positive core is boldly alive in all of the strategies, processes, systems, decisions, and collaborations and able to realize its dreams. They craft provocative propositions, affirmative statements of the future organization that are stated in the present tense and stretch the organization toward its dreams. While these are not statements of specific actions to be taken, they are actionable, for example, "At XYZ Company people have widespread access to knowledge, with liberty to make decisions." Such a statement, while highly desirable, will take action to fulfill. It represents the organization's commitment to move in that direction.

Specific activities of the Design Phase include:

- *Creation of the organization design architecture*—large group identifies organization design architecture best suited to their operation.
- *Selection of high-impact organization design elements*—large group draws on interviews and dreams to select high-impact design elements.
- *Crafting of provocative propositions for each organization design element*—small groups draft provocative propositions (design statements) incorporating the positive-change core into the design elements.

DAY 4–DESTINY. The final day is an invitation to action inspired by the prior days of Discovery, Dream, and Design. For some this is the day they have been waiting for, a time to finally get to work on the specifics of what will be done! At this point we invite personal and group initiative and self-organizing. We seek to demonstrate the large group's commitment to action and support for those who choose to go forward working on behalf of the whole.

Specific activities include:

* *Generation of possible actions*—small groups brainstorm possible actions and share with the large group.

* *Selection of inspired actions*—individuals publicly declare their intention for action and specify cooperation and support needed.

* *Emergent task groups form*—self-organizing groups meet to plan next steps for cooperation and task achievement.

* *Large group closing.*

A Dramatic Possibility for an AI Peacebuilding Summit

In May 2002, a videoconference brought together six courageous business leaders from Israel, Saudi Arabia, Egypt, and the United States to reflect on the crisis between Palestine and Israel. The session was happening at a time of the worst violence the region had seen in years. The six business leaders were shown together on a large split screen, an image telecast internationally with two hundred other chief executive officers (CEOs) from around the world watching.

The focus of the two-hour conversation was at two levels: What was happening for these business leaders personally, and what was happening with their businesses. At one point Mohammed, a Palestinian CEO, said, "I wrote the word 'hope' on the paper in front of me. The Palestinian people desperately need hope, any kind of hope that there is light at the end of the tunnel."

The teleconference was intense, with tensions and deep feelings expressed. The Israeli CEO Joshua started the session with a shaking voice as he told that members of his wife's family had just been killed by a Palestinian bombing. Mohammed, too, spoke at a personal level of the humiliation and endless delays of going to work each day through Israeli military checkpoints, even while trying to provide jobs for hundreds of employees. Amin, in Saudi Arabia, spoke about the collapse of his business. There were moments of tears, as the raw emotions shared by these business leaders spoke loudly.

The CEOs witnessing the event watched as dialogue shifted the relationships. At one point Mohammed spontaneously offered a prayer to Joshua, the Israeli, sharing the grief of the loss of family members. Others opened up about their fears, hopes for their children, and the sense of exhaustion. Soon there were proposals for collaboration and plans to help each other's businesses—to get supplies and products delivered, raise funds for social-change projects, and more.

Joshua observed that business, perhaps more than any other arena, could be a force for bringing people into positive contact and cooperation. Then someone commented half in jest: "We business leaders should hold our own peace summit, and then after a three or four days of finding pragmatic solutions and shared hopes, we will impose our plans onto the political arena. . . . With our governments paralyzed, it will all be a lot more simple if we get involved. Right?" Everyone laughed, grateful for a moment's comic relief.

Yet after the teleconference, another small group of CEOs met to debrief. One of them said that "many a truth is said in jest." Business might well be one of the few places where good conversation like this can happen, he suggested, and an idea was born. There could be a Middle East summit convened and co-chaired by Palestinian and Israeli CEOs working together. The title: "Business as a Force for Hope: Coming Together to Discover the Postconflict Future We Want to Create." Excitement grew, and someone proposed using Appreciative Inquiry to structure the summit. A foundation agreed to fund the idea.

Almost a year later, with the killing between these two peoples continuing and tensions heightened throughout the Mideast region, the moment has not yet arrived that provides the right kind of opening for this complicated work to proceed. But the possibility continues to give hope, and the idea and funding stand poised, awaiting the arrival of an opportune moment to carry it forward.

WHEN MIGHT WE USE APPRECIATIVE INQUIRY FOR PEACEBUILDING?

As we have introduced Appreciative Inquiry to businesses and communities around the world, we have encountered questions, hesitations, and even strong resistance. On the first day of a workshop in Austria, one participant stood in front of the group and called us naïve and uninformed about the realities of political life in her country. She argued that the situation there and in the world was so "dark and potentially dangerous" that we could not afford to ignore the problems. She was the leader of a growing and highly influential resistance group that was mobilizing against the neo-fascist forces that were then in the political ascendancy in her society. Then, on the third day of the workshop, she made a plea to the group: "Please help me. I see now that resistance is not the strongest way to build the future I want. We must help people believe in themselves and envision the future that they want. I now see that through Appreciative Inquiry can we help people create the world they want, not just resist what they don't want." Ⓠ

Many of our readers may be like this woman, wondering if it is possible to move beyond suspicion, suffering, injustice, abuse, and violence by reframing and dealing with such deeply challenging problems through positive approaches to peacebuilding. We believe it is not only possible, but essential that those of us who deeply desire a just and peaceful world set about creating it—and that we put our hearts, minds, attention, and best efforts to work creating enclaves of peace, points of light that will some day join together in a vibrant show of the best of humanity. And we believe that Appreciative Inquiry as a philosophy and methodology may have something to offer.

In this section we offer five areas we believe may be served by the adaptation and application of Appreciative Inquiry. Each of these ideas builds on those that come before. The result is a progression of possibilities for integrating AI into peacebuilding initiatives. Together they constitute a working hypothesis about how Appreciative Inquiry might be of service to the peacebuilding field.

Reframing the Issue: Transforming Helplessness to Commitment to Action

Appreciative Inquiry has the potential to transform the way people talk about, see, experience, and act upon the situations in their lives. In some cases a reframing of the issue followed by inquiry and dialogue into an affirmative topic may provide a safe opening for initiating communication.

A colleague phoned recently who has been working with a United Nations project in Africa to reduce HIV/AIDS. He told the story of using Appreciative Inquiry with a group of forty government leaders in one African country. Some group members asserted that a key factor contributing to the spread of HIV/AIDS in their country was disrespect for and abuse of women. At first the men among them felt defensive. All of them, men and women, felt helpless to change anything, until they engaged in an Appreciative Inquiry on the topic of "respect for women." Women and men interviewed each other and shared stories of times when men had given respect and women had felt it. Many wept as they heard these stories. Later the men shared what a relief it was to be recognized for the respect they give to women and their capacity to make a difference. The women, after telling their own stories of overcoming oppression and abuse and being listened to, expressed confidence that things could change. Altogether the group realized that education, in general, and health education that specifically supported the women's right to say no to men would increase respect for women and might help stem the tide of HIV/AIDS. They realized that these were indeed things this group of leaders could do, and they committed to doing so.

It is cases like this, as well as our work with conflict situations in business and international development, that give us confidence in the potential of Appreciative Inquiry for reframing situations from helpless to hopeful.

Bringing People Together Who Might Not Otherwise Talk

Among the things essential to peacebuilding is the creation of a safe climate for conversation and a vehicle for people to have equal voice in the process. One of the things that Appreciative Inquiry does best is bring people who might not otherwise talk into deep conversation. The positive focus creates a safe and inviting context for conversation. The choice of "homegrown" affirmative topics assures participants that what they want to discuss and create in their lives is not just *on* the agenda, it *is* the agenda. And the opportunity to meet as equals and tell and hear stories of deep personal meaning and significance can humanize the adversary or *the Other* as little else can. Indeed, the "freedom to be heard" is described by many as one of the key success factors of AI (Whitney and Trosten-Bloom 2003, 241–243).[12]

Some indigenous practices and contemporary restorative justice practice suggest that healing occurs when all parties involved sit in circle and talk—when victims, offenders, community members, law-enforcement officials, and judges join together for sharing and restoration planning. Restorative justice practitioner Thom Allena tells us he is finding that when Appreciative Inquiry is used, these conversations open up more quickly, people are more forthcoming, and resolutions are more collaborative.

Building Confidence and Courage—Healing Through the Positive Core

The theory and practice of trauma healing sees the need for trauma survivors to give voice to their loss and pain. Appreciative Inquiry suggests that healing also requires a remembering of strengths and capacities, a recollection or re-creation of dreams, and a reclaiming of identity in community. These all can occur through the 4-D Cycle.

The developing field of positive psychology (Seligman 1998) concurs with noted psychologist Carl Jung who commented at the end of his career that he had never seen people grow *from* a problem. Instead, he suggested, they grow *toward* some more compelling life force.

We wonder if there might be a three-step process for using Appreciative Inquiry in situations of violence, abuse, and trauma: first, *within groups* of trauma survivors as a way for them to discover and articulate their forgotten strengths and visions and to build confidence and courage to go forward in relation to the Other; second *between groups* in the conflict as a way for parties to meet safely to discuss both their experiences of suffering and loss and also their hopes and dreams for the future; and third, when the *par-*

ties together conduct the process, including interviewing, envisioning, and designing a just and peaceful shared future.

A gradual process such as this might provide time and safety for people who have been harmed to build confidence and heal as they discovered and discussed first their own and then their counterparts' strengths, hopes, and dreams. And finally, it would provide them with an important shared task— the co-creation of their own future. We have found that often when people who consider themselves opponents work together on a task of significance, relational improprieties heal in the process.

Envisioning the Future Together

The Dream Phase of Appreciative Inquiry is different from other visioning methodologies in two important ways. First, it is grounded in stories generated during the discovery interviews. These stories create a context of possibility. If participants know, for example, that someone somewhere or some other community has created a particular kind of program, they are more likely to envision it as a viable part of their future than if they did not know of it. The knowledge of best practices lived elsewhere or experienced at other times enriches dreaming in Appreciative Inquiry.

Second, we ask people to envision the world a better place and then to imagine what and how they can contribute to that image. In this way a group's vision for themselves is integrated into their hopes and dreams for the world, and they become meaningful and essential to the creation of that better world.

Appreciative Inquiry might contribute to peacebuilding by giving people the time and space to discuss and envision the life they want together. Recognizing, however, the power of prevailing policies, politics, and oppressive structures in many conflict situations, the predominant challenges for Appreciative Inquiry would be (1) how to safely and viably get all the relevant and affected parties together and involved in the process, and (2) how to mobilize enough clarity and strength of vision and action to have the necessary transformative effect in changing policies, structures, and systems.

Designing Better Ways of Being Together

Appreciative Inquiry goes beyond values and relationships to the design of programs, policies, and institutions that foster justice, democracy, and health and well-being for all people. In business we use AI to facilitate the creation of democratic, self-organizing systems. In international development we use AI to facilitate the design and establishment of self-determined local organizations. In many peacebuilding contexts there is a profound need for policy and institutional transformation. We believe that the highly participatory, affirmative nature of Appreciative Inquiry might also serve the creation of cultures of peace, institutions that serve and develop the habits of peace, and ultimately communities at peace.

Give Peace a Chance, Give AI a Chance

At this writing, the philosophy and practice of Appreciative Inquiry is no more than eighteen years old. Its co-originator, David Cooperrider, suggests that even now it is has reached only 5 percent of its potential as a methodology for social transformation and organizational change. In this chapter we've attempted to give an overview of what has been achieved and a taste of what may be possible. The invitation is now for you, the reader, to take up the call and experiment with Appreciative Inquiry, to adapt it to your work and see what more we can learn from it and what new ways the peoples of the world can benefit from its principles, ideas, and practices.

We welcome collaboration among AI practitioners and peacebuilders. We welcome research about Appreciative Inquiry and its potential for peacebuilding at the relational, local, and global levels. We welcome continued opportunities for building bridges across fields to enhance and expand the positive core of peacebuilding. And most importantly, we welcome you into the community of advocates for positive approaches to peacebuilding, a community of people who are being the change they want to see.

ENDNOTES

1. The GEM Initiative was a program of Case Western Reserve University from 1994 to 2001. Funded by the United States Agency for International Development, it provided innovative capacity-building programs in leadership, organizational strengthening, and partnership building for NGOs all over the world. Its signature approach was based on the use of positive-change methodologies, with a special focus on Appreciative Inquiry. Through the GEM program, some one hundred NGOs were exposed to these methodologies and had the experience of using them successfully, often in the most trying of circumstances.
2. This section is excerpted from Whitney and Trosten-Bloom (2003, 18–19).
3. The following account is drawn from Dorsey (2000).
4. This section is drawn from Whitney and Trosten-Bloom (2003, 133–134).
5. For an explanation of how to craft appreciative questions, a description of what to do with the stories collected, and forty sample questions, see the *Encyclopedia of Positive Questions* (Whitney, Cooperrider, Trosten-Bloom, and Kaplin 2002).
6. This account, here and continuing in a section below, is drawn from IISD (2001).
7. This is the title of an annex to the project's final report (IISD 2001, 23–30).
8. For more on GTE's use of Appreciative Inquiry, see Cooperrider and Whitney (1999, 7–9) and Whitney, Cooperrider, Garrison, and Moore (2002).

9. This section is drawn from Hlatshwayo, Khalsa, and Muyoya (2000).
10. For an overview of the various forms of engagement for Appreciative Inquiry, see Whitney and Trosten-Bloom (2003).
11. For a comprehensive description of the AI Summit and its uses, see Ludema, Whitney, Mohr, and Griffin (2003).
12. The other five freedoms commonly associated with Appreciative Inquiry are: the freedom to be known in relationship; the freedom to dream in community, the freedom to choose to contribute, the freedom to act with support, and the freedom to be positive (Whitney and Trosten-Bloom 2003, 238–251).

REFERENCES

Ashford, Graham, and Saleela Patkar. 2001. *The Positive Path: Using Appreciative Inquiry in Rural Indian Communities.* Winnipeg, Canada: Institute for Sustainable Development. http://www.iisd.org/pdf/2001/ai_the_positive_path.pdf.

Christian Reformed World Relief Committee (CRWRC). 1997. *Partnering To Build And Measure Organizational Capacity.* Grand Rapids, Mich.: Christian Reformed World Relief Committee.

Cooperrider, David L., and Diana Whitney. 1999. *Appreciative Inquiry.* San Francisco: Berrett-Koehler.

Dorsey, David. 2000. "Positive Deviant." *Fast Company* (December). http://www.fastcompany.com/online/41/sternin.html.

GEM Initiative. n.d. [1998]. "Breakthrough Illustrative Stories." Internal evaluation report, GEM Initiative, Washington, D.C.

Hlatshwayo, Godwin, Gurudev Khalsa, and T.S. Muyoya. 2000. "The Dawning of the Development Centre in Malawi: A Case Study of North-South Cooperation In Transforming World Learning's SHARED Project." A study conducted by the Institute for Development Research, Boston, Mass.; MWENGO, Harare, Zimbabwe; and GEM Initiative, Washington, D.C.

International Institute for Sustainable Development (IISD). 2001. *Integrating Aboriginal Values into Land-Use and Resource Management: Final Report, January 2000 to June 2001.* Winnipeg, Canada: IISD. http://www.iisd.org/pdf/skownan_final_nopics.pdf.

Kinghorn, Meg. 2001. *The Partnership Toolbox: A Facilitator's Guide to Partnership Dialogue.* Baltimore: Catholic Relief Services; Washington, D.C.: Pact Publications.

Lederach, John Paul. 1997. *Building Peace: Sustainable Reconciliation in Divided Societies.* Washington, D.C.: U.S. Institute of Peace Press.

Ludema, James, Diana Whitney, Bernard Mohr, and Thomas Griffin. 2003. *The Appreciative Inquiry Summit.* San Francisco: Berrett-Koehler. Forthcoming.

Rainey, Mary Anne. 1996. "An Appreciative Inquiry Into the Factors of Culture Continuity During Leadership Transition." *Organization Development Practitioner* 28:1 and 2, pp. 34–41.

Schiller, Marjorie. 2002. "Imagining Inclusion: Men and Women in Organizations." In *Appreciative Inquiry and Organizational Transformation: Reports from the Field.* Ronald Fry, Frank Barrett, Jane Seiling, and Diana Whitney, eds. Westport, Conn.: Quorum Books.

Seligman, Martin E.P. 1998. "Building human strength: psychology's forgotten mission." *American Psychological Association Monitor* 29:1 (January). http://www.apa.org/monitor/jan98/pres.html.

Whitney, Diana, David L. Cooperrider, Maureen E. Garrison, and Jean P. Moore. 2002. "Appreciative Inquiry and Culture Change at GTE: Launching a Positive Revolution." In *Appreciative Inquiry and Organizational Transformation: Reports from the Field.* Ronald Fry, Frank Barrett, Jane Seiling, and Diana Whitney, eds. Westport, Conn.: Quorum Books.

Whitney, Diana, David L. Cooperrider, Amanda Trosten-Bloom, and Brian Kaplin. 2002. *Encyclopedia of Positive Questions.* Cleveland, Ohio: Lakeshore Communications.

Whitney, Diana, and Amanda Trosten-Bloom. 2003. *The Power of Appreciative Inquiry: A Practical Guide to Positive Change.* San Francisco: Berrett-Koehler.

The world we have made as a result of the level of thinking we have done thus far creates problems we cannot solve at the same level of thinking at which we created them.

ALBERT EINSTEIN

CHAPTER THREE

APPRECIATIVE INQUIRY IN PEACEBUILDING:
IMAGINING THE POSSIBLE

Claudia Liebler and Cynthia Sampson

This chapter integrates insights from the two previous chapters by relating the theoretical underpinnings and practice of Appreciative Inquiry to those of conflict resolution and peacebuilding. It also relates the foundations of Appreciative Inquiry (AI) to a number of the case studies of positive approaches to peacebuilding in this volume. The chapter concludes by exploring how the AI 4-D Cycle of Discovery, Dream, Design, and Delivery has been, or might be, applied in peacebuilding contexts; and it illustrates some of the ways in which the design of the AI process can be contextualized for different types of conflict settings.

☙

*T*his chapter weaves together the threads of what has come before and also provides a "gateway" to the chapters that follow. In chapter one, we looked at the evolution of the peacebuilding field, key assumptions and principles of peacebuilding, and examples of positive elements in existing peacebuilding practice. In chapter two we were introduced to the theory and practice of Appreciative Inquiry as it evolved from organizational settings, primarily in business, to applications in international development and other social-change arenas. The second chapter ended by offering a vision of five possible ways in which Appreciative Inquiry (AI) might be brought to the service of peacebuilding: by helping transform a sense of helplessness to a commitment to action; by bringing people together who might not otherwise talk; by building courage and confidence for posttraumatic healing; by assisting conflict parties in envisioning the future together; and by designing better ways of being together.

In this chapter we pick up the threads of that vision and look more concretely at how Appreciative Inquiry has been and might be applied in peacebuilding.[1] We begin by exploring the conceptual and theoretical underpinnings of Appreciative Inquiry with reference to peacebuilding and then relate AI's 4-D Cycle—Discovery, Dream, Design, Delivery—directly to the practice of peacebuilding. A key purpose in the latter task is to illustrate some of AI's potential for adaptation and improvisation in peacebuilding contexts.

This chapter continues in an exploratory spirit. It does not presume to have glimpsed all of the possibilities or to have all of the answers. Far from it, we offer it instead as a further invitation to you, the reader, to explore, expand, adjust, and adapt the ideas and practices presented here. As you do, we hope you will share with us your experiences, your challenges, and your triumphs, however small or large.[2]

CONCEPTUAL AND THEORETICAL UNDERPINNINGS OF APPRECIATIVE INQUIRY

Appreciative Inquiry has been described as,

> the cooperative search for the best in people, their organizations, and the world around them. It involves systematic discovery of what gives a system "life" when it is most effective and capable in economic, ecological, and human terms. AI involves the art and practice of asking questions that strengthen a system's capacity to heighten positive potential. (Cooperrider and Whitney 1999, 10)

An Appreciative Inquiry might be viewed as a journey—but not the kind that you plan three months ahead and have all of your rooms and excursions booked in advance. This journey involves improvisation and a certain amount of risk. It begins with a general vision of the direction and an idea of the type of trip you're embarking on, but leaves a lot of room for the unexpected to happen along the way. As on any journey, there are certain provisions to take along. In this section we explore the major concepts and theories that drive the Appreciative Inquiry process, particularly as they relate to peacebuilding.

Major Concepts of Appreciative Inquiry

Appreciative Inquiry was developed in the mid-1980s by David Cooperrider and his colleagues studying organizational behavior at the Weatherhead School of Management of Case Western Reserve University. Drawing on research from such fields as organizational behavior, psychology, medicine, education, and sociology, as well as their own extensive experience in working with organizations, they challenged the traditional theories of change and created a new set of ideas that have been tested and further shaped by practitioners in the intervening years. Some of the most important concepts that underlie Appreciative Inquiry are the following:

IMAGE AND ACTION ARE LINKED. Cooperrider's research, drawing examples from diverse fields, has shown quite clearly that our actions are linked to our image of the future (1990). Perhaps the best known of the theories demonstrating this are the placebo effect, from the field of medicine, and the Pygmalion dynamic, from education.

The widely documented placebo studies dating from the mid-1950s in the United States have shown that people given sugar pills but believing they are taking real medicine get well at about the same rate as those taking actual medicine. Though controversial for some twenty years, most in the medical profession now accept that anywhere from one-third to two-thirds of all patients will show marked physiological and emotional improvement in symptoms simply by believing that they are being given an effective treatment (Beecher 1955; White, Tursky, and Schwartz 1985).

The Pygmalion studies, carried out in U.S. classrooms in the 1960s (Rosenthal and Jacobson 1968), demonstrated the power of the image that another person holds of us, positive or negative, in affecting both that person's behavior toward us and also in shaping our performance. In these studies teachers were told that one group of students was not very intelligent, tended to do poorly, and was often not well behaved in the classroom. The second group was described as bright, hard working, and successful. The teacher believed this to be fact, while in actuality the division of students into these groups was completely random. Within one semester, almost without exception, those labeled as poor students were performing poorly and those labeled good students were excelling. It was shown that the image the teacher held of the students' future potential affected the teacher's actions in displaying more patience with the positively construed students, having more eye contact, offering more praise, and so forth. These experiments were considered so damaging that they were discontinued.

Groups that are successful tend to be those that have a positive guiding image that is widely shared and galvanizes action. In the Appreciative Inquiry 4-D Cycle, therefore, participants spend a great deal of time in creating a shared vision. Likewise in peacebuilding, linking images and actions is the ultimate objective for the practitioner using processes designed to replace the negative image of war and the enemy or dehumanized *Other* (linked to negative and destructive actions) with a different set of images and actions. In this volume, for example, we see how the development of a common vision for peaceful community by former adversaries helped develop a culture of peace in the violence-prone Usulutan province of El Salvador (chapter five); and how a transformed image of the Other led to breakthroughs in understanding and establishment of relationship between former adversaries in the aftermath of World War II in Europe (chapter eleven), in South Africa (chapter fifteen), and in Bosnia (chapter seventeen).

GROUPS MOVE IN THE DIRECTION OF THE QUESTIONS THEY ASK. The kinds of questions people ask determine what they will find, and what they find then sets the direction for the journey toward change. In peacebuilding, this has tremendous implications for interveners first entering a conflict situation, not only with regard to the substance of the questions, but also with regard to how the questions affect the parties' perceptions of themselves, the Other, and their collective potential for constructive change. A motivating question in the peacebuilding arena is, "What resources, conditions, practices, and relationships are present in the system that promote peace?" This approach is well illustrated in a strategic opportunities assessment of Guinea-Conakry conducted by the West Africa Network for Peacebuilding, which sought out the peace-generating capacities inherent in Guinean society (see chapter eight).

ALL HUMAN SYSTEMS HAVE SOMETHING TO VALUE ABOUT THEIR PRESENT OR THEIR PAST. All systems, no matter how troubled, can find practices, experiences, or ways of being that work well or have at some time in their history. (See, for example, the remarkable history of creative coexistence between Muslims, Jews, and Christians in Muslim Spain and the medieval Mediterranean, described in chapter seven.) Appreciative Inquiry draws the analytical focus to these types of factors—the root causes of success—as the basis for change action, instead of looking for deficits or what is problematic or lacking in the system.

Mary Anderson writes, "Even when war erupts, local capacities for peace exist. Peace capacities are important because they provide the base on which future peace can and must be built." She identifies five categories of peace capacities as systems and institutions, attitudes and actions, shared values and interests, common experiences, and symbols and occasions (1999, 24). In the language of Appreciative Inquiry, peace capacities such as these are *positive-core elements* in the conflict system, which are discovered through inquiry and provide the foundations for visioning, planning, and implementing system change. By preceding the visioning process with inquiry aimed at discovering these affirmative values, social strengths, cultural and religious resources, indigenous conflict resolution practices, successful experiences in living with difference, and other positive-core elements, action toward change is grounded in the realities of the system at its best.

Five Principles of Appreciative Inquiry

Appreciative Inquiry is guided by five key principles. In many ways, peacebuilding is guided by these same principles, although they are often not made explicit in theory or practice. In this section we define each of the principles and discuss how they relate to peacebuilding.

CONSTRUCTIONIST PRINCIPLE. We can create what we can imagine. The *constructionist principle* states that we collectively make meaning of our world based on our habits, traditions, teachings, and how we view our very identity. What we believe to be real in the world is created through our social discourse and the conversations we have with one another.

These conversations lead to agreement about how we see the world, how we will behave, and what we will accept as reality. The ways in which we commonly understand the world, the categories and concepts we use, are historically and culturally specific. Our categories depend on when and where in the world we live.

This impacts our experience of conflict. For John Paul Lederach: ". . . a constructionist view suggests that people act on the basis of the meaning things have for them. Meaning is created through shared and accumulated knowledge. People from different cultural settings have developed many ways of creating and expressing as well as interpreting and handling conflict" (1995, 10). Meaning is not fixed, and new meaning is created continually through new experiences and new forms of shared and accumulated knowledge.

The effective peacebuilder in any situation, therefore, must be skilled in the art of reading, understanding, and analyzing conflict as a living, human construction. What we believe to be true about a conflict—that is the way that we "know" it—will affect the way we act and the way we approach change in that system. (See, for example, the role that the rewriting of conflict narratives had in transforming a formerly adversarial relationship in post-apartheid South Africa [chapter fifteen].) The first task for a peacebuilder, then, is to understand how people have shaped their meaning systems in regard to their own community and their constructed enemy.

We note here, however, that the social constructionist reading of conflict is not universally held by practitioners and advocates of positive approaches to peacebuilding, or at least is not seen as a fully adequate explanation of conflict behavior and dynamics. In considering the potential contribution of Appreciative Inquiry in complex peacebuilding and development contexts, Mary Hope Schwoebel and Erin McCandless challenge the notion that we have ultimate power to create our life opportunities and re-create our life circumstances (see chapter ten). They argue that we are born with or into many conditions of life or that they may be structurally determined by the institutions, environmental conditions, or cultural practices that surround us.

POETIC PRINCIPLE. In any culture, a people's past, present, and future are endless sources of learning, inspiration, interpretation, and possibility, just as a good poem is open to endless interpretations. The *poetic principle* acknowledges that people and their culture are open books, constantly being coauthored by the people themselves, as well as by those outside who interact with them. The poetic principle values storytelling as a way of gathering holistic information that includes not only facts, but feelings, and of getting beyond the verifiable data to the most meaningful and inspiring moments in the life of the individual, group, community, or society. In dialogue groups involving gay and evangelical Christians in California, for example, intimate and moving stories of religious and personal experiences were shared that enabled a deep level of connection among Christians who were otherwise deeply divided on theological interpretations regarding homosexuality (see chapter fourteen).

Stories carry meaning and truths that elude even the most sophisticated documentation systems. In peacebuilding, using approaches that elicit meaningful stories it is possible to access learning that is embedded in cultures and people's experiences to create culturally appropriate and sustainable strategies for peace.

PRINCIPLE OF SIMULTANEITY. The seeds of change are embedded in the questions we ask. The *principle of simultaneity* recognizes that inquiry and change are not separate moments, but are simultaneous, and therefore inquiry is also intervention. Not only does the way we go about analyzing conflicts and assessing needs determine what we find, but the questions lead to the stories that create the conversations that shape how people in conflict will construct their future.

One of the most impactful things a peacebuilder does is to formulate questions. To draw an example from this book, appreciative interviews on the topic of posttraumatic healing and growth, which were conducted with peacebuilders who had themselves survived trauma, not only yielded meaningful insight on the topic for the researcher conducting the interviews, but also provided new insight and perspective for the interviewees. This helped several of them appreciate how far they had come on their own healing journeys and strengthened their confidence and resolve to continue to support the trauma healing of others (chapter sixteen).

ANTICIPATORY PRINCIPLE. We anticipate the future based on the images we hold in the present. These images are guided by habits of the collective imagination. The *anticipatory principle* recognizes that our behavior is based not just on what we were born with or have learned from our environment, but also on what we anticipate, what we think or imagine will happen in the future.

This principle is critical in peacebuilding. People in conflict anticipate negative, hurtful behavior on the part of the Other, based on past experience. Sometimes this anticipation continues even in the face of new evidence to the contrary. Working to dislodge the deeply held images of conflict and allow more positive images to emerge is at the core of peacebuilding.

Examples abound in this volume of efforts to engage the positive imagination in giving birth to new images of the future. To cite one particularly creative example, an original song and storytelling project, created in response to the "9/11" terrorist attacks in the United States, put forward a vision of how one high school could change the world and bring an end to wars. As this vision reached wider and wider audiences, it triggered ripples

 of response in that high school and far beyond (see appendix to chapter six and compact disc included with this book).

AFFIRMATIVE PRINCIPLE. A positive stance is just as contagious as a negative stance. There is power in positive questions. The *affirmative principle* carries the key idea that if image leads to action, a positive image leads to positive action. In peacebuilding, the accessing of hope in situations that appear hopeless is essential if parties are to persevere in creating a different future. Positive inquiry can be an antidote to cynicism.

This principle does, however, depart from the mainstream of peacebuilding practice, which is focused on analysis of the root causes of conflict for the purpose of eliminating them. In peacebuilding, as we shall see in number of chapters in this book, a stance of "both-and" is most often warranted. We must give voice to the stories of trauma, loss, and pain *and* help the survivors recognize their own resilience, courage, and strength to move on and grow beyond trauma. We must allow respectful acknowledgement of past injustices *and* encourage positive visioning of the future as a way of creating positive change. We saw, for example, in chapter two how the sharing of "war stories" allowed the staff of the Christian Extension Services in Sierra Leone to appreciate their own and their agency's strengths exhibited during the war crisis and to plant the seeds of new vision.

JOURNEYING WITH APPRECIATIVE INQUIRY: AN INVITATION TO EXPERIMENT

We turn now to exploring how Appreciative Inquiry has been or might be practiced in peacebuilding contexts. Typically when people hear about Appreciative Inquiry for the first time, whether practitioners or prospective participants, a number of questions come naturally to mind.

Can Appreciative Inquiry make a difference in situations of deep-rooted ethnic and political conflict? Can this way of working that has grown out of the field of organizational development be used with whole societies as they work toward the transformation of relationships, structures, and systems? Can it redress injustice and transform unequal power relationships? Can AI help people dealing with intolerance, fear, mistrust, and hate?

For those involved in destructive conflict, the questions can be quite personal. Will focusing on the positive oversimplify the complicated situation I find myself in and trivialize, suppress, or overlook my grief and pain? Will my voice be heard? Will my grievances be fully aired and considered? How can I trust my enemy with personal stories of violation and loss?

We invite you to take up questions such as these and try on these ideas, by using the full 4-D Cycle of Appreciative Inquiry or parts of it and adapting it to the specifics and needs of your context. Far from a rigid, formulaic process, there are almost as many potential applications of AI as there are practitioners who use it. In the remainder of this chapter we suggest some ways to think about using AI in peacebuilding, beginning with identifying some of the other arenas of practice where helpful resources might be found.

Arenas of Appreciative Inquiry Practice

Although the bulk of the experience with Appreciative Inquiry has been in building organizational capacity in businesses and nonprofit organizations, AI has also been used to

- build global and regional coalitions and networks of social-change organizations, such as the Mountain Institute (Kaczmarski 1996) and the United Religions Initiative (see chapter nineteen; and Gibbs and Mahé [2003]);

- strengthen partnerships between international and indigenous non-governmental organizations (see Catholic Relief Service's *Partnership Toolbox* [Kinghorn 2001]);

- empower communities to discover and more effectively use their distinctive strengths and assets in building a better future (see Imagine Nagaland [chapter nine], and the project that inspired it, Imagine Chicago [Cooperrider 1996; Browne 2001; Belsie 2001]; see also Chupp [2002] on the use of AI in an interracial conflict in a Cleveland neighborhood);

- design and implement a wide range of literacy, education, health, agriculture, and other types of socioeconomic development programs (see examples in chapter two; see also Ole Sena and Booy [1997]; Liebler and Roche [1998]; Odell [2002]).

In addition, much healthy experimentation is taking place with appreciative ideas, for example, in the integration of appreciative processes with Future Search, a large-group visioning and change-action methodology (Weisbord and Janoff 1995; Kaczmarski and Khalsa 1997; United Nations Children's fund 2000); with Open Space Technology, a methodology for organizing meetings through self-managed work groups and distributive leadership (Owen 1997a; 1997b; Open Space Institute n.d. [2003]); and in the strengths-based approaches created by the Asset-Based Community Development Institute (Kretzmann and McKnight 1993).

Around the world today, Appreciative Inquiry and other positive-change approaches are being tried and adapted to local peacebuilding settings, as many of the chapters in this book attest. AI and peacebuilding practitioners are part of a larger movement of those exploring positive approaches to transformation in order to invigorate change processes with hope, possibility, creativity, and self-directed change.

APPRECIATIVE INQUIRY PROCESS IN PEACEBUILDING

In this section we look at some of the ways in which the AI 4-D Cycle might be used in peacebuilding settings. But first we look at some preparatory steps to assess the appropriateness of using Appreciative Inquiry in a particular setting and, if deemed appropriate, to lay the groundwork for doing so.

Preparing for an Appreciative Inquiry Process

To engage effectively in an AI process in peacebuilding, the conflict parties must be ready to turn toward building a new future together. It is important to allow time to explore whether Appreciative Inquiry is the right vehicle for them to take a next step. By sharing an overview of the philosophy and the 4-D Cycle, discussing the level of willingness to engage in a positive process for change, and sharing hopes, expectations, and fears about what could emerge, a safe space for beginning this work can be created

There are a number of indications as to whether a situation is particularly well suited for this approach. They include:

- Is there a shared sense that the time is right to begin working toward a positive future?
- Do the leaders have some level of comfort with appreciative ideas?
- Is there some experience among group members of using participatory processes?
- Are there some group members who are risk takers?
- Are there some who are able to see possibilities that others cannot?
- Does the environment (do stakeholders, the government stance, conflict dynamics, global events, etc.) support change?

If these conditions exist, the potential for change is present. Even when these indications are not present, however, the process might be used to help create them, for example, by doing some initial appreciative work with the parties individually (see below). So Appreciative Inquiry may still be a valuable way to move forward.

DESIGNING THE AI PROCESS IN PEACEBUILDING—VARIATIONS ON A THEME. Once a decision is made to proceed, the preparatory phase moves ahead with designing the overall process to be used for the Appreciative Inquiry. Each situation is unique, and AI has the capacity to adapt and adjust to take advantage of the resources within each situation and be informed by its constraints.

In the peacebuilding context, it may be appropriate to move through the 4-D Cycle more than once or to use the first steps in the cycle, Discovery and Dream, in some initial work with the conflict parties individually before attempting to undertake a full joint process. In that case, the first round would involve an inquiry into the positive-core elements—the values, strengths, capacities, resources for peace, and experiences of cooperation across differences—as well as some initial visioning within the individual groups. These stories and dreams would then be exchanged between the groups as the first step toward bringing them into dialogue. If the groups have some history of living in relationship, the second round would then be a joint inquiry into the positive core of their intergroup relationship, to discover the possibilities for creating a constructive relationship and provide the basis for visioning a shared future of peaceful coexistence. We see this two-phased approach illustrated in the model for an Appreciative Dialogue Workshop proposed to address an interstate conflict between Bolivia and Chile (see chapter thirteen).

The scope and conduct of the Discovery Phase inquiry may be varied in other ways as well. If the inquiry includes all parties touched in some way by the conflict, it could potentially involve hundreds of interviews with people from all sectors of the affected groups or societies. An inquiry of this scope might take several months to complete. Once the data has been collected and compiled, a representative group of the various stakeholders might then come together to work with the data and move through the 4-D Cycle in creating a vision of the future, designing the social architecture needed to support the vision, and charting next steps toward implementation.

Or, the inverse configuration might be warranted in which interviews (or the full 4-D Cycle) are conducted in microcosm in a workshop setting and then replicated with a larger group if momentum is created for further engagement. A third variant in process design would be for all participants, whether a dozen or dozens, to come together to work through the 4-D Cycle over a several-day period, in which case the Discovery Phase would take place on day one. (See the day-by-day description of the Appreciative Inquiry Summit in chapter two).

Finally, two variants in the actual conduct of the interviews are worthy of note for the peacebuilding context. The typical approach is to have one-on-one interviews, either in pairs of participants at an AI workshop or summit or by dispatching interviewers to conduct interviews with individuals in the larger society. One peacebuilding variant would be to have interviews conducted by pairs of individuals coming from different sides in the conflict, so that both may engage interviewees and their stories from different sides of the conflict and so the interviewer pairs can begin to build a common narrative out of the shared experience. The second would be would be for individuals to spontaneously conduct informal interviews virtually on the spot, as opportunities presented themselves, using an interview guide prepared in advance. This approach might work well in situations in which hostility between the parties or logistical restrictions (e.g., on travel) do not allow members to work together as a group at the initial stages of the process.

There are many ways in which the inquiry can be conducted, but the purpose in every case remains the same: to discover the positive-core elements in the system and to use this discovery data to help create an image of the future. Additional purposes served in the peacebuilding context are that parties discover new ways of viewing the conflict and that conflict meaning systems are transformed through personal connection and through exploring affirmative topics with individuals deemed "the adversary."

Once agreement has been achieved to use Appreciative Inquiry and an overall plan developed, the process moves to the first stage of the 4-D Cycle, the Discovery Phase.

Discovery Phase: Collecting Stories of Peace Capacities

The core task in the Discovery Phase is to uncover and appreciate the best of "what is" and "what has been." Empowering and hopeful ideas almost always emerge from stories that are grounded in a system at its best. The goal is to help the participants come to understand their relationship as one of positive possibility rather than a static, problematized set of conditions or events.

In peacebuilding this involves focusing on the local capacities for peace within the individual groups and in the intergroup relationship. In conflicts with longstanding hostilities, discovery may mean inquiring into and learning from even the smallest examples of constructive interaction in what is otherwise a highly conflictual relationship. For parties with no shared history of positive relationship, inquiry focuses on analogous situations of building relationship across other lines of division in the experience of the parties.

AFFIRMATIVE PEACEBUILDING TOPICS. Appreciative Inquiry begins and ends with valuing that which gives life to human systems—the discovery of the "life-giving" story, which in the peacebuilding context is the "justpeace-promoting" story—as it is understood and related by the people involved. The path to discovery is through the selection of affirmative topics for inquiry. AI topics are those qualities of the system that members want to discover more about and that will lead to conversations about the kind of future they most desire.

In peacebuilding, if identification of affirmative topics proves challenging for groups in conflict, it may be easier for them to identify things that are undesirable and then reframe them affirmatively. If, for example, a group wants to stop outbreaks of violence between two factions, reframing would be prompted by the questions: "What is it that you would like to see instead of violence? How would things look if the violence ended?" The affirmative topic might be "caring and cooperation across boundaries." Some other possible peacebuilding topics are:

- "improbable pairs"—finding partners for peacebuilding on the other side
- religious and cultural resources for peace
- breakthrough moments in understanding the Other
- courageous acts of compassion
- fearlessly witnessing the truth
- forgiving and being forgiven
- new growth out of the ashes
- boundary spanners (people who move across lines of division)

APPRECIATIVE QUESTIONS IN PEACEBUILDING. The next step is to develop interview questions to fully explore the selected topics. Good appreciative interview questions spark the appreciative imagination by helping the person locate experiences that are worth valuing; evoking essential values and aspirations; bringing out that which is inspiring, energizing, mobilizing; instilling hope; and opening up possibilities for positive change.

Three interview guides illustrating many types of appreciative questions that were developed for peacebuilding contexts are included in Appendix A to this chapter. The first guide was used at the conference "Positive Approaches to Peacebuilding: A Practitioners' Exploration" in September 2001. The second was designed to elicit stories of inner strength and personal growth out of difficult or "trying times." The third was used to initiate dialogue and planning at the founding meeting of a forum of religious leaders in November 1998.

Dream Phase: Visioning the Justpeace Ideal

The mental images and conversations of people in a system both drive and limit its activities; therefore to expand, enhance, or change the system, its image must be reconstructed through conversations among those who participate in and are impacted by it. The Dream Phase involves participants in bold conversations that challenge the way things are done and push the creative edges of possibility in realizing the ideal.

In peacebuilding, dreaming and visioning of a better future is crucial to sustaining hope and fortifying the resolve of individuals to continue to work for peace. Keeping their dream alive may be a matter of survival for people in a conflict zone. Yet for most people locked in conflict with one another, this will be the first time they have been invited to think great thoughts and create grand possibilities together. The process of jointly imagining and constructing a shared future with one's adversary requires courage and risk taking, but if accomplished, it can empower and provide a strong impetus for joint action. The story of Imagine Nagaland (see chapter nine) illustrates how AI discovery and dreaming creatively involved a diverse group of stakeholders, from children to government officials, in developing compelling visions for strengthening the social, political, and economic infrastructure of that northeast Indian state, which has seen decades of often-armed struggle for self-determination.

During the Dream Phase, participants create possibility statements (or provocative propositions) that describe their most desired future, as if it were already a reality. These statements stretch the way things are, challenge common assumptions or routines, express real desires, and suggest possibilities for system change. One of the ways facilitators assist participants in accessing and creating their vision of the future is by using a guided imagery exercise. A sample guided imagery exercise on the topic of "creative coexistence in my community" is included in Appendix B.

Possibility statements are visionary blueprints for pursuing the joint dreams of the AI participants. They are both imaginative and real. They contain the seeds of hope for a different future and yet are realizable. An example of a possibility statement that captures a dream for peaceful coexistence in Jerusalem, drawn from the real history Muslim-Jewish-Christian coexistence in medieval Spain (see chapter seven), is found in Figure 1.

Figure 1
SAMPLE POSSIBILITY STATEMENT

In Jerusalem's bustling markets, Muslims, Jews, and Christians come together to build a world of enlightenment. It is a time when these three communities are living together in harmony, neither oppressing nor being oppressed. The society in this era is being studied worldwide, not only for its intellectual excellence emanating from new knowledge being jointly created in the arts, sciences, medicine, engineering, philosophy, and literature, but also for its principles of tolerance and creative coexistence. Coexistence is modeled not on the melting-pot theory, but rather on the interchange of different points of view through wide-ranging dialogue.

Design Phase: Creating the Infrastructure to Realize the Dream

The Design Phase involves aligning values, structures, and processes with the vision for change and designing the social architecture that will be needed to support the envisioned future and ensure the feasibility of its implementation. Here, the participants begin to think about the kinds of changes that are needed in the institutional, social, political, and economic arrangements currently governing the system to allow their vision to be realized. One way for doing this is to write more detailed possibility statements about each part the system and its ways of functioning.

In peacebuilding contexts, social architecture might include some or all of the following elements, among others:

- laws, policies, agreements
- institutions, structures, systems
- communication mechanisms
- dispute-resolving mechanisms
- education and training
- multicultural approaches
- relations with the broader community.
- joint activities and projects
- strategies for sustainability

For peacebuilding, the Design Phase must address desired change at three levels: interpersonal, subsystem, and macro systems. Special attention is also needed to support the transfer of attitudinal change into the participants' home communities and to design elements that will sustain their energies and ensure their safety upon returning home.

Delivery Phase: Organizing to Begin Implementation

In the final, Delivery Phase of Appreciative Inquiry, the group plans concrete steps for realizing the vision and implementing the design. Typically, task groups form to initiate planning around different aspects of the vision and design; and in the best case scenario, dialogue continues beyond the immediate session, with new rounds of inquiry carried out at key junctures in the implementation process or as new members become involved. The Delivery Phase is a time of continuous learning, adjustment, and improvisation.

Action planning is, of course, integral to virtually any conflict resolution intervention as a necessary step toward implementation. Sound implementation planning is vital in peacebuilding contexts in which so often agreements are signed and celebrated yet crumble or face major challenges in their implementation. Increasingly, emphasis is being placed on delivery and monitoring mechanisms as equally crucial to the sustainability of peace as the terms of the agreement. An added serious concern in peacebuilding, alluded to above, is the "reentry factor," which involves the immediate safety and credibility of participants as they return to their communities and risk facing hostile constituencies who perceive them as having met with "the enemy." Thus the nature, scope, and intensity of the delivery and monitoring mechanisms carry the added weight of the real issues of participant credibility and safety, as well as of not undermining or working at cross purposes with the larger peace process within which the Appreciative Inquiry process may be embedded.

If full implementation of the vision and design seems daunting and beyond the ability of the participant group to fully plan for, they can look at delivery through the lens of "appreciate-influence-control." This involves identifying the parts of the social architecture and the specific aspects of the design that are within their immediate purview and ability of to either influence or control. This can help establish a strategy for setting implementation in motion, with checkpoints identified and additional rounds of Delivery Phase planning convened as appropriate and necessary along the way.

CONCLUSION

We close by touching briefly on some of the conjunctions between Appreciative Inquiry and peacebuilding and some outstanding questions that must be carried further into the book's explorations.

In chapter one, Mohammed Abu-Nimer presented a number of core assumptions and principles of peacebuilding. Peacebuilders assume, for example, that conflict is often a source of needed change and as such is neither good nor bad except in the ways in which it is pursued. Conflict can be a creative, constructive force for dealing with competing values, interests, goals, and needs, provided it is resolved nonviolently and in ways that empower all of the parties to collaborate creatively in problem solving. Peacebuilding assumes that "people are not the problem," and peacebuilders seek to treat every individual with dignity and respect. It is also assumed, however, that a change in the parties' perceptions of and communication patterns with one another is essential both to the resolution of the issues in the conflict and also to the creation of sustainable relationship among them.

Except for the difference in the analytical focus of Appreciative Inquiry, namely, its lack of problem orientation, these peacebuilding assumptions are all congruent with the AI philosophy of change and principles of practice. AI shares two core assumptions with peacebuilding that empower all parties to participate collaboratively and creatively in producing change. The first is that diverse participation in the process produces better outcomes, not only by ensuring that a range of viewpoints is represented, but also in providing a source of creativity and innovation. The second is that outcomes are more sustainable when all stakeholders participate in creating them. The AI process honors each individual and empowers every participant to contribute fully out of the best of who they are and what they can be.

It has the potential to transform perceptions and relationships by connecting participants with the goodness and humanity of the Other, as well as by engaging them together in creative visioning and mobilizing for action.

A second set of peacebuilding assumptions outlined by Abu-Nimer relates to systemic issues. It is assumed that the sustainability of outcomes also requires the transformation of dominant power relationships in the society and that agreements be supported concrete actions of social, political, and economic change. It is to these types of relational and systemic changes that Appreciative Inquiry as a methodology for whole-system change is dedicated and for which it has been tested in organizational systems of many kinds, including very large and complex organizations. Exactly how this experience will translate and adapt to social systems in conflict, however, is perhaps the leading question before us in this book.

This brings us to the take-off point of delving more deeply into what is known so far about Appreciative Inquiry in peacebuilding and positive approaches more broadly. The coming sections present seventeen chapters on applications, most of which are case studies and all of which give some clues to the answers for—or at least help to further illuminate—this and other real and compelling questions about positive approaches to peacebuilding.

ENDNOTES

1. Parts of this chapter have been adapted, with permission, from the practitioner's handbook of the Global Excellence in Management (GEM) Initiative of Case Western Reserve University (GEM Initiative 1999). We wish to extend warm appreciation to five colleagues who met with us for a day and contributed from the wealth of their experience and ideas in relating the theory and practice of Appreciative Inquiry to that of peacebuilding: Mohammed Abu-Nimer, Mark Chupp, Jayne Docherty, Susanna McIlwaine, and Nancy Good Sider.
2. Please contact us at: Positive Approaches to Peacebuilding, c/o Pact Publications, 1200 18th Street, NW, Suite 350, Washington, D.C. 20036 (tel: 202-466-5666, fax: 202-466-5669).

REFERENCES

Anderson, Mary. 1999. *Do No Harm: How Aid Can Support Peace—Or War.* Boulder, Colo.: Lynne Rienner.

Belsie, Laurent. 2001. "'Look for what's right': Theory of 'appreciative inquiry' takes on a community's mental atmosphere." *The Christian Science Monitor* (September 13), pp. 15, 18.

Beecher, H. K. 1955. "The Powerful Placebo." *Journal of American Medical Association* 159, pp. 1602–1606.

Browne, Bliss. 2001. "Imagine Chicago." In *Lessons From the Field: Applying Appreciative Inquiry*. Sue Annis Hammond and Cathy Royal, eds. Plano, Tex.: Thin Book Publishing Company.

Chupp, Mark. 2002. "From Culture Wars to Cultural Harmony." *Mennonite Conciliation Service Conciliation Quarterly* 21:1, pp. 4–5.

Cooperrider, David L. 1990. "Positive Image, Positive Action: The Affirmative Basis of Organizing." In *Appreciative Management and Leadership: The Power of Positive Thought and Action in Organizations*. Suresh Srivastva and David L. Cooperrider, eds. San Francisco: Jossey-Bass.

———. 1996. "The 'Child' as Agent of Inquiry." *OD Practitioner: Journal of the Organization Development Network* 28:1 and 2, pp. 5–11.

Cooperrider, David L., and Diana Whitney. 1999. *Appreciative Inquiry*. San Francisco: Berrett-Koehler.

GEM Initiative. 1999. *Appreciative Inquiry: Practitioner's Handbook*. Washington, D.C.: Global Excellence in Management (GEM) Initiative.

Gibbs, Charles, and Sally Mahé. 2003. *Birth of a Global Community: Appreciative Inquiry as Midwife for the United Religions Initiative*. Cleveland, Ohio: Lakeshore Press. Forthcoming.

Kaczmarski, Kathryn M. 1996. "Evolution of the Mountain Forum: Global Organizing for Advocacy and Mutual Support" and "A Conversation with Dr. Jane Pratt, President and CEO of the Mountain Institute." *Global Social Innovations* 1:1, pp. 21–30. Also at http://ai.cwru.edu/gem/mtnforum-v1i1.html.

Kaczmarski, Kathryn M., and Gurudev S. Khalsa. 1997. "Chartering and Appreciative Future Search." *Global Social Innovations* 1:2, pp. 45–52. Also at http://ai.cwru.edu/gem/chartering.html.

Kinghorn, Meg. 2001. *The Partnership Toolbox: A Facilitator's Guide to Partnership Dialogue*. Baltimore, Md.: Catholic Relief Services; Washington, D.C.: Pact Publications.

Kretzmann, John P., and John L. McKnight. 1993. *Building Communities from the Inside Out: A Path Toward Finding and Mobilizing a Community's Assets*. Evanston, Ill.: Institute for Policy Research.

Lederach, John Paul. 1997. *Building Peace: Sustainable Reconciliation in Divided Societies*. Washington, D.C.: U.S. Institute of Peace Press.

Liebler, Claudia, and Gregory Roche. 1998. *An Appreciative Inquiry Workshop: Sharing Our Strengths—Creating Our Dreams; An Approach for Revitalizing Ourselves and Our Schools*. Washington, D.C.: GEM Initiative and U.S. Peace Corps.

Odell, Malcolm J. 2002. "Issues in Participatory Development: From *Participatory Rural Appraisal* to *Appreciative Planning and Action*—A Former Volunteer's Personal Journey of Discovery. Kathmandu, Nepal, and South Hampton, N.H.: Habitat for Humanity International.

Open Space Institute USA. n.d. [2003]. *Open Space World Website*. http://www.openspaceworld.org.

Owen, Harrison. 1997a. *Open Space Technology: A User's Guide*. San Francisco: Berrett-Koehler.

————. 1997b. *Expanding Our Now: The Story of Open Space Technology*. San Francisco: Berrett-Koehler.

Rosenthal, Robert, and Lenore Jacobson. 1968. *Pygmalion in the Classroom: Teacher Expectation and Pupils' Intellectual Development*. New York: Irvington Publishers.

Ole Sena, Sarone, and Dirk Booy. 1997. "Appreciative Inquiry Approach to Community Development: The World Vision Tanzania Experience." *Global Social Innovations* 1:2, pp. 7–12. Also at http://ai.cwru.edu/gem/tanzania.html.

United Nations Children's Fund. 2000. "The Children of Southern Sudan." Thirty-minute video on a UNICEF-sponsored Future Search conference, held April 12 in Nairobi, Kenya. Livonia, Mich.: Blue Sky Productions.

Weisbord, Marvin R., and Sandra Janoff. 1995. *Future Search: An Action Guide to Finding Common Ground in Organizations & Communities*. San Francisco: Berrett-Koehler.

White, Leonard, Bernard Tursky, and Gary Schwartz, eds. 1985. *Placebo: Theory, Research, and Mechanisms*. New York: Guilford Press.

ADDITIONAL RESOURCES

AI Practitioner. Online newsletter. http://www.aipractitioner.com/Pagefiles/newsletter.htm.

Appreciative Inquiry Discussion List. Hosted by David Eccles School of Business, University of Utah, Salt Lake City, Utah. http://mailman.business.utah.edu:8080/mailman/listinfo/ailist.

Institute for Sustainable Development. n.d. [1999]. "Appreciative Inquiry—A Beginning." Thirty-five-minute video on experience with Appreciative Inquiry of development workers and community members in southern India. Winnipeg, Canada: Institute for Sustainable Development; Bangalore, India: MYRADA.

Liebler, Claudia. 1997. "Getting Comfortable with Appreciative Inquiry." *Global Social Innovations* 1:2, pp. 30–40. Also at http://ai.cwru.edu/gem/getting.html.

The Appreciative Inquiry Commons. Online resource of Case Western Reserve University, Cleveland, Ohio. http://appreciativeinquiry.cwru.edu.

Whitney, Diana, and Amanda Trosten-Bloom. 2003. *The Power of Appreciative Inquiry: A Practical Guide to Positive Change*. San Francisco: Berrett-Koehler.

Wilmot, Timothy B. 1996. "Inquiry and Innovation in the Private Voluntary Sector." *Global Social Innovations* 1:1, pp. 5–12. Also at http://ai.cwru.edu/gem/intro-v1i1.html.

Zander, Rosamund Stone, and Benjamin Zander. 2000. *The Art of Possibility*. Boston: Harvard Business School Press.

MOMENTS OF MAGNIFIED MEANING

Each of us, over the past couple weeks since September 11, at some level wonders what possible good—what new understandings, awareness, energies, relationships, spiritual insights, and perspectives—will come out of this moment? Surely there are many answers, most of which are not yet visible.

- What compels or draws you to this conference, and can you share some of the heartfelt hopes that are stirring in you, both about this conference on Positive Approaches to Peacebuilding and your hopes for the world? What is the most important thing stirring in you right now, and how do you sense that it relates to your future work or your larger sense of purpose?

- Moments like this offer the opportunity for shifts, big and small. But openings do not last forever, and one way to keep such openings vital and expansive is to magnify meaningful stories through conversation with others. Will you share one story, image, or powerful quote—either from the news or your own experience of recent days—that provided you with a precious image, new understanding, or appreciation of what we as human beings, in the positive sense, are capable of?

PEACEBUILDING EXPERIENCES: AN IMPORTANT STORY FROM YOUR LIFE

You, as well as everyone here, have been active in peacebuilding—in relationships, in organizations, in communities, in societies. Certainly there have been ups and downs, peaks and valleys, high points and low points.

- As you do a quick scan of your experiences in peacebuilding, please share a story of one powerful experience or initiative that stands out as something of an exceptional or extraordinary nature—a time when you felt particularly effective, challenged, alive, transformed, and found yourself learning? We're especially interested in a story when you felt

---

* This interview guide was developed for the conference, "Positive Approaches to Peacebuilding: A Practitioners' Exploration," held at American University in Washington, D.C., September 28–29, 2001.

like you used your full capacities and felt you were able to draw out the best in the others you were working with.

- If we now had a conversation with some people who know you the very best and asked them to share, what are the three best qualities they see in you—qualities or capabilities that you bring to peacemaking—what would *they* say?

LEADING EXEMPLARS WHOSE EXAMPLE YOU WANT TO MAGNIFY

- In your life, who is someone who has stood out to you as a great example of a peacemaker? What was or is it like to be around this person? How has he or she inspired you? How did this person do their work and live their life?

VISION OF A POST-TERRORIST WORLD AND ROLE OF PEACEBUILDING

- Let's assume that today, after this conference, we were to go into a sound sleep. When we awaken, it is ten years into the future—the year is 2011. While we were asleep, many small and large miracles happened, and the world changed and was constituted in ways you would most like to see it—for yourself, for children, for grandchildren, for nature, etc. Now you awaken. You go out into the world and get a panoramic view. You are happy with what you see. It's the kind of world you most want to be part of. So now, share highlights of what you see: What do you see happening that is new, better, healthy, and good?

- Now, more specifically, how did the field of peacebuilding, however you would define it, help bring about this change? Visualize the kinds of partnerships, projects, practices that were created and used. What do they look like?

CREATING EPIDEMICS OF POSITIVE CHANGE

Jonas Salk, M.D., would ask people three simple but powerful questions. None were medical questions about illness. In Salk's view "health" was not simply the absence of disease. It was qualitatively different and vastly more. He wanted people to discover, through systematic study and positive awareness, those things that they do that make them healthy. He was amazed with the wisdom people possessed and the varieties of techniques, behaviors, and lessons they identified. He would conclude each conversation with a request: Please share your insights with as many people as possible. Salk's great hope was to discover the means and methods "to create an epidemic of health." He realized that no action, no conversation, no thought was too small, in fact, that most tipping points have very small beginnings, but they reverberate.

- If anything at all imaginable were possible, how would you ignite or catalyze an epidemic of positive change?

SAMPLE INTERVIEW GUIDE 2

Trying Times**

DRAWING ON INNER STRENGTH

Life is full of challenges, failures, and even tragic events that we cannot avoid but must live through. Often during these times we discover an inner source of strength, a hidden reserve of energy and love, that is just what we needed to make it through.

- Describe a time when you discovered an inner source of strength and used it to get through a difficult time. Describe the quality in detail. How did it make itself known to you? What did it enable you to do? What did you learn about yourself? What did others say about you as you drew on this source to get through your ordeal? How were you able to draw on this source at other times?

FOOTPRINTS IN THE SAND (DEEPENING OR DISCOVERY OF FAITH)

When events reel out of our control, we feel powerless and small. It may be only by tapping into a higher power and giving our lives over to our faith that we are able to find the will to survive and to carry on.

- Describe a time when you felt a presence in your life that quietly and gently assured you that you were not alone and provided you with the support, encouragement, understanding, and love you needed. How did you feel the presence? What did it feel like? What need did it fill at the time?

PERSONAL GROWTH

Times of adversity are often times of tremendous personal growth and self-discovery, when we are open to the lessons to be learned. Sometimes these learnings don't occur until long after an event is over.

- Describe a time of great personal growth born of adversity. What was the event? What did it challenge you to do? How did it change how you

---

** This interview guide was developed by Elizabeth Lincoln, principal, Peach Tree Consulting, in Philadelphia, Pennsylvania.

see yourself? What specifically did you learn, and how have you applied that learning in other instances in a way that helped make a difference to you and to others?

HELPING HANDS

Often it is the selfless giving of others that gets us through bad times. Friends, family, even complete strangers who reach out to us, sometimes in unexpected ways, can often make the difference between despair and hope.

- Share a story of when someone helped you during a time of great need. What did they do? How did it help you? How did it make you feel about yourself, about them? How did it change the way you interact with others?

BEST MOMENTS

It was once said that our greatest gift as people is that we are at our best when things are at their worst.

- Describe a worst moment when you were able to step in and do what was needed to rescue the situation. What was the situation and what did you do? How did others describe you during that time? What did you learn about yourself? How have you applied that learning to other situations?

SAMPLE INTERVIEW GUIDE 3

Creating a Forum Where Leaders of the World's Religions Can Gather in Mutual Respect and Dialogue***

OPENING DIALOGUE

A Story From Your Life Journey

One could say a key task in life is to discover and define our life purpose and then accomplish it to the best of our ability.

- Can you share a story of a moment, or the period of time, where clarity about life purpose emerged for you—for example, a moment when your calling happened, when there was an important awakening or teaching,

---

*** This interview guide was developed by David Cooperrider for use at a meeting of religious leaders held in Washington, D.C., on November 9, 1998.

when there was a special experience or event, or when you received some guiding vision?

- Now, beyond this story . . . what do you sense you are supposed to do before your life, this life, is over?

Insights from Important Interfaith Encounters

We have all been changed both in outlook and in our lives because of encounters with people from other spiritual traditions or religions. In your work as a leader you might have had one, two, or perhaps many encounters with people of other traditions that stand out as particularly significant.

- Can you share a story of one experience that stands out in your memory—for example, an encounter outside the normal "safety zone," where you were surprised or humbled, or where there was an experience of healing and hope, or where there was a genuine experience of compassion, joy, love, or friendship?

- Whether it was difficult or easy, what did you come to respect most, not just about that person, but about their particular religion or practice?

INSIGHTS FROM THE PAST

World Events and Trends Over the Past One Hundred Years

Taking steps to create an enduring dialogue among leaders of religions does not happen in a vacuum.

- Think about the five most important historical events that have occurred over the past one hundred years—global or local events and trends that give you a sense of urgency, readiness, or calling for our work here. What trends or challenges do you see as most significant?

ASSESSMENT OF THE PRESENT: OUR WORLD AND THE HARD ISSUES

The Emerging Story of Interreligious Relationships

The *1996 Encyclopedia of World Problems and Human Potential* lists over fifteen thousand global problems and documents, for example, that half of the armed conflicts in the world early in 1993 were not between nation-states but between groups from different religions. Against the background of many world problems and conflicts there is also a hopeful story that offers a glimmer of what is possible when we find ways to promote peace rather than war, cooperation rather than prejudice, and sustainability rather than environmental degradation and human oppression.

The century since that historic gathering in 1893 in Chicago— the Parliament of the World's Religions—has seen a vast widening of interfaith dialogue, interreligious prayer and meditation, pilgrimages, joint action, and study in world religions. Indeed, it appears there is a worldwide urge for enduring, daily cooperation among people of the world's religions, to make peace among religions, and to serve, in the presence of the sacred, the flourishing of all life. As leaders in these arenas, what are we most proud about? What are we most sorry about?

• Think about the most significant achievements, milestones, developments, and infrastructures that have happened locally or globally in your lifetime. What developments are you most proud about?

• Conversely, as you look at events or trends in the world and the current responses of religious leaders, including yourself, what are you most sorry about? More important, what should we be doing more of or differently?

LOOKING TO THE FUTURE: VISIONS OF A BETTER WORLD

Your Vision of a Better World

Dag Hammarskold, former United Nations Secretary General, said: "I see no hope for permanent world peace. We have tried and failed miserably. Unless the world has a spiritual rebirth, civilization is doomed. It has been said that the next century will be a spiritual century or it will not be."

Put your thinking about thirty years, a generation or so, into the future. Even though the future is, in so many ways, a mystery, we want to begin to visualize the kind of world you feel we are being called to realize, a better world, the kind of world you really want. What do you see in your vision of a better world?

• Specifically, what are three changes or developments in your vision? What is happening in the world a generation from now that is positive and different, and how do you know? How would you feel if these three things were realized?

Your Vision of the Relationships Between the World's Religious Leaders

The assumption in the invitation to today's meeting is that there needs to be, in today's complicated and interconnected world, an ongoing and sustained conversation among the religious leaders of the world. The simple hypothesis: The world will be a different place, a better place. It is easy to see the value of something like this, is it not?

Let's imagine a scale from one to ten, where a rating of ten represents the ideal kind of relationship among leaders of the world's religions and spiritual traditions.

- What does your "ten" look like? The quality of relationships? The kinds of contact and communication?

- Let's assume a significant and growing number of leaders from the world's religions do choose "to get to know one another"—and it begins to succeed. A safe, confidential, ongoing, and non-binding forum is created. How might the world benefit? How might you and your faith community or organization benefit?

Appendix B

SAMPLE GUIDED IMAGERY EXERCISE

Topic: Creative Coexistence in my Community

The facilitator instructs participants as follows:

"Get comfortable, close your eyes if you like, and bring the topic, 'Creative Coexistence,' into your mind's eye. Imagine that creative coexistence has been implemented fully in your life and the lives of everyone in your community.

"Imagine that as you wake up, you are excited because you know that you'll find a flourishing community, one that is more harmonious, equitable, and alive because people from diverse groups live in dynamic, creative inter-relationship.

"As you think about the racial, ethnic, religious, or some other group that you most identify with, what are some of its most outstanding qualities and capacities that it brings to this lively and constructive interaction with other groups in the community?

"Wander around your community and as you meet people in the course of the day, what pictures emerge that are inspiring and energizing? What are you feeling? What are people doing differently—in neighborhoods, in the marketplace, in the workplace, in government? What skills are children learning in school? What kinds of programs are on TV? What new kinds of activities do religious congregations engage in?

"What is your day-to-day life like, and how has it changed? What conversations do you have with family, friends, and coworkers about these changes happening in the community?

"Congratulate yourself for being a part of such a healthy and meaningful social transformation. Open your eyes and return to this room at your own speed."

PART II

TOWARD CULTURES OF PEACE

Let there be peace on Earth, and let it begin with me.

JILL JACKSON AND SY MILLER

CHAPTER FOUR

PEACE CULTURE FOR TODAY AND TOMORROW

Elise Boulding

History has shown that positive images of the future have empowered creative action for social change in societies of the past. Recognizing this, the author has for many years conducted workshops on "Imaging a Nonviolent World," with groups of many kinds. In this chapter, she describes the encouraging findings of one such workshop, as participants made commitments to actions they were personally willing to make to bring about the nonviolent world they had imagined twenty years hence. The author then shares her own vision, from the vantage point of the year 2032, of a new sense of three-dimensional citizenship that has come into being in that world. The manual for facilitating this type of imaging workshop is included as an appendix to the chapter.

⚜

The United Nations General Assembly has named the first decade of the twenty-first century as the Decade of Education for a Culture of Peace and Nonviolence. Responding to that mandate, a group of educators, students, and peace activists met for a weekend discussion of peace culture at Tufts University in the early spring of 2001. What kind of mindset about peace culture would one find in a group already committed to peace studies, a group already familiar with many of the conceptual analyses of the structures, institutions, and processes involved in the social phenomena of conflict, violence, and peacebuilding, and already acutely aware of the obstacles to peace in the present world situation? Having been asked to lead a session of futures-imaging about a world in which peace culture prevails, I can report some surprising and, to me, encouraging findings.[1]

Futures imaging needs to be grounded in a sense of the present as process, so participants were invited mentally to enter the two-hundred-year present—from the birth year of today's centenarians to the centenary year of

83

the babies born today. We did this by first reviewing the social movements and events of the past century (positive and negative) and, second, by focusing on positive personal experiences of social-change activity. Only then did we step into the second half of the two-hundred-year present and concentrate on how a world at peace might look in 2031, thirty years forward from the midpoint of the time span (a year most participants would live to see). After a period of personal reflection, participants divided into groups of six and shared with each other positive images of a 2031 in which diversity was celebrated on a green and flourishing planet where conflicts were settled nonviolently. The walls of the auditorium were then filled with sheets of newsprint prepared by each group depicting a colorful, joyful, peaceable 2031.

Because this was a *mini*-workshop, conducted in a two-hour time frame, there was no time to reflect as a group on *how* 2031 came about, but I did point out that the future would, to a significant degree, be a product of the social movements and political, economic, and cultural developments taking place in 2001. After reflection on that, I asked them to choose what they would be willing to commit to doing *now* to help bring about this world they had just imagined, and to write down their personal action commitments on a sheet of paper.

After a few minutes of thinking and writing, the entire group of over a hundred participants joined hands in a giant circle to affirm the commitments they had just made, and then placed their slips of paper in a container I was holding as they left the room. The atmosphere was electric, and I could hardly wait to get home to begin studying what they had written.

The results really surprised me. I expected the commitments to be social action commitments, and many were. But what I did not expect was that 43 of the 107 sheets turned in contained one or more commitments and statements that related to the participants' personal growth and development as human beings. This response suggested that many participants felt that they had not given enough attention in their own lives to the inner development required to become effective peacemakers. Often, but not always, these personal-development statements were accompanied by community action statements. And some of the teachers present also developed new ideas about their teaching. The themes for all three categories—personal development, community action, and teaching—covered a wide range of approaches. But together they represented a level of deep thoughtfulness about what peace culture entails that goes beyond the usual categorization of social change activities.

Personal Development

My favorite response was just two words, beautifully printed on a single sheet of paper. BREATHE PEACE. That makes a good exercise for meditation! The most frequent personal development theme (11 responses) involved living a simpler life style, including driving less, walking and biking more, living in cohousing, using old-fashioned postal mail instead of e-mail, when possible (surprise!). This theme was followed by one on children: raising children to be peacemakers, adopting a child, working at peace in one's own family (10 responses). Developing inner peace, practicing non-violence in personal life, both in spiritual development and social behavior, also appeared in ten responses.

Then a new note: laugh a lot, play more, be more relaxed (6), followed by becoming a better listener, more empathic (5). Next, write a book about peacemaking (4!), followed by commitments to: developing independence of spirit, finding one's own voice, affirming others, love a new person every day (3), find a job in which I can contribute to peacemaking (3), become a teacher (3), and finish what I start, be more focused in my life (3). The following commitments each appeared twice: devote more time to learning, and become more aware of social injustice. Finally, the following commitments appeared once each: become more aware of self and planet, change the world one person at a time, help others develop inner peace, come out of the closet as a gay feminist, and become more fluent in Spanish.

In short, these conference participants felt that peace culture calls for attention to one's inner life, lifeways, and life styles. Historically, peace cultures have always been marked by special life styles, and that insight has not disappeared in our fast-paced consumer culture.

Community Action

Community peacebuilding commitments show a similar awareness of the qualitative dimensions of peace culture. There was an underlying theme of becoming more familiar with the local community and building on the resources for peacebuilding that already exist, combined with a focus on creating meeting spaces for local peace and justice groups of all ages and for intergenerational interaction. Community-building themes included: developing more cohousing; working with rural and urban children to build non-violent conflict resolution skills in cooperation with schools, local colleges, and faith groups; encouraging peacebuilding through the arts; and working with restorative justice programs.

There was also a strong theme of community mobilization for action on international issues: abolition of nuclear weapons; aid to victims of war and violence in Iraq, the Balkans, and Central America; work with peace organizations to move U.S. policy in the direction of conflict prevention; and campaigning to elect a woman president. Other more general commitments included working for economic justice for the poor, undertaking projects for local sustainability, and *just being there* for the community and its needs.

Clearly, most of the participants were thinking of peace culture in terms of peacebuilding at the local level, but this was also accompanied by a recurring theme of networking and linking with other nongovernmental organizations around the world on a range of peace, justice, environmental, and human rights issues. An emphasis on the uses of modern technology, including information technology, was, however, notably absent. Face-to-face interaction was central to most of the activities mentioned.

Teaching

Then there were the commitments that focused on teaching roles. First and foremost was the commitment to develop or expand peace studies at one's college or university, and to include peace studies in teacher training programs aimed at the next generation of teachers in the public schools. The most common commitments included: developing a course on nonviolence that would specifically include peacemaking skills and an emphasis on cultural diversity, working with and encouraging student peace groups, and working for peace education programs in the local public schools. The concern to do more teaching about peace issues was combined with a commitment to focus on community internship opportunities to empower young people in their development as activists.

Of the 107 slips of paper turned in, only two contained the simple message: TBA (to be announced). I am hoping those two participants will eventually write me to tell me what they have decided!

The Power of Positive Images

Because imaging the future workshops were originally designed to empower social activists, based on futurist Fred Polak's concept of positive images of the future acting as releasers of social energy in the societies holding such images,[2] it was encouraging to find that even in a primarily academic environment, participants responded so concretely to the request to verbalize specific commitments on behalf of the visualized future. These commitments went well beyond traditional campus and community-based activities to include a strong focus on nurturing personal and community development, as well as on the skills of nonviolent social change and accompanying strategies. Since these participants were well aware of rising levels of violence around the world, it is significant that they chose to focus on building peace culture at the levels most accessible to them—personal and community—with a backup strategy of networking nationally and internationally.

The focus on personal growth and locally based activities by a group possessing considerable knowledge of a highly complex world system reflects an ancient wisdom that has survived through the ages and is well expressed in the familiar phrase: "Let there be peace, and let it begin with me." The presence of that wisdom in peace studies practitioners is certainly to be celebrated.

NEW CONCEPTS FOR PEACE CULTURE IN ACTION

Yes! The old wisdom is still to be celebrated. But now, in the post–September 11 era, I feel the need to reflect on the sudden turn by a United States presumably at peace to a worldwide war on terrorism in defense against a small assault on its sovereignty (small in relation to massive deaths from aerial bombings in Japan in World War II, and in the Balkans more recently). What have we been missing in the peace studies field? In dealing with the complexities of an interdependent world, are we paying enough attention to a serious fear of diversity that characterizes many national communities?

That fear of diversity is not only a problem within states but between states, and keeps the United Nations from playing the peacebuilding role in the world that it was designed to do. How slow and hesitant states are in signing treaties that limit their "uniqueness," their sovereignty—especially the more powerful states. Yet the states themselves harbor societies within them that are also unique, and few states recognize their own internal societies—the *ethnies*, the cultural identity groups, each with its own history. The 190 states that comprise the United Nations actually consist of various groupings from among the world's ten thousand societies,[3] the cultural identity groups spilling every which way across their borders. Many current wars involve those identity groups, fighting within states as well as across national borders. Some of them—not all—get labeled "terrorist groups." What will bring these struggles to an end?

Let us take a fresh look at the world that lies thirty years into the future. In 2032, I can imagine all the valuable developments in the field of peacebuilding, so well described in this book, as expanding to include the development of a new sense of citizenship that encompasses the local in all its diversity and the global in all its diversity. The old citizenship was a wonderful social concept that addressed in a balanced way the twin human needs of bonding and autonomy, calling for love, loyalty, and sense of responsibility to the national entity. But in 2032, citizenship will come to be understood as being essentially three-dimensional. The first dimension is the local, the ethnic/cultural identity that shapes our human becoming in family and community, the identity that is primary in the ten thousand societies.

The second dimension is the national—the state whose institutions serve the well-being of the ethnies within its borders, and attracts their loyalty and support to the extent that they are acknowledged and respected. The third dimension is international—the United Nations itself, formed to protect the well-being of the six billion humans living in the ten thousand societies spread across the 190 states.

Back in 2002, we had forgotten that the United Nations came into being as an association of "we the peoples," as its founding charter says. It was not "we the states." The purpose of the association was to put an end to war. That means that we are, all six billion of us, citizens of the United Nations and have as much stake in its survival as in the survival of the state we live in and the identity group we belong to. Taking up this citizenship involves our own personal growth at the deepest level, as well as the development of our intellectual, social, and civic capacities. It involves a different and unfamiliar way of being in the world. Put in terms of our civic responsibility, we must see to it that our national representatives to our United Nations General Assembly and its associated regional organizations sign the necessary treaties that protect the security of all humans (as well as all life on the planet).[4] We need to be familiar with the United Nations, to know it and to love it, as we need to know and love our own country. All those treaties that the United States failed to sign at the turn of the century stand as signals of poor citizenship on our part. It also signifies a failure to love the United Nations as it needs loving, warts and all!—as we love our country, warts and all.

We are not born citizens. Becoming citizens is a process of social learning and personal growth. Our challenge is to learn "how things work" so we can exercise that citizenship. School systems must play an increasing part in this, along with those critically important bodies in the civic arena: nongovernmental organizations (NGOs)—especially international nongovernmental organizations, or INGOs. Those INGOs, roughly twenty-five thousand of them, provide the critical links that help activate our three-fold citizenship. They do this by bringing our concerns for peace, justice, human rights, and the environment from the local chapters where we live (including our local faith communities) to national offices and international headquarters of these organizations, and then right to the United Nations itself.[5] It is at the United Nations conferences and commission hearings and treaty negotiations on key world issues that INGO voices are heard and where our delegates can make a difference with their skills at negotiation across differing national interests.

As at the turn of the century, now in 2032 INGOs themselves are still in the learning stages on how to make the most of these opportunities for mutual learning and collaboration at every level, from the local to the

 United Nations. Thousands of citizen hours have gone into continuing dialogue with diplomats and government officials and U.N. officials, to produce the programs, agreements, and treaties now in effect after years of effort.[6] It is a slow and difficult process, but that is the only way in which new norms of governance and new models of behavior, based on problem solving rather than the exercise of force and violence, come into effect.

The peacebuilding approaches described in this volume will come to be seen as part of the evolution of a new, inclusive citizenship that embraces the riches of the cultural and biological diversity of the planet. Will there not be an accompanying change of consciousness about what it means to be human that will make of planet Earth a delightful place to live?

ENDNOTES

1. Part one of this chapter detailing the futures-imaging event held at Tufts University originally appeared as "Peace Culture and Social Action" in Boulding (2001), and is reprinted here by permission of the publisher, Taylor & Francis, Ltd. (www.tandf.co.uk).
2. The Dutch historian Fred Polak was the first to write a macrohistory showing how positive images of the future have empowered creative action for social change in societies of past times, and how the lack of positive images of the future have led to social decay (1961; 1972).
3. *Ten thousand societies* is a term referring to the existence of thousands of ethnies, and appears in UNESCO's report on "Our Creative Diversity" (1996), as well as in Ankerl (2000).
4. For insight into the workings of the U.N. process in relation to peace issues, see Peck (1988).
5. For examples of the activities of INGOs in relation to peacebuilding, see Boulding (2000).
6. A vivid description of citizens' involvement in the development of the law of the sea is found in Levering and Levering (1999).

REFERENCES

Ankerl, Guy. 2000. *Coexisting Contemporary Civilizations.* Geneva: INU Press.

Boulding, Elise. 1990. *Building a Global Civic Culture: Education for an Interdependent World.* Syracuse, N.Y.: Syracuse University Press.

———. 1995. "Image and Action in Peace Building." In *The Future: Images and Processes.* Elise and Kenneth Boulding, eds. Thousand Oaks, Calif.: Sage.

———. 2000. *Cultures of Peace: The Hidden Side of History.* Syracuse, N.Y.: Syracuse University Press.

———. 2001. "Peace Culture and Social Action." *Peace Review* 13:4, pp. 567–570.

Levering, Ralph B., and Miriam L. 1999. *Citizen Action for Global Changes: The Neptune Group and Law of the Sea.* Syracuse, N.Y.: Syracuse University Press.

Peck, Connie. 1998. *Sustainable Peace: the Role of the U.N. and Regional Organizations in Preventing Conflict.* New York: Rowman and Littlefield.

Pollak, Fred. 1961. *Image of the Future*. Elise Boulding, trans. Dobbs Ferry, N.Y.: Oceana Press.

———. 1972. *Image of the Future*. Abridgement by Elise Boulding. San Francisco: Jossey Bass/Elsevier.

UNESCO. 1996. "Our Creative Diversity." Paris: UNESCO Publishing.

Appendix

FACILITATION MANUAL FOR WORKSHOP ON THE FUTURE: IMAGING A NONVIOLENT WORLD IN THE YEAR 20xx*

Elise Boulding, Workshop Facilitator

INTRODUCTION

Since it is hard to work for something we can't even see in our imaginations, and since visions can guide and empower action, we will spend the next several hours exploring a _____ (name of a context) in which the twentieth-century cultures of violence have been replaced by peace cultures.

After an initial introduction to the process, participants will

1. list their hopes for the future,

2. engage in a brief exercise of "remembering," to discover how the imagination works in a future space,

3. spend a few minutes in _____ (the context), exploring what is going on in this future time, what a peace culture looks like,

4. in small groups, share individual experiences of _____ (name a type of experience) and then examine those experiences analytically to discover how this future world functions,

5. as a group, construct a history from the future to the present—how did all this happen?

6. choose action strategies for the present (present date) that may help bring this future about.

---

* This workshop is adapted from "Imaging a World Without Weapons," a workshop format developed by Elise Boulding and Warren Ziegler, which is fully described, complete with workshop instructions, in Boulding (1990).

IMAGING THE FUTURE

Choosing Your Hopes for the World

What specific social goals in relation to the overall goal of the abolition of the war system and the creation of a diverse, inclusive, nonviolent world community would you like to see realized three decades from now? Think in the most hopeful and optimistic way you can. Do not let yourself be confined by what you expect or fear will happen.

Exercising the Imagination

In a few minutes we are going to enter the world of thirty years from now through the door of our imagination. First we need to get into the imagining mode. To do this, each of us will enter our personal memory world and pick one memory to re-experience. It should be a "good" memory, one you will enjoy reliving. You will be able to describe in detail the setting, the people involved, the smells, sights, sounds, the feel of the place. The longer you explore the memory, the more you will see. Make some notes about the memory so you do not forget the details. The way you imagine (remember) the actual past experience will let you know how your imagination works, and this same mental mode will now take you into the future, where you will imagine (remember) something that has not yet happened.

Notes and Sketches of the World in Thirty Years

Now you have passed through a hedge separating the present and the future. You are in the year (give the year). Move around freely, observe carefully, ask questions of the people you meet. Make notes here of what you find. Make a pictorial or diagrammatic representation of the world you are experiencing on poster paper that will be provided.

World Construction

In small groups, share your individual images of the future world, then begin to ask more analytic questions of your combined imaging material. What kind of world is out there? Refer back to your goal statements for a theme to "build" your world around. Draw on each other's future memories. For the purposes of this exercise, you are still in the future-present. Use the present tense in speaking of the future-present. If you wish to refer to the present time, do so in the past tense. What structures must exist in this world you are in to account for what you have seen? How is family life organized? What is the economic, political system? How is education organized? How does civic and cultural life maintain itself? What makes this society tick? Account for your society locally, and move as far out as you can in terms of regions and the planet as a whole. Are there nation-states?

Time will be a limiting factor here, so begin with those aspects of the society that interest you most. You can add others later (even after this workshop is over). Take turns helping each other analyze the structure of the world you have each seen individually. On the basis of this analysis, the group will create a pictorial or diagrammatic representation of what you know about that world on poster paper, which will be provided. Each group will share their future world with all workshop participants in plenary.

Remembering History

Again working in small groups, stand in this future world and look back. How did this future come about? Remember/imagine some key events. Include major benchmarks in world trends as well. Last year? Five years ago? Ten, fifteen, twenty, twenty-five? Each group will create a time line for the events. These will be shared in plenary to develop a common remembered history.

ACTION IN THE PRESENT

- *Step 1.* Back in your small groups, think through what you individually might do now, this year, to help bring about this future world you have experienced in imagination. First think about the action settings available to you. List them: your family, neighborhood, community settings, work place, organizations you are involved in, where you shop, etc.

- *Step 2.* What objectives might you set for yourself—concrete, specific goals that you could achieve in the short term, in other words, in the coming months? Who will be your allies? How will you relate to decision makers?

- *Step 3.* Now begin to flesh out a specific project based on your answers to the above.

- *Step 4.* In the closing plenary session, share this project with all of the workshop participants.

To create this new society, we must present outstretched and friendly hands, without hatred and rancor, even as we show great determination and never waver in the defense of truth and justice.... [W]e know that we cannot sow seeds with clenched fists. To sow we must open our hands.

ADOLFO PEREZ ESQUIVEL

CHAPTER FIVE

CREATING A CULTURE OF PEACE IN POSTWAR EL SALVADOR

Mark Chupp

The Usulutan province of El Salvador was pivotal in the country's civil war. After the war, the area lacked infrastructure and state support for thousands of families who settled in the region. A group of villages formed a grassroots organization, La Coordinadora, to prevent disasters and promote sustainable development. In 1998, they declared themselves a Local Zone of Peace and established the Culture of Peace Program (CPP) to overcome rampant violence and teach peace. Rather than adopt a foreign conflict resolution model, CPP selected international consultants with an elicitive approach to create an indigenous process. The CPP process involves a core group of peasant leaders who facilitate dialogue and reflection circles as a means of educating villages, resolving conflict, and promoting democratic processes. The consultants promoted an inclusive, whole-system approach, active nonviolence, a positive vision of the future, and an experiential-reflective program-design process. Although slow, the effort avoided dependency on outsiders and is transforming communities into a zone of peace.

❧

*C*ivil war is the ultimate breakdown of a society's ability to peacefully manage its differences. After the guns cease to fire, regardless of the outcome a defeated outlook pervades. In an effort to rebuild society, postwar countries often look to foreign experts to reassemble polarized factions, introduce new approaches to conflict management, and teach people lost skills in communication and cooperation. Supported by international aid agencies, mediation consultants and trainers stream into postwar countries to rebuild nonviolent mechanisms for handling differences. If there is a lack of appreciation of indigenous resources, however, the introduction of foreign models and methods can further erode the confidence people have in their own capacity to handle differences.

El Salvador, the smallest and most densely populated country in Central America, faced such a dilemma in the 1990s after decades of civil unrest and twelve years of outright civil war. Usulutan, located in the southeastern part of the country on the Pacific Ocean, was one of the most affected departments (i.e., provinces). During the war guerrillas occupied Usulutan, strategically located across from Nicaragua on the Golf of Fonseca. Today, the department continues to struggle toward peace, as it is comprised of communities of former military personnel and their families, as well as communities of former guerrillas and their families. Previously a sparsely populated region of cotton plantations, the newly formed police force and public infrastructure were ill prepared to provide security and promote healthy relations. Many believe their ineffectiveness was part of a government effort to undermine the peasants and drive them out of the area, to make way for large-scale farming and tourist development (Cowan 2001).

A grassroots movement formed in 1996, when seven communities joined together to prevent flooding caused by the release of a government controlled dam. Known as La Coordinadora (The Coordinated Communities),[1] this movement did not rely on the government, an educated elite, or foreign experts to bring change. They embarked on an alternative path, building on the strengths of their own people and culture to transform the region. Eventually, dozens of communities joined to prevent natural disasters and promote self-sufficiency in response to poverty and government inaction. By 1999, eighty-six communities representing thirty thousand people constituted La Coordinadora, and the mission expanded to include peace and democracy (Cowan 2001).

Inspired by a United Nations concept, they declared themselves a Local Zone of Peace and developed community circles for rediscovering nonviolent problem-solving methods in their culture. To actually develop peace in the zone, they initiated their own home-grown Culture of Peace Program. A comprehensive approach, the program promoted peace through three components—restoring human rights and responsibilities, promoting peace and indigenous methods of conflict resolution, and fostering the transformation of organizational life to reflect peace and democracy.

This is their story. This chapter offers a brief overview of the civil war and the Usulutan context, describes the development of La Coordinadora and, in particular, its Culture of Peace Program (CPP). The ways in which this effort reflects an appreciative orientation is also examined. Specific methods and examples are given to illustrate how the CPP departed from the traditional North American mediation model. The chapter concludes with a discussion of the challenges and opportunities encountered in this positive approach to grassroots peacebuilding.

POSTWAR EL SALVADOR

Peacebuilding in a postwar context presents a series of challenges that must be addressed simultaneously. Politically, the country is typically polarized with military and economic structures linked to one side of the conflict. Economically, the means of production are so disrupted that food is in short supply, trade is reduced, and unemployment soars. Socially, the institutions that would normally be expected to provide health, education, and other public services are in disarray, if functioning at all. Culturally, peaceful ways have been replaced with an over-reliance on violence in response to interpersonal, political, and economic differences.

El Salvador, the smallest and most densely populated country in Central America, faced all of these realities in 1992, with the signing of the United Nations-mediated peace accords. After twelve years of war that left over seventy-five thousand dead, El Salvador was reeling from one of the most intense modern conflicts in Latin America. The country fit the classic revo lutionary scenario—a dictatorial regime with outside (United States) support, grave inequality of land holding, middle class opposition, and peasant grievances. The *Farabundo Martí para la Liberación Nacional* (FMLN), a national liberation front established in 1980 among five revolutionary movements, created the strongest revolutionary alliance in the hemisphere. These forces were stronger and more organized than Peru's Shining Path and the successful revolutionary movements in Nicaragua and Cuba (McClintock 1998).

The difference between outcomes in El Salvador and its neighbors was the strong commitment by the United States to stand by the country, partly out of a fear that if El Salvador fell, Guatemala and the rest of Central America would fall to leftist revolutionary movements. The United States commitment included extensive military training and support as well as economic aid. In 1987, the United States provided El Salvador $574 million in aid, which was more than all the country's exports. By the end of the decade, the United States had spent more than $200,000 per guerrilla, yet still failed to produce a victory over the FMLN (McClintock 1998).

In 1989, after years of fighting, both sides recognized they could not win the war. The government had lost the upper hand militarily and in terms of public will. Even aid from the United States decreased after a U.S.-trained Salvadoran military unit killed six Jesuit priests. That same year, the FMLN realized they could not win the war outright after failing in their final offensive. Under the auspices of the United Nations, both sides entered into negotiation over the next two years, leading to the 1992 signing of peace accords. The peace accords eliminated the most notorious military divisions linked to death squads, restructured the national police force with former guerrillas joining their ranks, stipulated some land reform and the resettlement of refugees, and implemented political and electoral reforms that would assure a place for the FMLN as a political party.

While successful in bringing the armed conflict to an end, the peace accords were not fully implemented and did not mean an end to violence. By the end of the 1990s, El Salvador, Colombia, and South

Africa became the countries with the highest per capita violence rates in the world. But unlike Colombia, violence in El Salvador was not primarily politically motivated. Violence stemmed from economic causes, the newly formed gangs, and simply as a common response to even the most petty conflicts.

LA COORDINADORA AND CULTURE OF PEACE PROGRAM

There were multiple factors that adversely affected the southern Usulutan Department, providing the impetus for the creation of La Coordinadora and their Culture of Peace Program. The war exacted a heavy toll on the region. For example, the only major bridge crossing the Lempa River, the largest river in Central America, had been destroyed in a guerrilla attack. The resettlement of entire communities into a previously unpopulated area meant the necessary infrastructure was nonexistent. Given the fact that the FMLN had controlled the region during the war, a high percentage of pro-FMLN families were in the area, which was further strengthened by the influx of refugees. The government was slow in providing resources and assistance in rebuilding the area, partly due to the enormity of the task, but also because it was trying to get the peasants to move away, offering them a pittance for their land. At any rate, the right-wing government did not want to strengthen the base of a leftist stronghold. To further complicate matters, the government attempted to establish a more politically balanced region by resettling former military personnel and their families in new communities strategically located next to leftist communities.

La Coordinadora emerged in response to these needs. Initially, seven communities came together to address the high risk of natural disasters. Heavy rains and the release without warning of a large dam up river frequently triggered flash flooding along the Lempa River. A network of volunteers established two-way radio communication and a rapid response system. La Coordinadora also lobbied the government to bring about policy changes to build flood walls and have the government hydro-electric agency give notice before releasing the dam.

Seeing this success, other communities joined La Coordinadora, forcing internal changes in its structure and institutionalization. Committed to democratic decision making and local participation, each community held an assembly and voted to join La Coordinadora and elect a representative. As the number of communities grew to twenty-six and then to three times that many within two years, it was no longer possible to make all decisions and carry out all work through the commission of elected representatives. In 1998, the group adopted a plan to establish a nongovernmental organization (NGO).[2] To assure community control in a democratic process, the constitution of the NGO linked its governance to the commission of elected representatives. Known as the Mangrove Association,[3] the organization was incorporated in 1999, with a purpose of not simply generating funding and projects, but also empowering people to become self-sufficient. In 1999, in an effort to be more democratic, La Coordinadora restructured itself again to create eight local groups—grouping together member communities from the same micro-region (Communitas Charitable Trust 2000).

Even with a separate NGO with its paid professional staff, La Coordinadora remained at the forefront. Mission and program direction were set by the peasant representatives, not by the NGO board of directors. La Coordinadora set as its mission "to engender in the population the basic conditions in organization, participation, and individual and collective skills and capacities that lead to integrated development." The areas of focus included organization, disaster prevention, local participation, culture of peace, production, and the environment. With an overall goal of promoting self-sufficiency, the NGO began securing funds and hiring agriculturists and other specialists to promote the development of collective shrimp farms and family cash crops.

While increasing production and preventing disasters greatly improved the quality of life in the communities, it did not address another major threat—community violence. An often-cited statistic declared that, at the current rate, more people would be killed in the twelve years since the Salvadoran civil war ended in 1992 than were killed during the twelve years of war. Interpersonal conflicts erupt into gunfights. Many feel violence has become a way of life, infused into the culture, a means of solving even petty disagreements. In addition, families have returned from living in exile, bringing back with them their teenage sons who were involved in gangs in Los Angeles and other U.S. cities. The U.S. government also routinely arrests and deports Salvadoran gang members, sending them back as free citizens to start gangs in their home communities (Wallace 2000). Even small communities live in fear as these imported gangs, the 13th Street and 18th Street gangs,[4] rival each other for turf.

Local Zone of Peace Declared

In response to increasing violence, on August 15, 1998, La Coordinadora, with the support of many other local organizations, declared themselves a Local Zone of Peace. They had explored, with the International Center for the Study and Promotion of Zones of Peace in the World, the concept outlined in numerous United Nations' proposals and a declaration presented by UNESCO. The U.N. first initiated the concept when it declared the Indian Ocean as a zone of peace in 1971, and later the South Atlantic as a zone of peace and cooperation. A study by the U.N. University of Peace in Costa Rica between 1987 and 1990 culminated in a proposal to declare Central America and the Caribbean a zone of peace and cooperation. On December 17, 1990, the presidents declared Central America a "Region of Peace, Cooperation, and Development." The U.N. General Assembly ratified the treaty in 1991 (Salvadoran Human Rights Institute 1996).

These earlier declarations were all top-down approaches to the creation of a zone of peace, including one for Central America in 1990 and one for El Salvador in 1993. The United Nations intent in launching the zone in El Salvador was to transform postwar zones into demilitarized civil societies. Unfortunately, all these efforts around the world were unsuccessful in actually creating a visible and known presence. The Usulutan initiative was the first grassroots initiative by the communities themselves. The declaration stated, "in a Zone of Peace, the principal actor is the community . . . and all efforts will be dedicated to sustaining life and the resolution of conflicts without violence." The government's role was stated as assigning resources and empowering communities.

The extreme violence in the region impeded La Coordinadora's efforts to develop the region and led them to embark on a zone of peace and conflict management project. The Local Zone of Peace (LZP) was based on a number of principles and values held by La Coordinadora as well as a commitment to create a new identity for the region. With the new theory of their region as a peaceful one, the LZP activities and definition would take shape over time. La Coordinadora facilitated annual commemorations, including a walk from one town to another that drew two thousand people in 1999. José "Chencho" Alas, a former priest from El Salvador who collaborated and supported La Coordinadora through his Foundation for Self Sufficiency for Central America (FSSCA),[5] played a pivotal role in promoting the principles and values behind the LZP. He provided nearly fifty workshops on human rights and responsibilities that brought people together in their communities to learn and affirm these rights and responsibilities.

The Local Zone of Peace was a declaration around a geographic place— in many ways initially more symbolic than substantive. A newly formed Culture of Peace Program created by La Coordinadora put flesh on the LZP skeleton. They faced a dilemma, however, as it was not clear whether to create a distinct Culture of Peace Program or to consider all programs and activities a reflection of a culture of peace. The original LZP declaration reflected not only a commitment to promote human rights and social justice, but also to assure local participation, democracy, and self-sufficiency. If the Culture of Peace Program was going to be one component of the organization, then it must affect all other components yet somehow not have authority over them. This dilemma required repeated dialogue among all the representatives and their communities. The program definition evolved over time, much of it taking shape after a team was organized, received preliminary training and was doing some pilot work in the communities. Practice informed program policies and procedures.

La Coordinadora sought international financial support and consultation in order to more fully transform the area into a zone of peace. The Foundation for Self-Sufficiency secured a grant from the U.S. Institute of Peace in 1999 and later one from the Hewlett Foundation to develop the Local Zone of Peace. The original funding proposals, developed in consultation with La Coordinadora by Richard Salem, a North American international conflict management consultant supportive of La Coordinadora, followed a traditional North American model of training local people to operate community mediation centers. As soon as the program was funded, FSSCA retained three Mennonite consultants to work at an elicitive design with the Usulutan communities. La Coordinadora recognized the communities would need to help develop the structure and methods for promoting peaceful conflict management.

CULTURE OF PEACE PROGRAM DEVELOPMENT

While a general vision and commitment to peace existed, the Culture of Peace Program evolved over time. The first two years of the LZP, from August 1998 through 2000, consisted of annual commemorations of the Local Zone of Peace and internal organizational changes to assure that the organization reflected peace and democracy. La Coordinadora restructured its governing commission to increase representation and reinforce democratic decision making. They educated themselves around issues of gender and recruited women to the commission staff positions. They established policies with clear criteria for selecting program recipients that was not based on personal relationships or biases.

The actual Culture of Peace Program received international funding and went through key stages in its development, beginning with the first trip made by the international consultants. Internal dialogue, pilot projects, and input from the consultants led to the development of principles of practice and policies that led to the current program structure and methodology.

Three Mennonite peacebuilding consultants, Phil Thomas, Luzdy Stuckey, and Mark Chupp (the author), assisted in the development of the Culture of Peace Program.[6] At Salem's recommendation, we were chosen as much for our approach as for the extensive experience we had in Latin America. We provided a combination of training and facilitated dialogue around the theoretical framework of conflict transformation. From the first trip in early 2000, we did not assume mediation as the model and only briefly introduced it as a method for transforming conflict. Six principles of practice guided us as consultants and were reflected in the first workshop.

Use an Elicitive Approach

Rather than arrive with predetermined objectives and a training agenda, the consultants first interviewed the staff and commission members. The interviews helped them build relationships, understand the history of the area and organization, discover the needs and vision that led to the Local Zone Peace, and learn the local parties' expectations for the upcoming training. Together with the key leaders, we established the objectives of the first workshop, which were to (1) understand what it means for us as individuals to live in peace, (2) together reflect on what it means to be a community of peace, and (3) discover the role and function of La Coordinadora in relation to the vision for a culture of peace. Only then did the trainer-consultants sit down and finalize the workshop activities.

The first workshop and subsequent training used a popular education model, which looked at where the group was in its development and then used exercises that allowed participants to experience the content firsthand and reflect on the experiences and its relevance to their communities. Abandoning preconceived notions of training a group of mediators, we focused on the theoretical foundation of conflict transformation and conflict management skills. Aware of the many failed attempts at establishing mediation centers in Central America,[7] we encouraged the program participants not to commit to any one model.

Building on the framework established by our colleague, John Paul Lederach (1995), we used an elicitive model in which we were catalysts and facilitators who attempted to make explicit the knowledge of the participants. Rather than import a model, we sought to create a discovery process in which they could identify the meaning and methods indigenous to their culture for transforming conflict from destructive to constructive. This type of training framework can be seen as an integration of contributions from popular education, appropriate technology, and ethnography. As primary resources, the participants presented case studies from their communities and then role-played how they would naturally incorporate the communication and conflict management skills to help transform the conflicts. Exercises and simulations evoked awareness and validation as they experienced the dynamics of their culture in the training itself.

Promote the Transforming Power of Nonviolence

More than simply teaching conflict resolution, the trainers brought an understanding that within each person there is a transforming power of peace and nonviolence. Drawing from the Quaker-based Alternatives to Violence Project,[8] the concept of transforming power posits that each person has a choice. The trainer's task is to increase each person's awareness of his or her strengths and the benefits of tapping into this internal source of nonviolence. The workshop included a small group exercise in which each group developed the "tree of life." Divided vertically, one half of the tree represented violence and the other half nonviolence. Each side detailed the elements that made up the roots, trunk, branches, leaves, and fruit of violence or nonviolence. At the same time, nonviolence was not the prescribed response, simply presented as an often forgotten alternative that can potentially transform a destructive situation.[9]

Promote an Inclusive Community and Whole-System View

Both La Coordinadora and the group of trainer-consultants placed a high value on an inclusive, nonhierarchical approach. The first training included commission members (grassroots community leaders), administrators, program staff, and even secretaries and the bookkeeper. One of the first team-building exercises was the Spider Web, where the group must pass, one-by-one, through a web strung between two trees without touching the web and without using the same web opening more than once. This exercise was a high point. The entire group cheered as the last member was helped through the web. It encouraged an atmosphere of mutual support, demonstrated the diverse needs and abilities of each, and stressed the importance of finding a place for everyone.

Inclusion took on a more serious tone on the last day of the first training. One question raised by the consultants was whether the Local Zone of Peace included all those in a specific geographic region, or simply the communities that had joined La Coordinadora. The earlier interviews revealed that some leaders and communities felt at odds with or alienated from the organization. Using Maire Dugan's nested paradigm (1996), the trainers illustrated how a specific conflict can be analyzed to see the causes and impact it has at multiple levels, from the individual, relationship, subsystem (e.g., organization), to the system. The workshop reinforced their commitment to democratic processes and inclusive participation and led them to extend the reach of the Culture of Peace Program to all communities in the region.

Create Experiences to Taste the Transformation We Seek

The training design (see Figure 1), beginning with the Spider Web, used an experiential learning approach to create the conditions in which participants could experience transformation personally and in the group. Exercises, followed by reflection, stressed the multiple levels of transformation—self, relationships, culture, and system.

Figure 1
FIRST TRAINING WORKSHOP—FEBRUARY 2000
La Coordinadora

Activity	Explanation
Day One	
Introductions in Pairs	Name, community, something you value about La Coordinadora, and something no one else here knows about you
Workshop Objectives and Agenda	Discussion of popular education approach and development of group norms (ground rules)
The Spider Web	Objective: to get all team members through web without touching the web and without using any space more than once
Violence-Nonviolence	Brainstorm list for each term; reflection
Conflict Transformation • Tools for analysis • Dugan's nested paradigm • Reflection on transformation	Discuss how conflict and violence affect all spheres (individual relationships, organization, community, society/world)
Light and Lively	"Big Wind Blows"—a type of upset-the-fruit-basket game
Tree of Life • Creation in groups • Presentation and reflection	In small groups, create a detailed drawing of the tree of life, split vertically between violence and nonviolence
Concentric Circles • Sit in two concentric circles • Rotate one chair after each question	Two minutes for each person to tell one other person their response to questions of self-esteem, personal strengths and successes, experiences of forgiveness.

Figure 1, continued

Activity	Explanation
Evaluation and Closing	
Day Two	
Integration Exercise	
Synthesis and Review of Day One	Trainers summarize participants' reflections from day one into synthesis of content
Peaceful Vision of Community in Ten Years • Small-group work • Presentation • Discussion of the roles of civil society and the state in a peaceful El Salvador	Divided by municipality, each group draws their community after ten years of peace • What makes it democratic? • What makes it peaceful? • How are differences handled?
Light and Lively	"Fire and Storm" group mixer
Simulation Exercise: Foundation for Development, Democracy, and Harmony • Competition to receive funding • Proposals must include how the collaborative will make decisions and deal with minority opinions	In small groups, determine how to develop project for funding that requires collaboration with local government and other organizations
Reflection and Observations by Trainers	Strengths of La Coordinadora; possible areas of risk
Work Session: Building on Strengths to Overcome Risks	In small groups, brainstorm what can be done to overcome each major area of risk
Evaluation	Oral, with several focus questions
Closing	Each person states something that inspires them

The workshop began with the individual level. Participants interviewed each other in pairs, focusing on something no one knew about them and what each person valued in La Coordinadora. Rather than presenting themselves to the group, each person presented their partner, speaking as if she or he were that person. This stimulated great camaraderie and tapped into the self-worth of each person and what the group valued about the organization. Even the skill-building exercises focused on the participants' knowledge and skills. To teach listening skills, for example, the trainers asked each person to identify the person they go to who best listens to them. A list of what the best listeners do served as the basis for practicing active listening skills.

At the relationship or group level, many of the exercises had a team-building quality to them. All plenary sessions were held in a circle, where the group served as a resource to one another during the reflection times. "Light and livelies"—short, interactive, cooperative games—appealed to the playful child in everyone. At a deeper level, a listening exercise called "concentric circles" invited participants to systematically share personal stories individually with other participants. Topics included "a way I show respect for myself," "a time when someone forgave me," and "an occasion when I did the right thing, even though I was afraid to do it."

At the cultural level, the entire training elicited the peaceful qualities indigenous to the group and their communities. Creating trusting and cooperative experiences and reflecting on the impact they had on the group provided the basis to explore how a culture of peace could be more fully realized in the region of southern Usulutan.

Create a Positive Vision of the Future

The impetus for the Culture of Peace Program was twelve years of war and a culture caught up in violence. Unfortunately, there was a greater sense among participants of what they wanted to move away from than there was of where they wanted to go. Using Elise Boulding's vision of a peaceful future (1991; see also chapter four), the trainers divided participants in the first training into groups from the same geographic areas and asked them to draw a picture of their municipality after ten years of peace. The trainers invited each person to reflect in silence and then contribute to a common group vision of their peaceful community. We guided them in the group work by asking how the future municipality would be democratic, what would make it peaceful, and how differences would be handled. Each group gave special attention to the roles and functions of the state and civil society in their vision of a peaceful future. Reporting back in plenary, the entire group reflected on appropriate roles of the police and courts, the meaning of integrated development, cultural rituals, and civil-sector mechanisms for promoting peace. There was a palpable excitement generated from these visions and they were later displayed in the central office.

At the conclusion of the first trip, the trainer-consultants and leaders from La Coordinadora arrived at a consensus about the appropriate ongoing role of the consultants. There were three roles: (1) explore with La Coordinadora the vision of a Local Zone of Peace, (2) offer experiences in conflict transformation from other parts of Latin America, and (3) facilitate a process for developing the Local Zone of Peace.

The program developed naturally over the next year and a half. One or two of the international consultants visited the program every three or four months. I served as the primary consultant and was present on each of the trips. Eventually, La Coordinadora appointed seven grassroots representatives from a number of communities to serve as the CPP team. The consultants visited to listen, learn, and share—mirroring back what they heard and observed, accompanying the group as it reached out to the communities, and providing training in specific skills. Much like the first training, the training focused on making explicit how the communities worked at conflict. Topics such as communication and restoration of trust involved an exchange of indigenous knowledge and that from the trainers. Ultimately, the program team determined how they would implement what they gained from the training sessions. As they gained experience, team members and consultants co-facilitated sessions with the staff, commission members, or community groups.

An Experiential-Reflective Program Design Process

A pilot effort in July 2000 in the town of Tierra Blanca gave legs to the program. A dilemma in using the elicitive approach—not having a clear model to follow—had created some confusion or uncertainty as to how the program would affect real conflicts. In an effort to provide a more formal intervention, I conducted a three-day training on participatory action research for the team. As part of the training, the team developed criteria for selecting a community for the intervention, an interview protocol, and a general strategy for approaching the community. With support from La Coordinadora's leadership, the team selected Tierra Blanca because of its strategic location, size, and high levels of violence.

The fieldwork consisted of working over five days with co-researchers from the community (grassroots leaders) to interview seventy-three households and the institutional leaders of Tierra Blanca. Interviews were tabulated, patterns and themes were categorized, and a focus group was held with key informants from the interviews. The final analysis and recommendations were then presented to more than fifty community members at the end of the week. The number-one concern in the community pertained to two rival gangs that had terrorized the community.[10] Even though all the youth and young adults in the gangs were from Tierra Blanca, many residents feared going out after dark. The written report and community assembly empowered the community to openly name the problem and identify a provisional committee to work on the gang conflicts and other needs in the community.

As a result of the participatory action research, the team, under the leadership of José "Chencho" Alas, held two mediation sessions over the next few weeks. In a dramatic turnaround, the gangs agreed to stop fighting and to seek ways of coexisting together. They developed personal goals for turning away from drugs and alcohol and sought vocational training and jobs. Unfortunately, the local police entered the Catholic Church at the end of the last mediation session and seized one of the gang members. Despite the fact that the arrested youth walked the streets of Tierra Blanca every day, the police felt this was the moment to act on a six-month-old warrant. The mediation team's credibility was at stake as both gangs wondered if this was all a plot to clamp down on the gangs. The team followed the police, advocated on the youth's behalf to the prosecutor, and eventually secured his release. In the end, however, the incident reinforced the community's sense that the police were still as much a problem as a resource.

In part because of this controversy and increased expectations created by developing close working relationships with the gangs, the commission that governs La Coordinadora held an evaluation of the program in October 2000. The burning question was whether the Culture of Peace Program had turned into a gang-intervention program, as word spread across the province and people sought out the team. I facilitated a self-evaluation in which commission members, the CPP team, administrative staff, and members from Tierra Blanca met in small groups to review all previous training sessions. The group collectively developed a list of values and principles for guiding the work. They also analyzed the Tierra Blanca pilot project as a case study, identifying the concerns, needs, contributions, relationships, and decision-making role of each of the groups present in the evaluation. They also discovered a long list of achievements that resulted from the Tierra Blanca project.

The three-day evaluation had a future orientation: How would the CPP work in the communities, make program decisions, and not overextend themselves beyond their capacity? The diverse group came together to develop a set of program goals, objectives, and policies to guide the project into the future. They developed policies that spelled out the roles and responsibilities of all stakeholders. They also considered various international organizational models before deciding to adopt an itinerant model, where a regional team would serve as promoters to develop the program in a limited number of micro-regions. Once established in these regions, the program would expand.

The document from the evaluation was adopted in 2001 by the commission and serves as the program's theoretical and programmatic framework. The overall emphasis is on promoting a comprehensive culture of peace, with mediation as one small component. The three major thrusts of the program are presented below, along with the objective and components of each.

CULTURE OF PEACE PROGRAM COMPONENTS

Conscientization and Education for Peace

The objective is that the communities in the Local Zone of Peace appropriate the principles, values, attitudes, behavior, and practical applications of peace. The three components of this education include (a) concepts of peace, (b) human rights and responsibilities, and (c) conflict transformation.

Methods for Transforming Conflict

The objective is that the communities in the Local Zone of Peace recognize the nonviolent mechanisms already present and develop and utilize new negotiation and mediation alternatives for improving conflict management and minimizing violence. The three components include (a) discovering and reviving existing nonviolent methods, (b) conflict management skills and processes, and (c) conflict intervention.

Organization and Participation for Peace

The objective is that the communities in the Local Zone of Peace participate in dialogue and reflection circles, in the formation of local Peace Initiative Committees, and in reflecting peaceful principles and values in all their organizational structures. The two components of this objective are the building of democratic participation internally in the Culture of Peace structure and building of democratic participation in community institutions.

In October 2000, the program hired as the full-time coordinator Mario Mejia, a Salvadoran with experience working on human rights in Guatemala. Although not a mediator, he brought expertise in program development and organization. An educated professional, the coordinator provided on-the-ground leadership as he quickly incorporated conflict transformation theory and practice. The program therefore became less dependent on the international consultants. The team was also gaining valuable experience as promoters in their micro-regions.

Over the next six months, the team developed a clearer methodology, having faced confusion about the itinerant model. The new approach centered around the newly created dialogue and reflection circles.

These informal circles, often taking place under a shade tree in a central part of the village, gathered residents together around a specific theme or topic. Less intimidating than a training workshop, the circles created a safe space for people to reflect on their own experiences and thereby make talking through conflict normative. The circles have an educational benefit but equally important, they create a trusting community. As a circle gains confidence, the facilitative role of the team member becomes less significant.

In order to accomplish the program objectives, the methodology incorporates different sectors of the same community and also integrates groups from different communities in the same micro-region. The current methodology is given in Figure 2. The third objective—organization and participation for peace—is worked at through the methodology by working jointly with sectors that typically do not cooperate and by expanding program involvement to communities not involved in La Coordinadora structure (the local group). The CPP team anticipates providing more direct training in organizational issues once the first two components are implemented.

A POSITIVE APPROACH

The Culture of Peace Program and La Coordinadora are founded on a positive approach. Clearly, the impetus for the organization and CPP program were problems and difficulties facing the communities, yet these peasant leaders had the foresight to avoid dependency models. They created structures and programs to promote self-sufficiency and a culture of peace. This orientation affected their choice in consultants, program development, staffing, even the strategies and methods they developed for advancing a culture of peace.

After considering several potential consultants, La Coordinadora invited consultants affiliated with Mennonite Conciliation Service to work with them. The Mennonite approach incorporated a strong commitment to peace and conflict transformation, a bias toward community building, and a style that fostered empowerment and self-development. All three consultants had lived in Latin America and accompanied peasant groups. The elicitive model, articulated by John Paul Lederach (1995), reflected in part the approach Mennonites had been taking in development work for decades around the world under Mennonite Central Committee. All three consultants were therefore convinced of the importance of working from the ground up in building a movement and structure that would be sustainable long after funding and consultants were gone. More than problem solving, the effort needed to create a safe and trusting space for communities to dialogue and build a peaceful future (Chupp 2000).

The most significant factor, however, that propelled the peacebuilding effort in a positive direction was the decision to become a

Figure 2
CULTURE OF PEACE PROGRAM METHODOLOGY

1. Collect basic information on the community.

2. Approach the community.

3. Identify and select reference persons or sectors to participate in the Culture of Peace Program.

4. Introduce the CPP program within the vision of La Coordinadora.

5. In coordination with the reference persons, motivate and invite receptive sectors of the community to participate in the CPP.

6. Promote dialogue and reflection circles with the local group of communities and among interested sectors.

7. Train persons selected from the dialogue and reflection circles who are willing to serve as trainers in their communities.

8. Train and strengthen the community in organizational processes that promote peace.

9. Accompany and follow up with existing organizational processes.

10. Promote the organization of those interested in continuing with CPP.

11. Internal exchange between diverse sectors of the communities from the same local group, and the communities from the same micro-region that have not been involved in the La Coordinadora local group.

12. External exchange to share experiences with different micro-regions.

13. Train selected persons in conflict transformation and conflict management.

14. Train those with interest and skills from previous training in mediation.

15. Organize and plan with the communities in light of their needs and priorities.

16. Accompany the communities in the implementation of activities that further generate a culture of peace.

17. Evaluate and systematize the process.

zone of peace, boldly declaring that an area of overt hostility and violence would become a place where a culture of peace pervaded. The war was due at least in part to a breakdown in democracy; the Local Zone of Peace declared peaceful democracy must be restored. In so doing, La Coordinadora proclaimed as fundamental the free exercise of economic, social, and cultural rights and the preservation of the natural environment. In addition, they were inviting government institutions and other organizations to join together with La Coordinadora to guarantee the sustainability of life (Local Zone of Peace Agreement 1998). Violence as a way to solve problems was out, replaced by a commitment to use human and financial resources to promote and develop peaceful alternatives that preserved human rights.

The declaration and orientation of the trainer-consultants coincided in a joint commitment to promoting the transformation of conflict as a negative force to a constructive one. Conflict, after all, is a social construction in which one's beliefs influence perceptions and responses. If one approached conflict with a sense of fear and a conviction that conflict never results in anything positive, the person's response would likely be negative, produce destructive results, and therefore reinforce those negative beliefs. If, on the other hand, people could come to believe that differences and conflict are a natural part of our diverse world, their responses would likely be more respectful, produce constructive results, and promote these same positive views of conflict. The task was to reconstruct notions of conflict as normative and a means to mutual understanding, self-realization, and peace.

This commitment to be positive has its roots in the positive core of Salvadoran culture and the nature of La Coordinadora. From their first disaster-prevention work, the organization did not assume a victim role but sought to create the conditions that would preserve and sustain life. Going beyond simply serving as advocates for their communities before the government, the organization mobilized people around the resources they held to effect change. From the programs it developed to the very structure of the organization, La Coordinadora built on existing human and financial resources to create a social infrastructure that embodied their principles and vision.

Peace, democracy, and self-sufficiency formed the basis of the new culture they were creating. La Coordinadora demonstrated the power of civil society through its accomplishments. It enabled citizens to act, educated its constituents, focused light on abuses of power, and critiqued the government. Through advocacy, organizing, and coalition building it created local structures and networks and alleviated the pain of poverty. These efforts represent the possibility of sustainable democracy; La Coordinadora demonstrated a new way when the future was not clear (Cowan 2001).

The approach also built on the best of Salvadoran culture.
 Decades of poverty and lack of government support gave rise to a

spirit of self-sufficiency and prompted grassroots organizing. Unlike the Nicaraguan revolution movement headed by comandantes, the FMLN operated as a collective and developed sophisticated democratic decision-making processes. Aristides Valencia, the executive director of La Coordinadora and a former leader in the FMLN, had not used his FMLN position to demand results but frequently sought the participation of the communities in decision making, seeing himself as a facilitator of democratic process. A dialogue about the principles of democratic participation often preceded a discussion and decision about the matter at hand.

These were living laboratories, creating internally the methods for peaceful relations that were so needed in the communities. The structure of the organization evolved and added layers of participation as more communities joined to assure that democratic process could still take place, although more efficiently. Funding and staffing of programs reflected these beliefs. If a new potential source of funds emerged, La Coordinadora first asked who would control decisions—the communities or the funder—and how the funds would support self-sufficiency. At times they decided to alter a proposal in order to avoid entering into a relationship that would promote dependency. They also made a commitment to hire few professional staff, relying instead on the peasants themselves to carry out the work. In the case of the Culture of Peace Program, they appointed the team of peasants before they hired a full-time professional coordinator.

The Culture of Peace Program emerged over time and followed a natural course of development. Reflecting on training in specific skills and learning about other experiences in conflict transformation, the team developed the appropriate methods that fit their context. Leery of focusing too much on workshops, the team developed its own strategy for introducing the program into a community—the dialogue and reflection circles. Informal, nonthreatening, and less focused on imparting knowledge, the circles drew in people who wanted to talk. The focus clearly invited participants to share about their conflicts, but not as an opening for the team to solve the problem. It was a process of mutual discovery—how the conflict affected them and what resources were available in the community to help out. Building strong trusting relationships within the village—relationships where people could express themselves freely and give or receive support—was essential to the creation of a culture of peace.

Another positive aspect to the program pertained to the team itself. They were not selected because they were the most powerful members of their communities. This helped prevent others from seeking them out as experts who would solve their problems for them. In fact, the experiential training approach meant that the team focused as much on their own transformation and development. They modeled the possibility of drawing out of people the life-giving forces that could be used to create a culture of peace. As they worked through their own conflicts on the team, using methods and skills discovered in the training sessions, they shared their own stories in the circles.

The Local Zone of Peace and Culture of Peace Program represent a combination of positive and traditional problem-solving approaches. Their motivation stems from deep concerns about violence and conflict. When reflecting on their past or current situations, the dialogue often revolves around the problems, not the best of what already exists. Yet they are guided by a vision of the future that embodies self-sufficiency, democracy, and peace. The program drew on both problem solving and community building. There is a new language emerging that is transforming the culture. People are shifting from old thinking, where others solve their problems, to the possibility that there are nonviolent resources within them and their communities that can be tapped to create harmonious communities.

There are several challenges as the program moves forward. Trying to obtain more measurable outcomes, such as those associated with local mediation centers, is still a temptation. Funding sources like to see tangible outcomes. Some people have difficulty giving up the notion that an expert must come in and solve their problem. There is a paradox in the approach. The commitment to popular education means that they must start where the people are, but somehow the team needs to transcend negativity to embrace the positive elements and values in the communities. Listening can give legitimacy to negative thinking. The trust-building and cooperative exercises, however, create new possibilities in people's minds as they experience the joy of coming together to meet a challenge.

A FUTURE OF POSSIBILITIES

Where is the program headed? The current methodology anticipates expanding the circles and then drawing from them a core group to receive additional support and training. Ideally, these people will serve their own villages, facilitating circles and offering to accompany those in conflict. More than creating mediators or mediation centers, the program envisions creating a transformed culture centered around human rights and responsibilities—a space in each community where people practice a transformative process that evokes respect and care for one another and democratic, inclusive organizations. As people learn the ins and outs of conflict, they can serve as resources to one another, informally offering help to those who know and trust them. Not necessarily an appointed group carrying the name mediator, people will emerge who exercise a combination of indigenous and learned methods that facilitate peaceful relations.

Admittedly slower than training a group of educated leaders as mediators, this positive grassroots approach offers a more sustainable model. Not relying on foreign experts or a local elite, the Culture of Peace Program breaks the dependency model—possibly for the first time for a conflict management program in Central America. The program is guided by a commission of peasant leaders inspired by the prospects of a culture of peace and self-sufficiency. The team becomes less and less dependent on outside training and consultation. Ongoing training now occurs within the country, provided by a growing Salvadoran conflict transformation resource group, Yek Ineme ("well being"). Networks of rural communities are forming as the CPP team is in dialogue about their vision and experience with a group of peacebuilders in the northern province of Chalatenango.

Breaking from the dependency model, La Coordinadora anticipates creating a strong civil society empowered to work at building healthy relationships, organizations, and communities. Government institutions and political leaders will become key sources for public services and will be accountable to the community. Hopefully, a balanced relationship with clear and mutually supportive roles for civil society and the state will emerge over time.

The promise of such a vision already exists, albeit in miniature. Seeing the team discover within themselves skills and knowledge is truly inspiring. In November 2002, the team discovered their potential after a training-for-trainers workshop when I invited them to carry out the workshop we had just designed. They were expecting me to serve as the lead trainer for the upcoming four days of workshops for representatives from six local groups (micro-regions). After their initial shock, they reached within themselves and found the confidence to facilitate the entire workshops themselves. They exuded surprising confidence as each member deftly facilitated exercises, led group reflections, and expressed in their own language the concepts of peace and conflict transformation. I was moved and convinced again of the power of peasants creating their own peaceful future.

A new sense of community is emerging in southern Usulutan. Diverse groups are joining together to discuss their future and are beginning to live into a new vision of inclusion, mutual support, holistic development, and true democracy. The fabric of society is being recreated. Social capital—the networks of trust and cooperation—extends freely to span all people, regardless of past affiliations. While many strangers still begin to get to know one another through a litany of their past military or political activities, these conversations soon give way to discovering what they hold in common. Twelve years of war are not easily forgotten. In a region of great conflict and polarized repatriation, a local zone of peace emerges based on a vision of ten more years of peace.

ENDNOTES

1. In Spanish the full name is La Coordinadora de Comunidades de Bajo Lempa y la Bahia de Juiquilisco, literally the Coordinator of Communities of the Lower Lempa River and Juiquilisco Bay. The organization prefers to use "La Coordinadora" as both their English and Spanish name.

2. El Salvador law requires that NGOs be structured with two organizations—one the social entity and the other the administrative/fiscal entity.

3. The mangrove is a threatened habitat for aquatic life and a source of self-sufficiency for the peasants living along the many miles of Usulutan shores. The organization chose this name to reflect its commitment to the indigenous way of life in the region and its commitment to preserving the natural environment.

4. These gangs have been transformed and carry their own names in El Salvador, *Mara Salvatrucha* 13 and 18. Even many active gang members are not familiar with the origins of these numbers with Los Angeles street gangs.

5. The Foundation for Self Sufficiency in Central America, a U.S. foundation dedicated to supporting La Coordinadora, employs Chencho and serves as a bridge between North Americans and the program (see www.fssca.net). For more on José "Chencho" Alas, see chapter sixteen of this volume.

6. The proposals were initially written by international consultant Richard Salem, who accompanied the group of three Mennonite trainer-consultants in the first visits. The trainer-consultants were all fluent in Spanish and had lived in Latin America for extended periods. Thomas had lived in Guatemala and El Salvador; Stuckey is a Colombian now living in Arizona; and Chupp had lived in Guatemala, Nicaragua, and Costa Rica. All had worked previously under the Mennonite Central Committee.

7. The trainers provided an overview of various efforts to establish mediation centers in the region, most of which were based on North American mediation practice. These efforts failed in part due to the short time frame expected to train and organize such centers. In other cases, the efforts lacked sufficient local ownership.

8. The Alternatives to Violence Project began in New York in the mid-1970s, when Quakers and civil rights workers developed workshops for prison inmates. Today there are community and prison-based projects throughout North America and numerous other countries.

9. Aware of not having themselves lived through the Salvadoran civil war, the trainers were careful not to prescribe nonviolence as the preferred response to a given situation.

10. Gangs in El Salvador are a relatively new phenomenon, emerging as Salvadorans living in exile in Los Angeles returned with their sons who had joined gangs. Some hardened gang members returned to the streets of El Salvador after being arrested and deported from the United States. The 13th Street and 18th Street gangs are the imported rival gangs in this community and throughout the country.

REFERENCES

Boulding, Elise. 1991. "The Challenge of Imaging Peace in Wartime." *Futures* 23:5, pp. 528–533.

Chupp, Mark. 2000. "Creating Space for Peace: The Central American Peace Portfolio." In *From the Ground Up: Mennonite Contributions to International Peacebuilding.* Cynthia Sampson and John Paul Lederach, eds. New York: Oxford University Press.

Communitas Charitable Trust. 2000. *Two Peasant Organizations in Central America.* An evaluation by the Communitas Charitable Trust, conducted by Harold Baron, Chicago, Ill.

Cowan, Ruth B. 2001. *The Contribution of a Civil Society Organization to Developing Democracy in El Salvador.* Unpublished essay.

Dugan, Maire A. 1996. "A Nested Theory of Conflict." *A Leadership Journal: Women in Leadership—Sharing the Vision* 1 (July), pp. 9–20.

Lederach, John Paul. 1995. *Preparing for Peace: Conflict Transformation across Cultures.* Syracuse, N.Y.: Syracuse University Press.

Local Zone of Peace Agreement. 1998. *Convenio para la Creacion de la Zona de Paz Local en Centroamerica,* in translation. Unpublished document signed August 15 in Ciudad Romero, Usulutan, El Salvador.

McClintock, Cynthia. 1998. *Revolutionary Movements in Latin America: El Salvador's FMLN and Peru's Shining Path.* Washington, D.C.: U.S. Institute of Peace Press.

Salvadoran Human Rights Institute. 1996. *Zona de Paz Local: Un Rio que Busca su Cauce.* San Salvador: Libros de Central America.

Wallace, Scott. 2000. "You Must Go Home Again." *Harper's Magazine* (August).

Dream, dream
We're coming out of the night.
Let's close our eyes
And dream of the light.
Dream of new tomorrows
From the rubble of today.
Dream of things that we can do
To build a better way.
Let's dream.

HERM WEAVER

CHAPTER SIX

THE "WOW FACTOR" AND A NON-THEORY OF CHANGE

John Paul Lederach

This "thought piece" conceives of the positive approach to peacebuilding as a "composite moment" in which the creative process lifts sight to a new, more holistic view and motivates action not directly on "the problem," but rather in the relational spaces surrounding the problem. In changing the people, relationships, and environment, the process ultimately changes the problem itself. This "non-theory" of change is derived in part from author's experience with a storytelling project, "Dream the Light," following the terrorist attacks of September 11, 2001, in the United States. An appendix to the chapter tells the story of the storytelling project and then presents the story itself, together with an original song created to accompany it. A second appendix, this one a compact disc found in the cover of this volume, presents the song and story as performed by the songwriter and storyteller.

My experience over the years suggests that there are two axiomatic questions for peacebuilding. "What creates a catalyst for constructive change?" and "What sustains the change process once it starts?" Both questions circle back to a critical platform of inquiry for the broader field that has not been adequately explored: "What are our theories of change?"

These kinds of questions have a direct bearing on our conceptual frameworks and practice, and in particular, they have implications for positive approaches to peacebuilding. If we take as our point of departure the need to make more explicit our underlying assumptions about how constructive social change happens, particularly in settings of deep division and polarization, we may arrive at some useful observations about our guiding-but-implicit theories. I find that these observations, by articulating the promises and challenges of theory, complexify our often too-simple notions of change. Let me give two examples.

One guiding-but-implicit theory of change in the justice and peacebuilding fields proposes that increased awareness about injustice and other sources of conflict translates into motivation for pursuing change. Hence, much effort is placed on publishing, speeches, and campaigns aimed at increasing people's exposure to facts and information, to motivate them to make a response. The promise implied in this theory of change is that cognitive knowledge coupled with emotional impact creates response and action.

Not explored to any great extent, however, are the questions of how, when, and for what reasons people who hear or read something about a situation actually translate that exposure into action, particularly when the information is aimed at contributing to their cognitive knowledge about the situation. Does information create insight and enlightenment that impel action? Does information instill of a sense of responsibility that motivates action? Must information employ the social hook of guilt to drive action? If we probed these questions deeply, we might in fact discover that the electronic age of instant global news, Internet, and email creates an overload in which awareness is numbed by too much information, and responsive action is actually diminished.

A second guiding theory of change is that solving problems is the key to constructive change. Implicit in this theory is the assumption that increased process skills will increase social change. More specifically, if people increase their skills in the various aspects of conflict transformation such as communication and problem-solving processes, there will be a corresponding increase in their interest in applying these skills to problems of real life. In this orientation, training often carries the day. The more training, the greater the social change.

Not explored in depth, however, are the presumed socio-political, cultural, and economic connections that underpin this theory. Who is drawn to training and from what groups in the society? For what purpose do people pursue training? What skills are taught and for what kinds of "market" demands? How exactly does the skill base translate into social-change processes? What is the impact of defining change in relation to the problem, and how does that create a platform for broader social transformation? Might it instead impose a limitation?

What do positive approaches to peacebuilding suggest about theories of change? While this is still a new and rising facet of the field, my experience suggests that, like all other theories of change, there are promises and challenges. A quick review may be useful.

I find positive approaches to peacebuilding to have the greatest impact when they create a composite moment that draws upon some aspects of the above-mentioned theories, but with a twist. There are several keys to creation of the "composite," while innovation and creativity provide the "moment."

The first key is that a positive approach does not define itself by the problem, but rather by the quality of the "beyond the problem." A social problem per se is often the manifestation of something that is deeply stuck, as reflected in the metaphors of "loggerheads" and "dead-end streets." These are situations in which social energies collide over issues, facts, and decisions and create incompatibilities of both social analysis (how the problem is understood and broken down into logical pieces) and social solutions (whose answer to the issue is best, usually based on analysis). A positive approach is not defined so much by a pollyannaish view of the possible, but rather by its willingness to see life beyond the boundaries of the problem. It looks for change not in the problem, but in the relational spaces that surround it. This is like trying to focus intently on an object in a dark room. The harder you look at it, the more difficult it is to see. If, however, you look around the object, placing it in your peripheral vision, the object becomes clear and settled.

A second key to a positive approach is paradoxical: It involves finding a social action that creates energy independent of the problem, but that ultimately affects the problem. This requires that a paradox be embraced. The action has to be practical (as in "Wow, this can be done and I can do it!") and also engaging ("Wow, this is great!"), providing a proactive and hands-on component that people feel and see making a positive difference.

In the story and compact disc, *Dream the Light* (see appendices to this chapter), the common response received by teenagers was simple. As one of the students commented in an interview, "The events of September 11 left us numb. The possible responses seemed like they were so far away from what we could do. But in the story there were very specific things we could do and [they were] immediately available. We could learn a language. We could talk with people from the mosque. We could find a pen pal in the Middle East and actually develop a relationship. It was, like, 'I'm not paralyzed. I can do something and it actually makes a difference'" (Kniss 2002).

The third key to a positive approach is innovation and creativity. I would call this the "wow factor." It can only be understood in parallel with arts and the creative process, as opposed to sciences and the analytical process. Understanding in the sciences comes, for the most part, through cognitive processes of breaking a phenomenon down into parts that can be studied. We "see" analytically by pieces. The artistic process, on the other hand, goes beyond the view seen through a parsimonious lens to capture the whole. It provides a way for us to "see"—to discern and grasp—what is visible but not seen with the eyes. That is the capacity of a painting, poem, play, or photograph. In its small wholeness, a deep truth about something is revealed and understood. When applied to peacebuilding, such a process is not set into motion by logical intent and cognitive design, but rather, as many artists would say, by intuition and an "I fell into it" quality. From my spiritual interpretative understanding, I refer to this as "divine naiveté." It is the intervention of an energy that goes beyond cognitive understanding and penetrates to a new level of understanding, motivation, and action.

When these three things come together—a willingness to not look for change in the problem, but in the relational spaces around it; a social action taken independently of the problem but ultimately affecting it; and a creative process that reveals a holistic new view of the situation—something is created that engages people, provides an avenue for meaningful action, and adds something new and creative to the situation. That new social "thing" has an impact on the problem and the process; on the past and the future; and on the individual and the system. Paradoxically, like a painting it often can only be grasped cognitively in retrospect.

What is the underpinning theory of change? To my current understanding, it is a non-theory in that it is not designed to systematically go "straight at the problem." Or perhaps it is a theory of social relativity. It is akin to the energy released by the splitting of an atom into the relational environment around the atom. When you create a catalyst that goes beyond the problem, you spark a creative process of engagement that is independent of the problem and yet changes the environment, the people and relationships, and ultimately, the problem itself.

REFERENCE

Kniss, Sharon. 2002. Interview with John Paul Lederach (April 3). Harrisonburg, Va.

Appendix

"DREAM THE LIGHT": THE POWER OF STORYTELLING FOR PEACEBUILDING

John Paul Lederach and Herm Weaver

The single greatest challenge facing positive approaches to peacebuilding is found in the paradox of how people in an ongoing violent conflict can develop unexpected creative action, while living in the grips of genuine tragedy, deep injustice, oppression, and trauma. This paradox hit home for North Americans in the wake of September 11, 2001. For the two of us this did not pop up as a rhetorical or theoretical question, though as academic professors each of us has written about the processes of reconciliation and healing. The paradox was, so to say, in our face.

Nearly a year prior to September 2001, we had agreed to facilitate several back-to-back events that unwittingly came on the heels of the violence unleashed in New York and Washington. On the surface, our tasks involved relatively routine, local, and in the bigger global picture, insignificant activities. We were to be the masters of ceremony for the annual variety show of our home congregation, Community Mennonite Church, in Harrisonburg, Virginia. We were also to provide input for a national meeting of elementary and secondary school educators who teach in private Mennonite institutions. Finally, we were to serve as the resource people for the spiritual renewal week at Eastern Mennonite High School, also in Harrisonburg.

These engagements came literally "on the heels" of the terrorist attacks. Working in Guatemala on September 11 and unable to fly home, John Paul was caught shuttling from airport to airport. The church retreat was Saturday, September 22; the plenary session with five hundred educators in Maryland was Friday, September 28; and the five morning sessions with four hundred junior high and high school students was the week of October 1–5. Local and personal? Yes indeed. But what an opportunity to practice Carl Roger's notion that that which is most intensely personal is also most universal, and Kenneth Boulding's proposal that change happens by demonstrated potential. If something exists it is possible.

We did have a certain advantage. For some years we had dabbled and experimented with the arts and peacebuilding. (Well, some may not call what we do "the arts.") We tell stories and sing folk music, at times bordering on the irreverent, but always aimed at insights and lessons from life experiences. With tragedy before us we felt we had to change most everything we had planned to do. The night before the church retreat variety show, we decided to end the evening of fun with a story and song that would propose a positive response to September 11. The story was intensely personal, based roughly on John Paul's life story as a peacebuilder and on resources and real-life people found in our congregation, in particular, a computer language program that had been developed by one of our church members. In previous variety shows, John Paul had told stories about the quirks of life and growing up that always started with the line, "Everything in this story is true, except for the parts that I changed to make it a better story." On the evening of September 22, under the night stars of the Shenandoah Valley, we started the story with the phrase, "Everything in this story is true, except for the parts that haven't happened yet."

That evening we were overwhelmed with the response of people in our congregation to the simple proposed action of learning Arabic and developing people-to-people contacts among children, teenagers, and schools in Central Asia, the Middle East, and the United States. A week later, we delivered the story and song to the educators instead of giving a lecture on peace education. There were tears and encouragement. But more importantly, teachers wanted to know how they could actually get connected to "doing the plan" with their students. Most significant was the feedback from several people on how to improve the story so that it had less "reaction" to political leaders and a more positive spin on the concrete steps that could be taken. We tweaked the story into version three and a week later delivered it to its original intended audience, "the high school that changed world." The following day we engaged students in a simple process of generating proposals for what could be done next. Suggestions ranged from language study and getting pen pals in Central Asia, to inviting guest speakers from the Middle East into the school and seeking connections with the local mosque, to activating the school to send relief supplies to Afghanistan.

With strong encouragement from several church members, three weeks later we recorded a compact disc (CD), *Dream the Light—A Story and Song.* By then Herm had written a new song, "A Dream of the Light," that provided the introduction and closing to the story, "How a High School Changed the World." The costs of production were defrayed by generous support from our church, which made available hundreds of free *Dream the Light* CDs to high school teachers across the United States. It was a homespun adventure. The church youth group and high schoolers gathered to stamp labels and package the first five hundred CDs. Within six months a total of 2000 CDs had been given or sold at cost.

Meanwhile, back at the high school in the months that ensued, seventy-five kids started Arabic lessons, with free computer language programs going to anyone who would commit to studying at least five hours a month for three months. Other schools finding out about the possibility wrote and received the same. Other students pursued pen pals, finding high school friends in Lebanon to correspond with by email. In their weekly "neighbor groups" the entire high school made "afghans for Afghans," and a significant number of blanket comforters were sent via a relief agency to Afghanistan. A small set of students chose to fast and pray on Fridays during Ramadan as an act of concern and solidarity with those who were suffering.

Now, nearly two years later, another two thousand CDs have been circulated into the public and a follow-up CD, "In Your Song I Hear My Voice," has recorded the original song in twenty-two languages. In an unexpected move just before his death in 2002, the owner and inventor of the Rosetta Stone language programs, Alan Stoltzfus, through a family foundation put in motion a gift of $3 million that will make the Arabic language CDs available to high schools across America. And on the one-year anniversary of the September 11 attacks, the story and song were used in a number of memorial services.

Amanda Maust, one of the students thinking back over the events of fall 2001, noted that the key impact of the story was that she could think about "doing something immediate to connect with real people. And I could actually do that with people over there and right here in the United States, in our own town." Amanda proposed the Ramadan solidarity fasting at home, and then she brought the idea to the Peace Club at school because "it was a way to show support to people who were different than us that said we do not look down on you. We want to understand and support you. So on Fridays, instead of eating lunch we would gather to email our pen pals in the Middle East" (2002).

Another student, Sharon Kniss recalled that she felt a sense of "empowerment." "Up until we heard the story, it was like we were watching things happen, looking at it all from a distance and not knowing what to do. Here in the story we had ideas about specific things to do, if we were willing to put forward the effort. What I liked best was that for a period of time, the whole school came together in committees—a committee to get language study going, one to connect to people that were affected in New York, another to get local people from the Middle East into our school, one to find pen pals. People were willing to do something rather than just say 'we should do something.' We had a course of action" (2002).

Did the entire program and movement described in the story actually happen? No, at least not to date. Did the high school actually stop the war or change the world? No. But then again, maybe. We still get more requests that we can fulfill to perform the story. High school educators continue to write us, from Louisiana to Alberta, out of the blue asking about the CD, the language program, and the initiative. Websites were created. Songwriters have asked permission to record the title track. Eastern Mennonite University sent thousands of copies of the story as a Christmas gift to its entire alumni list.

We cannot assess the impact of this adventure in traditional quantitative measures. What we do know is that the most important feedback we receive consistently from the song and story is simple. As one person said, "Thank you. In the midst of this tragedy I have struggled to know what to do. You have given me simple ideas that are possible for me to do with my children." As we wrote for one of our introductions, this was a small response to a big challenge, but one that suggests that no matter how small, all that is good starts with hope, faith, and a step of love. We are grateful for the opportunity to share this song and story with you.

Ⓠ

HOW A HIGH SCHOOL CHANGED THE WORLD

(Chorus)
Dream, dream
We're coming out of the night.
Let's close our eyes
And dream of the light.
Dream of new tomorrows
From the rubble of today.
Dream of things that we can do
To build a better way.
Let's dream.

It happened in the sunlight of the day
Filled with fear that would not go away.
A rising pile of rubble in the haze
And I couldn't even find the strength to pray.

(Chorus)

Fear turned into anger from that day.
"Revenge" it could be heard along the way.
Somewhere in the night
A soft voice would say,
"Hold fast and dream about the light of day."

(Chorus)

I want to tell you a story. The title of this story is "How a High School Changed the World." This is a true story. Everything in this story is true, except for the parts that haven't happened yet.

There was once a very old man who had lots of grandchildren. He loved to tell stories. And at night the children would come and beg him for a story. He would gather them up in his lap and ask, "Now which story do you want to hear?"

"Tell us, Grandpa," they would all shout, "tell us the one about the war that never started." And then the grandpa began. . . .

Once upon a time, a long time ago, there was a young man who went on a trip to the Bible Lands. He visited Lebanon, Egypt, and Jordan. He crossed over the Jordan River into Palestine and Israel. He visited refugee camps, holocaust museums, and stayed in people's homes. He even got sick and spent a couple of nights in a Jerusalem hospital.

One afternoon on the trip, he met an American volunteer working in Beit Jala, at a Palestinian boys' school. He was so impressed with how this American could speak Arabic. It just flowed. He felt a deep stirring in his tummy. He wanted to come back. He wanted to go to Beit Jala. He wanted to learn Arabic.

When he returned to the United States, he applied immediately to the volunteer agency. On the form where it said, "Where do you want to serve?" he wrote by the line for Preference Number 1: "Beit Jala", Preference 2: "Beit Jala"; Preference 3: "Beit Jala." He mailed off the application. And then he waited. Three months later the agency called. "We are closing the position in Beit Jala. We cannot send you to the Middle East. Too dangerous. Too much fighting. Too many problems at the school." But they had other suggestions. "We can send you to a horse farm in Poland, or a university-student housing project in Belgium."

The young man went out that night and looked up at the stars. Perplexed and confused he called into the sky, "Why, God? Why not Beit Jala?" But he did not hear any answer.

So he chose Belgium and he learned French. And lived with Africans, Arabs, Asians, and Latin Americans. And late at night around a chessboard he learned about the world. After three years he went to Spain and learned Spanish. He visited people who were in jail because they did not want a military dictatorship. He walked all over Spain, seeking people's stories about the war and their desire for peace. And he learned about struggle.

After about five years, he came home to finish college. He got a degree, but more importantly, he got fifth-degree burns being swept off his feet by the most beautiful, vivacious, olive-skinned, A-1 choice of a young woman he had ever expected to meet, and there she was right there in Hesston, Kansas. Can you believe, right there in Hesston, Kansas. They got married and went back to Spain, then on to Central America. They got into all kinds of good trouble and got chased around. But in the end they helped hundreds of new friends end a war in Nicaragua. The young man learned about suffering and commitment. He learned peace might be possible. They came home to teach young people about this idea, and that is how the young man came to be at a community church in Harrisonburg, Virginia.

One Sunday at church a man with a funny walk and crooked glasses stood up and said, "I have a dream that I am going to teach the world to speak languages through computers. And our world will be better for it." The young man smiled. He liked languages. He told the man with the crooked glasses it was a good idea.

Time went on. The young man and his wife had children. They grew up. The children played basketball. They sang in choirs. Actually the young man was not so young any more. He had some gray hair and his belly started to flop over his belt. He traveled to a lot of places where people were fighting. He had a weird job nobody could explain.

When his son was asked by a teacher at school, "What exactly is your daddy doing in

Somalia?" his son replied, "My dad has gone there to tell them to put their guns away and eat their food." That is what he did, this not-so-young man.

Then one day he was flying on a plane to Tajikistan, and he picked up the airline magazine. And right there on the back cover he saw an advertisement for the Computer Language Program straight from the friend at church with the funny walk and the crooked glasses. His finger went across all the languages until it stopped at Arabic. Then he thought about Beit Jala. And his stomach stirred.

When he got home he looked up his friend with the crooked glasses in church. "Listen," the not-so-young man said, "I saw your advertisement in the magazine. I have just come back from Tajikistan and nobody there speaks any English, and they really need to see your program. And . . . I want to learn Arabic. I have a laptop with a DVD. And I want to learn Arabic." His friend with crooked glasses gave him an Arabic-language CD.

On his very next trip headed for Colombia and Guatemala, the not-so-young man took along the new Arabic-language CD. On the plane he put on his earphones, fired up the laptop, and started his first lesson.

"Walad!" "Kalb!" he would repeat the words as the pictures on the DVD flashed by. He noticed his seatmate on the plane looking at him as if he were an odd-ball.

"I'm learning Arabic," he said a bit embarrassed. "Walad wa kalb. The dog and the boy," he said in Arabic pointing at the screen.

Then it happened. Before he could return from his trip, some men hijacked and crashed three airplanes into New York City and Washington, D.C., like a knife in the heart of

America. It was horrible. It made the not-so-young man sick to his stomach. And angry and sad.

Late one night, stuck in Guatemala, he went out onto the hotel rooftop and looked up at the stars. Perplexed and confused he shouted into the sky, "Why God? Why now? Why so many innocent people?" But he did not hear any answer.

The not-so-young man wished he were home with his family. But it could not be. No planes were flying. Everyone was afraid. He listened to the news reporters. They said the hijackers were Arabs. They found Arabic manuals and books in the rented cars.

The not-so-young man felt his stomach stir. He sat all alone in his hotel room, took out the Arabic-language CD and looked at it. "What should I do?" he wondered. They were pulling people off the airplanes with Arabic connections. He sat for a long time.

Then he pulled out the only compact disc jewel box he had in his luggage. It was from his daughter's high school choir. The title said, "I Can Tell the World." He put her CD in his computer and listened to track three. "Now Is the Cool of the Day."

Ah, the music felt good. He looked at his Arabic-language CD. He looked at the high-school-choir CD jewel box. Then the not-so-young man smiled and said out loud, "That's it!"

He put the Arabic-language disc from his friend with the crooked glasses into his daughter's high-school-choir CD box, walked to a post office, and mailed it home.

A week later, the not-so-young man spoke at a church retreat and told his community his story, all about Beit Jala, learning Arabic, the computer-language CD, and the high school choir. Then the next week he told the same story to five hundred school teachers at a big conference. And then he told the story at his daughter's high school. Each time he ended with the same idea.

"You see," said the not-so-young man, "just like the high-school-choir CD box 'I Can Tell the World' nestled its loving arms around the Arabic-language CD, so, too, can we wrap our arms around those we are told to hate. We have to find a way to understand each other in this world, and I have a proposal. With financial support from churches and the Computer Language Program, we will make available free Arabic-language CDs to all American high schools so they can learn Arabic, with two conditions: first, that each school agrees to find and develop a relationship with a sister high school in an Arabic-speaking country; and second, each high school must convince one other high school in the United States to do the same."

Of course the not-so-young man had not consulted with his friend with the crooked glasses who owned the Computer Language Program, but he figured his proposal might have greater moral persuasion if it had the whole community behind the idea.

And behind it they came.

His daughter's high school got so enthused, they started an after-school Arabic club. Sixty kids signed up for free Arabic CDs and started lessons. They invited local Arabic speakers into their classes. They found their way to sister schools, one in Jordan and one in Syria. And their U.N. club convinced two other high schools to join them. But more importantly, a local newspaper published an article about their efforts. Once it got onto the news wires, Good Morning America called and interviewed a couple of the kids, and the choir even sang on national TV.

Within a month the idea spread.

The man with the crooked glasses said he gave away five thousand Arabic CDs and a whole bunch of English ones to the Middle East.

Exchange programs jumped up all over the place. Soon there were hundreds of high schools all over America learning Arabic and writing emails to new friends in the Middle East who were learning English. It was no longer an idea. It had become a movement.

Why, the whole thing got so big that it finally reached Washington, the national security advisers, and even the President's cabinet. It seemed this movement had better connections in the Middle East and Central Asia than anyone else in the country. There were pen pals everywhere, and some were even going for visits. The advisers were curious and just had to know more. They invited the leaders of this movement to Washington. They were surprised when three teenagers showed up.

The advisers did not waste any time. "How in the world do you propose we achieve peace?" they demanded.

"Walad!" said one. "Kalb!" said another. "The boy and the dog," smiled the third.

"What kind of answer is that?" A security adviser could hardly believe his ears.

"Learn Arabic," the teenagers responded. "And remember Abe Lincoln!"

The grandpa paused, the last words still hanging in the air. The children watched his face carefully until one of them could wait no longer.

"But Grandpa," she burst out, "what about Abe Lincoln?"

"Well," the grandpa responded, "Ole Abe Lincoln once said that the only way to truly get rid of an enemy is to make him your friend."

"And so did that war ever start, Grandpa?" another one asked, looking at the old man.

"Oh the war started," said the grandpa. "But the amazing thing was that the second and third wars never did. Too many children grew up speaking Arabic. And I guess maybe they just finally understood what President Lincoln meant."

All was quiet again. Then one of the children asked, "Did the young man ever get back to Beit Jala?"

The grandpa thought for a while and then shook his head. "He never went back to Beit Jala. But you know, Beit Jala never left his heart."

Late that night, when all the children had gone off to bed, the grandpa went outside and looked up at the stars for a long time.

Then he just whispered, "Wow, God. Wow!"

(Sing)
Some dreaming has been done since that day
Singing, telling stories 'bout some day.
We shall overcome, they used to play
Building new tomorrows
From the rubble of today.
Building new tomorrows from today.

Dream, dream
We're coming out of the night.
Let's close our eyes
And dream of the light.
Dream of new tomorrows
From the rubble of today.
Dream of things that we can do
To build a better way.
Let's dream.

© *How a High School Changed the World*, John Paul Lederach; *A Dream of the Light*, Herman Weaver (www.dreamthelight.com)

REFERENCES

Kniss, Sharon. 2002. Interview with John Paul Lederach (April 3). Harrisonburg, Va.

Maust, Amanda. 2002. Interview with John Paul Lederach (April 3). Harrisonburg, Va.

A vivid imagination compels the whole body to obey it.

ARISTOTLE

CHAPTER SEVEN

CREATIVE COEXISTENCE IN MUSLIM SPAIN AS A MODEL OF POSITIVE PEACE

Joseph V. Montville and Heidi Paulson Winder

In order to build upon the positive history that the Muslims, Jews, and Christians shared in Muslim Spain and the medieval Mediterranean, seven historians have contributed to a book detailing how in the eighth to fifteenth centuries, peoples of these three faiths were able to create the greatest civilization that Europe north of the Pyrenees had seen. This chapter documents how the book project has been at the heart of efforts by the former preventive diplomacy program of the Center for Strategic and International Studies to combat Israeli-Palestinian pessimism by focusing attention on the principles of tolerance and pluralism at the heart of Jewish and Muslim teachings. The project aims to provide a roadmap for creative coexistence for Israelis and Arabs. With the book as a cornerstone, the plan is to launch a multi-level, multimedia information campaign among Israelis and Palestinians so that they can draw on their positive past to generate a vision for a collaborative future.

❖

As devastating conflict continues to escalate between the Israelis and the Palestinians, each side increasingly despairs that they will ever be able to make genuine peace. The derailed Oslo peace process serves as a touchstone for pessimism. Each side blames the other for the continuing violence and failure to make peace. Many people on both sides believe it is no longer possible to negotiate with the other. This attitude not only makes it much more difficult to launch an effective new peace process, but people become more dangerous when they feel that violence is their only viable option. It is our belief that the Jewish-Muslim relationship within and beyond Israel and prospects for stability in that relationship require a major initiative to deal with the deep pessimism among the Jews of Israel that they can ever build community with the Muslims and among the Palestinians that they will ever be treated with dignity and respect by the Israelis.

A basic reason for the distrust and fear between Jews and Muslims, which long predates the collapse of the Oslo process yet exacerbates current pessimism, is what could be called the "value gap" between the two cultures. There is a palpable sense that the two sides can never coexist peacefully or even functionally, as envisioned in the Oslo agreements, because they share no values in common. The two peoples are psychologically separated by perceptions that each has no meaningful connection with the other, except for their mutual distrust and disdain. This belief has been brought home with shocking emphasis as the death toll continues to mount on both sides, as homes are destroyed, civilians are blown up, and peace talks are stalled before they have barely begun.

This distrust has been rooted in stereotypes, years of violence, and competitive psychologies of victimhood. Israelis have been deeply affected by enduring and episodically brutal anti-Semitism in European Christendom (the creation of the state of Israel was ultimately the result of the obscene climax of anti-Semitism—the Holocaust). The Palestinians, for their part, have suffered the humiliation and degradation of losing their homeland and living under occupation. With these sad histories so present in their collective memories, the Israelis and the Palestinians both struggle with a profound sense of loss and injustice that, taken together, is a toxic combination. As Joseph Montville, a scholar of ethnic conflict, writes:

> Making history and absorbing historical change is one way of describing ethnic conflict over time. . . . [T]here is a direct correlation between intensity, scope, and continuity of interethnic violence—the absorption of history—and the difficulty in making peace between the ethnic groups involved. In other words, the higher the level of victimhood felt by aggrieved groups, the harder it is to get the conflict resolved. A situation is particularly difficult if both ethnic groups in conflict feel victimized—that is, if there is a competition of victimhood over which group has suffered more. (1990, 537)

The Middle East is a place that is struggling with its present, yet is crippled by its history. Both the Palestinians and the Israelis have experienced historical losses to a degree that they both approach the conflict with the mentality of victims. It is our belief that their painful histories must be addressed before real peace can be possible.

But negative memory can be fought with positive memory. In psychologically sensitive political-historical analysis of ethnic and sectarian conflict, the task is to discover where and when the blows to collective self-esteem of the peoples involved occurred. Strategies to transform conflicted relationships depend significantly on restoring self-esteem and a sense of justice to the groups that feel victimized.

 Often the people mired in the Middle Eastern conflict forget or are unaware that the Jews and Muslims have a history that was for the most part devoid of conflict. They actually share positive history. There are broad periods of history when neither was victimized and both excelled. By re-introducing these positive histories—stories of Arab and Jewish cooperation, stories of how that cooperation lead to a golden age for both the Arabs and Jews—the parties involved in the conflict can begin to imagine the shared future that is essential in a peace process.

Dissemination of positive information can have a strong social impact under certain circumstances. There is empirical evidence to support the efficacy of a broad-gauged information campaign. W. C. Adams affirms that research on persuasive mass communication shows that in most cases it will strengthen already held views, rather than change them. In particular, when it is a question of public attitudes toward disliked or distrusted groups or nations, both sociological factors—from social networks, value systems, and influential leaders—and psychological factors—family, peer, and/or ethnic biases—act as barriers to the receipt of new, favorable information. Yet even these barriers are vulnerable if the dissonant "good" news is conveyed by mass media and if it comes from a credible source, is repeated with variation, is disseminated via multimedia, is reinforced by personal contact, and if it presents balanced, "two-sided" accounts (Adams 1987, 263–267).

Everett M. Rogers, professor of communications at the University of New Mexico, agrees that mass-media channels are effective in creating knowledge of new ideas, but less so in persuading people to adopt them. Change of attitude depends instead on interpersonal communications networks in which respected opinion leaders and then near peers accept the new information as valid and thus change their attitudes. He reports consistent empirical findings that once an innovative idea is accepted by 15–20 percent of the population, it takes on a diffusion rate that cannot be stopped (1998).

THE IDEA

How, then, might one launch a "cognitive assault" on the collective consciousness of the Israelis and Palestinians? How could one bring a focus to the positive histories, the memories of peaceful and creative coexistence?

One of the most positive eras in Islamic history, an era that Muslims still talk about with pride, extends from the eighth to the fifteenth centuries C.E., when Jews, Muslims, and Christians created a level of civilization in Spain that was the envy of Europe and compared favorably to Constantinople and Baghdad. Although there were bad patches, this is a positive history for people on all sides of the current conflict in the Middle East. Muslim Spain, as seen in the history of al-Andalus, was not only a time of intellectual and material excellence, it was also a time when Muslims, Christians, and Jews lived together in relative harmony, neither oppressing nor being oppressed. It is an era worthy of study today, not only for its art and architecture but also for its principles of tolerance and creative coexistence.

The former preventive diplomacy program of the Center for Strategic and International Studies (CSIS) has designed a project that studies the roots of that tolerance and how it can apply to the current conflict between Muslims and Jews in the Middle East. The goal is to confront the current despair in the Israeli-Palestinian and Jewish-Muslim relationship by reminding these peoples that there is a precedent of peace, tolerance, and respect in their history and that that combination resulted in extraordinary cultural achievement. The principles of tolerance that flourished in Muslim Spain and the medieval Mediterranean region could be revived today, and the people of the Middle East could benefit from revisiting the creative history of that period.

The Muslim rulers of medieval Spain applied Koranic tolerance toward Judaism and Christianity and created an environment for cooperation, economic prosperity, and scientific achievement that not only preserved ancient knowledge, but also added significant contributions to the arts, sciences, medicine, engineering, philosophy, and literature. As historian T. A. Perry has written of Andalusia, "Coexistence was not modeled on the melting-pot theory, but rather on the interchange of different points of view, on a dialogue that could range from commonly shared tenets of moral philosophy to religious confrontation and polemic. This attempt at cultural *convivencia* has not only been of historical interest, but also has ongoing importance for modern pluralistic culture in search of models of coexistence" (1987, 4).

Muslim scholar Abdulaziz Sachedina explains that this tolerance is at the heart of the Koran and the practice of Islam:

> Islamic revelation presents a theology that resonates with the modern pluralistic belief that other faiths are not merely inferior manifestations of religiosity, but variant forms of individual and communal responses to the presence of the transcendent in human life. All persons are created in the divine nature *(fitrat allah)*, with a disposition that leads to the knowledge of God, the Creator, to whom worship is due simply because of the creation. This universal knowledge of the Being in creation holds equally for the believer or non-believer, the worshipper of One Being or of idols. More important, both a monotheist and an idolater can understand that God, by inspiring faith in divine mercifulness and forgiveness, can guide anyone He wills to save. (2001, 14)

Middle East scholar Fouad Ajami, in a retrospective essay on the millennium at A.D. 1000, writes with obvious enthusiasm:

> In Andalusia's splendid and cultured courts and gardens, in its bustling markets, in academies of unusual secular daring, Muslims and Jews came together—if only fitfully and always under stress—to build a world of rel-

ative tolerance and enlightenment. In time, decay and political chaos would overwhelm Muslim Spain, but as the first millennium drew to a close, there had arisen in the city of Cordova a Muslim empire to rival its nemesis in the east, the imperial world around Baghdad. . . . In the seven or eight decades that followed [Abd al-Rahman III's ascension in the early tenth century], the city would become a metropolis of great diversity. Blessed with a fertile countryside, the city had some 700 mosques, 3,000 public baths, illuminated streets, and luxurious villas on the banks of the Guadalquivir River, and countless libraries. Legend has it that the caliph's library stocked some 400,000 volumes. (1999, 45–50)

Erna Paris, another scholar of the era, writes:

The ambience that marked the early centuries of Arab rule in Spain could not have been further removed from the brutal Visigoths, or from Christian Europe in general. While Europe embraced ignorance and superstition, the Moors promoted scholarship. While Christianity denigrated the senses, the feel of Arab Spain was nothing short of sensual. . . . Public literacy was a government priority. Successive caliphs built libraries that were open to all; in fact, one tenth-century ruler, Hakam II, was so obsessed with books that he sent emissaries to Baghdad with orders to buy every manuscript that had ever been produced. . . . The Jewish poets of Andalusia were profoundly influenced by their Muslim compatriots, and from the tenth to the twelfth century, during the justly named Golden Age of the Spanish Jews, they, too, wrote remarkably beautiful verse. (1995, 40)

There is a rich inventory of published works on Andalusia dealing with political history, Muslim-Jewish-Christian relationships, literature, art, science, economic relations, and even water systems engineering. There are numerous subjects that can be explored to document the collaborative creativity of Muslims and Jews, early in the "Golden Age"; and when Christians regained ascendancy in Northern Andalusia, the tolerance and teamwork of Jews and newly subject Muslim and Arabized Spaniards made Toledo an historic entrepôt for the translation and transmission of scientific works, philosophy, and literature, which sparked the Renaissance in Italy.

Some people will argue that the model of Andalusia is irrelevant to the current situation in the Middle East and that coexistence in Andalusia was based on Jewish and Christian minorities' subject to Muslim rule. They argue, correctly, that Israel today would never give up its sovereignty. We agree that Israel will not submit to Muslim or Christian rule. Rather, Andalusia offers a template for today based on its principles of tolerance, cooperation, and coexistence. For example, Israel is a Mediterranean and Middle Eastern country; the countries that surround it are Arab, as are the Palestinians in the West Bank, Gaza, East Jerusalem, and almost 20 percent of the citizens of Israel. In this social and cultural context, it is conceivable that if the Eurocentric Jewish population of Israel could bring itself to recognize and respect the culture and history of the Arab world that surrounds it, there might emerge a new basis for political peace. Similarly, the Arab world could learn from the principles of tolerance practiced in Muslim Spain to enable it to accept the Jewish state in their midst.

THE PROJECT

The project begun at CSIS is a unique, if highly experimental, approach to peacebuilding in the Middle East. Although the fighting in Israel and the Palestinian territories has dominated the consciousness of both peoples, Project Director Joseph Montville was able to win consistent support from Israelis and Palestinians during an October 2001 visit to the region. The concepts they approved were as follows.

Through multimedia dissemination and a variety of academic and popular cultural events and ongoing educational programs, an attempt will be made to revive the memory of Muslim Spain and the medieval Mediterranean and to confront current Israeli-Palestinian pessimism with new knowledge, or perhaps more accurately, to launch a cognitive assault on both peoples. The message would be that not only can (you) Arabs and Jews build community, you did so in Andalusia, and in the process created the greatest civilization that Europe north of the Pyrenees had seen.

By convening working groups of experts to evaluate the source material, we are developing a collection of themes that illustrate the remarkable interreligious creativity of the era. These discussions produced a team of seven outstanding historians, each of whom has written a chapter about actual lifestyles and daily practices of the Jews, Muslims, and Christians of that period—how they interacted, how they tolerated, and sometimes fought with one another. The resulting book, with an introductory chapter by Montville, will be translated into Hebrew, Arabic, French, and Spanish.

The project will then launch a multi-level, multimedia information campaign among the Israelis and the Palestinians. This part of the project will be shaped through consultations with distinguished social psychologists on the most effective methods to convey and disseminate information and imagery of Muslim Spain and the medieval Mediterranean, especially Egypt, to Jews, Muslims, and Christians in Israel and Palestine. Models and mechanisms will be developed for testing the campaign's effectiveness with the goal of making this grand experiment transferable to other interethnic conflicts.

The project will encourage and support the creation of elementary school, high school, and college curricula to teach the newly revived knowledge. We will seek out journalists, television and radio documentary producers, and other responsible people in cultural institutions. We will promote historical tours of al-Andalus for Jewish and Arab high school and university students, and establish paired Israeli and Arab university study projects on the period. We will also explore the creation of temporary and permanent exhibitions of art, science, and culture in Israel, Palestine, Jordan, Egypt, and Lebanon, which might be transferable to Damascus and Baghdad. This work will build on an alliance already established with the Center of Andalusian Studies and the Dialogue of Civilizations in Rabat. All of this activity will contribute to the overall goal of enhancing the credibility of Israeli-Palestinian community as a goal of the peace process.

THE USES OF KNOWLEDGE

This project actually began with another book, unrelated to Muslim Spain. *The Islamic Roots of Democratic Pluralism,* by religious scholar Abdulaziz Sachedina, was conceived with and co-produced by the preventive diplomacy program. Written for Muslims and non-Muslims alike, the book undertakes the important task of highlighting the universal human values at the heart of the Koran that undergird democracy everywhere, especially with regard to religious tolerance. The analysis in this study goes a long way in bridging the value gap between Islam and the West. Although *The Islamic Roots of Democratic Pluralism* does not deal specifically with Muslim Spain, it is intrinsically linked to the project because it addresses Muslim religious values that explain why pluralism could flourish in Spain and the entire medieval Mediterranean.

Chapters in the current book, which should be published in 2004, include a study of Muslim and Jewish merchants in the medieval Mediterranean world, by Olivia Remie Constable of Notre Dame University. Diana Lobel of Boston University has written a chapter on Sufism's influence on philosophy in Muslim Spain. Stanford historian Kathryn Miller has written an account of the collaboration between Muslim and Jewish physicians. Raymond P. Scheindlin of the Jewish Theological Seminary has written a chapter on the poem, "The Battle of Alfuente" by Samuel the Nagid. The poem demonstrates a blend of Hebrew and Arabic literary techniques, as well as describing the high position Samuel the Nagid, a Jew, held in the Muslim court of Granada. Thomas Glick of Boston University has written on Jewish and Muslim collaboration in mathematics and science; and Ahmad Dallal of Stanford University has written a chapter on the legal status and rights of the Jews in medieval Yemen. Finally, Mark Cohen of Princeton University has written a chapter on the coexistence of Jews and Muslims in Egypt.

The project has also established strong partnerships with people in Israel and Palestine. Sami Adwan of the Department of Education, Bethlehem University, and Dan Bar-On of the Department of Behavioral Sciences, Ben-Gurion University of the Negev, co-directors of PRIME

(Peace Research Institute in the Middle East), have pledged to support this project to revive the memory of Muslim Spain in the Middle East.

In addition, the project has supported publication of and is promoting in the United States the translation from Hebrew to English of *The Upright Generation,* by Dan Rabinowitz and Khawla Abu Baker. The book is a social anthropological portrait of the young generation of Palestinian citizens of Israel. It is also an autobiographical account of the coauthors, a Jew and a Muslim of the same age, growing up separated in the same city, Haifa.

This project will rely heavily on systems of mass communication, television, radio, drama, and literature and will incorporate the knowledge of Muslim Spain into Arab and Israeli school curricula. Ultimately, we hope that knowledge and understanding of Jewish-Arab creative coexistence in Muslim Spain will become part of the conventional wisdom in the Middle East. When Arabs and Jews can recognize that there is a precedent for harmonious coexistence and the cultural and religious values that made it possible, they can begin to incorporate this understanding into their own lives and imagine that real peace is possible.

We hope to contribute to the building of a viable and lasting peace in the Middle East by offering a vision of a positive future based on an authentic past.

REFERENCES

Adams, W. C. 1987. "Mass media and public opinion about foreign affairs: A typology of news dynamics." *Political Communication and Persuasion* 4, pp. 263–267.

Ajami, Fouad. 1999. "An Iberian chemistry." *U.S. News and World Report* (August 16), pp. 44–50.

Montville, Joseph. 1990. *Conflict and Peacemaking in Multiethnic Societies.* Lexington, Mass.: Lexington Books.

Paris, Erna. 1995. *The End of Days: The Story of Tolerance, Tyranny, and the Expulsion of Jews from Spain.* Amherst, N.Y.: Prometheus Books.

Perry, T. A. 1987. *The Moral Proverbs of Santob de Carrion: Jewish Wisdom in Christian Spain.* Princeton, N.J.: Princeton University Press.

Rogers, Everett M. 1988. "Diffusion of the Idea of Beyond War." In *Breakthrough: Emerging New Thinking.* Anatolii A. Gromyko and Martin M. Hellman, eds. New York: Walker.

Sachedina, Abdulaziz. 2001. *The Islamic Roots of Democratic Pluralism.* New York: Oxford University Press.

PART III:

SOCIAL TRANSFORMATION

One cannot throw the baby out with the bath water.

AFRICAN PROVERB

CHAPTER EIGHT

PROVENTIVE PEACEBUILDING IN THE REPUBLIC OF GUINEA:
BUILDING PEACE BY CULTIVATING THE POSITIVES

Sam Gbaydee Doe

This chapter advances a new model of peacebuilding—"proventive peacebuilding"—which identifies, affirms, celebrates, and strengthens the values, instruments, and processes that nurture and sustain peace in a society. It focuses on the conflict-carrying and peace-generating capacities of the society. Conflict-carrying capacities assure relative stability or negative peace, while peace-generating factors nurture and sustain positive peace. Guinea Conakry is cited as a case study in which proventive peacebuilding has been applied. The peace-generating factors identified in Guinea Conakry are history, interethnic coexistence and cohesion, economic potentials, and religion, while the culture of silence is identified as a conflict carrying capacity.

❧

*S*everal sometimes contradictory definitions for the term *peacebuilding* have emerged in the last two decades. The landmark report to the United Nations Security Council, *An Agenda for Peace,* by former U.N. Secretary-General Boutros Boutros-Ghali, places peacebuilding at the end of a conflict cycle, as a process of repairing what has been damaged during violent conflict (1992). It describes *preventive diplomacy* as peacemaking, peacekeeping, and post-conflict peacebuilding. Similarly, Ernie Regehr describes peacebuilding as the immediate process of stabilizing society after a violent crisis. This differs from the long-term pursuit of common security by focusing on short-term, emergency measures in a crisis context (Regehr 1995). Jonathan Goodhand and David Hulme, on the other hand, define peacebuilding as the promotion of institutional and socio-economic measures at the local or national level to address the underlying causes of conflict (1999). John Paul Lederach describes peacebuilding as a comprehensive, integrated, and interdependent process by which we identify root causes of conflict, manage crises, build structures that will mitigate the likelihood of violent conflicts recurring, and facilitate the building of a new vision for post-conflict societies (1997).

147

A world that has experienced some of the most appalling violent conflicts in recent times can no longer tolerate this level of deadly conflict. The United Nations, now under the leadership of Secretary-General Kofi Annan, has made conflict prevention a major priority, pledging to move the international body from a culture of reaction to a culture of prevention (Annan 2002). Governments and multilateral agencies such as the European Union and the Bretton Woods financial institutions now operate conflict prevention units. The primary activity has been assessing societies for risks. The various agencies have oriented themselves to seeing the world through the single lens of conflict. Development initiatives are also adopting this approach. "Conflict impact assessment" is the common language spoken by development workers today. This essentially addresses how to implement development projects without generating, exacerbating, or sustaining conflicts.

While I do not dispute the claims that peacebuilding includes conflict intervention, nor do I discount the new and noble efforts of the United Nations and Bretton Woods institutions to nip conflicts in the bud before they become deadly, it would seem to me that linking peacebuilding and human security exclusively to conflict or the effects after conflict is a terrible limitation of a grand process that encompasses everything that has to do with the quality of life of the human person.

In a small way, I have set out to argue for an alternative to the problem-oriented lens with which many well-intentioned peacebuilding practitioners and world leaders have viewed the world. I name this alternative paradigm, *proventive peacebuilding*. John Burton first coined the word *provention* to signify a proactive response to conflict by addressing structural or systemic factors (1990). He posits that conflict is rooted in the lack of opportunities to satisfy one's needs. As I use the term, provention is a combination of proactivity and intervention. It is proactive—rather than reactive—intervention. Proventive peacebuilding is about celebrating the values, instruments, and processes that nurture and sustain a healthy society. It takes the focus away from what is wrong to what is right, from conflict-generating factors to peace-generating factors. Proventive peacebuilding is a continuing process of building and sustaining the human society. The process is different from the traditional problem-focused intervention; it cannot be a process that only repairs damages to societies ravaged by conflicts. Proventive peacebuilding begins with the identification of the good in a society. It argues that the problems in society are a consequence of either the deviation from its quality values and institutions or that the institutions are nonprogressive and therefore unresponsive to current exigencies. By asking what generates peace in a society and how responsive the peace-generating resources are to current situations, proventive peacebuilding sets itself apart from other processes.

 In this chapter I seek to demonstrate how beginning with the positive in understanding any human situation opens windows of opportunities and possibilities. It also invigorates communities that might otherwise become resigned to their fate, simply because others have branded them as wretched and irredeemable. To argue my case, I use an empirical study that was conducted by the West Africa Network for Peacebuilding, in collaboration with the Forum on Early Warning and Early Response. Out of the case study I offer some propositions for proventive peacebuilding (or positive approaches to peacebuilding). Proventive peacebuilding is not a marginal activity or a mere twist of jargons. It requires a significant paradigmatic shift from conflict orientation to peace orientation, from risk to opportunity, from impossibility to possibility.

THE CASE OF GUINEA CONAKRY

In February 2000, the West Africa Network for Peacebuilding (WANEP), through the Forum on Early Warning and Early Response (FEWER), was contracted by a United Nations agency (which prefers not to be named) to conduct an early-warning study on Guinea Conakry, to alert the international community to potential threats for violent conflict in that country, especially as it moved towards its presidential elections in 2003. A basic definition of early warning is the collection and analysis of information with the aim of providing strategic options for preventive action. Early warning is generally geared towards anticipation rather than prediction of possible outcomes of a given situation. It is designed to fulfill an alerting function by identifying critical situations with a high potential for conflict escalation, so that timely action can be taken to reverse the trend or at least to soften its impact through contingency planning (Jongman and Schmid 1994).

Warning, as construed by the theoreticians, is therefore about assessing threats in order to minimize them. Contrary to traditional warning systems, proventive peacebuilding is more oriented to assessing opportunities for peace and social cohesion in order to build on them. What was striking for us, while discussing this offer, was the seeming lack of interest in what accounts for the stability of Guinea Conakry, in the face of violent conflicts in all of the bordering countries and the resultant influx of refugees into the country for more than a decade. We were convinced that by assessing Guinea's capacity to endure the composite stresses of internal transitions, massive influx of refugees, and regional threats, the world could learn from the people of that country. So instead of designing the strategic risk assessment study requested by the U.N. agency, we designed a strategic opportunities assessment study (Doe and Suifon 2000).

The aim of the study was to analyze Guinea's potential for stability, conflict carrying capacity, and resiliency in the face of adversity. We hoped the study would: (1) mobilize the people of Guinea to develop awareness on the rapid and radical socio-political and economic changes being demanded by their evolving democracy; (2) create an atmosphere for cooperation and mutuality between state actors and leaders of civil society; and (3) call on the international community to support Guinea on the difficult road to economic development, good governance, and sustainable peace.

The core question for us was, "What accounts for the resiliency of the country and its people in the face of rapidly increasing economic, social, political, cultural, and military debility?"

The study lasted six months, with a number of visits made to the country and regular contact with key actors in the social, religious, and political life of Guinea. At the end of the study, we conducted a two-day roundtable conference with a cross-section of Guineans and other international actors in the country. This gave Guineans the opportunity to debate our findings and provide clarifications where needed. The minister for interior, responsible for internal security, though publicly disagreeing with some aspects of the report, officially accepted it and challenged his fellow compatriots to learn from its lessons.

Traditional early warning emphasizes confidentiality, and a large part of most early warning reports tends to be classified. Assessments conducted in proventive peacebuilding are not only public, they are thoroughly discussed by key stakeholders and actors who can effect the desired changes in the society, among them local religious, traditional, business, and political leaders. The media are also invited to build awareness around issues and resources identified.

For our present purposes, this chapter highlights key findings and draws conclusions that may contribute to the theoretical development of positive approaches to peacebuilding.

THE CONTEXT

A small country of about seven million people on the Atlantic coast of West Africa, Guinea Conakry is bordered by Sierra Leone, Liberia, Côte d'Ivoire, Mali, Senegal, and Guinea Bissau. The largest ethnic groups are the economically dominant Fullah or Peul with approximately 35 percent of the population, the Sousou with approximately 30 percent of the population, and the Malinke with approximately 25 percent. Members of the Malinke group are also found in Senegal, Mali, Burkina Faso, Côte d'Ivoire, the Gambia, and Liberia. Guinea is also home to a number of forest tribes—the Guerze or Kpelleh, Manon or Kono, and Kissi.

In the thirteenth century, the Malinke established hegemony in the region, including Upper Guinea, and by the fourteenth century, Guinea in its entirety was absorbed into the powerful Empire of Mali. In contemporary times a French colony, a landmark in Guinea's fight for independence came in 1958, when independence leader Ahmed Sékou Touré urged

Guineans to refuse "quasi" independence from France. In French President Charles de Gaulle's referendum, Guineans massively voted "non," to the surprise of the international community and the humiliation of France. Sékou Touré's defiance, despite all pressure to the contrary, shattered de Gaulle's vision of a Franco-African community and made Sékou Touré a great figure in the history of Africa's independence movements. His position was epitomized in his words: "We prefer freedom in poverty to riches in chains." De Gaulle's colonial administrators prepared to leave as Sékou Touré declared, in 1958, the independence of the second African colony, after Ghana (which negotiated and gained independence from Britain in 1957).

The battle for Guinea did not end with independence. A number of Western powers, including France, made attempts to destabilize Guinea. The abortive invasion by Portuguese and other foreign mercenaries in 1970, allegedly supported by West Germany, strengthened Sékou Touré's image as a true hero and Pan African who successfully opposed imperialism and neo colonialism in post-independence Africa. By portraying the West as the enemy of Guinea and successfully crushing the Portuguese invasion, Sékou Touré won admiration and successfully mobilized nationalist fervor within Guinea.

Sékou Touré's reign ended abruptly in 1984 with his death from heart failure while visiting the United States. Just three days after his burial, Guinea's armed forces staged a bloodless military takeover, deposing the prime minister and acting president. Headed by Col. Lansana Conté, the Military Council for National Redressment described Sékou Touré's rule as a bloody and ruthless dictatorship characterized by widespread corruption. Radio Conakry announced that the armed forces had taken over power "in order to lay the foundations for a true democracy, to avoid any personal dictatorship in the future." That same day one thousand political prisoners were set free. The message, however, also acknowledged and praised Sékou Touré's achievements, describing him as a great proponent of African unity.

In 1985, a few months after the military takeover, the Military Council announced revolutionary measures aimed at revitalizing an economy exhausted by twenty-six years of isolation. With the help of the International Monetary Fund (IMF), a structural adjustment program was initiated, and the economy began an upward trend, according to IMF reports.

In 1991, after considerable national and international pressure, the Conté-led military government agreed to reinstitute a multi-party political system. Eight candidates competed for the presidency elections in 1993, including the incumbent Col. Conté. The pre-election period was tense, marked by incidents of violence between government and opposition supporters. Conté won under doubtful circumstances by a slight majority of just over 50 percent. The legislative elections of 1995 were also characterized by allegations of fraud, vote rigging, and violence. The ensuing political tension culminated in a military mutiny in February 1996, when a group of disgruntled rank-and-file soldiers protested against inadequate salaries and poor living conditions. Conté quelled the uprising by agreeing to improve conditions for the soldiers.

In 1998 Guineans again tested their young democracy with a second presidential election. History repeated itself, as Conté was re-elected, defeating his closest challenger and political rival, Alpha Condé. Condé was later arrested and held without charge for over fifteen months, later to be convicted of planning a military invasion and sentenced to five years in prison. A few months later President Conté extended executive clemency to Condé.

By decree in 2001, Conté conducted a referendum that now allows him to have a third term. The process was blatantly manipulated, but he nonetheless got away with this action. Many believe that the passive nature of the Guinean people coupled with increased security threats, especially from the government of Liberia, and the international community's support for the Conté regime as a key ally in the Mano River basin, gave the president a free hand to violate Guinea's democratic and constitutional processes with impunity.

SALIANT CONDITIONS FOR STABILITY

The WANEP study identified five salient conditions as forces for peace and stability in Guinea: history, interethnic coexistence and cohesion, religion, economic growth, and the culture of silence. We argued that Guinea provides the international community with the occasion to build peace positively by learning from and acting on the lessons spawned from these conditions. The culture of silence that pervades the Guinean society is, however, a permissive condition that assures negative peace, in other words, the mere lack of violence. In an increasingly globalized and rights-based world, culturally prescribed silence or the subjection of a society to passivity is fundamentally unjustifiable within the context of the contemporary understanding of justice, freedom, democracy, and human dignity.

History

The traditional political and social arrangements that existed in pre-colonial Guinea continue to shape modern Guinean society. Anti-colonial leaders such as Diana Salifou, Alpha Yahya, and Almamy Samoury Touré, the legendary Emperor of Wassoulou who led the Fullah and Malinke in resistance to colonial domination, are acclaimed as undisputed national heroes, although the French colonialists crushed Almamy Samoury Touré's Malinke rebellion in 1898 and captured him. Thus the seeds of discord and animosity between Guinea and France were sown. This rift was to become more evident with the rise to power of Ahmed Sékou Touré, kinsman of the former emperor. The present Guinean government, though headed by a Sousou, has erected a monument in honor of the legendary Malinke emperor, and in 1999 sponsored an international conference in his honor in Gabon.

The majority of post-independence African states are burdened with the past. Bloody interethnic cleavages, colonial preference for one ethnic group over the other, conflicting interpretations of historical events, and manipulation of history by political demagogues have fragmented the present socially, politically, and economically.

Individuals and societies are the construct of memory, of history. As Robert Schreiter correctly concludes, "To trivialize and ignore memory is to trivialize and ignore human identity, and to trivialize and ignore human identity is to trivialize and ignore human dignity" (1992, 19). By extension, to trivialize and ignore human identity is to trivialize and ignore the identity of an entire group or society. Reconciling and healing history is a painful exercise that many nations have preferred to abandon, hoping that by turning their backs on the past, it will fade away. A few such as South Africa have come to the unhappy truth that without redeeming the past, they are unable to build a new society, let alone appreciate the future. The past has remained a painful and disrupting reality in most African societies (Botman and Peterson 1996).

Vamik Volkan has identified two extreme subjective interpretations of the past—"chosen glory" and "chosen trauma"—both of which are potent sources for building individual and group identity (1988). Wrapped in myths, these interpretations determine the way individuals and their community perceive themselves and the world around them. While both interpretations are psychological, based on perception, one—the chosen glory—engenders self-appreciation or even inflated self-esteem, as well as an enhanced capacity to face the future. The other—the chosen trauma—engenders fear, hatred, low self-esteem, and a perpetual desire for revenge. The stability and peace of a nation will depend on the proximity of the estranged *Other* and the level of awareness on both sides regarding their histories.

Guinea is on the lucky side. History is in her favor. Situated at the heart of the Great Malian Empire, the cradle of civilization in sub-Saharan Africa, Guineans are unanimous in interpreting historical events that only describe them as victors. Present-day Guinea still possesses historical artifacts that were the symbols of the Malian Empire. The victory of the Wassoulou emperor of the Malinke nation over France, concluded by his distant nephew Ahmed Sékou Touré, has been a unifying force in Guinea.

Long years of warding off external threats created inward-looking people whose internal cohesion is strengthened by external threats.

The best thing that can happen to any government in Guinea is to have an external enemy attack the country. In September 2000, for example, in spite of heightened internal political tension, an insurgency allegedly supported by Liberia and the Revolutionary United Front of Sierra Leone instantly reduced the tension at home and united the country against the military incursion. Retired officers of the Sékou Touré army dusted off their uniforms and arms to defend the motherland. Students and youth volunteers mounted guard and ensured the defence of their villages and towns. Unlike Liberia and Sierra Leone, where during their respective civil wars, the national armies quickly disintegrated, with large sections conniving with the rebels and with businessmen and politicians negotiating profitable deals with rebels, the reverse happened in Guinea. The Guinean business class created a war fund. Musical caravans of peace led by the griots, traditional praise singers, chanted old patriotic songs of the Sundiata, Samouro, and Sékou Touré eras. It was like the entire nation was in a trance. In less than a month, the Guinean government drove the insurgents out of the land.

At the roundtable conference where findings of this study were discussed, a number of the participants slipped into nostalgia. "The patriotism of yesterday is no longer experienced today," said one former minister. "The young generation is losing our past and even the adults are no longer demonstrating patriotism at their work places." "Sékou Touré's legacy of revolutionary sacrifice is fast disappearing," lamented another. "Sékou Touré's soldiers and police were trained and imbued with an exceptional sense of patriotism and were always ready to defend their country."

Inspired by reflections on the past, roundtable participants spontaneously suggested a "National Renewal Commission." The emphasis would be placed on the positive opportunities available for "preserving Guinea's assets and maximizing its opportunities and gains." The commission would initially focus mainly on selected "nonpolitical" problems such as health, poverty, and wealth generation, and then as it gained acceptance in the country, it would promote public dialogue on specific political problems of national concern.

History has the potential to engender positive or negative, divisive or unifying sentiments in any given society. It possesses a cumulative strength from which current events can draw inspiration. Such inspiration can either elicit complicity and belief in the inevitability of the status quo, or provide grounds to fight for change when other possibilities or alternatives become available. In Guinea's case, historic gains remain the ideal for the older generation, while the young are fast turning their backs on the rich past of their country. The nation's survival will depend on concrete efforts to translate historical gains from idealism to pragmatism. Love for Guinea must come to

 be seen in the ways people care for the common good, how civil servants conduct themselves in the work place, how the government distributes the nation's wealth, and how Guineans collaborate with external corporate interests, which exploit other African countries through their own governments and citizens. Patriotism must be demonstrated in constructive ways when there is no external enemy or threat.

Without a shred of doubt, Guinea stands to be a great nation in West Africa's Mano River basin if its historical accomplishments are sagaciously exploited. This task is much easier in Guinea than in other African countries where there is first the need to heal, reconcile, and rewrite history before educating the young. The international community, especially UNESCO, should help Guinea to uphold her history. The story of each Guinean community possesses rich resources that can build social cohesion and self-appreciation. An internal revolution is required, especially in the schools, to revive and lift up these stories among the younger generation.

Another group that needs support in order to revive Guinea's life-giving stories are the griots or praise singers, formerly the custodians and narrators of history. Woven in poetry, proverbs, and parables, each community's story is beautifully told through the griots' music. Griots are still an integral part of many West African societies, but their rich values and roles are now reduced to singing primarily for the wealthy. With a minimum of support (training, finance, and equipment), griots could resurrect dead memories and inject new life into communities.

The media are another institution that could support a historical revival. Unifying historical events could be dramatized and aired on radio and television. The national media already place emphasis on promoting local music and drama. This should be encouraged further.

Interethnic Coexistence

Interethnic social cohesion is another asset that deserves maintaining and strengthening. Guinea is one of the few African countries where ethnic conflicts have been kept to a minimum. Our research uncovered a number of factors related to peaceful coexistence. First, Guinea is united as a nation by a strong history of a common external enemy. From Diana Salifou to Almamy Samoury Touré, Guineans were mobilized to work together to save their nation from outside invaders. Second, there are no restrictions on an individual's choice of partner. Intermarriage is encouraged, even among bigger groups like the Sousou, Malinke, or Fullah, as well as among the smaller tribes. Communities are bonded through marriage. A third and most outstanding element is social relation. Guinea is a closely-knit society. The free thinking and individual liberties that characterize Western civilization have yet to prevail in Guinea, and the control that a community has over its members, whether educated or uneducated, remains strong in Guinea.

Most Guineans with whom we spoke could not imagine trading community safety and security for their individual freedom. Community values and harmony are emphasized over individual needs. Educated and employed members of communities take full responsibility for other members who are not educated or employed. "The choice of who stays with you or whom one is to support in school is not made by even the individual who is to foot the bill. It is made by his external family and community," one respondent indicated. "This is our own social security system—each community cares for its own."

Some of these social assets are not without excesses, but excesses do not justify the complete replacement of the socio-cultural values and system of any people by another group. They should be addressed continuously in order to make the system functional. Participants at the roundtable conference emphasized problems of nepotism and the suppression of meritocracy because of the uncompromising obligations an individual has to his social group. If there is a vacancy in a given agency, it is generally accepted that the employer will first look within his own group before considering anyone outside of that group. Guinean private entrepreneurs find it difficult to progress because of responsibility to their community. "A trader will only employ his relatives, whether they are qualified or not, and will be responsible for their welfare," an interviewee explained. "Responsibility to the community most times exceeds profit," another concluded.

Our inclusion of interethnic cohesion in this study is not to suggest that it is unique to Guinea, but to note that in Guinea such cohesion has not been destroyed by political manipulation and the "divide and rule" strategies that thrive in other parts of Africa. Guinea does not have a history of politically motivated interethnic hostility. While his Malinke ethnic group enjoyed preferential treatment from the state, Sékou Touré, the founding and longest serving president, extended patronage to all other ethnic groups. People perceived as threats to his authority were punished individually and not on the basis of ethnicity.

There are more homeless people in some of the richest cities in the world than in Conakry. It was nearly impossible, in fact, to find anyone sleeping in the street. This is essentially explained in the social security system of Guinea, with each family, kin, or community caring for its own. The integrity and success of any family is measured by the success, character, and fate of its individual members. This strong traditional system is undermined by capitalism in which the profit motive is the predominant value. External pressures from the World Bank, IMF, transnational corporations, and other market-oriented investors are pushing Guinea to structurally adjust, privatize, produce, and become current in servicing debt owed to rich countries. Indeed, Guinea may need to subscribe to market capitalism and turn its back on its more caring, humane, and civilized value system. If that happens, its weak economic infrastructure will not be able to accommodate those who are left out, and the left out could turn to prostitution, theft, armed robbery, etc., in order to survive in the new system. Already, these vices are on the rise in Conakry.

In spite of the high level of interethnic coexistence, it has still not produced national cohesion in Guinea. Until faced with an external threat, Guineans are first Peuhls, Malinke, Sousou, Kissi, or Kono. This is explained in the loyalty paid to ethnicity-based political parties. Violent ethnic conflicts are caused by the politicization of ethnicity by politicians who exploit difference and fear for political gain. As long as politics are driven by ethnicity based parties in Guinea, there is the potential of undermining and fragmenting the otherwise high level of interethnic coexistence, which is currently an important source of stability.

To imagine that African countries can become purely capitalist societies is to grossly disregard their social-cultural reality. Such a blatant disregard for Africa's values of caring for the weak and needy is to strip the continent of its identity, as well as a major source of stability. A people without identity are easily manipulated or can readily slip into anarchy. Liberia, Sierra Leone, Somalia, Angola, the Democratic Republic of the Congo, to name a few, typify a consequence of identity and institutional crises, resulting in disaffection, despair, frustration, and eventually, anarchy. So far these factors are not yet prominent in Guinea, but current political and economic trends suggest that Guinea's stability and cohesion are under threat. There is an urgent need to evolve a workable system, one that is inclusive and community oriented.

Religion

Religion is one of the most important factors responsible for social stability in present-day Guinea. Muslim traders from Morocco and Algeria introduced Islam in West Africa around A.D. 900 West African rulers of the famous Mali and Songhai empires easily accepted the alien religion. By skillfully combining aspects of Islam and traditional religion, these leaders made the new religion acceptable to the population, making Islam the predominant religion in contemporary West Africa.

More than 80 percent of Guineans are Muslim. Unlike other African countries that have seen a rise in fundamentalist Islamic movements and a corresponding rise in violent conflict, Islam is, at least for now, a stabilizing factor in Guinea. Influential imams in the Conseil Nationale Islamique (National Islamic League) have assumed the role of mediator in family and community disputes. The League also keeps a watchful eye on excesses such as Islamic extremism and safeguards against the imposition of *sharia* law, which has threatened social cohesion and state institutions in Algeria, Sudan, Egypt, and recently, Nigeria. Guinea has yet to produce religious extremists, demonstrating that it is not religion that produces extremists, but rather various forms of privation that cause individuals and communities to reinterpret their beliefs to draw inspiration and energy for the fight against oppressive regimes and systems.

According to the National Islamic League Secretary-General, El Hadj Mamadou Saliou Sylla, Islam is "peace." His organization uses prayer meetings and mosques to sensitize Guineans to the values of peace and living in harmony with all non-Muslims, especially Christians. The last Friday of every month, according to one interviewee, the League organizes prayer meetings along borders with countries suffering from civil war. These widely attended monthly ceremonies are used to pray for peace in Guinea and to sensitize people to the devastating consequences of war. Government officials, including sometimes the president, are seen on state television offering prayers for peace with the people along the borders.

In addition, the National Islamic League does not outlaw marriage between Christians and Muslims, and this has helped facilitate peaceful religious coexistence. Islam plays an influential role in the political life of the state as well. Politicians seeking state power at local, regional, and national levels are required to undergo apprenticeship with and/or acquire the benediction of the League. Political leaders consult the organization on any major decision-making process in the country. In a world where Islam is increasingly linked to those who perpetrate terror, the imam's task of preaching the Islam that means peace is even more noteworthy. Guinea could become recognized as a model state where Muslims and Christians coexist in harmony and could share this experience with other countries where the two children of Abraham cannot live in peace.

Conversely, some people at the roundtable conference indicated that the Sékou Touré and now Conté administrations have exploited this religious asset to their personal benefit. In this view, Islam is used as an opiate to keep the people in spiritual bliss, while the government exploits their fundamental rights. Messages such as "acceptance of the divine, love for fellow human beings, acceptance that the chief is appointed by God and is always a chief," are commonly heard in Friday sermons. Imams are not paid, and many of them depend on handouts from political leaders to subsist. Consequently, there is a tendency to overlook corrupt practices; as one interviewee succinctly put it, "there is a moralization of crime in Guinea."

At somewhat of a turning point, religion, especially Islam, will maximize its positive impact on the Guinean society if it operates independently of government. This does not suggest the separation of state and religion, which is not allowed in Islam. Instead, it means that to ensure that each plays its respective role in the sustenance of the state, imams should work against the temptation of being supported by individual members of government in exchange for prayers, a practice that currently prevails in the country. At present Islam's moral and prophetic voice is fast eroding in today's Guinea, and moral laxity is replacing adherence to the values of the Prophet. Innovation will be required from the National Islamic League to address the increase in social vices and engage the government more constructively. In a society that remains attentive to the imams, Islam could become a potent force for the building and institutionalization of social justice and respect for the dignity and sanctity of life, provided the imams return to the values of the Prophet.

Economic Growth

Western economic experts believe Guinea has made more economic progress than most African countries. In 1996, with the help of the IMF and World Bank, the Guinean authorities began reforms to restore economic and financial equilibrium. These efforts were prompted by the need to revitalize Guinea's economy after years of upheaval due to a drastic drop in revenue, as well as poor management of public funds.

Guinea is blessed with significant mineral wealth. It possesses approximately two-thirds of the world's known reserves of bauxite, accounting for more than 80 percent of the country's export earnings, as well as iron ore, gold, uranium, and diamonds. Guinea is also endowed with exceptional potential for hydroelectric power.

Natural resources can be a force for stability or instability. With strong, creative, legitimate leadership and the right infrastructure, natural resources can bring not only prosperity but also peace to a country. Libya is an example of a country whose oil wealth has been used to keep society together and to extend altruism to parts of the Middle East and sub-Saharan Africa. In sub-Saharan Africa, however, the presence of natural resources has typically been a source of corruption and conflict, notably in the Democratic Republic of Congo, Sierra Leone, Liberia, Angola, Cameroon, Sudan, and Nigeria.

In neighboring Côte d'Ivoire, former leader Felix Houphuet Boigny cultivated the agricultural sector as an instrument for stability and prosperity. Today, Côte d'Ivoire is the world's largest producer of cocoa, and food is in abundance. By comparison, Guinea is even more richly endowed with arable land, although no effort has been made to develop the appropriate infrastructure and policies to promote the agricultural sector. Guinea's agricultural potential cannot be overemphasized; a well-developed agricultural sector will not only ensure food self-sufficiency, but will also earn large amounts of foreign exchange in the subregional food markets.

One outstanding economic difference between Guinea and her Mano River neighbors of Liberia and Sierra Leone is the level of private ownership that is in Guinean hands. In Liberia and Sierra Leone, foreign nationals (especially Lebanese) own 90 percent of private investment in the extractive industry and trading of imported goods, while in Guinea 70 percent of private ownership is in the hands of Guineans (especially the Peuhls). This concentration of national wealth in its own citizens' hands is, in Guinea's experience, a major source of stability given that the decision to go to war or to endorse violent confrontation can be largely contingent on how much one has to lose or gain in doing so.

If Guinea's full economic potentials were deployed, its young people would not be disillusioned as they are now, with some even daring to fly in the cargo bays of European planes in an attempt to escape to a better future. Guinea needs the appropriate infrastructure and a farsighted, accountable leadership system to gain from its plentiful endowments of minerals, land, and water.

A Culture of Silence

From the years of Sékou Touré until today, Guineans have been generally passive and demonstrate a nonchalant attitude to sensitive issues that would provoke massive mobilization and perhaps uprising in some other countries. Fear of constitutional authority and government officials is a strongly ingrained behavior for many Guineans. This apparent Guinean culture of silence and laissez-faire can be traced to ancient traditional and socio-cultural arrangements maintained over generations. Strict hierarchical structures, social classes, and the supremacy of certain families or clans remain largely unaffected by Western values of equal rights and individualism. The privileged dominate the underprivileged, and the latter unquestioningly accept their fate as predestined. Amongst the Malinke and Fullah, these class divisions have been cemented by the endorsement of a preferred interpretation of Islam, which supports strict loyalty to hereditary or "sacred" leaders. Sékou Touré's twenty-six-year dictatorship further contributed to this passivity. Dissent was violently suppressed, and traditional institutions and leaders were basically destroyed and silenced, making the state the only authority in Sékou Touré's Guinea.

Whether this attitude of submission in the face of provocation and hardship is a positive stabilizing factor is debatable. Some see it as a weakness and predict that sooner or later the situation will be reversed. The belief that everything is predestined and thus unchangeable may give way to the conviction that the freedom from socio-cultural or political bondage and domination that Western democracy promises is never a given but must be fought for. Passive societies can only be maintained in a dictatorship or, at best, a one-party democracy. Control of the masses through violence or the threat of violence or through socio-cultural manipulation is a gross violation of human rights, which is a universal law to which all societies must adhere.

The state system in Guinea still uses Sékou Touré's baton of violent control to govern. It seems resistant to change. In addition, the regime is finding it more and more difficult to adapt to the tenets of Western multi-party democracy. The society, on the other hand, has yet to engage the regime constructively so that both the society and the state can uphold the universal values of human rights and good governance. The tension between the social, cultural, and political inertia of the regime to adopt new rules of governance and democracy and an impatient external demand to pull Guinea into the world of democracy, free market, human rights, and good governance is becoming stronger and stronger. The success of human rights protection, peacebuilding, and other facets of civil society will depend largely on widespread and carefully planned popular education. Doubtless, the government and other power structures will resist these initiatives.

Confrontation with the government would be tragic. Constructive engagement that wins the government over as a partner for constructive change for sustainable peace and development is clearly the best option. This means targeting government institutions for the educational process as well. At present human rights organizations in the country emphasize reporting of human rights abuses by government institutions, which often antagonizes the government and leaves no room for engagement. We are not suggesting a compromise with injustice; rather, our argument is that in order to change a system that spans centuries, persuasion, education, and dialogue are the best tools.

PROPOSITIONS FOR PROVENTIVE PEACEBUILDING

Lessons learned from this study allow us to make the following propositions about proventive (or positive) peacebuilding:

PROVENTIVE PEACEBUILDING TAKES THE FOCUS AWAY FROM WHAT IS WRONG TO WHAT IS RIGHT, FROM CONFLICT-GENERATING FACTORS TO PEACE-GENERATING FACTORS. It identifies history or experiences, actors, instruments, structures, and systems that are the foundational bedrock for peace, justice, and social cohesion in a society and celebrates them. Proventive peacebuilding cultivates the constructive capacities and strengths of a society.

Our experience from Guinea and other West African countries where we have applied this approach to peacebuilding shows three immediate outcomes: First, it inspires hope in a society, and hope is an essential stimulant for positive change. Second, people become more independent and confident. Identifying a society's abilities and opportunities can engender positive attitudes towards change. Third, proventive peacebuilding allows one to have access to the whole picture of a society. When one enters a society to access risk, at least in West Africa, many things are kept from your view, either because your telescope is limited by a problem orientation or that stakeholders protect information that could threaten their credibility. Those who assess risks of society often overlook the potential that exists in that society. Emphasis is put on external intervention.

By pointing to the peace-generating resources—history, interethnic coexistence, economy, and religion—we helped mobilize a renewed spirit and engender self-appreciation, which was then demonstrated (in the story told above) as a massive, country-wide mobilization when in September 2000, just two months after the study was completed, rebels invaded the country from the Liberian border. Prominent leaders who attended the roundtable consultation had just been refreshed about their history, social, and economic assets. We do not want to claim that the consultation was the only impetus for the national mobilization, but the renewed energy, according to one participant, contributed to the mobilization of civil society groups. In any case, the national mobilization supported our analysis of the Guinean society as one that responds effectively to external threat.

PROVENTIVE PEACEBUILDING IS A PROCESS WHEREBY WE DISCOVER. The success of our study was in the fact that we went to Guinea with open, curious, and inquiring minds. Instead of asking questions about what was wrong with Guinea, we asked, "What gives life in Guinea? What do Guineans value about their society? What holds their society together?" We literally asked the people we met in Guinea to teach us about their peace, how they live together, who they are. Proventive peacebuilders are mere witnesses, not purveyors of change, therefore they must have inquiring minds. If we all agree that "positive" peace is essentially a healthy and whole relationship, we should also be guided by the truth that relationships are personal, relevant, and understandable only to those who own and experience them. Proventive peacebuilding is an exciting journey in which both the peacebuilder and the community discover exciting potentials about themselves. In our experience, no group or individual has ever travelled this road and emerged unchanged.

PROVENTIVE PEACEBUILDING IS A NEVER-ENDING PROJECT FOR ENHANCING AND BETTERING THE QUALITY OF HUMAN RELATIONSHIP. Peace is about human relationship. And the human story does not begin with violence or conflict. It begins with being, belonging, generating, sharing, and building. The essence of society is relationship, for society is a collection of relationships. This includes interlocking and interdependent groups, ideas, values, and physical, emotional, and psychological spaces. Peacebuilding is therefore synonymous with society building. The vitality and health of any society is peace. In Guinea Conakry, like other traditional societies, peace is synonymous with closely-knit and cohesive social groupings. The bond between the individual and community cannot be severed. Economic and political systems must speak to the social reality of Africa. The African is not an individual who must satisfy his own interests. He is a member of his community, his society. He cannot turn his back on this demand for if he does, he will be stripped of identity, of personhood, of existence.

PROVENTIVE PEACEBUILDING IS ABOUT WITNESSING AND UNDERSTANDING CHANGE. There are two basic sources of change: endogenous (from within) and exogenous (from without). Endogenous change is not imposed; it is a product of the inherent regenerative capacity of the society. Endogenous change happens out of encounters. Every encounter presents opportunity for learning, for growth, for development. It takes a reflective person or society to identify the lessons that that encounter presents. When the lessons are identified and the society learns from them, new meanings are constructed from which the society forms new attitudes, and eventually, new cultures and structures.

Often times the society loses the opportunities presented by encounters or challenges that confront them because people tend to put emphasis on the stresses or pains associated with the encounters and lose sight of the lessons to be learned and growth to be experienced. The Conflict Indicator for Foreign Policy of Carlton University in Canada, for example, devotes its risk assessment project to identifying stresses in society, referred to as structural indicators. These include demographic stress (increase in the number of people relative to the society's capacity to provide for basic needs), political stress (tension emerging from external demands for democracy and resistance of regimes to give up old systems), stress from refugee movements, etc. These are essential indicators that must be monitored to assure stability in any society.

When the focus is only stressors or causes of stress in a society, however, the usual reaction is to eliminate the symptoms, and not to strengthen institutions and social structures to alleviate the stressors so that learning can take place. For population increase, for example, more resources are directed to contraception, and for urban migration emphasis is placed on forced relocation of communities. None of these responses, however, have contributed to eliminating the stressors that produce the social patterns of high rates of birth and migration. Another example is the constant use of elections as the panacea for addressing civil conflicts in Africa. The assumption is that one can remove the stress of war by simply replacing a regime. Sufficient time is not given to understanding why civil wars proliferate and what opportunities for change these conflicts present to us. Because of our unwillingness to fully understand the dynamics of the endogenous evolutions in most African societies, the responses we have applied have often exacerbated the pain and anguish of the stresses. That is precisely what classical peacebuilding has been doing—building institutions to avoid the pain of encounter and even, sometimes, the encounter itself!

Another factor that affects the learning from endogenous processes of change is the role of bystanders. Bystanders or outsiders are those who are not directly affected by the change process but attempt to describe and give meaning to what they observe. Instead of those who are experiencing the encounter naming what they are encountering, the bystanders or outsiders usually give meaning to that which they are *not* experiencing and thereby decide what should be done about the change. There is no way a bystander can adequately describe what he or she is not experiencing. This is not to say that bystanders' contributions are not important, but their interpretations or conclusions are rooted in their own experience and socialization and should not be imposed on those involved in the encounter. Making meaning out of an encounter is the exclusive right of those experiencing it, and the bystanders' role should mainly be to facilitate the discovery process for those directly involved.

Exogenous change, by contrast, assumes that existing cultures, instruments, structures, and systems are flawed and must be replaced immediately with new ones that are inherently different from the ones known by the society to undergo the change. Exogenous change comes from outside. It is drawn from the experience of an outside group which that group feels obliged to impose on the group facing change. Usually the outsider is terribly convinced that the change will be for the good of the other and is even surprised that the other is hesitant in embracing it. The British Empire, French expansionism, and recently, America's rights-based, individualistic, capitalist democracy are but a few examples of the imposition of exogenous changes on many states and nations, whether the society is suited and ripe for the change or not, and whether the society has the appropriate structures to support and sustain the change or not.

There are several sources of stress engendered by exogenous change processes. These include the outsider's demand for change versus the society's inertia resisting the change; the level of elasticity or responsive capacity of the society to be changed; the palatability of the change to the society; and the process by which the change is negotiated.

Guinea as a society has existed for more than two thousand years. Its peoples have had a tremendous number of encounters with both endogenous and exogenous conditions. Consciously or unconsciously, these encounters have shaped the understanding of Guineans about the world and hence their culture. Inquirers or bystanders are needed only for the community to discover itself and understand the change it is undergoing. Nonstructured interviews driven by curious and learning attitudes allowed WANEP to elicit tremendous amounts of information from which we have learned, not only about Guinea, but also about our own intervention strategies and ourselves. In the process Guineans and other communities with which we have worked have also learned about their assets and the challenges that threaten their stability and peace. Proventive peacebuilding is a journey of mutual learning. The roundtable conference at the end of the process is the dialogue space where the body of knowledge is collated and joint-response actions are designed by the members of the community themselves.

CONCLUSION

My journey as a peacebuilder began with stories of tragedy. I witnessed a brutal civil war that tore apart the fabric of my home country of Liberia, a small country of just three million people. More than three hundred thousand people (one of every ten persons) were killed in seven years of barbarity. That war extended to neighboring Sierra Leone, the place of my birth. Since 1990 I have been working with communities ravaged by violent conflicts in Liberia, Sierra Leone, and many other parts of Africa. Everywhere I have travelled, especially outside of Africa, I become a prime recipient of sympathy. People hail me for my work simply because I work with people who are suffering the agony of violence. Yet deep inside I know that the source of the energy that drives my work is not from these terrible stories. My energy comes from the glimpses of hope, the stories of small, seemingly insignificant individuals and communities that show inexplicable courage and resiliency in the face of terror. Their smiles and their hope for a peaceful tomorrow sustain me and make my work possible.

These experiences forced me to begin to rethink the traditional peacebuilding processes that emphasize conflict analysis, crisis management, and post-conflict rehabilitation. I realized that peacebuilding which was oriented towards conflict was not telling the whole story, nor doing justice to the concept. It seemed limiting to me and was not inspiring hope and mobilizing the energy needed for growth.

Three years ago I began testing the idea of positive approaches to peacebuilding. My emphasis was on resiliency. I wanted to know what accounted for the resilience of some societies in the face of adversity and what could be learned from that. My interest grew in societies like Guinea, Kenya, the Gambia, Ghana, and Cameroon, with high volatility quotients but yet still relatively stable. I increased my visits to those countries and started asking questions about their strengths.

I identified two categories of resources that explain the relative stability of these countries. Conflict prevention experts call these conflict-carrying and peace-generating capacities. *Conflict-carrying capacities* are those social, political, cultural, economic, and religious structures that accommodate or absorb tensions in a society. They do not, however, promote peace. Instead, they ensure that conflicts are kept at the latent level. *Peace-generating capacities* are those social, cultural, political, and religious institutions that promote the values of positive, sustainable peace. They are the dynamic institutions that build peace continuously.

The strategic opportunities assessment study of Guinea highlights these two categories. The first four conditions—history, religion, economy, inter-ethnic coexistence—can become generators of peace, while the culture of silence was considered a conflict-carrying resource. A number of societies have survived on their conflict carrying-capacity, which serves as a negative stabilizer but with no guarantee of preventing conflagration of violent conflict in the future.

At the West Africa Network for Peacebuilding we are currently applying this approach in two peacebuilding programs:

Through the Proventive Peacebuilding Program's Early Warning and Response Network (WARN) we are conducting numerous action-oriented studies in various countries. The inquiries we conduct have helped both us and the communities we study to discover potentials needed to change their conditions. Since the study discussed in this chapter, for example, civil society groups and government agencies in Guinea are cultivating healthy relationships to address their social, political, and economic problems. Guinea will need more work, however, to evolve a strong civil society that will hold the government accountable for human rights and political violations.

In 2000 WANEP launched its Active Nonviolence and Peace Education Program in seven West African countries. This program seeks to strengthen the social processes that promote justice, peace, and social cohesion in communities through the school setting. It is promoting the history, literature, and other arts in West African societies that advance the values and attitudes in support of these social processes. The first stage of the program focused on the "attitude of teaching." It has demonstrated the role teachers play in building society and how their attitudes contribute in building individuals who have either a positive or a destructive sense of their identity. Especially in Liberia, teachers are discovering that affirmation, giving constructive feedback to young people, and including them in decisions made in the classrooms are making a significant difference in the lives of children. Young people who benefit from the program show significant improvement in academic performance and social skills.

Our three-year experience in West Africa demonstrates that by building positive images, we are able to mobilize the resources needed to address obstacles and challenges in many communities. Proventive peacebuilding does not deny structural injustices that must be named and addressed. What it has done is to mobilize bolder and more courageous people. The courage they draw on to engage these structures comes from the hope that there is certainly a liberating future.

REFERENCES

Annan, Kofi A. 2002. *Prevention of Armed Conflict.* New York: United Nations.

Botman, H. Russel, and Robin M. Petersen. 1996. *To Remember and To Heal: Theological and Psychological Reflections on Truth and Reconciliation.* Cape Town: Human and Rousseau.

Boutros-Ghali, Boutros. 1992. *An Agenda for Peace: Preventive Diplomacy, Peacemaking and Peace-keeping.* New York: United Nations.

Burton, John. 1990. *Conflict: Resolution and Provention.* New York: St. Martin's Press.

Doe, Samuel Gbaydee and Takwa Suifon. 2000. *Guinea Conakry: Potential for Stability and Instability.* Forum on Early Warning and Early Response, www.fewer.org.

Goodhand, Jonathan, and David Hulme. 1999. "From Wars to Complex Political Emergencies: Understanding Conflict and Peace Building in the New World Disorder." *Third World Quarterly* 20:1 (February), pp. 13–26.

Jongman, A. J., and A. P. Schmid. 1997. "Preventing Violent Conflict: Methods and Actors in the Field of Preventive Diplomacy." Milan: ISPAC.

Lederach, John Paul. 1997. *Building Peace: Sustainable Reconciliation in Divided Societies.* Washington, D.C.: U.S. Institute of Peace Press.

Regehr, Ernie. 1995. "Rebuilding peace in war-torn and war-threatened societies." *The Ploughshares Monitor* XVI:4, pp. 1–3.

Schreiter, Robert. 1992. *Reconciliation: Mission and Ministry in a Changing Social Order.* New York: Orbis.

Volkan, Vamik. 1988. *The Need to Have Enemies and Allies: From Clinical Practice to International Relationships.* Northvale, N.J.: Jason Aronson.

O future Nagas, let's stop this evil
Let there be peace again
Stop the gun culture
It's not ours
For we cannot survive this pool of
Hatred, conflict, and corruption

NAGA YOUTH

CHAPTER NINE

IMAGINE NAGALAND:
THE COURAGE TO BE POSITIVE

Peter Delahaye and Bharat Krishnan[1]

The United Nations' Global Movement for Children (GMC) has heralded an unprecedented challenge to leadership to unite in the service of children. Listening to children speaking out was a central focus of the Special U.N. Session on Children in May 2002, as well as in many GMC projects all over the world. Independently, this work has also been going on through a series of "Imagine" projects around the world, which were inspired by the original Imagine Chicago, in 1992. Among them is Imagine Nagaland, which was created by the United Nations Children's Fund (UNICEF) in 2001. The intergenerational dialogue that took place in the complex setting of India's Nagaland inspired "imaginings" and hope for many parts of the world facing similar challenges. By involving children and youth in dreaming about the future, taking only the positive possibilities from history, a way for development for peace is created.

❧

*N*agaland, a small and remote state bordering Myanmar in India's North East, has had a troubled political history over the last fifty years. What began as a nonviolent struggle for self-determination in the 1950s later took the form of an armed conflict. The political issues remain alive even today. In 1963, Nagaland became the sixteenth state of the Indian Union. Since then, the situation of Nagaland's two million people has changed dramatically and a "see-sawing process has led alternately to despair and hope," according to Sanjoy Hazarika.[2] "With the coming of statehood, Nagaland entered the era of planned socio-economic development, ending centuries of isolation and neglect, although the wounds and hurts of the past still caused pain to those who had suffered or lost their loved ones in the armed struggle."

The situation has improved significantly since the signing of ceasefire agreements by the government of India in 1997 and 2001, respectively, with the two major groups leading the armed struggle. Although there are occasional complaints of ceasefire violations, the situation is noticeably better than in the past. What is reassuring today is that there is a genuine desire among the people for ushering in lasting peace and a firm determination that all contentious issues should be resolved across the table in a nonviolent and democratic manner.

"I am never tired of saying that Naga society needs change," said Nagaland Chief Minister S.C. Jamir, the most senior political figure in the state, in his inaugural speech at the Dream/Design Summit of Imagine Nagaland in July 2001. "I say this with deep conviction, because I feel that we as a people tend to live in the past, while ignoring the present and the immediate future. Learning from the past and emulating the values which we have inherited is healthy, but living forever in the past is only a means of escaping hard realities and avoiding what needs to be done. Nobody can deny that Nagaland has been a very troubled place for many decades and has seen far too much violence for such a small society. The Naga people have suffered a lot. Many wounds are yet to be healed. There are many political issues that need to be resolved and many economic issues that trouble us. For a small state, we seem to have a disproportionately large number of problems. But living in the past will not help to solve any of our problems. They have to be resolved in the present and with strategies that are relevant today. Living constantly in the past will only reopen old wounds and cause more pain."

Caught between the imperative of asserting the rule of law while at the same time having to face the consequences of the continuous conflict and violence in the state, it has not been easy to maintain the balance between ensuring development while simultaneously maintaining peace. As a result, the alternatives of pushing forward an agenda of "peace for development" or "development for peace" remain a conundrum that begs an appropriate answer. A large presence of security personnel continues to be clearly visible in the state as a top-down means of strengthening the rule of law and ensuring security. A large number of peace rallies and peace resolutions by civil society are a bottom-up response that reflects the determination to make peace endure.

Government service is currently the major avenue for employment in this underdeveloped corner of India, as would-be investors are just beginning to understand the North East Region and its special developmental needs. It is a moot question whether their interest would be sustained even if the ceasefire holds, given the locational disadvantages and inadequacy of infrastructure. Nevertheless, Nagaland cannot stand still and remain caught in a time warp in relation to progress and growth the world over. It has to move forward from being a spectator to a participant in the global initiatives for improving the quality of life. In any blueprint for transforming Nagaland, a critical question—and indeed a serious challenge—is to reorient the attitude and approach of government employees and officialdom to play the historic role expected of them. Given the large number of government employees in the state, it is imperative that they see themselves as lead players and strategic catalysts in the mission to transform Nagaland into a state that is responsive and sensitive to the needs of its citizens. Nagaland should aspire to become a model state, where development has a human face, is fair and equitable, and respects ecology and the environment.

Nagaland's key strengths are many and can be seen at three levels. The first level would include low population density; absence of caste and social discrimination; remarkable social capital made up of clans, villages, and tribes; strong community spirit; and social bonding. At the next level, one can see a highly literate population; an established and empowered local governance system built around village councils and village development boards; and strong religious bonds. At the third level, Nagaland has tremendous natural resources in terms of forests, oil, gas, and minerals, which await sensible, eco-friendly exploitation.

In early 2000, the chief secretary of Nagaland, the highest ranking bureaucrat in the state, initiated a loosely structured visioning exercise for his departments. Essentially a top-down process, "Vision Nagaland" was aimed at combating "fatigue and cynicism" in the state. At the same time, UNICEF in India (and globally) was in full preparation for the Global Movement for Children. A fortuitous lunch meeting between UNICEF personnel and the Nagaland chief secretary set the ground for the Global Movement for Children and a possible "Imagine Nagaland" to come together, as part of the Imagine series,[3] to meld with the top-down visioning exercise already in progress. This also provided an opportunity for UNICEF to work with children in Nagaland and amplify their voices as part of the consultative process that had been envisaged. It was therefore agreed with the government of Nagaland that children and their voices would be very much at the center of this project.

DISCOVERY PHASE

Peter Delahaye and Bharat Krishnan (the authors) constituted the core team and initiated a series of Appreciative Inquiry (AI) workshops in Nagaland, starting with the first Discovery Workshop in early April 2001. In their message to the chief secretary, the two facilitators requested his office to invite up to one hundred participants for the workshop, to constitute a "Nagaland glue,"[1] a Noah's Ark, representing all stakeholders of the state. In the final count there were seventy participants of whom more than thirty were children and youth. Using the Appreciative Inquiry philosophy (Cooperrider and Whitney 1999), participants were asked to inquire into "what gives life to Nagaland?"

These exercises led to the development of six major themes, chosen by participants, for detailed inquiry across the state: "unity, peace, and respect for all," "education and employment," "ecology and development," "equitable development," "respect for the rule of law," and "Nagaland of our future." (See appendix for interview guides.) For many of the adults this was their first experience of interacting on an equal footing with children and youth. The participants, comprised of children, government servants, probationers (trainee bureaucrats), nongovernmental organization members, legislators, media persons, teachers, doctors, human rights activists, etc., eventually set a target of twenty thousand discovery interviews to be conducted over a period of ten weeks, representing one percent of the Nagaland population.

In order to cover people in all eight districts of Nagaland, the team had to adopt a cascading interview method whereby each person interviewed was asked to interview two more, and so on, with the numbers multiplying geometrically. A need was also felt for enlarging the number of first-level interviewers and to ensure that all districts were adequately covered. A second Discovery Workshop was therefore conducted the next month in which one hundred people participated, nearly sixty of whom were children and youth. The themes remained the same in this workshop, but participants were given more intensive training in AI interviewing. This included first interviewing their best friend, then interviewing a workshop participant, and finally interviewing a significant segment of the "Nagaland glue."

Discovery Phase Process Highlights

Culturally, Nagaland is a place where children are expected to remain silent spectators and speak only when spoken to. The first major challenge for the facilitators was how to get this mixed group of children and adults to interact on an equal footing in the Discovery Workshop and later to give children the confidence to interview adults. The workshop agenda was therefore designed like a DNA molecule, with separate streams of dialogue for children (who in any case could not be expected to feel comfortable with AI theory) and for adults. At appropriate times the two groups were brought together to share their findings.

Towards the end of the first day, children and adults were asked to "guess" what the other group might have captured as dreams, hopes, and expectations. Adults presumed their output would be more realistic and based on experience, while children were confident that they would have pictured a more exciting future. When the two groups came together, the resulting discussion was a turning point in the workshop. Adults were truly overawed by the power of the children's dreams, and the children felt adults had come up with "the same old thing." The group of adults openly admitted their respect for what the children had come up with and from then on, adults and children decided to work in combined groups. A crucial barrier had been overcome.

The facilitation team had a person who had tremendous experience of working with children, and this also proved to be invaluable in getting them to participate fully.

Once the six themes were chosen by the participants, crafting the lead-in statements and the questions proved to be quite challenging. In the practice interviews, children needed special coaching, but in the end proved to be the best interviewers! One young boy needed a lot of guidance (and confidence building) to get through even the first interview. Having done that, he went on, as he proudly announced in the second workshop, to complete twenty-eight interviews with senior bureaucrats, police personnel, teachers, and community members.

One of the young participants designed a wonderful, brightly colored logo for Imagine Nagaland (see Figure 1), which became a symbol of hope for the participants and something of an icon for the entire state. To another of the participants, the colors in the logo symbolized the richness of Nagaland; the bonded hands—unity and strength; the hills—peace, serenity, and values upheld for ages to come; the birds—life; and the rising sun—the dawn of a new beginning.

Figure 1
NAGALAND LOGO

The dozen or so probationers became deeply engaged in the process, as did the Administrative Training Institute (ATI), the apex training institution of the state government. In the second workshop, the probationers developed into great co-facilitators—a natural, unplanned, and very welcome development! Participants in this workshop actually came from each of the districts and were to go back and interview hundreds of people over the next few weeks. The probationers felt the need to reach out further and deeper into districts and so led a one-day workshop, on their own initiative, in each of the districts. Local stakeholders—villagers, students, government officials, teachers, and student-union leaders, among others— participated and took the cascading interview process to new frontiers. The power of this "reach" could be seen from the fact that many village-level stakeholders were deeply influenced by the process. One example is that of a local church leader, who had attended a district workshop admittedly "with quite some reluctance." He was so taken up by the process that he ended up doing sixty-four interviews with farmers, village leaders, local government functionaries, and children, an invaluable contribution to the Discovery Phase of Imagine Nagaland.

A steering committee had been formed, consisting of representatives of all the major stakeholder groups in the first workshop. This committee led the review meetings in the period between the Discovery workshops and the Dream/Design Summit, and ensured that interviews and data mining were on track.

DREAM AND DESIGN PHASE

By the time the Dream/Design Summit was held in late July 2001, six thousand interviews had been completed and mined for stories, best practices, and dreams by a band of tireless student volunteers, probationers, ATI staff, and a few dedicated bureaucrats. Hundreds of interview forms were still pouring in each day at the time of the Dream/Design Summit. To enhance the state's capacity to continue the AI philosophy, ATI was strengthened in terms of literature and presentation materials and books on Appreciative Inquiry. An open invitation was sent out that the core team would train anyone interested in the art of facilitation, using AI. Nearly forty people signed up and were trained immediately prior to the Dream/Design Summit. Many of them acted as invaluable co-facilitators during the summit.

The Dream/Design Summit had nearly two hundred participants. Many of them were from the earlier two workshops, but about a third were new to AI, pulled in by the power of Imagine Nagaland. Nearly half of the participants were children and youth. The challenge was to facilitate the identification and ownership of a common ground between the dreams of children, adults, and also the government team that had been "visioning" for the past few months in the parallel, top-down Vision Nagaland process. The initial two days of the three-day event were spent, repeating the "DNA methodology," in working with these three sets of stakeholders separately and then developing the common ground through plenary sessions. Two new facilitation tools were used with great success in this workshop: mind mapping for group brainstorming and market stalls for plenary (see below).

Dream/Design Summit Process Highlights

Participants were asked to form teams for each of the six topics from the Discovery Phase, with children and adults in separate teams.

Each team generated a *mind map* to graphically organize and show the linkages among the mined data from the discovery interviews and their members' own aspirations and personal knowledge of the areas they came from. Once again, as in previous workshops, children and youth were astounding in their imagination, the power of their dreams, and the courage of their convictions. The younger generation overwhelmed the adults with their magical combination of exuberance and wisdom, and their "provocative propositions" about the future reflected the boldness of their dreams.

Combined teams of adults and children then merged their provocative propositions into one powerful proposition per team for each topic. These acted as a beacon for the Design Phase.

A challenge for the facilitators was how to hold a plenary for such a large number of presentations and participants and yet make it exciting and meaningful. The facilitators decided on a methodology called *market stalls,* in which each team was provided a space (pin board or wall space) to "display" their presentation in the most attractive manner, using decorated Naga shawls and handicraft items. Each team had the opportunity to present their own stall and visit other stalls to sell and buy ideas, within a stipulated time frame. This brought excitement to the plenary and a sense of healthy competition and cooperation amongst the presenters.

The market-stall methodology was used, first, to present the provocative propositions, and on the third day, to present ideas for development opportunities. In this final step in the process, participants were divided into teams for each of the eight districts and one for the state as a whole. The nine teams each created a "Tree of Achievement," a broad-brush prioritization of about a dozen development programs that each team felt were essential, keeping in mind the outputs from the Discovery Phase interviews, mind maps, plenary discussions, and the unique characteristics of the district, as well as the centrality of children's dreams. Project ideas that could bring early results were represented as low-hanging fruits, while those with longer-term potential were high-hanging fruits. The market stalls of these district-level trees, taken altogether, were seen as the "Garden of Achievement" and laid the foundation for further detailed work leading up to the Destiny Phase.

Since Imagine Nagaland was intended to feed into the state's tenth five-year plan, as well as ultimately to attract funds (private and corporate sector donors, etc.) for programs that could not be funded from the government resources, the pulling together of these "trees" into a "Garden of Achievements" was facilitated by a key functionary of the State Planning Department. This was an individual who had spent eighteen years in rural areas, visiting nearly one thousand of the eleven hundred villages in the state.

**VOICES OF CHILDREN AND YOUTH
ON IMAGINE NAGALAND**

- "It is time to take education out of classrooms and bring it to our homes, villages, and communities."

- "Obviously what we are facing now would be the consequence of what our predecessors had already committed. So it is the right time to reshape our society again. Or else the future situation will again be the result of the present, and we will be held responsible for that."

- "If we neglect our ecology, then we are our own prosecuting lawyer, judge, jury, and hangman."

- "Any kind of human understanding is a two-way traffic."

- "Children are the leaders of tomorrow, so we must educate them properly if we are to be led properly."

- "A child should be allowed to focus and develop her emotional balance, and we should help to nurture their talents and abilities. A child should not be given importance only on the basis of 'intelligence,' based on academic performance."

- "I imagine a Nagaland where people have less complaints and criticism, children [are] eagerly involved in school because of the good facilities and extracurricular activities, villages [are] involved in their own development, and everyone [is] involved and aware of their cultural heritage."

- "Nagaland, with all its diversity, can still remain united because of the innate desire for harmony of our people."

- "Nagaland is a land of festivals, and that is when we are all 'one'—so why can't we be in that frame of mind all through the year?"

- "Let peace be forgotten for some time and preach for unity. Peace will come into the picture as unity is developed."

VOICES, continued

- "Better to light one's candle rather than cursing the darkness."

- "I'd like Nagaland to be a 'united nations'."

- "Women should be given chances to give and talk about their ideas. Also, women should be encouraged that their active participation is a must for the development of a society. This should start with their equal participation in all platforms."

- "Students should not be subordinated to the teacher— rather the teacher should coordinate (facilitate) to allow students to reach their real capacity."

- "Wildlife parks and sanctuaries tell more to a child than a thousand books."

One of the serendipitous events that came about as a bonus from the second Discovery Workshop was the "discovery" of a brilliant young artist who thanked the facilitators by quickly sketching out a beautiful visual image of how he saw the process of Imagine Nagaland. This young boy then produced a set of stunning paintings for the Dream/Design Summit—a painting for each of the topics of Imagine Nagaland.

Kelhousedenuo: The Beginning of Life

Mahesh Bhatt, one of India's top film directors, captured the Dream/Design Summit on video. The product, entitled *Kelhousedenuo: The Beginning of Life,* captures the dreams, the energy, and the participation of youth and children in visioning for the future. As part of the briefing of Mahesh Bhatt, who had not heard of Appreciative Inquiry before nor ever traveled to Nagaland, the facilitators asked him to just be "overwhelmed" by children and then let himself be led by the momentum of the process and its outcomes. He was asked to view the summit from the perspective of a three-tiered stage setting, with the front tier being the voice of children, the next one being the Imagine Nagaland project, and the last one being the reconciliation process that was on in the state.[5]

The film as finally envisioned by him has captured the experience of a person visiting the state for the first time, with all the trepidation created by stories of the Nagaland armed struggle. The film captures the exciting journey of entering a "dark tunnel"—a state and its people full of foreboding, hopelessness, fear, fatigue—and coming out into the light of energy, hope, confidence, and the strength and will to dream. The film has immortalized the indomitable spirit of the people of Nagaland and their determination to move forward with renewed hope and determination.

DESTINY OR DOING PHASE

As preparation for the final, Destiny or "Doing" Phase (at the time of publication), the state planning team has worked on getting a buy-in to the outputs of the Dream/Design Summit from more district-level stakeholders and to develop the program ideas on the "Trees of Achievement" into fundable proposals to take to prospective donors.

This strategic planning exercise, focused on children's dreams and expectations, has involved UNICEF and a team of consultants from the Australian Agency for International Development. The consultants spent considerable time with the state planning focal point and discussed how best to take this initiative forward. Their experience has shown senior government officials how to create a set of development-project proposals, in line with the "Approach Paper of the 10th Five-Year Plan for India," for potential fundraising. The recent novel creation of an ordinance for "communitization" of Nagaland's public institutions and services is one significant milestone.

The government of India has since led an effort to focus the attention of donors on the entire North East region by holding a donor conference, and Nagaland has been an active participant in this process. Areas like eco-tourism, education, and HIV/AIDS have already attracted donor interest.

CONCLUSION

The journey begun two years ago by the people of Nagaland, as part of the Global Movement for Children, is as exciting as it is challenging. What Imagine Nagaland has triggered is a change in the "inner dialogue" (the somewhat stereotyped thinking of helplessness, fatigue, and cynicism that characterized the people's perception) of a large number of people who live in this area of conflict. Intensely Christian, the Naga society looks for the forgiveness and reconciliation needed to overcome this conflict. But instead of getting lost in the past, Imagine Nagaland has managed to focus the energy and attention of children, youth, and adults forward by drawing on the positive possibilities from the best of the past. Thousands of people now dare to dream and design their future and look to a tryst with a destiny that they are co-authoring. A team of youth, led by a facilitator, participated in the "Global Imagine Meet" in Chicago in 2002, and the painting of the young artist (who was part of the team) was adopted as the logo for the meet. The Nagaland government is pursuing the planning and implementation process within its own framework. But what is more interesting is that other independent initiatives have taken root, using Appreciative Inquiry and Imagine Nagaland as a springboard. A chain of schools, for example, with branches in Nagaland and the rest of the North East is using AI for rethinking about their approach to education, as part of a long-term strategic planning exercise.

ENDNOTES

1. Imagine Nagaland was conceived by Peter Delahaye, deputy director, UNICEF India, and Bharat Krishnan, management adviser, as part of the Indian government's "Vision Nagaland."
2. Sanjoy Hazarika is managing trustee of the Centre for North East Studies and Policy Research. These comments were made on the occasion of the visit by Naga social reformist Niketu Iralu to Delhi in September 2001.
3. Involving citizens in sharing and working towards positive images of their community's future unleashes energy and commitment. Across the world, "Imagine" projects, inspired by the original Imagine Chicago, have begun in places as far ranging as West Australia, Scotland, Nagaland, Cape Town, London, Detroit, Denmark, and Vojvodina in Yugoslavia. These projects are discovering that hope can be cultivated through constructive dialogue, community engagement, and the forging of meaningful intergenerational connections.
4. The "glue" expression hails from Imagine Chicago's search for key people that made Chicago tick.
5. The Naga Reconciliation Initiative, begun in August 2001 by a resolution of representatives of various mass-based Naga organizations, called for "journeys of healing" internally among the Naga tribes and externally with other communities.

REFERENCE

Cooperrider, David L., and Diana Whitney. 1999. *Appreciative Inquiry.* San Francisco: Berrett-Koehler.

Appendix

IMAGINE NAGALAND INTERVIEW GUIDES

NAGALAND OF OUR FUTURE

We all share a sense of great pride in our culture, our people's hardworking nature, and the abundant flora and fauna that Nagaland has to offer. There have been unceasing efforts for peace and unity in the state, and we are now at a very opportune time where we can begin to build a new and prosperous future for ourselves. As adults, we are trustees and custodians of a wonderful future that our children expect as their legacy. And as children, we owe it to our elders to build on all the good things they bring to us from their hard work and values.

It is up to all of us now, whether we are adults or children, to work together for jointly creating a Nagaland that we will all be legitimately proud of—building on our strengths, learning from our mistakes, but all the time thinking positively about a common dream that we all share. We have a tryst with destiny, and it is our individual and collective responsibility to make sure that we undertake this wonderful journey of development of Nagaland in a spirit of oneness and optimism.

It is in this context that I would like you to share your stories, experiences, and dreams over the next hour or so. This will be a wonderful opportunity for you to be a partner in this exciting project of "Imagine Nagaland."

- As a citizen of Nagaland you do feel an attachment to it. What are the things that really make you feel a part of Nagaland?

- We all feel that perhaps if certain things improve, Nagaland would be a better place to live in. In your opinion, in what sphere do we have to concentrate to make our state better?

- Can you recall any incident that you have witnessed or heard of and that you wished for more of that kind to make Nagaland a better place to live in?

- Every child has the potential to develop his or her abilities. So how do you perceive the future of Nagaland where in ten years' time, every child with his or her potential can contribute towards the furtherance of the developed and civilized healthy state of society?

- Close your eyes and imagine you travel through a time machine seven to eight years into the future and see a fully transformed Nagaland. Can you describe what kind of a transformation (political, social, religious, economic, cultural) you see in this state?

EDUCATION AND EMPLOYMENT

Even as the winds of peace blowing over our state bring with them a sense of hope for peace and well-being, they have also carried the anguished cry of our children and elders for the delivery of quality education, particularly in the primary level. The yearning is now to ensure that all children, especially the girl child, are not only provided the opportunity to enroll in schools, but are motivated to carry on studying by a caring, appreciative, and encouraging school system that imbibes uniformly a love for learning and desire to scale new peaks in all fields of endeavor, building on the traditional values of the Nagas.

Much needs to be done to transform our schooling and education system to make it more learner friendly, joyful, and to impart quality education. Students should be taught the value of dignity of labor and learn that theirs is the task and challenge of creating a vibrant, humane, and prosperous Naga society.

The vital role of teachers cannot be overstressed. The teaching community needs to be made conscious that theirs is the momentous and historical task of molding the young minds of today to grow to be tomorrow's responsible citizens. It is in their acceptance of the responsibility of imparting joyful learning and being accountable to the critical task entrusted to them that the future of our society hinges.

- Today there is widespread recognition of the fact that education should be made more joyful and interesting. In what ways do you think our educational system can be made to impart joyful, meaningful, and relevant education at all levels—primary, elementary, secondary, and higher secondary levels?

- As a community, do we encourage children (boys and girls) to continue their education? What steps do we need to take to encourage parents and community leaders to ensure everyone gets a proper education in urban and rural areas?

- We see a lot of entrepreneurs in our society. What made them think and act differently from the rest of us? If you know an entrepreneur, can you tell us his or her story? Are you proud to know such a person?

- If you were the minister for education, what three steps would you take to make the present system more employment and entrepreneurial oriented?

- If you were the leader of your tribe or community, what specific steps would you take?

- For everyone in Nagaland to have a meaningful and sustainable livelihood (job or self-employment), how can we prepare our students and young people to realize this dream?

EQUITABLE DEVELOPMENT

Equitable development is the need of the hour for Nagaland! That means benefits of development reach every part of our society, in a proportionate manner. It also means decision making, accountability and development go hand in hand at different levels of our social system, whether it be a village, a district, or the state. Each community has the responsibility to plan for its own development, with support from the state.

Emphasis and focused importance is needed towards a well-balanced development in the spheres of

- balanced regional/geographical development, starting with basic amenities;
- equitable representation in all decision-making bodies and strata, with devolution of powers at all relevant levels;
- economic development and employment opportunities;
- equal opportunities for girl children and women for all-round development.

We aspire to promote these. But this requires leadership and participation of everyone in Nagaland. This is the subject we have come to discuss with you, to share your stories and experiences.

- Looking back on your community and society, can you remember any occasion when people (men and women) of different backgrounds came together and participated in taking decisions?
- Are we satisfied with the present status of women and children in Naga society? If not, where do we begin?
- Balanced and equitable development cannot happen without fairness, justice, honesty, and transparency. Can you think of examples of this in your community?
- If you were made the head of your district development committee, what would you do to ensure balanced participation of your people and equitable distribution of the benefits thereof?

ECOLOGY AND DEVELOPMENT

Nagaland is a beautiful land, gifted with a wide variety of rare and exquisite flora and fauna. The richness of Nagaland's ecological heritage sustains the people, but a need has come today to preserve, conserve, and protect this wealth that is under threat.

The cry of Nagaland today is for greater economic and social development, and the concern is that development has to be more sustainable, while ensuring ecological sustainability as well. The balance between protecting ecology and sustainable development is the answer to promoting the quality and meaning of life in Nagaland, and that is the challenge before all of us.

It is on this subject that we would like to spend some time with you.

- Balance between ecology and development leads to a better living. Can you think of some examples in your area of this balance?

- What do you think is the role of the people and the community, other than the government, in protection of this ecological balance? Draw on your traditional history for some examples.

- In what way do you feel that this delicate balance can be restored and promoted?

- Development usually means taking something away from our land and other natural resources. How can we repay nature for all that she gives to us?

UNITY, PEACE, AND RESPECT FOR ALL

Unity is a feeling of oneness without barriers of tribalism, communalism, and regionalism. All of us, leaders and led, need to learn to forgive one another and stay united in the larger interest of our people, recognizing that as human beings, we have all fallen short of living perfect.

Peace is the most important ingredient for any kind of meaningful human or economic development. We need to build bridges of understanding to transform our hopes into reality. The setting up of democratic structures in our society has become imperative.

Given the current context, we need a collective approach towards social well-being. How can each one of us contribute in this effort of building a Nagaland where the unity of our people and peace in society will help us to march forward into the future with the rest of the world?

This is the subject we would like your valuable inputs on.

- What does "peace" mean to you, and when was the last time you remember such a time?

- When was the last time you really felt proud of being a citizen of Nagaland? Can you explain the particular circumstances?

- Does diversity mean richness to you, just like diversity in flora and fauna are seen as the beauty of nature? Then, why do we as people struggle to respect diversity amongst ourselves?

- What role can we as individuals play towards bringing peace and unity?

- If you went in a time machine to the year 2010, what do you see as Nagaland? What can we do to make your dream a reality?

STRENGTHENING THE RULE OF LAW

The rule of law is the hallmark of a civilized society. It signifies respect for the rules and regulations framed through democratic methods, following good traditions and customs, self-discipline, fair play and justice, tolerance towards dissent, concern for other people, civic sense, and a host of other values that enrich life. The rule of law is particularly relevant for more vulnerable groups like women, children, and the differently abled.

Nagaland has emerged as a modern, educated, and enlightened society in this new millennium. There is a sense of hope and optimism in the air. The cornerstone of this progress has been a deep respect for values, traditions, and the rule of law. This march towards happiness, peace, unity, and development, including conservation of our natural resources, will depend a great deal on harmony, tolerance, and concern for others, all of which come from adhering to the rule of law—whether written or unwritten.

Recent trends in efforts for peace are a cause of great hope to many of us, and we would like to interact with you on this crucial subject so that we can strengthen the rule of law in Nagaland for the common good of all citizens.

- How is the rule of law helping our society?
- We are all striving to ensure the happiness of our citizens and to build a healthy society. Do you feel that adherence to the rule of law will strengthen this process and improve the quality of our lives?
- Would you share with us the most critical areas where strengthening the rule of law would most benefit society?
- Can you recall a personal experience where you observed a positive impact of the rule of law?
- Could you give us some practical suggestions that would make the rule of law more attractive to people and more effective in its implementation?

Let us be realists, let us do the impossible.

ERNESTO "CHE" GUEVERA

TOWARD THE THEORY AND PRACTICE OF APPRECIATIVE INQUIRY IN COMPLEX PEACEBUILDING AND DEVELOPMENT CONTEXTS

Mary Hope Schwoebel and Erin McCandless

This chapter discusses the potential applications of Appreciative Inquiry in complex peacebuilding and development settings and also in facilitating theory building and practice at the nexus of these two fields. The authors highlight common assumptions and approaches found in peacebuilding, development, and Appreciative Inquiry, which point to a potentially fruitful integration. They also address some of the epistemological and methodological critiques of Appreciative Inquiry, particularly as they pertain to contexts of structural and direct violence and poverty. An example from the Africa Community Publishing and Development Trust, a Zimbabwean nongovernmental organization, illustrates how appreciative approaches can be combined with problem-solving approaches to tackle such conditions in ways that empower people and communities to generate social and structural change, and to overcome some of the limits of appreciative approaches when used exclusively in such contexts. The chapter concludes by suggesting additional ways in which Appreciative Inquiry might be adapted to create positive peace and positive social change.

❧

*W*ithin the fields of peacebuilding and development, there is a growing recognition that sustainable approaches to transforming deep-rooted conflict and overcoming development challenges are those that empower people through bottom-up, participatory, and context-sensitive methods. Both fields are also paying greater attention to best-practices cases, or what works, with the aim of replicating them in other contexts. Replication of models, however, has historically too often proved to not bring about desired results, where local conditions and cultures are not considered when transplanting the model into different situations. Appreciative Inquiry (AI) is a dynamic method that does consider these issues, while focusing on what works with a vision for what could be. This creates an active space for social change, something desired by many academics and policy makers in search of alternatives to the dominant paradigms built upon pessimistic assumptions and reifying practices.

Critics, however, might view Appreciative Inquiry as a "feel-good" approach rooted in naive idealism. As academics and practitioners coming to AI with critical-theory leanings and a strong concern for the ways in which structures too often create violence and maintain peoples' subjugation, we believe that AI must be theoretically and methodologically adapted to tackle these concerns. This will include some consideration of its epistemological foundations, lest its constructionist biases ensure it is only useful to those of this persuasion. Not all believe that everything is "constructible," or that we have ultimate power to create our life opportunities and re-create the circumstances that steer our experiences. Many of these, it may be argued, we are born with or born into. Such conditions can be structurally determined by the institutions, environmental conditions, or cultural practices that surround us.

This reflective article aims to lay foundations for the adapting of Appreciative Inquiry to address the above issues, even as it makes a case for the utility of AI methods for those working in areas of peacebuilding and development where there is an a priori concern about how to facilitate positive social change. A case study of the work of the Africa Community Publishing and Development Trust in Zimbabwe is discussed, which draws on many of the same assumptions as AI, and employs strategies similar to AI to bring about personal and social change among participants in a context of unrealized human development and structural and direct violence.

Through the case study and accompanying analysis, we argue that Appreciative Inquiry is appropriate for addressing structural and direct violence as long as it remains dynamic and adaptive to particular contexts. This may require a comprehensive discussion by AI enthusiasts about which assumptions and principles are to remain as an unchanging core that defines AI and which are open to contextual adaptation. One such consideration, for example, is the question of problem solving, which AI theorists have argued is not within the realm of AI. As our case study illustrates, however, "positive" approaches and problem-solving approaches are not necessarily diametrically opposed. In this case, where economic, political, and social problems prevail, they are viewed as complementary. Impoverished and marginalized communities are first empowered to recognize and acknowledge their strengths and talents (the positive approach), which enables them to expand and hone the skills to tackle the enormous structural problems surrounding them (the problem-solving approach). Visioning new possibilities and creating new opportunities is a part of this process.

APPRECIATIVE INQUIRY'S APPROACH TO CHANGE

Appreciative Inquiry is defined as a cooperative search for strengths, passions, and life-giving forces that are found within every system and that hold potential for inspired, positive change. It is a process of collaborative inquiry based on interviews and affirmative questioning, which brings out and celebrates the best and highest qualities in a system, situation, or human being. These "good news stories" serve to enhance identity, spirit, and vision, eliciting strategies for intentional change that draw upon the best of what is to pursue dreams and possibilities of what could be (Cooperrider and Srivastva 1987).

A number of assumptions underpin Appreciative Inquiry, including: reality is co-created through peoples' language, thoughts, images, and beliefs about reality; the act of asking a question influences a system's reality in some way (questions are themselves a form of intervention); the types of questions asked determine the types of answers received; people manifest what they focus on and grow toward what they ask questions about; AI actively involves people in changing their organizations, communities, and societies; and AI is a holistic and systemic approach to change, which asks who is affected and who has a stake in the process (Cooperrider and Whitney 1999).

Fundamentally a dialogic process, AI carries such questions and concerns through to the planning and implementing of social change. An AI process is comprised of four stages, known as the 4-D Cycle. Once the focus area or topics of interest are selected, interviews are conducted to discover strengths and passions within the system and to identify patterns, themes, and possibilities. This is the Discovery Phase, which concerns appreciating and valuing the best of "what is." The second stage is the Dream Phase, which involves envisioning "what might be," and creating bold statements about ideal possibilities. The third stage is the Design Phase, which includes dialoguing about "what should be," particularly in terms of principles and priorities. The fourth and final stage is the Destiny Phase and involves innovating "what will be" by taking and sustaining action.

A central principle and epistemological foundation of Appreciative Inquiry is that of constructionism—the idea that human beings construct realities based on their experience, so that their knowledge and the destiny of the system are interwoven. Cooperrider and Whitney write:

> Constructionism reminds us that the "world out there" doesn't dictate our inquiries; rather, the topics are products of social processes (cultural habits, rhetoric, power relations). AI makes sure we are not just reproducing the same worlds over and over again through simple and boring repetition of our questions. . . . AI also says, with excitement, that there are great gains in linking the means and ends of inquiry. (1999, 26–27)

This *constructionist principle* is one reason why AI practitioners and theorists assert that the principles underpinning Appreciative Inquiry invest in it the potential to produce radical social change. Contrary to those who benefit from the current reality and the status quo, AI proposes that a better world is realistic, that there already exist success stories of positive change, and that people already have (at least some of) the resources necessary to bring it about. By recognizing and appreciating "what is," Cooperrider and Whitney argue, "future dreams are grounded in reality and hence believable" (1999, 21).

AI's radical social change potential is secondly attributed to the *principle of simultaneity,* which maintains that inquiry and change are simultaneous. AI engages all levels and all types of stakeholders in a cooperative learning and co-creation process. "When everyone's awareness grows at the same time, it is easier to believe that fundamental change is possible" (Cooperrider and Whitney 1999, 18).

Other change-promoting principles underlying AI are the poetic principle, the anticipatory principle, and the positive principle. The *poetic principle* states that the story of the system is constantly being co-authored, and the *anticipatory principle*, that what people anticipate determines what they find. The *positive principle* posits that as an image of reality is enhanced, actions begin to align with the positive image.

CASE STUDY: COMMUNITY PUBLISHING IN ZIMBABWE[1]

Gervase Bushe and Thomas Pitman (1991) define appreciative process as a theoretical and practical approach for affecting social change, which is based on the concept that change can be created by attending to what people want more of rather than attending to problems, but which maintains a balance between appreciative approaches and problem-solving approaches.

The Africa Community Publishing and Development Trust (ACPDT) in Zimbabwe is a nongovernmental organization that has developed a unique and highly successful methodology for empowerment of people and communities within difficult social contexts, where poverty and structural or physical violence prevail. They describe their work in the following way:

> . . . through a community based, participatory process of publishing, organizing and development, [community publishing] aims to enable marginalized groups to use their creative energies to build dynamic leadership, tackle poverty, take charge of their lives and make the decisions that shape their future (Bond-Stewart et al. 2002, 1).

While ACPDT does not directly refer to the terms Appreciative Inquiry or appreciative process, their work draws upon many of the same assumptions and employs many similar strategies. Comfortably falling into the realm of appreciative process, their work also often involves action research along the lines of the research inquiry processes involved in AI. ACPDT Director Kathy Bond-Stewart explains:

> Community Publishing works best in extremely difficult circumstances, as the creative energy it releases is directly proportional to the degree of oppression that its participants have experienced. (2002)

Zimbabwe is currently experiencing severe economic and political crises, which manifest in pervasive poverty (approximately 80 percent) and conflict that cuts across political and ethnic lines. The state-owned public media are used for propaganda purposes, and the ruling party foments political violence to generate a culture of fear and disempowerment, stifling activism and opportunities for social change amongst Zimbabweans.

Within this context, the Africa Community Publishing and Development Trust has developed an innovative method of development education, which builds the skills, confidence, and creativity of marginalized communities by involving them in the collective production and distribution of books. The starting point of transformation, they believe, is helping those with the lowest incomes and least power overcome mental oppression and dependency. In the process, people discover and develop their own capacities and skills. This enables them to enter into new, more equal, and enabling relationships, while contributing to the building of strong political and cultural organizations (ACPDT 2000, 28).

ACPDT's innovate approach evolved out of their research on poverty, which involved 150 youth (eighteen to thirty-five years of age), and culminated in the 1995 publication, *The Suffering are the Cornerstone in Building a Nation*. Through the process it became clear that while material deprivation is painful, psychological deprivation is much more painful. A critical first strategy, then, was to give people a sense of their strength and place in the world. The process for participants was developed and practiced through many of ACPDT's projects. This involves:

- writing about their life stories and self images (often of oppression);
- analyzing how their strengths allowed them to overcome such difficult circumstances and naming the skills and talents that enabled this;
- learning research, writing, and organizing skills;
- identifying and promoting all local forms of creativity with a positive focus, where a positive sense of self and potential is activated.

Utilizing this process, ACPDT has developed many books on critical developmental and peace issues with its hundreds of community researchers. Their books are accessible to popular and academic audiences, as well as policymakers. They are simple and yet profound in the way they handle complex ideas, with meanings derived from local people and contexts. In addition to the product, the process of community publishing has catalyzed processes of positive individual, community, and social change. According to one community activist:

> Those of us who are involved in the production of these publications ended up discovering within ourselves talents which had not been tapped. The world began to open before our minds. We began to see more clearly, think more creatively, reason more logically, and analyze facts more critically. Our minds became liberated. (ACPDT 2000, 28)

Guided by the same vision and in conjunction with community publishing projects, ACPDT runs local leadership trainings for village youth. The main vision of the program is to "transform marginalized communities from poverty to prosperity through an integrated economic, social, environmental, and organizational development process." In the first local leadership program in Chiyubunuzyo in Gokwe North, communities have been able to successfully campaign for a clinic, a community hall, improved roads, a greater role in wildlife management, and the introduction of preschools. Moreover, "the use of their own well-researched documents assists them in negotiating with local authorities and other service providers" (Bond-Stewart et al. 2002, 4).

At the national level, their civic publications were used by the National Constitutional Assembly civic social movement to ensure a "no" vote to the government's proposed authoritarian constitution—the first time in twenty years that citizens challenged the government. "Our low budget, community publishing constitutional pamphlets and imaginative debate process had more impact than the state's multi-million dollar media campaign, with unlimited use of radio, television, and the government newspapers" (Bond-Stewart et al. 2002, 5).

Bond-Stewart emphasizes that the approach builds people's confidence and skills, whereby they emerge from the process with new tools to analyze problems deeply and develop strategies to address these problems. She therefore emphasizes the complementarity of "a positive, confidence- and skills-building approach with the problem-solving approach" (2002).

Community publishing gives people an alert, energetic, critical, and creative set of skills that are useful in dealing with structural developmental and conflict issues. At the core of ACPDT's philosophy and method is a value of respecting the dignity of all—a foundational assumption in both peacebuilding and development work. The causes of violence and uneven development begin with prejudices and faulty assumptions, which ACPDT community researchers strive to address. They also learn how to give and receive criticism, particularly towards authority figures, and the importance of having respect for your opponents—that you can learn the most from those who oppose you. The process elicits and develops other skills complementary with peacebuilding and development, which include:

- motivation
- mobilization
- shared leadership
- communication
- democracy planning
- participatory community development

Community publishing as practiced in this way illustrates the utility of positive approaches in complex and structurally violent peacebuilding and development contexts. ACPDT's collaborative inquiry process, combined with the practical production and dissemination of concrete outputs of their work, reflect Bushe and Pitman's understanding of appreciative process. ACPDT's work shows how the principles of appreciative process, in accessing the strengths and building the positive capacities of individuals and communities, can produce meaningful research, as participants also learn new practical skills and contribute towards profound social change. In Zimbabwe, where the vast majority of the population are overwhelmed with poverty and lack of human development—in particular, lack of opportunities and choices—the practical skills and community-building aspects cannot be overestimated.

Theoretically, the case points to the need for contextual sensitivity and adaptation of AI methods and approaches and to the usefulness of these approaches where peacebuilding and development are transformational goals of the communities involved, as well as those offering some sort of intervention. In Zimbabwe as well as other conflict-ridden and structurally violent contexts, people need to work together in tackling problems, challenges, and traumas in new ways. Thus, while the concept of good-news storytelling is important in AI, with ACPDT people are encouraged to write, draw, act out, or in any other creative way tell their life stories, which are often not good news but rather stories of oppression and pain. This is part of a transformative healing process—learning to communicate, remember, forgive, and reconcile.

We now turn to a discussion of both of these aspects—the peacebuilding and development nexus and some of the theoretical challenges of AI—in an effort to illuminate ways in which AI can be utilized in complex peacebuilding and development contexts.

APPRECIATIVE INQUIRY'S APPLICATION TO
PEACEBUILDING AND DEVELOPMENT

As academics, policy makers, and practitioners are recognizing the important linkages between peacebuilding and development, the need for new methodological approaches to facilitate coordinated understanding and action between the two fields grows. AI has the potential to be a powerful methodology for peacebuilders and development scholars and practitioners—and one that can facilitate greater understanding and better practice between them. To develop these ideas, we start with a discussion of peacebuilding and development and the intersections between them.

Peacebuilding is generally understood as

> . . . a comprehensive concept that encompasses, generates, and sustains the full array of processes, approaches, and stages needed to transform conflict towards more sustainable, peaceful relationships. It simultaneously seeks to enhance relationships between parties and to change the structural conditions that generate conflict. The term thus involves a wide range of activities and functions that both precede and follow formal peace accords. (Lederach 1997, 20)

As we have written elsewhere, peacebuilding focuses on the context of the conflict—the experiences and socioeconomic circumstances of ordinary people who are affected by war and who will build the peace, rather than the on the military and the issues that divide the parties. Peacebuilding activities have come to include: generating contact and dialogue between communities; reconciliation; identifying overarching goals between communities; confidence-building; institutionalization for the respect for human rights; promoting political pluralism and the rule of law; accommodating ethnic minorities and ethnic diversity; strengthening the capacity of state structures and promoting good governance; and participatory community and human development (McCandless and Schwoebel 2001).

The human-development paradigm aims to enlarge people's choices. This begins with the formation of human capabilities, including improved health, the acquisition of knowledge, and access to resources for a decent standard of living. Secondly, human development encompasses the freedom for people to use their capabilities for being active in cultural, social, political, and economic affairs, as well as for their leisure. The human development paradigm is comprised of four essential components: productivity, equity, sustainability, and empowerment. In the development context, empowerment means that "development must be by people, not for people. People must participate fully in the decisions and processes that shape their lives" (UNDP 1995:12).

Understanding the nexus between peacebuilding and development requires some awareness of the relationship between development and conflict. Protracted, deep-rooted social conflicts usually have an economic, or development, dimension to their evolution and dynamics. Conflict may result, for example, from an abundance of resources (e.g., minerals in the Democratic Republic of the Congo) or resource scarcity or unjust distribution (e.g., land and natural resources in Rwanda and Burundi). Conversely, unwise practices of development often create greater inequality within society, which can lead to destructive forms of competitiveness and even violent conflict. Violent conflict also prohibits sustainable human development, where the livelihoods of ordinary people are destroyed or disrupted, health and education services are disrupted, and public monies are spent on militaristic approaches to problem solving.

The emerging nexus of peacebuilding and development is particularly concerned with structural violence, as described by Jeong:

> Poverty, hunger, repression, and social alienation constitute another way to characterize situations causing human misery. Quality of life is reduced by denial of educational opportunities, free speech, and freedom of association. These conditions are associated with uneven life chances, inequitable distribution of resources, and unequal decision-making power. Given its indirect and insidious nature, structural violence most often works slowly in eroding human values and shortening life spans. It is typically built into the very structure of society and cultural institutions. (2000, 20)

In other words, the peacebuilding field is concerned with any form of violence—direct or structural—that prevents sustainable human development. Studying the aims, methods, and values of sustainable human development, peace researchers would also find great convergence with the concept of positive peace.

Appreciative Inquiry converges with peacebuilding and development and becomes useful as a methodology for the academic and practical pursuits of both, because it is based on assumptions about the desirability and the possibility of fulfilling peoples' potential for human development. At the same time, it assumes (like both fields) that win-win solutions to problems are possible. This contrasts with dominant peace and development paradigms, in other words, the realpolitik approach to peace and the modernization approach to development, which rest on the acceptance of "winners" and "losers" in the social-change process. AI theorists view change systemically, and AI practitioners seek win-win solutions for all parties in post-change environments. These are principles adhered to by those who aspire to the notion of transformative conflict resolution, which views conflict as an opportunity rather than merely as a problem-to-be-solved.

In addition to common principles, peacebuilding and development intersect with Appreciative Inquiry at another critical juncture—the processes that embody those principles. Both fields, for example, are increasingly recognizing that for development and for peace to be sustainable, certain conditions must be met. These include process and outcome ownership by the population and productive use of existing local resources and indigenous capacities. Processes that are viewed as being effective at fulfilling these conditions combine participatory, elicitive, strengths-based, bottom-up, and system-wide approaches. Sustainability has also been linked with approaches that focus on empowerment (as a catalyst for, and result of, development) and transformation (as a result of conflict resolution). These processes appear to be valued in the AI discourse and practice.

A theoretical underpinning of the field of peacebuilding is that the sources of a given conflict are to be found at all levels and in all spheres of a system. Peacebuilding activities should therefore be undertaken at all levels and in all spheres, in a coordinated and integrated manner. This is a departure from quick-fix approaches that seek a panacea involving only one level or one sphere. Another way of articulating this is by saying that interventions must be integrated both vertically and horizontally within the system. More importantly, meaningful participation at all levels and in all spheres makes interdependence explicit.

Yet, the bureaucracies that design and implement peacebuilding and development initiatives tend to compartmentalize both the problems and the solutions. People living and working in conflict settings do not necessarily experience the sources or the impacts of conflict on their lives as compartmentalized. Appreciative processes, because of their elicitive nature, can facilitate integrative approaches based on people's experience of the problems and the solutions that they have already identified. Appreciative processes can also assist those charged with designing and implementing interventions in recognizing the strengths that each level and each sphere can bring to bear in peacebuilding and the building of human development. AI methods can facilitate the integrated practice and interdisciplinary growth of the fields of peacebuilding and human development. This would be an important contribution to the critical merger of these fields.

AI is a useful methodology for those working in both the fields of peacebuilding and development precisely because it assumes many of these best-practice notions in its application. It is thus a compatible method for those who want to ground their practice on a similar starting point and with a positive social-change vision, to which both peacebuilding and development policy makers and practitioners aspire. Moreover, this is useful to those working from post-positivist persuasions, such as critical theory, postmodernism, poststructuralism, where there is dearth of suitable methodological tools considered legitimate for academic research.

THEORETICAL AND PRACTICAL CHALLENGES TO AI

As with any methodological tool, challenging questions arise that, if well answered, strengthen it and enable its wider usage. What follows are some substantive, epistemological, and application-based critiques that we propose need further inquiry.

The social sciences have long grappled with the debate about how structures and ideas determine and/or motivate social change. In the conflict resolution and peacebuilding literatures is found a similar debate around relationships versus structures as the primary source of conflict. This debate has been summarized in a way that is useful to our discussion:

> Proponents of the structure-as-primary-source identify social structures as the source of conflict, as it determines the distribution of valued resources and positions, denying particular groups access to power, resources, or other human needs (for example, Mitchell 1981, Azar 1986, Galtung 1996). Relationships-as-source proponents alternatively focus on psycho-social explanations, in particular, *perceptions* of difference as conflict-causing (for example Kraybill 1996; Lederach 1997). Many nationalism and identity theorists, as well as social psychologists, would agree.
>
> This debate has implications for praxis. . . . Van der Merwe notes that identity issues can be structural also, arguing for a complementary approach that steps beyond issues of causality (1999). Lederach and Galtung both illustrate this complementary approach in recognizing the importance of both relationships and structures in their transformation pursuits (1997; 1996). (McCandless 2001, 211)

Jeong agrees, writing that efforts to resolve conflict need to be assessed in terms of an outcome as well as a process. "Subsequently, conflict resolution has to be geared toward finding solutions to the structural causes of problems that are responsible for contentious relationships. . . . Negotiation for peaceful relationships would not be effective without confronting the structural origins of problems" (1999, 15–16).

Given the importance of this debate within the social sciences, and in particular, with all fields addressing social change, Appreciative Inquiry will need to be much more explicit about the Design and Destiny phases of the process. These are where the psychological changes generated during the Discovery and Dream phases catalyze actions that create political, economic, and social change.

Another set of critiques that AI could more comprehensively address surrounds the question of "critical" versus "positive" thinking. Bushe has illustrated one way in which this manifests its potential to be indiscriminately applied. He has noted the potential for practitioners to develop

> a zealous attention to "appreciation" without any theoretical rhyme or reason to their practice. Promoting appreciation where there has been little can, of itself, generate a wave of energy and enthusiasm but that will go away just as quickly as the next challenge or tragedy to a social system rears its head. (Bushe n.d. [2002])

Bushe questions the blind ideological application of Appreciative Inquiry and calls for a "disciplined and reasoned approach." While it can be exceedingly helpful in the right time and the right place, he argues, a model for its application is necessary, as it will not always have a positive effect.

> From a purely practical standpoint I think researchers and consultants will find that systems full of deeply held and unexpressed resentments will not tolerate an appreciative inquiry until there has been some expression and forgiving of those resentments. From a theoretical perspective there is the question of what happens to negative images and affect if they are "repressed" from collective discussion by a zealous focus on the "positive." Experience from psychoanalysis, sociology, and medicine suggest repression usually results in some nasty side effects. (Bushe n.d. [2002])

Indeed, as accusations of being "unrealistic" can succeed in silencing proponents of social change, so too can accusations of being "negative" succeed in silencing victims of social injustice, since it shifts the focus away from the system and onto the individual. It is fine to seek out and acknowledge the positive, but it may also be insulting or insensitive to not fully recognize the realities that people face, which may prevent them from being able to consider only the good. Reconciliation and trauma theorists and practitioners have illustrated the need for people to share their traumatic stories as part of their healing process. Ultimately, we return to the problem of the limits of constructionism and the options and choices that are available to people who live under extremely oppressive political and economic regimes and/or under conditions of extreme poverty.

Related questions emerge with the debate about problem-solving paradigms versus AI's focusing on the positive, good-practice cases and possibilities. AI theorists critique the deficit-based orientation of problem-solving approaches, not unlike others from different epistemological persuasions. Cox writes:

> The ingrained beliefs and models from the dominant, problem-solving paradigm are not easy to overcome and people have a high stake in rationalizing what they have always believed and finding it hard to expand their vision to include a larger reality. The key is not to focus on saying the current way is wrong; rather, it is about freeing ourselves to see larger and more expansive realities that are right under our noses. (1998)

Cooperrider and Whitney have further argued that deficit-based change approaches "reinforce hierarchy, erode community, and instill a sense of self-enfeeblement" (1999, 22). While we agree that problem-solving paradigms can limit options and close down creative thinking, this is not always the case. As our community-publishing case illustrates, the practice of problem solving, particularly at the community level, can empower people, build community, and erode hierarchy, depending on the methods that are used. Participatory methods, for example, can ensure that problem-solving paradigms bring empowering outcomes. At the same time, critical thinking enables individuals and communities to identify and confront the structural conditions and constraints that prevent their empowerment. According to the renowned development and education philosopher, Paolo Freire (1972), this is *conscientization.*

CONCLUSION

Appreciative processes, theories, and practices, and in some cases Appreciative Inquiry methods, are well suited to the investigation and transformation of complex problems within challenged peacebuilding and development contexts. The caveats, however, are important. Genuine and thorough consideration must be given to the context within which the method is being applied. In some cases or at certain times, AI may not be appropriate on its own, for example, where severe trauma has been experienced and needs to be recognized and the grief needs to be owned and processed. Alternatively, where people face overlapping, complex sets of problems, they can critically and creatively employ appreciative processes to seek to create new conditions that address the very real challenges they face. This can be done in ways that are empowering to themselves and their communities, and in ways that simultaneously confront and transform the violent structures that oppress them. As illustrated above, contextual adaptation of Appreciative Inquiry may come through a form where problem-solving and empowerment approaches are viewed as mutually beneficial and reinforcing in community and social change.

We also argue that AI's epistemological orientation needs to be reconsidered if it is to be useful to academics and practitioners of different leanings. This is also likely to serve its ability to tackle complex social and structural problems, such as poverty and other manifestations of structural and direct violence. Given that Appreciative Inquiry has been developed and for the most part theorized among those working in the fields of organizational development and international development, this is a natural direction for its theoretical growth and expanded application.

The fields of peacebuilding and development have moved towards context-sensitive, strengths-based, bottom-up, participatory approaches and practices. AI, as a context-sensitive, strength-based, bottom-up, participatory process for planning and implementing social change, manifests the best practices identified by theorists and practitioners of both of these fields. While challenges related to structural and direct violence and structural resistances to change, which often characterize complex peacebuilding and development contexts, will continue to confront AI practitioners and theorists, we believe that Appreciative Inquiry offers inherent resources to address these. As a method designed to empower and transform, Appreciative Inquiry, specifically, and appreciative processes, generally, enable people to discover, dream, and design destinies that will sustain transformative action in their lives and in their communities.

ENDNOTE

1. Sources for this case study on the Africa Community Publishing and Development Trust (ACPDT) are primarily documents from the organization and several interviews with the organization's director. While this might seem limited, author Erin McCandless has also attended various workshops held by ACPDT, spoken with staff and participants of ACPDT programs in various parts of the country, and thus speaks with confidence about their work. Their highly favorable reputation with other civil society organizations in the country, which are in queues to work ACPDT and use its books, is an indication of the integrity and success of their methods and product.

REFERENCES

ACPDT. 2000. *Democratic Governance in Zimbabwe: Citizen Power.* Harare, Zimbabwe: Commonwealth Foundation.

Azar, Edward E. 1986. "Management of Social Conflict in the Third World." A paper presented at the Fourth ICES Annual Lecture, Columbia University, New York, New York.

Bond-Stewart, Kathy. 2002. Interview with Erin McCandless (March 20). Harare, Zimbabwe.

Bond-Stewart, Kathy, with Talent Nyathi, and Lucia Chikuhuhu. 2002. "Community Publishing as a Process of Change." In *Courage and Consequence: Women Publishing in Africa.* Mary Kay and Susan Kelly, eds. Oxford: African Books Collective.

Bushe, Gervase R. n.d. [2002] "Five Theories of Change Embedded in Appreciative Inquiry." Burnaby, B.C., Canada. http://www.bus.sfu.ca/homes/gervase/5theories.html.

Bushe, Gervase R., and Thomas Pitman. 1991. "Appreciative process: A method for transformational change." *Organization Development Practitioner* 23:3, pp. 1–4.

Cooperrider, David L., and Suresh Srivastva. 1987. "Appreciative Inquiry in Organizational Life." In *Research in Organizational Change and Development,* Vol. 1. Richard W. Woodman and William A. Pasmore, eds. Greenwich, Conn.: JAI Press.

Cooperrider, David L. and Diana Whitney. 1999. *Appreciative Inquiry.* San Francisco: Berrett-Koehler.

Cox, Geof. 1998. "Appreciative Inquiry." Edinburgh, Scotland. http://www.newdirections.uk.com/ai.htm.

Freire, Paulo. 1972. *Pedagogy of the Oppressed.* Harmondsworth, U.K.: Penguin Press.

Galtung, Johan. 1996. *Peace by Peaceful Means.* Oslo: Sage.

Jeong, Ho-won. 1999. "Research on Conflict Resolution." In *Conflict Resolution: Dynamics, Process and Structure.* Ho-won Jeong, ed. Aldershot, U.K.: Ashgate Publishing.

———. 2000. *Peace and Conflict Studies: An Introduction.* Aldershot, U.K.: Ashgate Publishing.

Kraybill, Ronald S. 1996. *An Anabaptist Paradigm for Conflict Transformation: Critical Reflections on Peacemaking in Zimbabwe.* Unpublished Ph.D. dissertation, Department of Religious Studies, University of Cape Town, South Africa.

Lederach, John Paul. 1997. *Building Peace: Sustainable Reconciliation in Divided Societies.* Washington, D.C.: United States Institute of Peace Press.

McCandless, Erin. 2001. "The case of land in Zimbabwe: Cause of conflict, foundation for sustained peace." In *Reconciliation, Justice and Peace in Interethnic Conflict.* Mohammed Abu-Nimer, ed. Lanham, Md.: Rowman and Littlefield.

McCandless, Erin, and Mary Hope Schwoebel. 2002. "Peacekeeping, Peacemaking, Peacebuilding." In *World at Risk: A Global Issues Source Book.* Washington, D.C.: Congressional Quarterly Press.

Mitchell, Christopher. 1981. *The Structure of International Conflict.* New York: St. Martin's Press.

United Nations Development Program (UNDP). 1995. *Human Development Report.* New York: Oxford University Press.

Van der Merwe, Hugo. 1999. *The Truth and Reconciliation Commission and Community Reconciliation: An Analysis of Competing Strategies and Conceptualizations.* Unpublished Ph.D. dissertation, Institute for Conflict Analysis and Resolution, George Mason University, Fairfax, Virginia.

PART IV:

CONFLICT RESOLUTION

Change is not threatening, so long as we keep firm hold of the values by and for which we live. We can travel with confidence, so long as we have a map. We can jump with safety knowing there is someone to catch us as we fall. It is when we lose these things that change creates anxiety. It is when we think that, because technology is changing, our values too must change that we create problems we cannot solve, fear we cannot confront.

RABBI JONATHAN SACKS

CHAPTER ELEVEN

INITIATIVES OF CHANGE

Michael Henderson

This chapter documents the distinct and innovative approach to peacemaking adopted by Initiatives of Change (formerly Moral Re-Armament). It does so through describing the post–World War II interaction of a Frenchwoman, Irène Laure, and German participants at Mountain House, which has been for more than fifty years a center for reconciliation in Caux, Switzerland. Hallmarks of the Initiatives of Change approach include an emphasis on personal moral and spiritual change as the starting point for bringing change to relationships and to society as a whole, a stress on the importance of apology and forgiveness, and the use of personal stories of change to convey a challenge to conscience and present a positive model for change.

⚘

In 1946 a group of Swiss, at great personal sacrifice, bought the rundown Caux Palace Hotel overlooking Lake Geneva as a place where the warring nations of World War II could meet. It was the fulfillment of a thought that had come to a Swiss diplomat, Philippe Mottu, three years earlier: If Switzerland were spared by the war, its task would be to make available a place where Europeans, torn apart by hatred, suffering, and resentment, could come together. Mottu and the other Swiss were associated with a worldwide work for reconciliation that was then called Moral Re-Armament (MRA) and is now known as Initiatives of Change (IC).

Renamed Mountain House, this distinctively turreted building, which in 2002 celebrated its centenary, is set in restful grounds with a panoramic view of the peaks of the Dents du Midi and has, since 1946, been host to several hundred thousand people from all over the world, many of whom met across contentious divides—whether it be Turkish Cypriots and Greek Cypriots; Muslims, Christians, and Jews from the Middle East; or Cambodians attempting to move beyond the killing fields.

It is only comparatively recently that the Caux center's role in world peacemaking has been appreciated by scholars, spurred by a study of the contribution of Mountain House to post-war reconciliation between France and Germany. The author, Edward Luttwak, had commissioned a search of some ten thousand monographs and articles in the academic literature on the history of Franco-German reconciliation and found no mention of the role of MRA. There, he says, the matter would have stood for eternity "but for the existence of both unpublished documents and indirect evidence that prove beyond all doubt that Moral Re-Armament played an important role at the very beginning of the French-German reconciliation" (Luttwak 1994, 38).

A more recent book by Scott Appleby highlights the service of Caux in providing a neutral and secure place, where antagonists can meet at a physical and psychological distance from a conflict zone and in an atmosphere of civility and mutual respect, to discuss their differences and what they hold in common. Of the role of Mountain House as a forum for the discussion and exploration of personal, religious, ethnic, and political differences, he writes:

> Transforming attitudes on a person-by-person basis was the goal of such forums, which embodied MRA's conviction that peaceful and productive change in hostile relations between nations or ethnoreligious groups depends on change in the individuals prosecuting the war; that process, in turn, requires individuals representing each side to listen, carefully and at length, to their counterparts. This approach proved productive in settings where other sources of moral authority, hospitality, and disinterested (i.e., nonpartisan) conflict management had been discredited. (Appleby 1999, 225–226)

THE STORY OF IRÈNE LAURE

A look into the MRA/IC archives will help us understand this distinct, innovative, and positive approach to peacemaking touched on by Luttwak and Appleby. This might best be done by taking the example of that Franco-German reconciliation, specifically focusing on the visit to Caux of Madame Irène Laure from France, a visit that took place in 1947, the second year of the existence of Mountain House. Drawing from it some idea of MRA/IC's mode of operation. Joseph Montville singles out the change of attitude of Laure at Caux as "perhaps the signature event in terms of psychological breakthrough in the Franco-German conflict" and "one of the most dramatic examples of the power of a simple appeal of forgiveness" (1991, 161). And Harold Saunders, a former U.S. assistant secretary of state, said at Caux in 1992, "If the changes in the human arena involving the French and German people who came to Caux after 1945, if that human relation had not been changed, there would be no institutions of the European community today, or they would at least have taken longer in coming" (1993, 17). The journey of discovery of comparatively few individuals has led on to a greater vision of cooperation and coexistence among many Europeans.

 That summer of 1947, five thousand people from some fifty countries attended sessions at Caux. They included the Swiss president

and the prime ministers of Denmark and Indonesia, Swedish U.N. emissary
Count Bernadotte, a U.S. congressional committee, twenty-six Italian parliament members, U Tin Tut, the first foreign minister of independent Burma,
and G. L. Nanda, a future Indian prime minister.

When Irène Laure arrived at the conference in September that year, she
would have felt at home in the presence of dozens of Allied service personnel recently demobilized, and been reassured by meeting former resistance
figures like herself. She would have appreciated the "physical and psychological distance from a conflict zone." She was not, however, prepared to
meet Germans, even those who had been anti-Nazi or had suffered because
of Nazism. Germans at that time were not welcome at other international
conferences. She might have been appalled had she known that the first
group of Germans was welcomed to Caux by a French chorus singing in
German. She was certainly not aware that the first words of Frank Buchman,
the initiator of MRA, on arriving for the opening of Caux the summer before
had been, "Where are the Germans? You'll never rebuild Europe without the
Germans" (Lean 1988, 341). And that, spurred by his challenge, high-level
efforts had been made to break through restrictions that prevented Germans
from leaving their country. Already in the first summer, 16 Germans had
come and 150 in 1947, with 4,000 more to come between 1948 and 1951.

This was an early illustration of a basic approach of Initiatives of
Change—that everyone should be welcome at the table. It is still emphasized today, for instance, in IC's work for racial understanding under the
aegis of the U.S.–based Hope in the Cities, or for interreligious unity in India
at another IC conference center, Asia Plateau, in Panchgani. Hope in the
Cities, in language that would have been as appropriate in 1946 as it is
today, calls for honest conversation that "includes everyone and excludes no
one, focuses on working together towards a solution, not on identifying enemies, affirms the best and does not confirm the worst, looks for what is right
rather than who is right, [and] moves beyond blame and personal pain to
constructive action" (Corcoran and Greisdorf 2001, 23).

The Germans came to Caux as equals. The Hamburg *Freie Presse*, in a
report from Caux, commented, "Here, for the first time, the question of the
collective guilt of the past has been replaced by the more decisive question
of collective responsibility for the future. Here in Caux, for the first time,
Germany has been given a platform from which she can speak to the world
as an equal" (cited in Henderson 1996, 24). Buchman biographer Garth
Lean writes, "Buchman insisted that the emphasis at Caux must be upon
Germany's future rather than her past, her potential rather than her guilt.
Whether dealing with an individual or a nation he was only interested in
reviewing past mistakes as a basis for discovering a new way forward. He
simply treated the Germans like everyone else" (1988, 351).

Irène Laure, a nurse from Marseilles, was an internationalist. Between the two world wars she had had German children in her home. But her experience in the resistance when Germany occupied her country and the torturing of her own son had given her a passionate hatred. When Allied bombers flew overhead, Laure rejoiced at the destruction that would be wreaked on Germany. After the war, she witnessed the opening of a mass grave containing the mutilated bodies of some of her comrades. She longed for the total destruction of Germany; she never thought that understanding was possible and never sought it (Henderson 1994, 17–27).

At the end of the war, Laure entered the French Constituent Assembly and became a leader of the three million socialist women of her country. Invited to Caux, she hesitated at first because she knew at some point she would have to come to grips with the question of Germany's future. But she finally accepted, welcoming the chance of a break from the political wrangling in Paris and the opportunity of some good food for her children, malnourished from the privations of the war. The presence of Germans was a shock. Every time a German spoke she left the hall. Although she also noted that the Germans were saying things she had not heard them say before, that they were facing the mistakes of the past and their own nation's need for change, her gut reaction was still, "I will never stay under the same roof as Germans." She packed her bags to leave and then ran into Frank Buchman. "Madame Laure, you're a socialist," he said to her, and, echoing his remarks the year before, "How can you expect to rebuild Europe if you reject the German people?" (Piguet 1985, 9).

Her immediate response was that anyone who made such a suggestion had no idea what she had lived through. Her second response was that perhaps there might be hope of doing something differently. She retired to her room. "I was there two days and nights without sleeping or eating with this terrible battle going on inside me. I had to face the fact that hatred, whatever the reasons for it, is always a factor that creates new wars" (Henderson 1999, 146).

Emerging, Madame Laure was ready to have a meal with a German woman. She hardly touched her food, but poured out all she felt and all she had lived through. And then she said, "I'm telling you all this because I want to be free of this hate." There was a silence and then the German woman, Clarita von Trott, shared with the Frenchwoman her own experiences from the war. Her husband Adam had been one of those at the heart of the July 20, 1944, plot to kill Hitler. It had failed, and her husband had been executed. She was left alone to bring up their two children. She told Laure, "We Germans did not resist enough, we did not resist early enough and on a scale that was big enough, and we brought on you and ourselves and the world endless agony and suffering. I want to say I am sorry" (Channer 1983).

After the meal, the two women and their interpreters sat quietly on the terrace overlooking Lake Geneva. Then Madame Laure, the Christian socialist, told her new German friend that she believed that if they prayed, God would help them. She prayed first asking to be freed of hatred so that a new future could be built. And then Frau von Trott prayed, in French. Instinctively, Madame Laure laid her hand on the knee of her former enemy. "In that moment," she later said, "the bridge across the Rhine was built, and that bridge always held, never broke" (Channer 1983).

Laure asked to be given the opportunity to speak to the conference. Many were aware of her background, but few knew what conclusion she had come to alone in her room or the effect that her conversation with Frau von Trott had had on her attitude. "Everyone was fearful," she remembers. "They knew what I felt about the Germans. They didn't know I had accepted the challenge" (Laure n.d. [1980]. It was a risk for the organizers. They did not believe that the best way to get across new ideas to Germans, who had lived all those years under Nazism, was to put them in the dock. It was not the best of days either for Laure to choose. It was to be a German-speaking session. At the preparation meeting it was suggested than an Austrian minister speak, but he refused: "I was in a concentration camp for four years. I cannot speak with Germans" (Lean 1998, 352). A young German said that if the Germans were guilty, the Austrians were no less so. Buchman, who rarely chaired a session, decided to chair this one.

Laure spoke to the six hundred people in the hall, including the Germans. She told them honestly and, as she says, disastrously, all that she had felt. Then she said, "I have so hated Germany that I wanted to see her erased from the map of Europe. But I have seen here that my hatred is wrong. I am sorry and I wish to ask the forgiveness of all the Germans present" (Lean 1998, 353). Following her words, a German woman stepped up from the hall and took her hand. To Laure it was such a feeling of liberation that it was like a hundred kilo weight, she said, being lifted from her shoulders. "At that moment I knew that I was going to give the rest of my life to take this message of forgiveness and reconciliation to the world" (Henderson 1994, 22).

Rosemarie Haver, whose mother was the German woman who took Laure's hand, said to Laure more than thirty years later, at Caux in 1984, "Your courage in bringing your hatred to God and asking us Germans for forgiveness was a deeply shattering experience. When I saw my mother go up to you, my whole world collapsed about me. I felt deeply ashamed at what Germans had done to you and your family. I slowly began to understand that these Germans who had also brought much suffering on my own family had acted in the name of Germany, which meant in my name also" (Channer 1983).

Peter Petersen, a young German who was later to become a senior member of the Federal German Parliament, also was in the hall that day. As he told the story:

> Ever since the age of seven I had been in a uniform of some sort so, at the end of the war, I had no civilian suit of my own. I arrived in Caux in an old suit of my grandfather's. It was too short in some places and too wide in others. My army coat I had dyed black so it was not too bad. I arrived in Caux with very mixed feelings. I fully expected people to say, "What are these criminals, these Germans doing here?" I was ready with counter accusations to whatever we were accused of. Instead, we were really made welcome. A French chorus sang, in German, a song expressing Germany's true destiny. Every door was open to us. We were completely disarmed. Three days after my arrival I learned of the presence in Caux of Madame Laure. I also learned that she had wanted to leave when she saw us Germans arriving. A violent discussion broke out amongst us. The question of guilt and who was to blame, the question that was so dividing Germany at that time, could no longer be avoided. We all recognized that this Frenchwoman had a right to hate us, but we decided that if she expressed her hatred we would reply with stories of the French occupation in the Black Forest. (Petersen 1947, as cited in Marcel 1960, 24)

When Laure spoke in the meeting, Petersen and his friends sat at the back, ill at ease and asking themselves if it would not be better if they left the hall. After her speech, Petersen said:

> I was dumbfounded. For several nights it was impossible for me to sleep. All my past rose up in revolt against the courage of this woman. I suddenly realized that there were things for which we, as individuals and as nations, could never make restitution. Yet we knew, my friends and I, that she had shown us the only way open if Germany was to play a part in the reconstruction of Europe. The basis of a new Europe would have to be forgiveness, as Madame Laure had shown us. One day we told her how sorry we were and how ashamed we were for all the things she and her people had had to suffer through our fault, and we promised her that we would now devote our lives to work that such things would never happen again anywhere. (Petersen 1947, as cited in Marcel 1960, 24)

Irène Laure could, with every justification, have blamed the Germans. She did not do so. In fact, she said many years later, "From the moment I decided to talk to them as friends instead of blaming them, the only thing I wanted to do was to apologize for my own hate" (1971). And as in myriad other examples over the years, this generous attitude on her part provoked a soul-searching in those to whom her words were addressed, whether they were Germans or other nationalities. Assessing the broader implications of Laure's experience, Bryan Hamlin writes, "One person apologizing to another is nothing new. Most people learn empirically that such exchanges are necessary for the maintenance of successful interpersonal relationships. And all religion teaches contrition. The further step is to take this same approach to the group and national level. To achieve that, strategies for such encounters between representatives of different countries or ethnic groups are consciously developed" (1992, 12).

THE CAUX EXPERIENCE

In her three weeks at Caux, Laure was exposed to many other aspects of the center's approach, which deepened her understanding, and she had the chance also to express her own convictions, speaking six times. Caux has the advantage, not always present in the work of Initiatives of Change in the field, of tending to draw people who are at least already predisposed to finding a new way of resolving conflict, even if they may not realize that some change may be needed in themselves.

Other elements that contribute to the center's effectiveness, along with the restful setting, are the nature of the meetings and workshops, the chance for leisurely talks at mealtimes, and the use of theatre and the arts to present universal truths. Undergirding it all is a gracious sense of hospitality, which expresses the esteem in which IC holds every person. Hospitality at Caux is expressed in the fact that Swiss families gave of their best to furnish the place, and by the teams of volunteers taking infinite care in the preparing of rooms, with fresh flowers there and in the public rooms, and meals that take into account the cultural sensitivities of different peoples.

In plenary sessions formal presentations are kept to a minimum, and the emphasis is on participants sharing their experiences briefly. In more recent times, it has become the custom to divide the conference into "communities," smaller groups where people can get to know one another better and explore conference themes. In sessions and conversations, Laure would have heard others tell personal stories of change, stories that were intended to inspire and motivate change in others, without preaching or advising, just as her own story has reverberated over the decades to far corners of the world.

As with Laure and the Germans, when adversaries meet at Caux, the IC approach may open the way to a change in relationship. Rabbi Marc Gopin observes, "Hearing the public testimony of parties to a conflict at Moral Re-Armament's retreat center is critical to its conflict resolution process. Empathy is evoked by the painful story of the other party, and, in this religious setting, both parties refer to God's role in their lives. This, in turn, generates a common bond between enemies that has often led, with subtle, careful guidance, to more honest discussion and relationship building" (2000, 20).

Unhurried meals are an integral feature in the IC approach at Caux, for meals are the prime venue for encounters. Meals are a means of "putting people in the way of others"— bringing individuals who are grappling with life's tough dilemmas together with others who have met similar challenges honorably—whether through careful planning by IC workers or by the chance "decisive encounter," as Marcel (1960, 17) called these interactions at Caux. Anthropologists tell us it is psychologically difficult to continue to hate someone with whom you have broken bread. As in the case of Madame Laure and Frau von Trott, many a mealtime at Caux has brought enemies to a place of new understanding and possibility.

Laure's own experience of a change of heart had been a soul-shaking one for her. Now she was to begin to believe that it could happen to others, even to employers. Another aspect of Caux would have been that she probably discovered early on that some of the persons serving her at table were from the class that she hated. It was through getting to know employers, particularly French ones with a new motive, that she was helped to move beyond her class-war attitudes. In fact, she had first thought Caux was "a capitalist trap." But by the end of her time at Caux, she was working with employers to plan an industrial conference in the north of France. The encounters he observed in Caux convinced the French Catholic philosopher, Gabriel Marcel, that he was seeing a new world conscience evolving: "What strikes me before all else is that you find there the global and the intimate linked together in a surprising way. For the first time in my experience, I sensed a true global awareness in the process of being formed. It is shaped through encounters" (1960, 17).

Some encounters will have been in the serving teams, which are a central feature of life at Mountain House. All guests are encouraged to take a share in the running of the house. Gopin notes: "The Caux center is organized by work teams, with the specific intention of creating relationships through shared work. This is cost effective, equalizing of relationships, and a powerful non-dialogic way of developing relationships" (2002, 253). He refers to the bonding that occurred between him and some Arab students at Caux in 1991, when they found themselves working together on a service team, having to cooperate to solve practical questions quite separate from the Middle East and being dependent on each other (173–174). At one point in its first years this aspect of life at Mountain House had a downside: A photograph appeared in the Italian press showing members of parliament washing dishes, and this put off some other members from attending! Laure's husband Victor, a merchant seaman, soon became a regular baker of bread in the Caux kitchen.

One of the first acts after the purchase of the Caux Palace Hotel had been to turn the hotel ballroom into a theatre. For, as Marcel observed, "Buchman and his associates have made a real discovery.

They have realized that people nowadays are far more profoundly influenced by seeing something acted than you could expect them to be by hearing a sermon" (1960, 13–14). Laure saw plays in the theatre, which sometimes presented vision, sometimes historical or biographical stories. One was *The Good Road,* a musical with humorous sketches of contemporary life and a moving pageant of history that proclaimed dramatically the basic ideas of freedom and the necessary conditions of a sound society. She saw *The Forgotten Factor,* an industrial drama that contained that basic principle of Initiatives of Change—it is not who is right but what is right that matters—and she recognized in the unfolding clashes between employers and workers something of her own experiences in Marseilles. Later she was to have that play staged in France, in French.

Also shown that summer was *And Still They Fight,* a dramatization of the life of a great Norwegian patriot, Freddie Ramm, who had helped his country be reconciled with Denmark and who died as he was being repatriated from a German concentration camp. With the horrors of the Holocaust shocking the world, Germans were very much on the defensive. After Reinhold Maier, minister-president of the state of Wuerttemberg-Baden, saw *And Still They Fight,* he slipped away from the theatre and threw himself on his bed "completely shattered" with shame at what his country had done. "It was a presentation without hatred or complaint and therefore could hardly have been more powerful in its effect," he later wrote (Maier 1964, 383).

PERSONAL STORY AS POSITIVE IMAGE FOR CHANGE

Laure had to return home from Caux for an election campaign. In a speech before leaving, indicating how far she had come in her thinking, she said, "I ask you to understand the suffering and needs of the working people, as I shall ask myself in campaign speeches to remember that employers are not always wrong either." To the Germans she promised that she would fight for reconciliation between France and Germany. "Here at Caux," she said, "my heart has been liberated from bitterness against Germany. I shall use my position in politics to see that France and other countries do not have any desire that Germany should starve. France, too, has been an occupied country just as Germany is today. We have all been wrong. Now we must build a bridge of caring across the Rhine" (MRA 1947).

Responding to Laure's words, Madleen Pechel of Berlin, who had been with her husband in a Nazi concentration camp, said, "I shall take Madame Laure's words to the women of Germany. Many times tears of joy have come to me at Caux. I do not think from 1934 to 1947 I have ever laughed with such a full and open heart as in the last eighteen days, here among people who would have every right to hate us Germans" (MRA 1947).

In 1948, Laure and her husband Victor traveled to Germany. For eleven weeks they crisscrossed the country, addressing two hundred meetings, including ten of the eleven state parliaments. With them went some of their compatriots who had lost families in the gas chambers, as well as men and women from other countries who only a short time before had been fighting against the Germans. Everywhere she repeated her apology. Laure reported that after hearing her speak, "Generals and other officers, politicians, and young former Nazis apologized to me" (Henderson 1996, 29). Of the travel of Laure and others to Germany at that time, Robin Mowat writes, "Such actions played their part in preparing the ground for the political decisions which made it possible for the statesmen to carry through on another level the work of reconciliation, and open a new way towards the future of Western Europe" (1991, 197).

In her lifetime Laure traveled thousands of miles to share her experience of the answer to hatred, sometimes alone, sometimes with her husband, often with small or large teams of people. This aspect of teams traveling together has continued to be a favored IC way of conveying to audiences the power and diversity of an answer, whether it is in recent years with senior Africans from the Horn of Africa visiting European capitals, or with a mixed faith team of Christians, Jews, and Muslims visiting Israel and Palestine, or with young people in "Action for Life" visiting South Asian nations.

In the decades that followed Laure's visit to Caux, the work of reconciliation on the basis of the principles outlined above continued. Appleby writes:

> MRA played important supporting roles in resolving dozens of conflicts in the decades that followed that impressive debut. Its loose organizational structure as a network of spartanly motivated professionals—"citizen diplomats"—based in Switzerland with small national branches operated by a few full-time staff and supported by local funds, was appropriate to its ethos of fostering personal relationships across battle lines. (1999, 225–226)

Caux became the hub of its peacebuilding work under the rubric Agenda for Reconciliation and through its NGO (nongovernmental organization) office at the United Nations in New York.

Around the world even today, fifteen years after Laure's death, there are men and women, active peacemakers, who owe their commitment to or were vitally influenced towards it by the life of Irène Laure, either by meeting her in person, by reading her biography (Piguet 1985), or seeing the film about her, *For the Love of Tomorrow* (Channer 1983). One is Renee Pan, now a Buddhist nun, whose husband, the deputy prime minister of Cambodia, was murdered by the Khmer Rouge when they took over her country in

 1975. She escaped to the United States where she struggled to become economically independent. But over time she felt that her mind had

been consumed by what her Buddhist religion calls the "three fires of the world"—greed, anger, and foolishness. At a low point when she felt her heart was numb and her brain empty, she had a talk with Laure that gave her the key to overcoming her hatred of the Khmer Rouge: the taking time for *le silence* (Henderson 1999, 29–41).

Central to the experience of Caux and to the continuing work of Initiatives of Change is that of taking time in quiet, recommended to Pan by Laure. This is not a religious doctrine so much as a practical experience. Each person interprets it differently. Laure, who wrote down her thoughts in a notebook, saw this practice in a broad dimension (Channer 1983). She called the quiet time the strongest weapon of all. "Instead of dropping bombs or firing guns, be quiet and listen. For some it is the voice of God, for others the voice of conscience; but every one of us, man or woman, has the chance to take part in a new world, if we know how to listen in quiet to what is in our hearts" (Piguet 1985, 50).

Laure also stressed to Pan the importance of forgiveness. Her message on this was clear: "What I learned at Caux was how to forgive. That is a huge thing, because one can die of hatred. If I had continued as I was, I should have spread hatred right through my family. My children would have started off hating the Germans, then the bosses, and who would have been next?" (Channer 1983). Pan's meeting with Laure led her to treat the Khmer Rouge differently. "It was very hard for me to forgive the Khmer Rouge for what they did to me, my family, and my friends," she says, "and especially to my beloved country. But the burden of revenge that I carried for a decade was lightened from the moment that I did so" (Henderson 1994, 33).

Another person influenced by Laure's life was Eliezer Cifuentes of Guatemala, who is lucky to be alive. One night in 1980, four carloads of attackers ambushed his car and shot him. With a bullet in his arm and crouching low in his car, using the outlines of houses to steer by, he managed to evade his pursuers, then jettisoned his car, and ran and found shelter in a shop for five hours. At midnight, borrowing the shopkeeper's car and disguised as a woman, he drove back to Guatemala City where he found asylum in the Costa Rican embassy. After four months of negotiations he was allowed to fly to San José, Costa Rica (Henderson 1999, 143–144).

In exile, Cifuentes' hatred of his would-be killers grew. He could not bear to see a policeman; he had terrible headaches. Then one day after seeing the film about Irène Laure, he had an experience that transformed his life. He recognized "the tigers of hatred" in his heart for the military and for the United States, which he felt was backing them. He realized that he had not practiced the love that he had repeatedly preached. "I found a renewal inside that began to change my feelings of hatred and my desire for vengeance. . . . Giving up hatred is a wonderful, personal experience, but my danger was to leave it at that" (Henderson 1999, 143–144).

Cifuentes decided to go and see a former Guatemalan intelligence officer, who he thought responsible for drawing up the lists of intended kidnap victims. Eventually, as they had further meetings, Cifuentes was able to be honest about his hatred of the military. This led to changes of attitude on the part of both men and to a meeting outside the country with senior army officers, who expressed their readiness to work with him for national reconciliation. After a struggle, his wife Clemencia and their children also decided to forgive. Of the experience of seeing *For the Love of Tomorrow,* Cifuentes says, "What the Germans were for this Frenchwoman in the film, the military were for me. God has laid on my heart a task—the reconciliation of the military and the civilian population of my country" (Henderson 1999, 145).

A third person influenced by Irène Laure's story was Abeba Tesfagiorgis, an author from Eritrea, who was suspected by the Ethiopian occupiers of her country of being in the underground resistance. She was imprisoned and at one point faced a firing squad as a ruse to extract information, but was spared. In prison Tesfagiorgis came face to face with the man who had betrayed her. She forgave him. She then tried to help the other prisoners see that it would be a disservice to their fallen comrades if they did not forgive their enemies. "We all pray together for our release and peace," she told them, "but God will not answer our prayers if we keep on nursing resentment and hatred for one another" (Henderson 1999, 43–53).

After her country's independence, Tesfagiorgis set up a center for human rights and development. Speaking to a symposium on regional cooperation, Tesfagiorgis said, "Let us get rid of our enemies not by imprisoning or killing them, as many African regimes are known to do, not by belittling them or humiliating them, but by resolving the conflict." It was the Frenchwoman's story that Tesfagiorgis told the other prisoners in her cell: "Just as Irène Laure could not hope to see a united and peaceful Europe without Germany, we could not say we love our country and then refuse to understand and forgive our fellow Eritreans" (Henderson 1999, 51–53).

We take for granted that hatred can be passed down from generation to generation. The experience of Laure suggests that love, too, in all its supposed softness, can have that same permanence. People who never met her have been moved by her example and taken her experience forward in unexpected ways. Peace dividends continue to come in long after she has passed from the scene. The idea that one day her actions would inspire not only these three people but thousands more around the world would have been far from Laure's mind during those nights in 1947, when alone in her room she wrestled with the question of whether she would give up her hatred for the sake of a new Europe. Her life is but one example of IC's strong conviction that the ordinary person can be used by God to do extraordinary things.

 More than fifty years later, Mountain House continues to operate on the same principles as it did in those first years. An honest facing up to the past still today evokes a dramatic response. One example comes from Lebanon.

In February 2000, just ten years after a civil war in which seventy thousand Lebanese died and seventeen thousand are still unaccounted for, a remarkable letter appeared in Beirut's dailies (Sennott 2000). It was an apology by Assaad Chaftari, a high-ranking officer in the Christian militia, for what he had done in the name of Christianity. For ten years he had wanted to make this apology. "We were all responsible," he said, "those holding the guns, those giving the orders, even the civilians applauding it." Charles Sennott, writing in the *Boston Globe*, said that Chaftari had "stunned Lebanon with a statement extraordinary in its simplicity and honesty" (2000).

Some months later at a conference in Caux, Chaftari repeated his apology before an international audience. He outlined his previous beliefs to the conference. Chaftari had regarded Muslims as a danger. They were brothers, yes, but of a lesser God. Because they looked toward the Arab world and he toward the West, Muslims were traitors for him. In the war he shelled Muslim areas or passed sentence on adversaries who had relations with Muslims, with what he thought then to be a clean conscience. "After a week of mischief I could go to church on Sunday at ease with myself and with God" (MRA 2000a; MRA 2000b).

Toward the end of the war, however, Chaftari had met some Lebanese who were associated with Caux and Moral Re-Armament and who were providing a forum for dialogue between Christians and Muslims. Here, again, there was a link with Laure, for one of the things that played its part, "perhaps subconsciously," he says, was the film about her life (Chaftari 2002). In these occasions for dialogue he heard about the dreams, the hopes, the grievances of the other Lebanese people. In March 2000, he had prayed in a mosque. As Chaftari told the Caux audience, "For the first time it felt like we were praying to the same God." He concluded, "I am ashamed of my past. I know I cannot change it. But I also know that I can be responsible for the future of my country" (MRA 2000a).

As the audience in Mountain House rose in a standing ovation, another Lebanese man, Hisham Shihab, came up to the platform and embraced Chaftari, shouting out, "I am a Muslim who was shooting at his countrymen from the other side of the 'green line'. I also apologize and accept his apology and will help him in any way I can." Shihab said that he had been trained as a young man to shoot straight with the admonition, "Imagine there is a Christian in your sights." He had shelled Christian areas and sniped at Christians. But his conscience had told him that all political causes were not worth the bloodshed. "I pledge to walk hand in hand with Chaftari," Shihab promised (MRA 2000b).

The next year, in 2001, on the same platform, Muhieddine Shihab, an elected official from Beirut, apologized for atrocities he had committed as a leader of a Muslim militia in the civil war. "Nothing in the world is more dangerous than a man who fears for his life and property," he said. "Self defense can quickly turn into vengeance and the wrongful taking of life. What motivated me and people like me to take up arms was absolutely evil." He was followed to the platform by Jocelyn Khoueiry, who had led a corps of Christian "girl soldiers" on the other side of the barricades from Muhieddine Shihab. Khoueiry, too, had found her attitude to the enemy shifting (Lean 2001, 5).

In 2002, Lebanese from different sides and different faiths, including Chaftari and the two Shihabs, came to Europe to speak together of their experiences of finding healing and unity. These former enemies had become friends, with an impressive depth of honesty and trust built between them. Wherever they spoke they gave moving accounts of their involvement in atrocities, not just against the other community, but also between rival groups of the same faith. For each one there had been a defining moment when they came to the realization that violence was not the way forward. At risk to themselves, they each had reached out to meet someone from the other side, discovering "they were a human just like me." Chaftari is still worried about his country's future, but welcomes these signs of hope. "Asking for forgiveness is difficult," he says, "and forgiving seems impossible, but is essential for the reconstruction of a country" (MRA 2002a).

IC'S PRINCIPLES FOR POSITIVE CHANGE

What, in essence, does Irène Laure's change and commitment and that of the others who followed tell us of the methodology of MRA/IC? Some who work with it would even deny there is a methodology. They would caution against reducing to a formula what is often spontaneous and driven by care for people. Certainly there is a serendipity about some activities, even coincidences or encounters that IC adherents might put down to God at work. They would definitely suggest that an openness to unexpected ways is vital. "One of their great strengths," writes Gopin, "has been the model of informal networking and relationship building, which has important theological roots for them, for it is in the 'surprises' of human connections and chance meetings that they see the Divine Hand guiding human beings toward reconciliation with others and with God" (2002, 161). Nonetheless, certain principles do stand out and are there whenever you meet IC's committed people and try to learn what it is they do.

It is no surprise that the word *change* should be enshrined in the organization's new name, *Initiatives of Change*. MRA often speaks of the "full dimension of change." As early as 1921, Buchman defined his aim as

"a program of life issuing in personal, social, racial, national, and superna-
tional change." In 1932 he stressed, "Lives must be changed if problems are
to be solved. Peace in the world can only spring from peace in the hearts of
men. A dynamic experience of God's free spirit is the answer to regional
antagonism, economic depression, racial conflict, and international strife"
(1961, 3).

Archie Mackenzie, a British diplomat who has been long associated with
Initiatives of Change and with Caux, writes in his recently published mem-
oirs that when at international conferences, he often reflected that the problems on the table were not so difficult as the problems sitting around the
table, and yet no one was doing anything about the latter. A feature of his
contribution to diplomacy was that he did try to do something about them,
and in some cases succeeded (2002, 54).

From the outset the heart of MRA's philosophy has been that if you want
to bring a change in the world, the most practical way is to start with change
in yourself and your country. Laure often made the point in later years that
if you have less to put right than the other person, then isn't it easier for you
to start first? The emphasis on starting with yourself and your own group
can help break the endless cycles of blame and retribution. It is certainly
extraordinary that at the Caux conference just two years after the end of
World War II, blaming of the Germans and Japanese happened only when
someone was overcome by their wartime experiences. Instead, British ex-ser-
vicemen, for example, went out of their way to express their regret for the
way Germany was treated by the Allied governments after World War I.
Buchman's question to Laure about rebuilding Europe reflected an element
of vision for the Germans, despite all that had happened.

Initiatives of Change puts forward the practice of taking a time of quiet,
alone or in community—*le silence* of which Laure spoke to Pan—helping
each individual find for himself or herself the right course of action. As aids
to identifying the next steps forward, and as standards for private and public
life, IC recommends universal benchmarks of honesty, purity, unselfishness,
and love. Laure said of these standards, "It is this that gives strength to the
quiet time. Otherwise one comes out of a time of meditation with a vague
feeling of personal uplift, but without having faced the reality of life. It is
through these times of silence and in obeying what was deepest in myself
that I have been able to accomplish things that were humanly speaking, for
me, impossibilities" (Marcel 1960, 26).

Gopin, who has studied the subject thoroughly, writes that MRA's methods of peacebuilding and relationship building involve

> a profoundly persistent pattern of relationship building with key individuals
> on either side of a conflict, and the use of spiritual awakening to
> provoke self-examination and transformation of one's relationships.

It also involves support for and evocation of a spirit of personal responsibility that recognizes primarily one's own part in the failure of one's relationships. Further, awakening to the "spirit of God" within you as well as
between you and others is critical, in addition to a very strong focus on personal morality. Indeed for many associated with this society, personal morality and the morality of one's culture are at the heart of their message and
teaching, with peacemaking taking a secondary role. (2002, 110)

Wanting the best for the other person does, indeed, take precedence
over the results, whether political, social, or economic. In other words peace
is a fruit of change in people. A vision is held before people of the wider part
they can play in their countries and what could be different as a result.
Those surrounding Madame Laure, for instance, wanted to build on her
desire to see a new Europe and her compassion where there was suffering.
It was not for them to tell her that hatred was wrong or to suggest that she
should apologize to the Germans. No one had any idea of the dramatic form
her change would take. It was Laure's spiritual growth that would have been
the priority for those who lived alongside her, helping her to be ready to
accept the next step God had for her, whatever that might be. Of her
encounter with Buchman in the hallway as she was preparing to leave Caux,
Laure said: "If at that moment he had pitied me or sympathized with me, I
would have left. He gave me a challenge in love. It was the quality in him
that arrested me. One felt his life corresponded exactly to his belief. He
transmitted the feeling of certainty to you, that if you accepted change, you
could have a part in the transformation of the world" (Lean 1982, 353).

Montville sees the experience of Madame Laure as a model for relieving
a sense of victimhood and the violence associated with it, which usually
defies traditional diplomatic attempts at a solution. Although it is rare for
national leaders to admit past national misdeeds, he believes that individual
representatives like Laure can assume such responsibility. By their acts of
forgiveness or contrition, they then become spokespersons for a new way of
thinking and a new image for their respective nations (1991, 161).

Laure's readiness to apologize not only for her own hatred of the
Germans, but also to admit to failings by France in North Africa and
Southeast Asia, was a key to helping nationals from those parts of the world
break free from their bitterness about the past. Such readiness has been
encouraged at all levels by MRA over the years, in the belief that an individual prepared honestly to acknowledge his or her own country's failings may
defuse the antagonism felt by a person from another country, whose heart
has been closed to any form of dialogue. As we have seen with the Laure
example and also the Lebanese, Caux conferences have often witnessed such
unofficial apologies. They are said to have had significant influence in
issues as varied as Tunisia achieving independence without bloodshed

and the resolution of the conflict between German- and Italian-speaking people in South Tyrol (see Henderson 1996, 37–43; 148–160).

The role of MRA has traditionally been an enabling one. A French Member of Parliament Georges Mesmin says that political figures who come to Caux find three things:

- *A respect for all opinions.* "Despite certain remarks which could be hurtful, people have not become angry. We have listened to everyone, and we have all benefited."

- *An openness to others and to forgiveness, even when one thinks another is wrong.* "We politicians are inclined to battle at the level of personalities. One thing we slowly learn at Caux is to distinguish between the battle of ideas and the battle with a person who is an adversary now but who tomorrow could become a friend."

- *An atmosphere of friendship.* "In this building you make friends who want nothing from you. Here we have a vision of a world of goodwill, a world where one cares for the real interests of others and not one's own. It is a well of living unselfishness" (cited in Henderson 1996, 15).

Hamlin puts it this way:

It should also be emphasized that after these intense animosities are removed or alleviated, all the political and economic differences remain to be negotiated. MRA has seen its role as enabling those who finally have to sit down to negotiate a settlement, to be better able to negotiate or even be willing to negotiate. It is therefore a precursor work to the formal diplomacy, rarely involving negotiation itself, but rather working privately behind the scenes at the different ends of a dispute, to prepare or enable the parties for negotiation. (1992, 14)

Richard Ruffin, executive director of Initiatives of Change in the United States, believes the challenge before positive peacemakers is to build long-term relationships of trust with people on all sides of a conflict. He adds: "For the first time in modern history, those shaping policies in the major nations recognize that traditional concepts of international relations no longer explain the interdependent world in which we live. Nor do traditional instruments of policy reliably produce the expected results. This . . . led to a recognition that current reality requires an approach to the resolution of conflict that involves the healing of wounds and the building of new relationships across a broad spectrum. This recognition, in turn, brought an understanding of a moral and spiritual dimension to statecraft, a dimension that should prompt the foreign policy community to draw on the resources and experience of spiritually motivated individuals and groups in quest for solutions" (1993, 10).

REFERENCES

Appleby, Scott. 1999. *The Ambivalence of the Sacred*. Lanham, Md.: Rowan and Littlefield.

Buchman, Frank N. D. 1961. *Remaking the World* (collected speeches). London: Blandford Press.

Chaftari, Assaad. 2002. Email message to the author (April 13).

Corcoran, Robert L., and Karen Elliott Greisdorf, eds. 2001. *Connecting Communities*. Richmond, Va.: Initiatives of Change.

Channer, David (producer and director). 1983. *For the Love of Tomorrow*. London: MRA Productions.

Gopin, Marc. 2000. *Between Eden and Armageddon: The Future of World Religions, Violence, and Peacemaking*. New York: Oxford University Press.

———. 2002. *Holy War, Holy Peace: How Religion Can Bring Peace to the Middle East*. New York: Oxford University Press.

Hamlin, Bryan. 1992. *Forgiveness in International Affairs*. London: Grosvenor Books.

Henderson, Michael. 1994. *All Her Paths are Peace: Women Pioneers in Peacemaking*. West Hartford, Conn.: Kumarian Press.

———. 1996. *The Forgiveness Factor*. London: Grosvenor Books.

———. 1999. *Forgiveness: Breaking the Chain of Hate*. Portland, Ore.: Arnica Publishing.

Laure, Irène. 1971. *Cross Road*. Juliet Boobbyer, Ailsa Hamilton, and Ronald Mann, playwrights. London: Westminster Productions.

———. n.d. [1980]. Conversation with the author. Portland, Ore.

Lean, Garth. 1988. *On the Tail of a Comet*. Colorado Springs, Colo.: Helmers and Howard.

Lean, Mary. 2001. "The house of love has many rooms." *For a Change* 14:5, pp. 4–7.

Luttwak, Edward. 1994. "Franco-German Reconciliation: The Overlooked Role of the Moral Re-Armament Movement." In *Religion, The Missing Dimension of Statecraft*. Douglas Johnston and Cynthia Sampson, eds. New York: Oxford University Press.

Mackenzie, Archie. 2002. *Faith in Diplomacy*. London: Grosvenor Books.

Maier, Reinhold. 1964. *Ein Grundstein wird gelegt 1945–47*. Tuebingen, Germany.

Marcel, Gabriel, ed. 1960. *Fresh Hope for the World*. London: Longmans.

Montville, Joseph. 1991. "The Arrow and the Olive Branch: A Case for Track Two Diplomacy." In *The Psychodynamics of International Relationships*, Vol. 2. Vamik Volkan, Joseph Montville, and Demetrios Julius, eds. Lexington, Mass.: Lexington Books.

Moral Re-Armament (MRA). 1947. Caux press release (September 23). MRA archives, Caux, Switzerland.

———. 2000a. "Former Lebanese militiaman now works for reconciliation." Caux press release (August 14). MRA archives, Caux, Switzerland.

———. 2000b. "Former militiaman pledges to work for reconciliation in Lebanon." Caux press release (August 15). MRA archives, Caux, Switzerland.

Mowat, R. C. 1991. *Decline and Renewal.* Oxford: New Cherwell Press.

Petersen, Peter. 1947. Transcript. MRA archives. Tarporley, United Kingdom.

Piguet, Jacqueline. 1985. *For the Love of Tomorrow.* London: Grosvenor Books.

Ruffin, Richard W. B. 1993. "Breakthroughs in Peacemaking." Transcript of speech given at Hubert Humphrey Institute, University of Minnesota, Minneapolis (December 8).

Saunders, Harold. 1993. "The Missing Dimension of Statecraft: Six scholars from CSIS report on their findings." Transcript from presentations given at Mountain House, August 1992. London: Grosvenor Books.

Sennott, Charles. 2000. "Apology of Lebanese figure breaks silence on civil war." *Boston Globe* (February 28).

If you are wise therefore you will show yourself a reservoir and not a channel. For a channel pours out as fast as it takes in; but a reservoir waits till it is full before it overflows, and so communicates its surplus.... We have all too few such reservoirs in the Church at present, through we have channels in plenty ... they (channels) desire to pour out when they themselves are not yet in-poured; they are readier to speak than to listen, eager to teach that which they do not know, and most anxious to exercise authority on others, although they have not learnt to rule themselves.... Be filled thyself then, but discreetly, mind, pour out thy fullness.... Out of thy fullness help me if thou canst; and, if not, spare thyself.

BERNARD OF CLAIRVAUX

CHAPTER TWELVE

ENGAGE CONFLICT WELL
TRANSFORMING CONFLICT IN THE
UNITED METHODIST CHURCH

Thomas W. Porter and Mark Conrad Mancao

The JUSTPEACE Center for Mediation and Conflict Transformation believes that creating justpeace through conflict transformation involves preparing the self and engaging others in processes that move in positive directions. "Engage Conflict Well" is an emerging model in The United Methodist Church, which explores these interrelated phases of conflict transformation. This chapter presents a summary of each element in the model and then offers more in-depth discussion of the three aspects that are most germane to this book—circle process, relational covenants, and appreciative questioning.

❧

he results of the 1998 National Congregations Study suggest that 26 percent of churches are highly conflicted (Chaves et al. 1999). Other studies project that one in every fifty churches is sued each year, amounting to a tremendous drain on financial and human resources and contributing to attrition in the membership rolls. A report prepared by the General Council on Ministries of The United Methodist Church (UMC) presents data on conflict in UMC churches collected by the Faith Communities Today project in October 2000. Approximately half of the 601 United Methodist churches surveyed had experienced some kind of conflict over money, mission, worship, or the pastor's leadership style during the five years prior to the study (This and Smith 2001). Envisioned as centers of peace and justice in their communities, churches today are experienced by many as places of controversy and destructive conflict. Headlines broadcast news of the latest scandals and stories of conflict and harm in churches that were either ignored or mishandled.

The JUSTPEACE Center for Mediation and Conflict Transformation, an organization of The United Methodist Church, was established in 2000, with the mission "to prepare and assist United Methodists to engage conflict constructively in ways that strive for justice, reconciliation, resource preservation, and restoration of community in the Church and in the world."

Recognizing that religion can be both a source of conflict and a resource for peace, the JUSTPEACE Center is practicing peacebuilding by focusing primarily on the positive resources for peace that exist within our Christian experience, tradition, scripture, and theology. This means looking to a theology of abundance and inclusion, as opposed to a theology of scarcity and exclusion. In developing our approach to peacebuilding, JUSTPEACE has also learned from positive resources beyond our own tradition, drawing mainly from the conflict transformation and restorative justice fields, as well as Appreciative Inquiry, which was developed in the organizational development field (Cooperrider and Whitney 1999).

The JUSTPEACE Center is integrating these various resources into a guide for conflict transformation in the Methodist Church, *Engage Conflict Well: A Guide to Prepare Yourself and Engage Others in Conflict Transformation* (2002). In this chapter we present an overview of the entire model, in summary form, and then discuss in greater detail three elements of the model: circle process, relational covenants, and appreciative process. We know that other faith traditions have similar resources from which to draw and hope that in putting forward this model, they too may be encouraged to introduce into the literature their own distinctive approaches, to enrich the learning and practice of us all. The model begins with individual preparation for engaging in conflict transformation and then proceeds to engagement of others.

PREPARE YOURSELF FOR CONFLICT TRANSFORMATION

Our societies devote vast resources and pursue disciplined training in preparing for war. What if we were as committed and disciplined in preparing ourselves to engage one another constructively? Preparation is a critical element in our ability to be peacebuilders. More than technique, this is about preparing our being, opening our hearts, and stretching to reach that place in those with whom we are in conflict that allows real communication to happen. The JUSTPEACE model for conflict transformation includes four elements of preparation.

Create a Well, Not a Wall

CREATE IN YOURSELF AN OPENNESS TO CONFLICT AS PART OF GOD'S CREATION, AS AN OPPORTUNITY FOR GROWTH AND REVELATION. Conflict is the result of differences that produce tension. It is our attitudes to conflict that determine whether our response is constructive or destructive. The usual attitude, that conflict is negative and destructive, generates defensiveness, fear, and anxiety, causing us to erect walls that we fight to maintain or hide behind. But we can choose to create a well, rather than a wall. We do this by seeing conflict as a natural and necessary part of a creation that is relational and diverse; as essential to overcoming injustice, oppression, and evil; and as a source of energy for doing so. Conflict can be a time of discovery and a catalyst for growth, learning, and positive change in ourselves, our relationships, and our society. To transform conflict in a positive way, we must be prepared with a constructive attitude, working to break the cycles of reactivity and violence and eventually to heal. Creating a well in the midst of conflict is a challenge that involves risk, hard work, and time.

Allow the Well to Fill

OPEN YOUR HEART AND MIND TO GOD'S LOVE, REDUCING YOUR ANXIETY AND DRAWING YOU TOWARD RECONCILIATION AND BEING A RECONCILER. It is fundamental to Christianity and many other faiths that God is love, and that all of creation is related in God, interconnected and interdependent. Walter Brueggemann notes the movement in the Bible from holiness as separation (God's chosen people as holy, set apart) to holiness as relational engagement (the capacity to be with and be for others in ways that heal). Such holiness means living out of God's abundant love, not living out of scarcity or anxiety. It means experiencing the generative power of forgiveness. Through relational engagement, everything can become new (Brueggemann 2000, 54).

Be Well Prepared

BE PREPARED TO LISTEN FOR UNDERSTANDING, SPEAK THE TRUTH IN LOVE, USE YOUR IMAGINATION, AND BE FORGIVING. Holiness as relational engagement requires skills. Listening speaks to one of our deepest needs—to be understood—and it creates the possibility of learning and being changed. The heart of good listening is authenticity, genuine curiosity, and caring. Speaking the truth in love means focusing on giving specific information about our needs, emotions, and the impact of the situation on us; not on blaming, mind-reading, or demanding. Using our imagination releases creativity and opens our minds and hearts to the leading of the spirit, which can carry us to ideas and places we never dreamed possible. Imagining involves letting go of our assumptions and positions, even if only temporarily, and letting go of our desire to control the outcome or the solution. Being forgiving involves freely choosing to release one who has harmed us from the bondage of guilt, giving up feelings of ill will, and surrendering any attempt at revenge, thus clearing the way for reconciliation and restoration of relationship (Marshall 2001).

In our experiences of training workshops and interventions, an individual's capacity in these basic areas has a tremendous impact on the direction of the conflict, even when only one of the persons involved in the conflict is skilled in this manner. These skills are by no means exhaustive but without them, the possibilities for transformation, reconciliation, and healing are diminished.

Be Well

ACCEPT FORGIVENESS AND HEALING SO THAT YOU CAN BE A MEDIATING PRESENCE IN THE CONFLICT. If we understand holiness to be wholeness, wellness, *shalom,* we need to *be well* to be able to bring healing and forgiveness to others. Drawing from our own well, we can each can *be a well* and bring wellness to others as a mediating presence that brings people together, helps to create a safe space for dialogue, encourages the telling and hearing of stories, acknowledges emotions, encourages the use of spiritual practices, and helps people to resolve their own conflicts, healing themselves and reconciling with each other. We can do this even when we are parties involved in conflicts, when we cannot be mediators or facilitators. By following this model, we are freed from believing that we can or should be the fixer, the healer, or the savior.

Preparation for conflict is a life-long process, and such preparation is critical for the moment of crisis. The better prepared we are, the better chance we will have of living out of the overflow of our well. We will always have to deal with our tendencies to fight or to flee. If we are well prepared, however, we may be able to break free of such reactivity and enter a constructive process characterized by nonviolence, healing, community, and a new creation.

ENGAGE OTHERS IN CONFLICT TRANSFORMATION

Constructive engagement of others in conflict transformation is a relational process that involves direct communication between the parties in a collaborative process. The following practices are seen as dynamically interrelated with one another and with the practices of personal preparation presented above.

Create a Common Well Together

TOGETHER ANALYZE THE CONFLICT AND DESIGN A COLLABORATIVE PROCESS IN WHICH EVERYONE CAN PARTICIPATE AND BE RESPONSIBLE. Process is as important as outcome—often more important where relationships are at stake. Everyone needs to feel valued and be treated fairly. Generally people can live with a decision they may not actually prefer if they have had a voice in that decision or resolution.

In the Gospel according to Matthew (18:15–17), Jesus taught his disciples to follow this process:

If another member of the church sins against you, go and point out the fault when the two of you are alone. If the member listens to you, you have regained that one. But if you are not listened to, take one or two others along with you, so that every word may be confirmed by the evidence of two or three witnesses. If the member refuses to listen to them, tell it to the church.

Jesus' direction in this sacred text ensures that the parties have been in direct communication, unless there are issues of safety. This approach helps to prevent others and us from being unnecessarily dragged into the conflict. We can, however, coach the parties in preparing for direct engagement, just as we have prepared ourselves. If direct communication fails, we then move to being a witness or mediating presence and to developing a collaborative process. Only if collaborative process fails do we consider that the conflict should be resolved by others.

In conflict transformation, good process begins with giving all key players a role in analyzing the conflict and designing a process for transforming it. Good process means being clear and open about purpose, agenda, timing, and how decisions will be made, and providing the opportunity for all the parties to be heard. The JUSTPEACE model employs circle process, a practice found in various indigenous cultures, as the preferred method for collaborative process. The circle (discussed in greater detail below) provides the "container" for positive engagement, providing the necessary safety, within a relational covenant (see next section), for participants to talk with one another. The process respects the experience and wisdom of each member of the circle, and each member has equal responsibility for the outcome of the process.

Share the Well

CREATE A RELATIONAL COVENANT THAT CLARIFIES AND AFFIRMS HOW EVERYONE WILL BE TREATED IN THE PROCESS. A covenant is a mutual agreement that binds people together, both honoring its members and requiring mutual accountability and responsibility. A relational covenant is a set of shared promises to one another and the community as a whole. It embodies the shared expectations and aspirations as to how the members will treat one another in community. More than rules of conduct and procedures for solving problems, relational covenants are affirmations of the vision and values of the community and the positive conduct that expresses them (Dukes et al. 2000).

Drink Deeply Together

ELICIT STORIES OF PEAK EXPERIENCES, GRACE-FILLED MOMENTS, AND DREAMS OF A PREFERRED FUTURE. We believe that as much as possible, a conflict transformation process should start with questions that open the participants up to remembering and telling stories of peak experiences—of times when relationships worked well for them, for example, or of meaningful engagement of problems or differences in church life. Such stories can generate energy for moving forward, building on the common themes and connections and addressing problems more easily and constructively. Powerful positive questions give everyone the freedom to dream and express their hopes for the future, which in turn inspires creativity, innovation, and out-of-the-box thinking. Sharing hopes and dreams can reveal deep values, desires, and strong preferences, and point the way to possible points of connection in defining a preferred future.

At JUSTPEACE gatherings, when conflict transformation practitioners have explored the telling of positive experiences as a possible tool for intervention, the participants have responded to this alternative to problem solving with a sense of hope. When they practiced the tool of crafting and asking positive questions, they noticed how quickly the tone and direction of the conversation could move toward constructive ways of relating in conflict.

Let It Flow

MOVE FROM POSITIONS TO INTERESTS AND NEEDS, GENERATING OPTIONS TO REACH CONSENSUS. MOVE FROM RETRIBUTION TO RESTORATION—HEALING THE HARM, AFFIRMING ACCOUNTABILITY, AND CREATING A NEW RELATIONSHIP. At some point it is necessary to generate and evaluate options for a solution and reach consensus. This is accomplished most effectively by discussing the parties' interests and needs, rather than their positions and demands (Fisher and Ury 1991). Positions are statements or demands that are expressed as solutions, and they often point to deeper interests and needs. Rather than challenging the demands that people put forward, we can move the discussion toward seeking information that draws out the underlying interests or needs. Parties often discover that they share many of these in common or that meeting their respective interests and needs is not mutually exclusive. The next step then is to generate options that meet both parties' interests and needs and to evaluate them accordingly. If consensus is reached on one option, the agreement is summarized in writing. If a full consensus is lacking, the agreement also states the remaining issues, what progress has been made on these issues, and what process has been agreed upon for continuing to deal with them.

At some point in a conflict transformation process, parties will need to name the problem and tell of the harm that was done them. JUSTPEACE believes that we need to move to a paradigm of *restorative justice,* which

focuses on the harm caused to people and relationships, rather than the approach in the prevailing systems of *retributive justice,* whose aim is to establish blame (guilt) and administer pain (punishment). A focus on the harm committed, rather than on blame and guilt, helps the parties move toward accountability, healing, and restoration of relationship (Zehr 1990). Specifically, a restorative justice process engages offenders, victims, and the community in a collaborative process of identifying obligations and solutions and promoting healing among the parties. It places emphasis on offender accountability—understanding the harm caused—and taking responsibility to make things right to the extent possible, both concretely and symbolically. Retribution or punishment, on the other hand, is often counterproductive to such accountability. In restorative justice, the community is involved in working to support real accountability and heal the harm; it recognizes its own role, if any, in causing the harm; and it works to restore both the victim and the offender to the community. Restorative justice is about creating community.

Be Well Together

CELEBRATE EACH STEP TOWARD HEALING AND COMMUNION. BE PRAYERFUL, PERSISTENT, AND PATIENT. The healing of relationships is a communal act. We can only truly be well if we are well together. The health and wholeness of our communities will be determined by our treatment of and relationship with the marginalized—by the welfare of our weakest members. If we work together to heal relationships and create right relations in all of creation, we can truly experience community as communion. We believe in celebrating the hard work that leads to healing and communion, including every small step forward. As Daniel Day Williams has said, "Love does not resolve every conflict; it accepts conflict as the arena in which the work of Love is to be done" (1968, 138).

SOME POSITIVE APPROACHES IN FOCUS

In this final section, we take a closer look at three of the practices introduced above—circle process, relational covenants, and appreciative process.

Circle Process

In the second phase of the model, the engagement of others in conflict transformation, we know of no collaborative process that is superior in working towards positive peacebuilding in the church than the circle process (Ross 1996). Participants in JUSTPEACE training seminars have often found this to be the most helpful and important process they have learned.

The process takes place with the participants seated in a circle, with each person equidistant from the center and having equal visual access to everyone else. In our practice of it, opening and closing prayers and ritual gestures form the whole time and space together as sacred, as a space safe enough for the speaking and hearing of truth. JUST-PEACE facilitators typically light a candle in the center of the circle as a reminder of God's presence.

A talking piece is used to help people listen for understanding and speak the truth in love. The holder of the talking piece is the speaker; all others listen. The talking piece may be something symbolic such as a feather, key, or a sacred text. By moving the talking piece consecutively around the circle, at least for the first few rounds, everyone knows when he or she will speak, and each person has an equal opportunity to be heard without interruption and commentary. A person may pass when it is his or her turn to speak, but the talking piece continues to be passed in order around the circle, and those who have passed may have the opportunity to speak again in a future round.

The facilitator—called a "circle steward" in the JUSTPEACE model—is responsible for maintaining the process. This includes starting and concluding the circle with ritual; getting agreement as to the relational covenants; asking the questions that elicit the stories; summarizing the contributions of the circle after each round; helping the circle focus on the issues and use its imagination to explore options and common ground; sometimes holding the talking piece to allow for group brainstorming; and summarizing consensus or, if no consensus, what has been accomplished and what has not been accomplished.

JUSTPEACE uses circles whenever possible, even for training workshops. Our experience has been that using the circle is instrumental in providing the opportunity for participants to share stories, often of difficult conflicts, and to be open to receiving support and wisdom from others around the circle. As a learning tool and as a tool for intervention, the circle provides the container for positive engagement with the necessary safety for participants to talk openly with one another. Safety in terms of the nature and content of the interactions is promoted by making the first task of a circle the development of a relational covenant.

Relational Covenants

Relational covenants are critical to the creating and nurturing of community. If creation of community is a goal of the conflict transformation process, we believe that the creating and living out of these covenants is as important, if not more important, than any other decisions made by the group. Relational covenants, in effect, establish a positive definition and image of the way group members want to be together in community. They

 express the vision, values, and strengths of the community, as experienced by the community and owned by its members.

Conflicts are still present but they are engaged constructively. Every community has many unexpressed and often conflicting rules as to how people should be treated. Being unexpressed, they provide no assistance in creating communal understanding and accountability. Being conflicting, they create more conflict. In churches, for example, conflict is often dealt with in parking lots after services, over the phone or by email, or in secret meetings. This undermines the honest, direct conversations that need to occur to correct misunderstanding and allow people to demonstrate their best intentions transparently.

We believe that creating together an expressed, shared relational covenant is the most important work we can do to prevent destructive conflict in the church. To be valued and valuable to a community, these covenants must grow out of the life of the community. Ground rules that are simply imposed on a community do not have the "buy in" that would make them covenants. They do not enter into the life or ethos of the community.

Some of the issues that can be addressed when developing a covenant are: How would you like to be treated? How do we create respect for each member as a child of God? How do we create sanctuary or safety for each member of the community? How do we listen for understanding, speak the truth in love, use our imaginations, and be forgiving? How are we going to make decisions? How do we deal with the issues of confidentiality and transparency? How do we deal with accountability to the covenant? How do we maintain an openness to revise the covenant as needed?

As the first collaborative action of a circle process, the development of a relational covenant shapes attitudes and defines shared aspirations for how every person will be treated. After agreement is reached on the covenant, the steward has the responsibility of asking the first question of the participants in the circle, as well as follow up questions. This is where we have found appreciative process to be most helpful.

Appreciative Questioning

The JUSTPEACE process begins, whenever possible, with appreciative questions that elicit stories of peak experiences and dreams of a preferred future. We believe that it is more constructive to build on strengths and what is known and appreciated than trying to imagine an abstract, unexperienced ideal of a better self or a better community.

The most powerful tool in this approach is an open-ended, positive question. Positive questions promote the forward momentum of good process, for example, "If your hopes for our meeting are fulfilled, what will our relationships, our church community, our world look like?" The overarching, driving question in the JUSTPEACE model of conflict transformation is always: "What is God's love calling us to be and to do?"

A good question is sometimes so big that the asking of it sets us off on a journey of self-discovery. We are reminded of the advice of Rainer Maria Rilke in his *Letters to a Young Poet:* "Be patient toward all that is unsolved in your heart and try to love the questions themselves like locked rooms and like books that are written in a very foreign tongue. Do not now seek the answers, which cannot be given you because you would not be able to live them. And the point is to live everything. Live the questions now" (1972, 4).

CONCLUSION

JUSTPEACE has sought to integrate positive approaches in every aspect of the Engage Conflict Well model, including the development of positive attitudes about the purposes and potentials of conflict; living out of a theology of abundance; affirming the importance of developing skills and well-being, individually and communally; and through engaging each other in collaborative processes that work toward healing and new relationship. At the heart of this positive model is asking powerful, appreciative questions in the context of a circle process after a relational covenant is created and affirmed.

REFERENCES

Brueggemann, Walter. 2000. "Vision for a New Church and a New Century, Part II: Holiness Become Generosity." *Union Seminary Quarterly Review* 54, pp. 45–64.

Chaves, Mark, Mary Ellen Konieczny, Kraig Beyerlein, and Emily Barman. 1999. "The National Congregations Study: Background, Methods, and Selected Results." *Journal for the Scientific Study of Religion* 38:4, pp. 458–476.

Cooperrider, David, and Diana Whitney. 1999. *Appreciative Inquiry.* San Francisco: Berrett-Koehler.

Dukes, E. Franklin, Marina A. Piscolish, and John B. Stephens. 2000. *Reaching for Higher Ground in Conflict Resolution: Tools for Powerful Groups and Communities.* New York: Wiley.

Fisher, Roger, and William L. Ury. 1991. *Getting to Yes.* New York: Viking Penguin.

JUSTPEACE Center. 2002. *Engage Conflict Well: A Guide to Prepare Yourself and Engage Others in Conflict Transformation.* Evanston, Ill.: JUSTPEACE Center for Mediation and Conflict Transformation.

Marshall, Christopher. 2001. *Beyond Retribution: A New Testament Vision for Justice, Crime and Punishment.* Grand Rapids, Mich.: Eerdmans.

Rilke, Rainer Maria. 1972. *Letters to a Young Poet.* New York: W. W. Norton.

Ross, Rupert. 1996. *Returning to the Teachings.* Toronto: Penguin.

This, Craig, and Karen Smith. 2002. *Do You Know How We See Ourselves? A Snapshot of The United Methodist Church.* Dayton, Ohio: General Council on Ministries, Office of Research and Planning.

Williams, Daniel Day. 1968. *The Spirit and the Forms of Love.* New York: Harper and Row.

Zehr, Howard. 1990. *Changing Lenses: A New Focus for Crime and Justice.* Scottdale, Penn.: Herald Press.

ADDITIONAL RESOURCES

Buber, Martin. 1958. *I and Thou.* New York: MacMillan.

Evans, Alice F., and Robert A. Evans. 2001. *Peace Skills Leaders' Guide.* San Francisco: Jossey-Bass.

Kraybill, Ronald S., with Robert A. Evans and Alice Frazer Evans. 2001. *Peace Skills Manual for Community Mediators.* San Francisco: Jossey-Bass.

Leas, Speed B. 1985. *Managing Your Church Through Conflict.* Bethesda, Md: Alban.

Lederach, John Paul. 1999. *The Journey Toward Reconciliation.* Scottdale, Pa.: Herald Press.

You can tell whether a man is clever by his answers. You can tell whether he is wise by his questions.

NAGUIB NAHFOUZ

CHAPTER THIRTEEN

APPRECIATIVE INQUIRY AS A TOOL FOR CONFLICT RESOLUTION

Mauricio O. Ríos and Scott D. Fisher

This chapter explores the potential use of Appreciative Inquiry within the arena of unofficial, track-two diplomacy as a tool for conflict transformation and reconciliation between conflicting parties. Through a guiding example of a longstanding, nonviolent interstate conflict in Latin America, the authors explore how the positive characteristics of Appreciative Inquiry might assist antagonistic parties in transforming their relationship. The proposed Appreciative Dialogue Workshop uses affirmative questioning to assist participants in the discovery of common values and goals, new possibilities, and in the co-construction of a shared ideal image of their future relationship. The chapter considers the potential contributions of, as well as some cautions in, applying Appreciative Inquiry within such a conflict scenario.

In the last several decades, significant progress has been made in the field of conflict resolution as scholars and practitioners have brought innovative approaches to the fore. In the 1960s, for example, scholar-practitioner John Burton began to develop the analytical problem-solving workshop methodology, which he initially used as a model of "controlled communication" to gather representatives of parties in conflict to discuss and analyze the underlying issues of their conflict (1969). Later, Burton went beyond this model by using a theory of basic human needs to explain that human motivations have more weight than structures in the generation and resolution of conflict (1990). Following Burton were other scholar-practitioners who made additional contributions to the structure of the analytical problem-solving workshop (see, for example, Doob 1973; Kelman 1990; Mitchell and Banks 1996; and Fisher 1997). Although the results of these international workshops and their impact on policy making and the resolution of conflicts have been mixed, the workshop methodology has nonetheless made a vital contribution to the development of the conflict resolution field.

As the level of conflict complexity increases in the contemporary world and violent conflicts persist, there is a continuing need for creative new approaches to conflict resolution. Within the arena of unofficial or track-two diplomacy (Montville 1995), Appreciative Inquiry (Cooperrider and Whitney 1999) holds significant potential to serve as a creative alternative— or complement—to established conflict resolution methods. Although Appreciative Inquiry (AI) has been applied primarily to large-scale transformation in organizations and communities, this chapter proposes extending its application through an Appreciative Dialogue Workshop. We employ the case study of a nonviolent interstate conflict, between Bolivia and Chile, as a guiding illustration of a proposed model. It is our hypothesis that the positive approach outlined in this chapter would not only facilitate agreement to address the underlying issues in the conflict using new frames of reference, but it would also help propel conflicting parties toward a transformation of their relationship.

The workshop methods in use today generally focus on the identification of key problems in the conflict system. They analyze the root causes of conflict, identify potential solutions, and develop action plans. While the problem-solving approach has produced constructive results in a variety of settings, AI theorists postulate that since human systems tend to grow in the direction of the questions they ask, emphasis on the problem has a tendency to perpetuate those problems over the long run. Since most human systems have been programmed to focus on problem solving as the means to achieve needed change, the systems remain caught in a negative spiral of deficiency (Cooperrider and Whitney1999).

The AI approach, on the other hand, relies on the assumption that a particular situation is a "solution to be embraced" rather than a "problem to be solved." It focuses on discovery, valuing, envisioning, open dialogue, and co-construction of a shared future. The positive energy and ideas generated from discovery and dialogue about what works well in the system (or analogous systems) leads to sustained, positive change in many cases. The ability to achieve positive results relies on the hypothesis that organizations or other human systems reflect the nature of their internal dialogue (the patterned ways that people in the system think about it and the stories they tell about it). While deficit-based internal dialogue tends to result in the proliferation of deficiencies, methodologies that elicit the positive aspects of experience can shift the internal dialogue, cultivate the ability to recognize and embrace strengths, and propel the organization or system into a realm of untapped potential for positive growth.

APPRECIATIVE INQUIRY PROCESS

The AI methodology is operationalized through the phases of the 4-D Cycle: Discovery, Dream, Design, and Delivery. Although the 4-D Cycle may span weeks or months, it is often carried out in the form of an Appreciative Inquiry Summit through which an entire organizational system or representatives of the various stakeholder groups are brought together to work through the process over a several-day period (see description of AI Summit in chapter two). Whatever the format, facilitators of Appreciative Inquiry work to unleash group genius, creativity, and untapped potential as they guide participants through the process using appreciative questioning, a method designed to focus on values, strengths, assets, and affirmative possibilities in the system. The success of the process depends on the ability to understand and apply the art of inquiry. "The more thoughtful the inquiry, the more innovative the response" (Cooperrider 2001).

THE SETTING

To illustrate the application of an Appreciative Dialogue Workshop within a conflict scenario, we begin with the characteristics of an appropriate setting, which share much in common with those of a problem-solving workshop. The following criteria would ensure that the environment is conducive to constructive dialogue:

- The facilitators are perceived as impartial and objective.
- Both parties perceive the setting as neutral ground.
- The setting serves as both physically accommodating and psychologically supportive and invigorating.
- The setting provides sufficient space for parties to subdivide and regroup as necessary.

Participant attitudes and expectations are also vital to the success of an AI process. Although the means by which the process is carried out will vary, we consider the following basic conditions would be necessary for an Appreciative Dialogue Workshop to take place:

- The participants have come prepared to engage in dialogue.
- The participants understand the purpose and objectives of the dialogue session.
- The participants are willing to collaborate in using an appreciative approach.
- The participants represent diverse sectors of civil society and have access to decision makers within their respective countries.

To illustrate the proposed model of an Appreciative Dialogue Workshop, we use the example of a longstanding maritime conflict between Bolivia and Chile in South America. As detailed below, we chose this conflict because we believe its characteristics reveal the potential for using Appreciative Inquiry in a situation of large-scale conflict transformation between nations.

BOLIVIAN-CHILEAN SEA CONFLICT

The Bolivian-Chilean sea conflict is rooted in the Pacific War of 1879, when Bolivia lost its sovereign access to the ocean in a war against Chile. Since that time, Bolivia has peacefully attempted to recover its maritime access through Chilean territory. Chile, on the other hand, maintains that there are no pending territorial issues with Bolivia and that its neighbor has "totally free transit facilities" to the Pacific Ocean through Chilean territory. As a result of the dispute—and after several failed attempts to resolve it—the countries have not engaged in full diplomatic relations since 1978.

The Bolivian-Chilean sea conflict was selected in a report by the International Peace Academy as one of five case studies that illustrate the complexity of contemporary hemispheric conflict situations and the range of approaches to resolve or contain them (Child 1987). One of our assumptions is that in the case of a nonviolent, deep-rooted conflict such as the Bolivian-Chilean example (although at one point in history the conflict was indeed violent, and it still has the potential of violent outbreaks), the AI methodology could initiate a process of reconciliation that acknowledges and addresses each country's underlying issues and needs by bringing both parties together to transform their relationship and ultimately the conflict at hand.

There are several reasons why this conflict is particularly suitable for an AI intervention. First, the co-creative aspect of the AI process is noteworthy since Chile has not favored mediation or arbitration, by which a solution would be imposed by a third party. With the AI approach, the solution would emerge out of the interaction between the parties and therefore would satisfy both parties' core needs.

Second, in contrast to the polemical, accusatory, and legalistic approach that conflict norms tend to support (Kelman 1990; Mitchell and Banks 1996), a dialogue workshop using Appreciative Inquiry could provide a setting that encourages open discussion, attentive listening to opposing views and needs, a focus on the positive aspects of the relationship, and opportunities for genuine creativity.

Third, the Appreciative Dialogue Workshop would serve a dual purpose: an educational one, which could produce changes in attitudes and perceptions and generate new ideas for transforming the conflict and the relationship; and a political one, since influential participants from different sectors of civil society would have the opportunity to influence the political debate within each country (Kelman 1990). This might in turn serve to dispel the negative stereotypes, mistrust, and mutual misunderstanding that plague the two countries' relationship.

Fourth, an Appreciative Dialogue Workshop could present advantages as a pre-negotiation and solution-generating instrument that would enhance the transfer mechanisms to political constituencies, leaders of different sectors, and diplomats. This is important for the Bolivian-Chilean case since both countries need to develop the appropriate political environment if they genuinely desire to renew their relationship.

Fifth, the AI approach might also help develop a "de-committing formula" that enables participants from both countries to break free from constraints on discussions that they have either inherited or imposed upon themselves (Mitchell and Banks 1996). A de-committing formula is precisely what Bolivian and Chilean leaders need in order to start a fruitful dialogue that focuses on the positive characteristics of the relationship.

Finally, this workshop would involve low political, financial, and human-resource costs in relation to the potential gains. A low political cost is particularly important in this case given that several official attempts to solve the maritime conflict have failed, and these failures have only added to frustrations—including the breaking off of diplomatic relations—in an already delicate bilateral relationship.

APPRECIATIVE DIALOGUE WORKSHOP: A PROPOSED MODEL

We now turn to the practical application by proposing a process framework (see Figure 1) for an Appreciative Dialogue Workshop around the improvement of strained interstate relations and, ultimately, conflict transformation in the case of Bolivia and Chile. We present here a model for an Appreciative Dialogue Workshop in some detail as we relate it to this maritime conflict between two nations. We note, however, that as with the analytical problem-solving workshop or other conflict resolution methodologies, the Appreciative Dialogue Workshop methodology would need to be adapted to each new context and, in fact, would require a flexible enough design to allow adjustments along the way during its execution. The model we present here is therefore intended to suggest possibilities for using Appreciative Inquiry in a dialogue workshop format.

The proposed Appreciative Dialogue Workshop would proceed through the 4-D Cycle over a period of at least four days. It would involve sixteen to twenty participants from a cross section of key civil society stakeholder groups in the two countries, to ensure the representation of diverse perspectives and varying areas of influence.

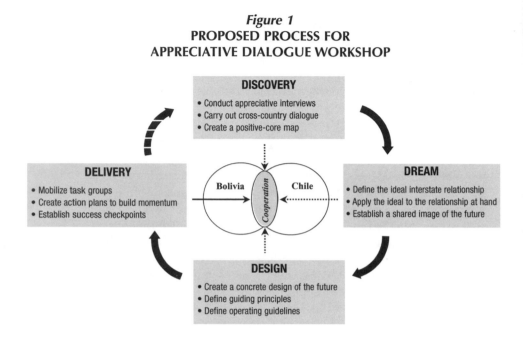

Figure 1
**PROPOSED PROCESS FOR
APPRECIATIVE DIALOGUE WORKSHOP**

Discovery Phase

The Discovery Phase in this model includes the first of several rounds of inquiry in the overall process. Through appreciative interviewing, the conflicting parties would uncover and come to understand both common and distinctive strengths and values of their respective countries and the core characteristics of an ideal interstate relationship—themes that would be used throughout the lifecycle of the dialogue session (or possibly sequence of sessions). Discovery would begin prior to the workshop with a series of twenty to thirty appreciative interviews carried out across the diverse sectors within each country. Stories captured from generations of men, women, and children in many walks of life would contribute a breadth of perspective to the workshop's Discovery Phase and provide a rich foundation for thought-provoking appreciative interviews among the session participants.

Using information gathered during pre-workshop interviews, two types of questions would be crafted for use at the workshop: (1) questions that draw out the strengths and distinctiveness of each country's history, culture, and national character, with the thought that deep understanding of differences can help to mobilize the best of those differences in future phases, and

(2) questions that elicit stories of shared history, culture, and examples of positive coexistence and other forms of interaction.

The Discovery Phase inquiry would involve participants in one-on-one appreciative interviews with individuals from the other country, to humanize the other party and allow participants to gain deep insight into the values, culture, attitudes, perceptions, and life experiences of their interview partner. Moving from interviews in pairs, to sharing key elements from the interviews in small groups, to further sharing and processing the discovery data in the large group, this first phase of the inquiry would allow participants to build their knowledge and understanding of one another and establish a more positive frame of reference with regard to interstate relationships. Some possible questions might be:

- What is the story of an experience you have had personally or an experience in the life of your nation that exemplifies its core values, distinctive strengths, and unique national character?

- Reflect upon a time when you experienced or were aware of an enriching and prosperous relationship—whether academic, professional, artistic, scientific, athletic, or some other form—between communities, groups, or individuals from two countries, if possible, including your own. What were some of the defining characteristics of the relationship? What opportunities for interaction and creative collaboration existed and how were they realized?

- Reflect upon an example of a strong bilateral relationship, between your country and another nation. What factors account for its longevity? In what ways have understanding, cooperation, mutual support, or even creative collaboration on a matter of common concern been expressed?

Themes that emerged in the Discovery Phase would be carried as discussion points throughout the dialogue workshop. Themes that emerged with regard to effective bilateral relationships (e.g., strong diplomatic ties, economic integration, cross-fertilization in the arts, education, sciences, etc.) would be carried forward to later phases of visioning the ideal interstate relationship and then specifically the ideal Bolivian-Chilean relationship. Key themes and insights might be captured in a "positive-core map" that shows both unilateral and bilateral strengths and assets (Cooperrider and Whitney 1999). Participants should depart the Discovery Phase with confirmation of their own national values and strengths, a deeper understanding of those of the other country, and insights into the diverse dimensions of an effective bilateral relationship.

Dream Phase

The process now moves to the Dream Phase in which participants would build upon their most valuable discoveries to define their ideal interstate relationship. They would work together to develop ideal images of the future, uncover themes across the images, and ultimately build consensus around themes for a design of the ideal. In our model, the focus at this stage is placed on each individual's depiction of the ideal, without reference to the existing relationship between the two contending countries. The purpose in this is to achieve displacement from the prevailing conflict framework and to help participants expand their thinking beyond their two countries' immediate conflictual relationship, which otherwise might have a limiting effect on the scope of the dialogue and range of possibilities imagined.

Participants might capture the comments, thoughts, and images that emerge from the group exercises in a collage of images for further discussion. Questions to consider during this phase might be:

- Picture your image of the ideal interstate relationship. What are the key characteristics of the relationship? What factors cultivate and maintain the relationship?

- What opportunities for cooperation and creative collaboration exist that would foster social, cultural, and economic prosperity within and between two countries?

- How do newspaper stories read that capture the living dimensions of this thriving interstate relationship?

Once this new round of appreciative interviews was completed, participants would have shared a multitude of images and ideas. As these images were shared with the large group, common themes and elements would be identified that could then be used to build a collective, shared image of the ideal interstate relationship. Some possibilities might include:

- resilient, constructive diplomatic relations
- synergy in the economic and trade sectors
- pioneering, creative business partnerships
- mutually enriching bi-national and cross-cultural educational opportunities
- cultural exchange programs sponsored by the governments or private sector
- scientific and technological advancements through joint research and development
- breakthroughs in environmental protection of shared air and water resources

Once they had imagined and discussed the *ideal* interstate relationship, participants would then mine that ideal in creating images and concrete ideas that were specific to the Bolivian-Chilean relationship. As they envisioned the contours of economic synergy, for example, they might see the interrelationship between two key assets: access to Chilean ports and the recent discovery of major natural gas reserves in Bolivia, which combined could open up major economic and development opportunities for both countries.

This visioning would open the way to powerful dialogue out of which a positive image of a shared bilateral future could emerge in increasing richness and detail. Once consensus was reached on the general contours of a shared image, it would then be carried into the next phase where the new, realistic relationship between Bolivia and Chile would be defined in its practical details.

Design Phase

Having defined a shared image of the ideal Bolivian-Chilean relationship, the dialogue process would then move to the Design Phase. In the first part of this phase, the envisioned ideal would be translated into a realistic design. Participants would capture elements identified in the Discovery and Dream phases in the design, checking to ensure the distinctive national strengths and characteristics identified previously were not compromised or undesirably altered.

During this phase, participants might agree to ambitious and challenging relationship goals such as stronger diplomatic relations and new economic agreements. To properly lay the foundation for the achievement of the design goals, a second round of appreciative interviews would be conducted to identify and define two key attributes: the guiding principles and the operating guidelines for interaction and cooperation. In order to achieve the goal of stronger diplomatic relations, for example, guiding principles such as mutual trust and respect for differences, open dialogue, and nonviolent conflict resolution might be offered. If participants agreed upon respect for differences as a guiding principle, they might craft operating guidelines that describe how respect would be demonstrated and nurtured on an ongoing basis.

While working to build consensus around a design, it is likely that the specific problems and issues plaguing the parties' conflictual relationship would begin to emerge. The facilitators should work to redirect problem-focused discussion toward the task at hand, while challenging participants to incorporate as much of the ideal image as possible into the new design. Although there might be a tendency for participants to fall back into traditional conflict frameworks as they move toward specifics in the Design Phase, facilitators would need to show that by weaving themes and ideas from the Discovery and Dream phases into the Design Phase, concrete responses to the issues in contention would emerge.

We believe that the focus on creating a *realistic* relationship would serve, not as an inhibiting factor, but rather as a means of generating excitement, confidence in, and commitment to realizing the design. At the same time, a balance would need to be struck between realism and challenging the status quo by reaching—stretching—for imaginative new possibilities. Presuming, for example, that the participants would identify stronger diplomatic ties as a key component of the ideal future relationship, they should be encouraged to outline means by which this could be accomplished. Some possible visioning questions for inquiry at this stage might be:

• Imagine that five years into the future, full diplomatic relations have been established between Bolivia and Chile, and both countries are flourishing from new opportunities and growth. What were the key relational principles and practices that enabled these accomplishments to be achieved? What innovative structures or mechanisms were put in place and activities undertaken that fueled this transformation?

• Which individuals played key roles in this accomplishment? How did they serve as catalysts for change?

Delivery Phase

Last comes the Delivery Phase in which the critical component of action planning takes place. Clearly, the large-scale transformation of an interstate relationship cannot be achieved in a group dialogue setting. Processes, actions, and events carried out upon the participants' return home would be essential to paving the way to a new beginning.

The Delivery Phase would involve work in small task groups to build consensus around and manage actions to be taken in the specific arenas that have been identified by the process thus far (e.g., political/diplomatic, trade, health, education, culture, sports, etc.). If the establishment of stronger bilateral diplomatic relations is one of the identified priorities, one action to be taken might be the development of a proposal outlining key measures and steps toward achieving that goal. Other actions might include:

• development of a plan for presenting the proposal to government leaders;

• awareness raising and education of the two countries' citizenries about the Appreciative Dialogue Workshop process and the opportunities identified;

• involvement of the media as bridge builders between the two societies by opening up spaces for the exchange of opinions, ideas, and hopeful stories;

  • identification of conditions and actions necessary to put new policies in place;

- identification of means for encouraging ongoing support from governmental leaders;

- initiatives to keep citizens engaged, such as exchange programs for journalists, artists, and high school students;

- plans to lobby educators for the inclusion of conflict prevention and management courses in the standard educational curricula.

Once specific actions were outlined, the focus would shift to defining a number of success checkpoints to monitor progress. Measurement of progress would not be used to police participants, but rather to maintain momentum and keep parties on track with fulfilling commitments made during the workshop. The success checkpoints would also provide opportunities for fresh perspectives and new ideas to emerge in the ever-unfolding and evolving process.

Since true relationship transformation between nations can take years or decades, the parties might agree to reconvene at some point or periodically to assess progress, discuss lessons learned, and make mid-course corrections as needed. Conducting periodic dialogue sessions at various checkpoints would allow them to evolve and enhance action plans and pursue bolder ideas in their bilateral initiatives. Another powerful option would be to hold an Appreciative Inquiry Summit with a much larger number of stakeholders. Results and success stories from actions taken by the first group of dialogue workshop participants could be used as inputs to a much larger follow-up effort to engage a large cross-section civil society groups from across both nations.

CAUTIONS IN USE OF THE APPRECIATIVE DIALOGUE WORKSHOP

Although Appreciative Inquiry applications in corporate and community settings have been successful in addressing complicated issues, scenarios of deep-rooted and longstanding conflict within or between countries can bring quite different challenges. In interstate conflicts such as the Bolivian-Chilean maritime conflict, a web of complex economic, political, military, ethnic, and social issues, as well as unique conflict dynamics (internal politics and restraints) and conflict norms (repetitive actions) exist that generally do not allow countries and their government officials much latitude to act in transforming their conflicts and moving them towards resolution.

Since Appreciative Inquiry has not yet been applied in the context of an interstate conflict, it is not clear how this methodology would help tackle the basic, unmet needs of the parties involved. Without addressing these basic needs, such as the need for territory or sovereignty or the need for dignity and international respect, parties might not be able to access the power of the AI process and simply "let go of negative accounts," or they might have difficulty in identifying the positive core of their relationship (Cooperrider and Whitney 1999).

It is also unclear how Appreciative Inquiry would help address the asymmetries (in economic and political power, in motivation to address the conflict, etc.) that the conflict parties often bring to the table. On many occasions, for example, Chile has conveyed the impression that everything would be much easier if Bolivia would simply forget about its maritime demand, thus neither favoring nor being motivated to pursue any real change in the status quo.

Furthermore, it remains to be seen whether participants involved in such deeply emotional conflicts as the example present would display the will or capacity to move through the AI process as it is intended without becoming overwhelmed by repressed feelings of negativity and anger. In the case before us, for example, Chileans are perceived as "indifferent" and "insensitive" to Bolivia's maritime demand, and Bolivians are perceived as not wanting to respect international treaties already in place.

Finally, it is not clear how Appreciative Inquiry would address the "re-entry" factor for the workshop participants. Although the rigorous action-planning exercises would provide for the ability to develop detailed next steps, it is understood that participants who re-enter their own countries or groups after an encounter with the adversary need to be prepared to deal with a hostile environment filled with recurrent negative feelings, perceptions, and stereotypes.

POTENTIAL CONTRIBUTIONS OF THE APPRECIATIVE DIALOGUE WORKSHOP

In spite of these uncertainties, we believe that this adapted Appreciative Inquiry approach, the Appreciative Dialogue Workshop, has the potential to unleash previously unseen results in the field of conflict resolution, whether at the local, national, or international level. Moreover, the workshop model as we envision it has a number of primary characteristics and advantages in common with the analytical problem-solving workshops advanced by Burton, Kelman, Mitchell, and Fisher. They include:

- a facilitative role in the larger change process
- a focus on relational concerns
- a focus on the generation of specific ideas, actions, outputs, and outcomes
- an educational and political role
   • a de-committing formula that provides space for contending parties to step out of entrenched positions and conflict frameworks

These commonalities with the problem-solving workshop reinforce AI's potential role in interactive conflict resolution processes. They also present the possibility that practitioners might complement other approaches (facilitated dialogue, negotiation, mediation, even arbitration) with selected appreciative elements, depending on the nature of the conflict, the objectives of the immediate process in use, and the state of play of the overall peace process. Appreciative Inquiry stands to enrich the conflict resolution field with unique contributions that could prove transformative, particularly in advancing processes of unofficial dialogue and reconciliation, as we have proposed in this chapter.

Affirmative Focus

One of the greatest contributions Appreciative Inquiry could make to the workshop format and to the larger conflict resolution field is the affirmative focus of appreciative questioning. Questions that uncover the life-giving factors of an organization, community, or country and bring to light what people most value and hope for can open new avenues for tackling some of the core underlying issues in a conflict. Appreciative questions can elicit deep and thoughtful responses, as well as inspire hope and elevate creativity.

Capacity to Involve Large Systems

Although the proposed model is tailored for a small workshop group of sixteen to twenty participants, another advantage of the AI methodology lies in its capacity to involve large numbers of people. The large-scale Appreciative Inquiry Summit has accommodated groups as large as two thousand participants at one time. The summit environment could provide a tremendous opportunity in the Bolivian-Chilean conflict, for example, for participation by representatives of all sectors of civil society in defining an ideal future bilateral relationship and in designing widely accepted strategies and action plans for achieving that ideal. Such large-scale participation of stakeholder groups would also translate into a more complete representation of the diversity of values and interests in the conflict, including the identification of the various perspectives and underlying issues affecting the conflict.

Since Appreciative Inquiry has the capacity to impact personal, relational, and group performance profoundly and simultaneously in an organizational setting, it should also have the potential to impact behavior country-wide, given a large and diverse group of members of the society who are committed to the process. Often, a nation-wide commitment is required to end longstanding and deep-rooted conflict. Thus the ability to involve thousands of participants in an AI process increases the potential for large-scale commitment to a co-created vision. As in other conflicts, the different political parties, factions, and sectors in Bolivia and Chile each have their own views and ideas about how to solve the maritime conflict. An AI Summit could provide a venue to hear and accommodate the many different opinions and sentiments in crafting strategies and action plans that could achieve consensus and sustain commitment.

We do, however, inject a note of caution here. If it is already delicate and difficult to bring a dozen representatives of two parties in conflict together in the same room, there is a question of feasibility in trying to bring hundreds or even thousands of representatives of antagonistic parties together under the same roof. While it is clear that even a small group would present challenges during a conflict intervention using Appreciative Inquiry, a great deal more planning and care would have to be given to safely manage a much larger group of people addressing a highly emotional conflict, such as the Bolivian-Chilean maritime conflict.

Improved Relationships Through Building Trust

The AI methodology also has the potential to radically transform relationships among individuals and groups and between nations. Improvement of relations between conflicting parties is a fundamental first step in the establishment of trust, which in turn is essential to addressing the core, underlying issues in the conflict. The ability for Appreciative Inquiry to transport participants beyond their traditional frames of reference could open new avenues for healing and reconciliation. It is not possible to imagine a transformation of both the maritime conflict and the Bolivian-Chilean relationship without the generation of trust between the two nations, their leaders, and their societies at large after decades of miscommunication, negative stereotypes on both sides, misperceptions, and lack of a shared understanding of the underlying issues of the conflict.

Partnership and Cooperation

Another advantage of Appreciative Inquiry in a conflict resolution context is its emphasis on building partnerships, moving from adversarial to cooperative relations, and uncovering positive attributes and traditions that support this transition. When Appreciative Inquiry is employed in a whole-system approach, the positive core becomes the explicit and common property of all (Cooperrider and Whitney 1999). This clears the path for defining a solution that is also held as common property and the legitimization of that solution in the society as a whole. In allowing all sectors to participate and, through inquiry and dialogue, to draw deeply from their own experiences, Appreciative Inquiry can transcend traditional societal barriers for it also allows for all sectors of the society to participate in the design of conflict resolution and reconciliation processes. In the Bolivian-Chilean maritime conflict, for example, this holds potential for bridging diverse sectors of the two civil societies in new ways and empowering them to participate in finding the best solutions to their shared conflict—solutions that have escaped the political and diplomatic leadership for decades.

Open Communication and Empowerment

Yet another advantage is the capacity of an AI process to cultivate relevant and much-needed communication across levels, from the grassroots to the policy-making levels of society. In large-scale organizational systems, Appreciative Inquiry has successfully led to the establishment of structures that liberate an organization's strengths and that enable individuals at all levels to empower one another to connect, cooperate, and co-create a new vision. This empowerment capacity is fundamental to the creation of "social ownership" of solutions to a conflict, and this is essential for the legitimization and implementation of solutions such as pre-negotiation accords, peace treaties, and reconciliation initiatives between and among parties. There can be little doubt that the generation of social ownership in the Chilean and Bolivian societies regarding a solution to the maritime conflict would enable political leaders in both countries to step out of their constrained and patterned behaviors and take bold actions in transforming the status quo on both sides of the border.

Flexibility to Meet Unique Challenges

Finally, appreciative questioning allows for each dialogue process to meet the unique challenges of the conflict at hand. This gives the methodology the necessary flexibility to adapt to differing conflict scenarios, whether international or domestic. Although the basic AI framework—the 4-D Cycle—would remain constant when applied across various settings, the art of crafting appreciative questions makes it possible to address each conflict from an appropriate vantage point.

CONCLUSION

As failed attempts at reconciliation and conflict transformation plague the international arena, there is no doubt that Appreciative Inquiry offers interesting new possibilities for the conflict resolution field and, specifically, for track-two diplomacy. In that regard, three significant opportunities seem to stand out.

First, the AI methodology can complement the efforts of traditional diplomacy as a pre-negotiation, pre-mediation, and unofficial-dialogue tool. Use of the modified AI methodology through the proposed Appreciative Dialogue Workshop might provide groundbreaking results out of which further negotiation and mediation strategies could be developed. This method must be tested in a variety of environments (one of them hopefully being the Bolivian-Chilean case) to determine the optimal conditions for its implementation.

Second, it is clear that the AI methodology differs from problem-diagnosis and deficit-based approaches to change that rely heavily on the analysis of conflict and its root causes. Only testing the AI approach in practice will determine whether it successfully thrusts parties beyond their pressing immediate concerns through greater emphasis on existing strengths and positive possibilities.

Third, if Appreciative Inquiry proves able to transform a conflict and the parties' relationship over time, it could play an increasingly important role not only as a conflict resolution tool, but also as a conflict prevention mechanism. The fact that Appreciative Inquiry produces strong relationships and coordinated actions that may lead to simpler and more effective solutions could represent a fundamental shift in the way both international and domestic actors deal with conflict. Additional effort must be placed on sharing the power of the AI model and the means by which it can be applied to a variety of conditions and conflicts.

Although a great deal of experimentation is necessary before the full potential of Appreciative Inquiry is understood and unleashed, there is no doubt that it presents an unprecedented and exciting opportunity for exploration and discovery. In today's increasingly complex global political environment, it is necessary and worthwhile to explore innovative, constructive, and positive approaches to conflict prevention and resolution. A new world is calling out for new interventions. We must answer.

REFERENCES

Burton, John W. 1969. *Conflict and Communication: The Use of Controlled Communication in International Relations.* New York: Free Press.

Burton, John W., ed. 1990. *Conflict: Human Needs Theory.* New York: St. Martin's Press

———. 1995. "Track Two: An Alternative to Power Politics." In *Conflict Resolution: Track Two Diplomacy.* John W. McDonald, Jr., and Diane B. Bendahmane, eds. Washington, D.C.: Institute for Multi-Track Diplomacy.

Child, Jack. 1987. "Interstate Conflicts in Latin America and the Search for Solutions: Five Illustrative cases." In *Regional Cooperation for Development and the Peaceful Settlement of Disputes in Latin America.* A report by the International Peace Academy, Jack Child, ed. Dordrecht, Netherlands: Martinus Nijhoff Publishers.

Cooperrider, David. 2001. A talk given at the "Positive Approaches to Peacebuilding Conference," September 28, American University, Washington D.C.

Cooperider, David, and Diana Whitney. 1999. *Appreciative Inquiry.* San Francisco: Berrett-Koehler.

Doob, Leonard W., William J. Foltz, and Robert B. Stevens. 1973. "The Fermeda Workshop: A Different Approach to Border Conflicts in Eastern Africa." In *Conflict Resolution Through Communication.* Fred E. Jandt, ed. New York: HarperCollins.

Fisher, Ronald J. 1997. *Interactive Conflict Resolution.* Syracuse, N.Y.: Syracuse University Press.

Kelman, Herbert C. 1990. "Applying a Human Needs Perspective to the Practice of Conflict Resolution: The Israeli-Palestinian Case." In *Conflict: Human Needs Theory.* John Burton, ed. New York: St. Martins Press.

Mitchell, Christopher, and Michael Banks. 1996. *Handbook of Conflict Resolution: The Analytical Problem-Solving Approach.* London: Pinter.

Montville, Joseph V. 1995. "The Arrow and the Olive Branch: A Case for Track Two Diplomacy." In *Conflict Resolution: Track Two Diplomacy.* John W. McDonald, Jr., and Diane B. Bendahmane, eds. Washington, D.C.: Institute for Multi-Track Diplomacy.

PART V:

HEALING AND RECONCILIATION

... so when you are offering your gift at the altar, if you remember that your brother or sister has something against you, leave your gift before the altar and go; first be reconciled to your brother or sister, and then come and offer your gift.

MATTHEW 5:23-24

CHAPTER FOURTEEN

THE BREAD AND THE WINE ON THE FRONTLINES BETWEEN GAY AND EVANGELICAL CHRISTIANS

Peggy Green

Addressing a painful struggle in the American church, First Be Reconciled, a proj-ect of the Pacific School of Religion, works to foster trust and build working rela-tionships between gay and evangelical Christians. This chapter documents its first two initiatives, designed to open avenues of cooperation and educate lay people, pastors, and seminarians in an ecumenical process that includes dialogue, discov-ery, and faith-based inquiry. Over a period of ten weeks, up to eight participants share meals, tell their personal stories, and join one another in silence and prayer. In the second half of the program, each participant unites with an "adversary" to craft questions and co-facilitate a session.

⚘

*J*oe is a gay man in his late thirties. As an evangelical Christian, confiding in his pastor from time to time, he struggled for years with his sexual orientation. He has three children who live in Ohio, the home of his entire family, of his former job as a third grade teacher, and of the Nazarene congregation he loved—all of which he fled when his pastor broke Joe's confidence before the entire congregation, after which Joe's sister accused him of molesting her two children, and Joe's lawyer advised him to forget about teaching—*forever.*

That was ten years ago. About a year ago, while looking for candidates for First Be Reconciled, a dialogue project bringing together gay and evan-gelical Christians, I found Joe's name on a website for gay Christians. I called him up. I left a message. We played phone tag. Finally one night, I answered the phone, and shortly afterwards Joe asked angrily, "Who are you—*a stu-dent?*" I carefully explained my past experience facilitating dialogue around issues ranging from abortion to race and said, "Yes, I'm a student again—at Pacific School of Religion."

If my computer hadn't expelled its hard drive and all that was in it, I could tell you exactly what we said after that. Suffice it to say that we agreed to meet at an artsy cafe in downtown Berkeley.

Somewhere on Shattuck Avenue, in a room where canvasses dripped from the wall, Joe talked about reconciliation in his own life. With the death of the grandfather they loved, Joe had forgiven his sister for the painful fabrications that resulted in his fleeing west and sending child-support payments home to Ohio, while selling vacuum cleaners door-to-door in San Francisco.

Unhampered by the concerto of juice blenders and Mozart, Joe put away a baguette sandwich while he talked about Ohio—about the second Church of the Nazarene into which he finally settled his family, the more liberal congregation within which Joe made a new home, the same congregation that refused, a year later, Joe's application for membership.

With a deep swig of lemonade, he said what he had come to say: *Yes*, he was going to join this fledgling group of peacemakers—some evangelical and straight, some evangelical and gay, some lesbian and way-liberal—for weekly dialogue. A few weeks later, a small cluster of us began meeting midweek, about a mile north of the University of California campus. For twelve consecutive Wednesdays, we met in a nearby church, told stories, ate grapes, and approached our differences through the door of things we all held dear.

By the end of the fourth week, the six of us were dipping pieces of a fresh roll into a glass full of red wine. It was the perfect way for a tired bunch of war-weary church-types to close an evening of dialogue about homosexuality and biblical inerrancy. We took turns ad-libbing the words that have been spoken in sanctuaries for centuries; we turned to each other, offering the bread and the Communion cup. No floggings, no drive-by Bible thumpings, no forced or overstated love stuff. Just a little stillness—and then we'd part for the week.

Was everybody *for us?* No, not everybody supports reconciliation between gay and evangelical Christians. Why would anybody be against us? First of all, most conservative evangelicals believe that "practicing homosexuals" are not Christian. We may go to church, study the Bible, take vows and wear stoles, *but* if we go home every night to a partner of the same gender, we are walking against the Word of God and are therefore ill-defined as "Christian." In support of these beliefs, conservative Christians offer the well-known citations, from Leviticus to Romans, now hotly debated in seminaries throughout the West.

Similarly, many in the lesbian/gay community believe that to reconcile with the enemy before justice is won is to dignify the perpetrator and to let the evildoer off the hook. In this view, "premature reconciliation" distances the oppressor from any incentive to look again at Christian love, to look again at the Jesus who lived and moved among the outcasts of his day, among the very people whom the Pharisees called "unclean" and "impure" because of what was written in the Scriptures.

A more powerful, if not universal, fear that accompanies most efforts towards reconciliation is the concern that conversation designed to "re-humanize the enemy" will not only create a Pollyanna-like attitude towards those working tirelessly against the truth, but it will also create a kind of amnesia on the part of participants, the dangerous forgetting that theologian Robert Schreiter calls "a betrayal of the past" and "a betrayal of the dead" (1998, 55).

"To urge the forgetting of painful memories or events," Schreiter writes, "is to either trivialize the events themselves . . . or to trivialize the victim" (1998, 66). Martha Minow both echoes this alarm and pairs it with its opposite. She cites the twin dangers "of wallowing in the past and forgetting it" or of "too much enshrinement of victimhood and insufficient memorializing of victims and survivors" (1998, 2).

In short, the chief concerns regarding current efforts at reconciliation (something like putting the cart before the horse) are, one, that purveyors of falsehood, once "forgiven," will be removed from the error of their ways and from accountability for their crimes (as well as from any incentive to change) and, two, that victims of injustice, once "reconciled" to their perpetrators, will trivialize their own experience and, in so doing, no longer be moved to fight for their own freedom.

While both of these concerns reflect real-world fears about restoring balance to the scales of justice, and about the long-term impact of abuse on its survivors, they also highlight problems in the understanding of reconciliation itself. As I reflect upon my own role in First Be Reconciled, the above apprehensions not only bring to light a clear confusion about the *how* and the *why*—but more importantly, about the *who*—of forgiveness.

Why might a man like Joe be moved to reconcile with the sort of Christian who would break confidentiality and publicly shun him, beside his wife and three children, before all of his friends in the congregation? What's in it for Joe?

Consider the question, Who is forgiveness for? Who benefits?

Joe came to First Be Reconciled with a decade's worth of anger that almost anyone would say was perfectly justifiable. Enraged as he was, he chose to come and tell his story—and to listen into the lives of "heterosexual evangelicals." He was fractious that first Wednesday night we all met in Peace Chapel. But he came, he told his story, and he listened.

Writing about South Africa's Truth and Reconciliation Commission, Charles Villa-Vicencio argues that "telling one another stories is perhaps the only basis for recognizing and yet transcending our differences. It is perhaps the only basis for gaining an understanding of both ourselves and the hopes and fears of others" (1997, 31).

In First Be Reconciled, the story begins in that place where we have the most in common. Are we human? Let's examine our humanity—our hurts, our hopes, our moments of life-giving grace. Are we Christian? Let's talk about our faith—our very experience of God. In so doing, we stand a good chance of reducing hatred, restoring dignity, and dismantling stereotypes. As we transcend difference (as we call into question all those assumptions that commonly pass for fact), we "crack the code," thereby uncovering what Villa-Vicencio calls "common memory" (1997, 31).

Common memory. On a typical Wednesday night, the first question, which follows the Prayer of St. Francis, which follows a long and soothing silence, begins with the words, "Tell us a story. . . ." "Tell us a story about a time when God played a role in your life, which shaped your relationship with God today." Joe talked about the winter three years ago when he learned that he was HIV-positive, about the following Lent and "that season of death" which he could, at the time, "barely tolerate." While he could still pray to his Creator, he could no longer allow himself to think about Christ. But then summer came and with that, the story of Jesus—at the tomb of Lazarus—"weeping for this man that he loved."

By the time everyone has answered, thirty minutes have gone by, and each of us, having shared a rather personal piece of the journey of faith, has opened wide the hearts and minds of everybody in the room. Nobody strums her fingernails on the tabletop; nobody inches his way down the hallway to the bathroom. I posed a question about our relationships with God. One at a time, as each of us answered, we strode deeper and deeper into relationship with one another.

Too nice? Next question: "How does your experience of Jesus influence your views about relationships? About sex? About sex between two women or sex between two men?" While the first question warms people up, this second question cranks up the heat. Mysteriously, not one among us is sick on this rainy winter night. *Hmmmmmmm.*

Okay: *sex.*

Actually, we girls talked about intimacy, and how intimacy with God is one yardstick by which we've gauged the success of our relationships with our partners. While Bonnie, an evangelical, echoed this, she went on to tell a deeper story. A minister for nearly twenty years in a Bible-based denomination, Bonnie talked about the night when she knew she had to leave the very church in which she was raised, nurtured, and employed. "I was," she told us, "facedown on my bedroom floor." Alone but not without comfort at the moment of awakening, she described Jesus, "cloaking his body over me, embracing me for all I am, including my sexual being . . . as a lesbian."

Rather than "urge the forgetting of painful memories," we speak the truth. Rather than "trivialize the event," we tell our most transforming stories. It isn't wimpy, this kind of inquiry; it gets to the heart of the matter.

 And it does so in a way that builds rather than destroys relationships. While Joe and Bonnie get the Pulitzer Prize for pure poetry, Lee, a dyed-in-the-wool Pentecostal, gets the Purple Heart for courage. Not only because he talked about the first time he masturbated, but because after an evening of hearing stories and building trust, he risked hurting people's feelings—and risked feeling disliked.

Question: "If there was a prayer or a passage in Scripture that supports your point of view, what would that be?" Throughout this line of inquiry, Lee not only used his own sexual history to offer an example of sexual behavior he believes was wrong, but he also, in the midst of painful, touching stories, said what he believes is true: "If the Bible says that something is wrong, it's *me* who needs to change and not the Bible."

What I'll most remember about Lee, as he articulated the essence of his faith, is the care with which he acknowledged that people had been hurt. In First Be Reconciled, we make known our opinions but we do so in such a way that our naked humanness speaks first. We don't just talk about the inerrancy of Scripture; we talk about the time when we were most healed by this approach to the Bible. We don't just talk about homosexuality, we talk about the very instant when we finally knew that we were gay.

Still too nice? If you watch a lot of cop dramas (of the sort whose average scene is half the length of the average scratch), the very nature of a successful dialogue (which is neither a high-school debate nor hand-to-hand combat) may, by contrast, be too settling for some tastes. It may ask you to sit still—and in the meantime, to experience your own anxiety about stillness. In that sense, it isn't nice at all.

But what if you show up week after week and find you have no real adversaries, find that the "bad guys" are really there to hear you, that "the enemy" is really there to join you, is only there as an expression of God's surprising grace? What then? Does that mean the process isn't working? Does it mean the process is working really well?

Facilitated dialogue is designed, by and large, to create a safe place in which all may speak, be heard, and feel understood. A lot depends on who is in the room. We had a whole mess of conscious people this first time. So much so that the group agrees, after three months of chatting up everything from sex to salvation, that twelve weeks was at least two more weeks than we needed.

Joe, during the last couple of times we met, talked about an invitation he'd received from members of the Nazarene church that had refused him membership to come back and make a presentation about HIV during their three-week endeavor to better understand AIDS on the African continent. They had no idea that Joe himself was HIV-positive. He accepted the invitation to speak.

Two weeks before he was scheduled to address the congregation, the topic was suddenly revised, his presentation cut painfully short. "They didn't," Joe explained, "want to hear about gay men." He returned, at first, to a familiar despair. Days later, he mulled it over. "Because of my experiences in First Be Reconciled, I was able to remember what was motivating the evangelicals. I was able to see them as 'people in a struggle' rather than 'the enemy.'" He accepted the "watered-down proposal," believing that that was "the high road" that would enable him to remain in conversation, about a topic that mattered to him, with the very people who had once rejected him.

Still, all through the process of writing his remarks, he had planned to do it his way, to say what he really wanted to say, to tell them a story, through the eyes of an African gay man, that would "trick them" into hearing him. But the night before he was to speak, something he read in *Tales of the City* caught his eye and made him reconsider. "I realized I loved these people. And I didn't," he concluded, "*want* to trick them. So I rewrote my talk."

The next morning, standing before the congregation, he looked into old, familiar faces, took a deep breath and said, "These are my credentials for talking to you today: I'm a Nazarene, I'm a gay man, and I have AIDS.

"It was like Dorothy's house falling on the witch." As soon as the words were out of his mouth, Joe saw something in their faces that he had "never expected to see—profound sadness. I was expecting judgment. These . . .," he remembered, "were people I knew, people who taught me how to be a Nazarene."

At the end of his presentation, he sat down. The new minister sprang to her feet and ran over. "Joe," she said standing before him, "you've just told us something intensely personal and powerful about yourself. . . . I just want to acknowledge that." She looked into Joe's face and recited a psalm. She asked if he would like the congregation to join him. As she turned to the congregation and invited them to come forward, she asked Joe how he would like them to pray for him. "I need," he replied, "comfort and hope."

"After ten years of being angry and acting out," Joe, as his fellow Nazarenes laid their hands on him, reconciled "with the people who taught me everything I know about being evangelical." He forgave that church, and the church before it, and he knew it. Remembering their faces and the feel of their hands, he said, "They gave me a blessing, gave me something I couldn't give to myself. . . ."

"I'd felt such a broken heart around this congregation," he confided. "First Be Reconciled brought me to a place where I could reconcile. This is," he concluded, "truly a gift I can give to my children—for the first time in ten years, I can truly live—I want these years to be good."

"Forget 'the perpetrator,'" I thought. "Forgiveness is for the forgiver." While it may be construed as something one does for "the enemy," while it may be seen as letting the "bad guy" squirm down off the hook, forgiveness isn't about the bad guy at all. Freely given, forgiveness bestows peace upon the giver. Forgiveness, for those of us who live with anger as a fact of life, can help survivors transcend hate, can transform reconcilers into reservoirs of light.

THE SECOND GROUP

There is something about the Bread and the Wine on the dining room table before us— three Bay bridges spanning ice-cold waters in full view behind us—it reminds us that something we've done has something to do with the Oneness of God. In the last ten weeks, eight people have spent a total of twenty hours together. Something we've done, listening to one another as we hope God will listen to us, is a little bit beyond words. Good thing, because alongside several other ground rules we signed is the one about confidentiality. And anyway, it's hard to describe the feeling of being heard, the experience of being understood, by the very people with whom we are locked in ecclesial *jihad*.

We are about to begin our final conversation. I look around the table at the group that has met every Wednesday afternoon. We are three men and five women; three gay people and four evangelicals; two heterosexuals who are hopelessly liberal (even the one who is also evangelical); pastors, lay leaders, and a seminarian; Catholic and Quaker, Congregationalists and Presbyterians; and last but not least, two Asian men—Peter, the conservative Chinese immigrant from Hong Kong, and Pete, the gay Chinese-American from Idaho. On our final Wednesday afternoon together, there's only one thing wrong with this picture. Pete was sick that day. He caught a chill while volunteering in the parish office and was home in bed with the flu. That was sad. But then it was funny. And pretty soon, it was just perfect.

We began these conversations on September 11, 2002. In so doing, we wasted no time feeling lost on the global field of religious conflict. We knew right where we stood. And because of that, we neither belabored the point nor berated ourselves. Instead, we did something we would do a lot: we paired off, wherever possible, with an "ideological opposite." On this **first** day, one year after the twin towers collapsed in a heap of bone and ash, we asked our dyad partners to reflect on the aftermath, to "share a story, a picture, or a powerful quote—one that provided a precious image or a new understanding—of what we, as human beings, in the positive sense, are capable of." Stop for a moment. What comes to mind?

Imagine you are a native New Yorker, born and raised in a city famous for its warp-drive and sonic boom, whose inhabitants are lining the sidewalks in silence. You get off the bus, feel for your gloves, and head past the still life to ground zero. Helmet under your arm, boots up to your knees, the sound of applause—it takes you by surprise—filling your chest until your heart wants to burst. Morning after morning, weeks after the worst was over, rescue workers got that treatment from their fellow native New Yorkers.

Across the continent one year later—reaching down into the ugly rubble of the bloodiest thing to soak American soil since the Civil War—we were handing each other shards of hope. There was something about it; we got off to a good start. We didn't pretend that nothing bad had happened; and we didn't pretend that in the American church, nobody was getting hurt. It's just that we didn't start there. We started, as we would always start, with a moment of silence, followed by the Prayer of St. Francis, followed by a reading of the ground rules and guidelines. And then we summoned the spirit of New York for a little bit of help.

First Be Reconciled

The project, named for a passage in Matthew's Gospel, has a clear mission: to build trust and foster working relationships between gay and evangelical Christians. As of the second round of dialogue, only one thing has changed. Participants not only engage in dialogue, they engage in a "learning laboratory." As of the anniversary of September 11, First Be Reconciled not only brings both sides face to face but teaches both sides, week after week, how to co-facilitate. In other words, by the time ten weeks have gone by, eight participants have been invited to form a facilitation team.

A little history: The first round of dialogue (at press time a third has just begun) lasted twelve weeks, was designed, over untold numbers of doughnuts and lattes, by two women—myself, a lesbian and the director of this project, and Linda, a Southern Baptist scholar when she's not out planting Southern Baptist churches. The entire series was co-facilitated by a Pentecostal named Lee and myself. Between Linda, Lee, and myself, we wrote every question, we co-facilitated every inch of conversation.

But the second round of dialogue was a horse of a different color. For the first three weeks, I co-facilitated with an evangelical pastor, a nice guy named Steve. On the fourth week, we asked the participants to shout out a few topics. "What," we inquired after several weeks of building trust, "do you want to ask each other questions about?" (I filled a whole page on the flip chart.) On the fifth week, we asked the participants to join the facilitation team. (Not a single participant declined.) By the sixth week, Steve and I had joined the conversation while the participants began taking turns at co-facilitation. Determined to maintain the high level of respect, determined to shoulder the necessary risks, they were going for the "big issues." With a little coaching from us, they paired up, crafted questions, and took the stage. (See Figure 1 on how to craft questions.)

They asked questions about biblical inerrancy, sexual orientation, and the role of conscience in Truth and discernment. Pete and Peter wasted no time demonstrating that a gay Catholic and an evangelical

Figure 1
HOW TO CRAFT GREAT QUESTIONS

First Be Reconciled borrows from the Discovery Phase of Appreciative Inquiry, which assumes that people move in the direction of things they ask questions about. So, think about what it is you want to achieve in each session; look closely at what it is you want *more of*. Ask questions about *that*.

- Do you want to see the participants find common ground in their faith? Ask questions about their faith journeys, and how those journeys have brought them together.

- Do you want to see "high quality relationships" between gay and evangelical Christians? Do you want transformation? Ask a question about a relationship in their lives that crossed those lines— and gloriously! Try this: "Tell us the story of a time when you connected in a way that was unexpected and transforming with someone who was different from you?"

- Do you want to see them develop understanding around their approaches to the Bible and the Christian faith? Ask questions about their experience of the Bible and about the role that it plays in the practice of their faith. Ask how they use their faith to make difficult decisions. Get them to tell a *story*.

- Do you want them to make decisions together? To evaluate the process as they go? Ask questions that get them talking about the highlights of their reconciling journey; ask how these highlights represent a value they hold dear, ask what wishes they have for future sessions. And then, if it isn't already clear, ask specifically what topics they would like to cover during the next few sessions. If the group is ready, this should lead you into "dangerous territory."

- Look closely at the topics they wish to cover. In crafting related questions, look for the goal inherent in each topic and craft questions that elicit answers about the goal.

pastor can work together side by side, constructing the question that will become a turning point for the entire group. They weren't shy. They wanted to know how the people in the room had come to understand their sexual identities. Not only did they want to clarify the role of culture in that understanding, but they wanted to know: "Where was God in all of that?"

"We walk by faith and not by sight," writes the Apostle Paul. Approaching the mossy cliff of safety and trust, eighty toes wiggled over the edge. The risks people took in telling their stories left us with a feeling of intimacy that was surpassed only by the courage that had begun to pilot this group. It was an evangelical, Beth, who led us, blindfolded, on a trust walk through the thickets of her life as a young adult—through the years of promiscuity, the letter from God enveloped in a shocking dream, and the subsequent sexual awakening. It was a story, one of many told that afternoon, that left the group feeling gifted, trusted, and deeply united. Suffice it to say, we were different after that. Stepping off the soft turf of common ground into the thin air of the hard question, we came down—again and again—on a great big trampoline. Suffice it to say, we didn't need a ropes course to learn that we were all on the same team. Suffice it to say, by the time three more weeks had gone by, words like "liberal" and "conservative" were categories we were no longer able to use.

So what does that mean for the two kinds of people on either side of the searing fissure in the American church? Does it mean that openly gay people, denied both matrimony and Holy Orders in most denominations, can stop fighting for ordination and stop performing Holy Unions? Does it mean that evangelicals, who live their lives very close to the Word, will relinquish their belief in the authority of Scripture and embrace all manner of sexual diversity? What it means is, this group of liberal and conservative Christians has put aside bitterness and rage as a way to frame the scary questions that cause us real pain. What it means is, this motley group of eight, this cadre of believers gay and straight, is reaching across the table, quilting story after story into a blanket of common memory. As the fabric of world peace unravels everywhere from the Midwest to the Middle East, we follow the thread of higher truth that loops back through the human heart.

On our last day together, three pastors, two lay leaders, one seminary professor, one seminary student, and one new seminary alum sat around a dining room table in a North Berkeley home overlooking the Bay. I don't know which is the better metaphor, the three bridges or the Bread and the Wine (even if it is only pita bread and pomegranate juice). All I know is, as we served one another Communion—in the language of the server's tradition, in the style of the recipient's liking—an evangelical Quaker included the gay Chinese-American, who was home in bed with the flu, by tearing off a piece of bread, dipping it in the wine, and serving The Lord's Supper to the microphone on the tape recorder.

According to the afternoon's ritual, the one receiving Communion had about four minutes to say what he or she had learned from the people in the group. Following that, the same person got to hear what each of the others in the room had learned from him or her. (For Pete, home in bed, we passed the microphone and took turns blessing his soul, his unfettered passion, and his fabulous colorful shirts.) That was when Peter told Pete that he loved him.

And when it was Peter's turn to tell the group what he had learned from all of us, he, speaking as a Chinese immigrant, said that, although he knew what it was like to be treated "like a second-class citizen," he had no idea what it was like "to feel hated." Nor did he understand "the danger" that attended all the hate. Just the week before, a young man in a neighboring town who occasionally dressed as a woman and called himself "Gwen" was found strangled, bludgeoned, and murdered. (Meanwhile, students at Gwen's high school and students at a Catholic school nearby were rehearsing their parts in "The Laramie Project," a dramatic weaving of interviews in the wake of the unspeakable murder of a gay man named Matthew Sheppard.) In the aftermath of another murder, Peter wanted to be a better minister to gay people—and he wanted to continue to dialogue with gay Christians. The next to echo a desire to remain in conversation, another evangelical, was Beth, who felt our work had "just begun."

The thing I will remember most, in the midst of eight rounds of grateful farewells, was that a male pastor from one of the most conservative Congregational churches in the West, addressing a female pastor from one of the most liberal Presbyterian churches on the map, said, "I know you are not the pastor of our group but I want you to know that you have been a pastor *to me.*"

And before long, the whole group had decided to stay together. Perhaps we have had a taste of the real reason why Jesus spoke so much of reconciliation. Maybe the taste of real food has left us in touch with real hunger. All I know is that we're staying together. We will go a little deeper, with a little less structure; we will explore inviting others into the dialogue process; and we will continue to ask the questions that will help us better understand.

After that, it's out of our hands.

REFERENCES

Schreiter, Robert J. 1998. *The Ministry of Reconciliation.* Maryknoll, N.Y.: Orbis Books.

Minow, Martha. 1998. *Between Vengeance and Forgiveness: Facing History After Genocide and Mass Violence.* Boston: Beacon Press.

Villa-Vicencio, Charles. 1997. "Telling One Another Stories: Toward a Theology of Reconciliation." In *The Reconciliation of Peoples* Gregory Baum and Harold Wells, eds. Maryknoll, N.Y.: Orbis Books.

All the greatest and most important problems of life are fundamentally insoluble. . . . They can never be solved, but only outgrown.

CARL JUNG

CHAPTER FIFTEEN

REWRITING NARRATIVES IN THE NEW SOUTH AFRICA:
A STORY OF RECONCILIATION

Anastasia White

This chapter explores the notion of narrative in situations of deep-rooted conflict and, in particular, how the transformation of these narratives can open up space for reconciliation to occur. Using a lens of social constructionism and positive approaches to conflict resolution, the author reflects on her experience in South Africa in the post-apartheid period and how this led to the rewriting of narratives in the presence of a former adversary. From this experience, she draws lessons about the process of reconciliation and its attendant impact on existing narratives. The chapter concludes by arguing for the contribution of positive approaches toward humanizing relationships between antagonists and how this process of humanizing the Other creates a frame with which to understand reconciliation and notions of justice.

⚜

In January 2001, just four months into the second *intifadah,* the Palestinian uprising against Israel, I participated in an interfaith peace delegation to Israel, Palestine, and Egypt. In witnessing the Middle East conflict through the eyes of those who are living it, I began to access my own experience of conflict in my homeland of South Africa in a new way. I was consistently struck by how easy it was to locate myself in the stories that I was hearing from both sides. I, too, had been born into war, grown up as a participant who made choices to resist what I considered an immoral system, and finally became a peacemaker in that same conflict.

It has always been my belief that the theories and practices developed to resolve and transform conflict should be rooted in the lived experience of the participants themselves. It is only those who confront the harsh reality of war who can truly understand its nature and purpose; and it is ultimately those same participants who will have to find a way forward. The Mideast trip prompted new reflections for me about the field of conflict resolution and my work as a practitioner in South Africa. These, in turn, fed into my doctoral research, which is guided by the questions: "How do people who live in conflict experience and make meaning of it, and what implications does this have for conflict analysis and intervention practices?"

In this chapter I share part of my own story of transformation in the new South Africa, a personal process of reconciliation and healing as understood from a social constructionist perspective. I offer a set of lessons learned in this reconciliation process and conclude by arguing for the role of positive approaches to reconciliation.

I share this story in a spirit of inquiry and with the hope of contributing to the larger discourse about the prospects for using positive approaches to bring former "enemies" together in creating a joint future. This is especially important in South Africa where the whites and blacks share a deep love and commitment to the place they call home.

A SOCIAL CONSTRUCTIONIST READING OF CONFLICT

John Paul Lederach summarizes a social constructionist reading of conflict in a way that offers a helpful frame for this section:

> . . . a constructionist view suggests that people act on the basis of the meaning things have for them. Meaning is created through shared and accumulated knowledge. People from different cultural settings have developed many ways of creating and expressing as well as interpreting and handling conflict. A fundamental argument of this book is that understanding conflict and developing appropriate models for handling it will necessarily be rooted in, and must respect and draw from, the cultural knowledge of people. (1995, 10)

The social constructionist illumination of the role of meaning and knowledge in conflict can be explored through the idea of a "conflict narrative." The notion of a conflict narrative is relatively new in the field of conflict resolution and peacebuilding and is emerging as the field grapples with the deep-rooted and intractable nature of many of the current conflicts affecting our world. It is clear that new ways of understanding the nature and source of contemporary conflicts are needed, as well as new approaches to intervention.

In situations of protracted, endemic, deep-rooted conflict, the conflict itself becomes the all-consuming nature of existence. This in turn creates a conflict narrative, a story about the conflict through which people can locate their experience and give meaning to events. These narratives can best be understood as stories of group identity. They are the language that each party uses to construct their past as a people, the words that contain the meaning of their existence and which are faithfully passed on to each new generation. The narrative is the thread of continuity that feeds the life of a nation or people. The purpose of this narrative is to help members of the group navigate the questions of living and to serve as a lighthouse in the storm and a way to engage daily existence. In war, these stories become central, fixed notions of a "who we are" and a framework by which to understand daily experience. They order feelings and process cognitions, reinforce the boundaries of group identity, and bind the group together.

As such, the conflict narrative structures the relationship toward the antagonist and, in addition, forms the basis of an individual's experience of self. What makes conflict narratives such a challenge to peacemaking efforts is that each party constructs their own distinct narrative based on their relationship to the conflict and interpretation of events, which often leave minimal space for a common starting point. "From a postmodern perspective, these stories construct both identity and ideology as speakers claim experience/memory from within the constraints of context they did not make, and often cannot alter" (Cobb 2002).

One of the common aspects of the conflict narrative is the dehumanization of the enemy or *the Other.* The ability to justify violent acts relies on the underlying principle of negation of the human rights and dignity of the Other. This dynamic allows a participant in the conflict to frame actions as morally justified in the face of an immoral threat, and further allows each group to understand their actions as retaliations rather than as attacks or acts of aggression. This complex dynamic has very important implications for the way that a conflict unfolds. In particular, it provides the moral justification for participants to engage in what would normally be considered gross violations of human rights. The spiral of violence this engenders is very difficult to end because of the cycle of blame that it sets in motion. Each side perceives itself as the victim and the Other as the perpetrator, making traditional reconciliation, which relies on a perpetrator's apology to the victim, very difficult.

I have used a social constructionist view of conflict and the idea of a conflict narrative to explore my own experiences as both a participant in conflict and as a conflict resolution practitioner. What follows is a piece of my experience in South Africa, which deeply challenged my conception of conflict and created the impetus for me to develop a frame and worldview through which to understand the role that the generation of positive narratives can play in healing and reconciliation work.

MY PERSONAL NARRATIVE

They have a name for people like me. Well, a few actually. They call us "the lost generation," "children of war," or even "child soldiers." We have different names for ourselves. The affectionate name we gave ourselves in South Africa was "Young Lions," but we also called ourselves "comrades," "brothers in arms," "vanguards of the struggle." I don't know what images these conjure up for you, the reader. Perhaps video clips of young suicide bombers in Palestine, or ragtag armies of young cocaine addicts in Sierra Leone, or even those images on CNN that pan over the faces of children in war zones with weary and old eyes. But I look nothing like that actually. I am about five feet, six inches tall and have dark hair, green eyes, freckles. I am thirty-two now. The thing that most people comment on when meeting me is my voice—soft-spoken and a strange, unidentifiable accent. Looking at me it is hard to believe the story I tell. My friends often tease strangers that they could never guess my past. I am a contradiction of sorts, but then I come from a place of contradictions.

One of the common questions I encounter these days, studying in the United States, is how I could have been an anti-apartheid activist given that I am white. You see the blood that runs in my veins comes from the colonists of my country. My mother's ancestors came in the 1600s, either fleeing persecution or as convicts from France, Germany, and the Netherlands. My father's ancestry dates back to the 1820 settlers from England (and more recently, some Irish blood, thus the freckles). Given my ancestry, my anti-apartheid activism does not conform to a clean definition of the struggle in South Africa as being between races, but rather demonstrates some of the complexity of the situation. Although most whites were for apartheid and most blacks were against it, there were exceptions, and my family was one of them.

I grew up in a community of anti-apartheid activists, a community created and sustained by an ecumenical group of churches. In 1948, when the Apartheid government rose to power, a group of clergy came together and decided that this new system seemed to be aimed at the separation of races. They decided to purchase a plot of land where races could come together. Their sense was prophetic, and the place that they bought became a central meeting and training ground for anti-apartheid activists from across the political spectrum. The community is called Wilgespruit Fellowship Centre, and in 1964 my father was placed by the Anglican Church to be the warden. It is here where I was born and spent the majority of my life.

The story of Wilgespruit is the story of ordinary individuals challenged by their faith to live in community at a time when the larger society believed in separation. It also becomes a way to tell a larger human story, a story of faith and belief in human goodness in the face of great suffering and persecution. It is out of this larger story that I share a part of my own life journey, in the hope that this experience may speak to that of others who, like me, were born into a war that worked to shape their lives.

THE CONTEXT OF APARTHEID SOUTH AFRICA

The institution of policing is generally accepted by society as one that exists to serve and protect citizens. In the context of Apartheid South Africa, however, the police role was constructed as a protection of the state and the racial status quo against terrorists, communists, and other unwanted elements who were committed to a different political and social ideal. This put my family and community in direct conflict with the policing and security apparatus of the state. We had no recourse to their resources, or protection, but rather were a target of their activities. This was the parameter that defined my experience and my perception of police and other security members and, in particular, the Security Branch.

There were two implications of this system for us. First, because the Security Branch worked outside of the mainstream legal system, during a "state of emergency" they did not need a search warrant when entering private property. They could arrest you without charges or trial for an indefinite period of time, and they did not have to account to a legal system as to your location or even provide visitation rights for lawyers, family members, or medical practitioners. This meant that once in the hands of the Security Branch, they could do anything they wanted with you, including torture, solitary confinement, or murder. Activists knew that their life and safety depended on never being taken into custody by a member of this policing structure, and we developed elaborate strategies to stay out of reach.

Second, being the specific target of police attacks meant that there was no one to protect you or your family. Activists lived in a constant state of vulnerability within the society and were considered "fair game" by anyone. Throughout my childhood, for example, random white citizens would come onto our property and try to shoot members of our community. If we called the police, they either did not come or warned us that if we continued our "subversive" activities, they could not be held responsible for the actions of outraged citizens. Not one of the perpetrators of these activities was ever charged, arrested, or even given warnings to cease this behavior.

After South Africa's first multiracial democratic election in 1994, this situation was radically altered for activists. Months after the election, I would be driving in my car and it would suddenly hit me that Nelson Mandela was now the president of South Africa! I would think to myself, I never again have to be afraid. Now the beliefs of my family and community are the accepted legal and social agreements. It is the racists, the people who believe in apartheid, who are the marginalized voice in our country, and I *never* have to be afraid again.

It was in this context that I first met Colonel van der Merwe (not his real name).

AN IMPROBABLE PARTNERSHIP

After the 1994 election, I was asked by the new Ministry of Safety and Security in Gauteng, the province where I lived, to assist in setting up Community-Police Forums (CPFs) at each local police station in the West Rand. This area encompassed Soweto, South Africa's largest black township and a central flashpoint for anti-apartheid activity. The mandate from the newly appointed minister was to bring together community leaders and police personnel to rebuild relationships damaged under the Apartheid regime and to create a joint policing strategy for the area. This process was intended to provide legislative recommendations on the restructuring of the police service, as well as to write a new training material for police personnel. The need for reconciliation came out of the history of conflict between police and the community in Apartheid South Africa. What made this reconciliation process so crucial was that part of the transition agreement was a clause that guaranteed the jobs of all civil servants for three years, thus none of the policing personnel would change.

I was assigned a co-facilitator from the South African Police Service. My mandate was to convince community leaders to come to the table because of my substantial contacts with this group, while his task was to bring the relevant policing authorities.

During the initial meeting with my co-facilitator, Col. van der Merwe volunteered that he had been a member of the Security Branch, the specialized unit of the police whose mandate was to harass and eliminate anti-apartheid activists, and that he had been responsible for my family's file. This was the first time that I could attribute a face to the years of institutional harassment and intimidation that my family and I had endured at the hands of the Apartheid State. Since before I was born, the Security Branch had wire-tapped our phones and houses; intercepted and detained visitors to our community; raided the property on at least two occasions, attempting to confiscate arms (which we never had) and to arrest members of banned parties and dissidents (who often were present); and ignored calls for help when armed men entered our property and discharged firearms.

The decision to work with Col. van der Merwe resulted in one of the most intense and profound personal transformations I have ever experienced. The key to my being able to work on a professional level with him and subsequently to develop the necessary level of trust to make our co-facilitation successful was the challenging and rewriting of my own conflict narrative. This narrative, defining people like him as "the enemy," had worked to sustain my anti-apartheid stance and my identity in the Apartheid era. What made our work even more powerful was that our relationship mirrored the dynamic that was present in any meeting we facilitated between

 community and police members, giving us a level of insight that other facilitation teams did not necessarily have. It also increased our legitimacy with participants since we were fully aware of the transformation each person had to undergo for the process to be successful.

The following sections explore that process and capture the milestones and turning points in our relationship.

First Meeting

Our first encounter was in Col. van der Merwe's office of Community-Police Relations. This was a new department established by the Ministry of Safety and Security, although all personnel had been recruited from the existing police force. I walked in and introduced myself. His response was to say that he knew me already. Assuming that we had met in the past, I was embarrassed, knowing that I had a propensity to forget names, though very rarely a face. He quickly countered my apology with the revelation that we had in fact never met in person, but that he had previously been a member of the Security Branch and knew me from my family's security file. I was very taken aback and asked how he had been allocated to the Community-Police Relations department. It turned out that when the Security Branch was closed, most members were given the option of taking a severance package or moving to this new department. We continued our meeting in a stilted fashion, discussing our terms of reference and the guidelines of our approach as outlined by the new legislation on community policing. We parted with an agreement to address a meeting of community leadership the following week in Bekkersdaal, a black community on the West Rand, where severe fighting between local police and the community had taken place.

I left his office in turmoil. It was beyond my comprehension how the ministry could staff this department, mandated with a reconciliation agenda, with the worst of the perpetrators from the Apartheid era. Although I respected Col. van der Merwe's honesty, I was very mistrustful of his motivations for revealing his past to me. Was I entering a situation where my credibility and legitimacy within communities was going to be used for a covert police agenda? If this process was not authentically aimed at the empowerment of communities and creating accountability of the police, could I ethically give my backing to it? What would happen to my reputation and ability to work in the field if this project turned out to be a manipulation by police who had no interest in being held accountable for past or future actions? On the other hand, what if I was wrong? What if this process had a real possibility of leading to the kind of post-apartheid society I had dedicated my life to? Could I in all integrity walk away if this was the case? How could I allow my personal feelings to prevent a social restructuring of relationships to happen, if I did not want my children to grow up in a divided world filled with hatred? I felt that I was being challenged at the deepest level to commit to personal and social transformation. It would be the most difficult professional challenge to know whether this process was truly beneficial, and the cost of making a mistake would be my future credibility and my family's reputation.

Why did I choose to stay on the project? Partly it was the potential the project held for real engagement of social relationships at a local level. In my view, the Truth and Reconciliation Commission (TRC) was a political agreement that needed to be supplemented with civil-society initiatives if we were ever going to have true reconciliation in relationships. Partially it was also trusting that I had sufficient understanding of the issues at hand that I would be able to make a judgment call about whether to continue or not—and that being part of the process, I would have more ability to shape and influence this outcome. Perhaps most importantly, I felt there had to be a reason that out of the thousands of people I could have been assigned to work with—in this case, Col. van der Merwe—life was offering me an opportunity that I could not walk away from.

Community-Police Meetings

We soon adopted a routine for working together. Prior to each community-police meeting, we would prepare an agenda for discussion, divide up the facilitation tasks, and talk through the possible dynamics that could derail the process and that needed to be managed. During the Community-Police Forums, I would usually take the lead, and Col. van der Merwe would reinforce the important points by rephrasing them in the cultural language of the police. After each meeting we would debrief and decide on the next steps of action.

The second meeting we facilitated was at the police station in Meadowlands, a suburb of Soweto that had experienced some of the most intense violence of this area. Due to the severity of the antagonism between the community and police personnel, we agreed that I would meet with the station commissioner to brief him on how to approach the meeting. I found it ironic that I was considered an appropriate "coach" to this station commissioner, given that the first and last time I had ever entered that particular police station was when I was arrested at the age of twelve.

It was a huge psychological strain for me to enter the world and workspace of police. My life experience had taught me to avoid them at all costs, and the adrenalin of self-preservation kicked in anytime I was in a closed space with police. In addition, I found it very difficult to speak honestly and felt unsafe sharing my thoughts and ideas. Col. van der Merwe alleviated much of this stress by consistently briefing me prior to meetings on which police personnel had been in the Security Branch and who knew me from the files. This access to information helped me to enter each situation feeling a little less vulnerable and caught off guard if I was recognized, or when references were made to my background. I was especially grateful because I knew that he could easily have kept that information from me, and this would have hindered my ability to facilitate the process in a way that was beneficial to the community.

Personal Meetings

Due to Col. van der Merwe's consistent honesty and open information sharing, I became more interested in his personal story and openly shared my questions about his motivation. This led to a series of personal meetings that would often last for hours, which we labeled "mini TRCs." These meetings began by sharing perceptions around events that had occurred. For example, my family's house and office had been bombed when I was sixteen, and although we always suspected the Security Branch, we had no evidence. I asked him directly about the Security Branch's role in this incident, and he admitted that they had planted the bomb in order to destroy contraband they believed we were producing and distributing.

These conversations were difficult for both of us. For me it was painful to hear his rationalizations, which trivialized actions that had been very traumatic for us. For him it was difficult to acknowledge that what they had labeled as "pranks" to harass and inhibit our activities were very serious violations of our sense of safety and human dignity as a community. A feature of these meetings was that they became more and more confrontational as our comfort level in the relationship grew. Through this process I did, however, gain an insight into how he had framed his activities, as well as the narrative that sustained his sense of purpose. In time this led to my recognizing that we had both shared a common sense of struggle, although from opposing sides, and that I would probably have behaved in very similar ways if I had been in his place. The line between perpetrator and victim became blurred for me, and this allowed me to realize the humanity of Col. van der Merwe and, by extension, the groups with which I identified him.

Slowly, I came to trust his motivations for wanting to facilitate a successful restructuring of police-community relationships. His initial motivation for joining the police was to create safety and security for the civilian population, and now that black people were considered legitimate citizens, they fell within this realm of responsibility. I also witnessed his personal anguish that came with the realization that apartheid was a destructive system that had robbed people of their human dignity and rights as citizens. Through our conversations, he began to confront the myths of "white supremacy" and "Afrikaner identity" that had been used to propagate this evil. For both of us this process called into question many of our life actions and beliefs, leading to a radical rewriting of our personal narratives. When the Other attains a human face, all the justifications that have sustained one's sense of purpose are deeply challenged. It no longer becomes possible to retain the clear distinctions between causes once this humanization occurs, and this in turn leads to a reassessment of one's past actions in light of the human face of the Other.

Entering Personal Lives

Once we had worked sufficiently through this process, both of us made overtures to invite the other into our personal lives. I believe we both felt the need to integrate this transformed perception and narrative into our world, meaning our existing social group. Col. van der Merwe's overture was on two levels. First, I was invited to his home for dinner and to meet his wife and, then, with an ironic twist, into his community life. With the establishment of the Land Restitution Act, black communities that had been forcibly removed in order to establish racially hegemonic communities were now able to lay claim to their historic land, and the community to which Col. van der Merwe belonged was engaged in a dispute about land ownership. He asked me for assistance in mediating this dispute.

Given his role in the life of my family, introducing him to my parents was a huge step in our relationship. I felt very protective of him, wanting my parents to see what I had come to understand about his humanity. For his part, Col. van der Merwe was extremely nervous, knowing that he was partially seeking forgiveness for past actions. It was a strange dynamic in which I acted as a mediator and interpreter between Col. van der Merwe and my family. The outcome was a limited ability for each of us to begin operating in the world of the other, allowing us to develop a friendship. This friendship ultimately found tangible expression when I wrote a letter of recommendation for his promotion at the ministry, and Col. van der Merwe wrote a recommendation for my application to my Ph.D. program.

IMPLICATIONS FOR THE RECONCILIATION AND HEALING PROCESS

When reflecting on the milestones and turning points in my relationship with Col. van der Merwe, five elements emerged that made our shared transformation possible. I discuss each element below, explain how it was manifested within our interaction, and then draw from it a general lesson. I offer these implications as a starting point for understanding the process of recrafting previous narratives in order to allow a new relationship to emerge.

Opportunity to Interact with the Other

I had known from a very young age that the anti-apartheid struggle was my life. There would be no other life for me, and all my choices and ambitions would be subservient to this higher calling. I believed that it would not be for me to live in a "normal" society, but that this was the legacy I would leave to a future generation. The ending of the Apartheid regime and the transition to a new South Africa was therefore both the culmination of a life dream and an extremely confusing time. I felt as if suddenly the whole world had opened up for me. There was a lifetime of choices that now became available but which required a redefinition of self. What now would be my purpose, my contribution in life? Did I have the life skills to operate in this new environment? Who was I really, me, deep down, and what were my gifts?

The new space that this created within my own life was mirrored in that of the society, and each individual faced this challenge. The timing of my project with Col. van der Merwe thus allowed for a new flexibility in my responses to the Other in ways that were not available during the struggle. Prior to this, any movement toward understanding the humanity of the enemy would have been seen as treasonous. During the struggle, people were killed for less. With the national TRC process, however, and the necessity to build a new South Africa, reconciliation was the new national project.

The nature of apartheid was the segregation of races and the prohibition of racial mixing on any level, from marriage to use of the same amenities. The misunderstanding, stereotypes, and hatred that were generated among groups were therefore not founded in interpersonal relationships. It was the system that had structured the parameters of interaction, and with the restructuring of that system, people were brought into new relationship with one another. This new national project brought the opportunity to unveil existing stereotypes through humanizing of the Other.

The cost of not succeeding at this national project was the possibility of ongoing civil war. But South Africa was different from other African countries, whose colonial populations still held some ties and allegiance to European nations. White South Africans, in general, and Afrikaners, in particular, had nowhere else to go. Thus an inability to coexist would lead to either the annihilation of certain groups or a return to apartheid's separatist policies.

Lesson: In conflicts characterized by lack of personal interaction among social groups, and in which individual engagement with the Other is structured by conflict narratives, an opening in social space is needed to allow a restructuring of narratives so that a new manifestation of relationship can emerge. To the extent that the timing of a new interaction between conflict parties is congruent with and reinforced by larger social changes, it is more likely to succeed.

Peaceful Role Models

This process requires a deep questioning of a person's worldview and the way in which the person structures his or her responses to the world. In many ways this is uncharted territory, which is frightening in its possible implications. Part of what makes the conflict narrative so seductive is how clearly it allocates moral blame. You are right and they are wrong, a simple life philosophy that enables you to justify many behaviors that outside of war are considered inappropriate, even unthinkable. In this new moral wilderness, it is important to find voices with some moral authority that can help guide your quest. For me these were Nelson Mandela and Jesus Christ.

It was very soon after the April 1994 election that our Community-Police Forum held a rally in Soweto and invited opposing factions. This was the first time that people who had been in violent conflict with one another would attend a joint ceremony to celebrate the successful transition. As such, it was important to ensure that the new symbols such as the new flag and national anthem be given prominence. President Mandela was invited as the guest speaker. This was the first time I sang the new national anthem—a combination of the Apartheid-era anthem and the liberation-struggle anthem—in its entirety. As committed as I was to the national transition, I had until that day been unable to sing the Apartheid anthem, and would instead stand silently until the time to sing the anthem of my allegiance. Standing close to Mandela at this rally, I saw him sing the entire anthem and thought to myself, if Mandela can do this, then I can too. Since that time I have sung the entire anthem.

Role models can also give inspiration when you feel you are at the end of your own ability to understand or forgive. Being a committed Christian, I often found myself asking the question, "What would Jesus do in this situation?" His philosophy of forgiveness and treatment of one's enemy were important guidelines that allowed me to transcend my own bitterness and anger in my relationship with Col. van der Merwe.

Another aspect of role modeling is the power of becoming a role model yourself. Given the work in which Col. van der Merwe and I were engaged, participants in our meetings studied our interaction very carefully. In the end, the success of our project was tied directly to the success of our interaction. Through our own reconciliation process, we were able to provide an example of successful cooperation for the other project participants. There were many times when one of us could convince a participant to stay with the process only because we had shown ourselves willing to engage as well.

Lesson: The ending of the existing conflict narrative challenges previous static categories of right and wrong, which leads to a situation of confusion and personal reassessment of previously accepted behavior within which positive role models can help guide individuals in navigating the restructuring process.

Never Apologizing

Throughout our many conversations, neither Col. van der Merwe nor I ever apologized for our actions, our group, or our cause. It was not something that I required from him—and certainly nothing that I would ever have given. In fact, the Truth and Reconciliation Commission never had this as a criterion for amnesty. (The criteria for amnesty were full and complete disclosure of activities and being able to prove that your actions held a political agenda.)

This aspect runs contrary to theories of victim-offender reconciliation that require the perpetrator to acknowledge the harm committed in order for the process to move forward. In situations of ongoing conflict, however, the distinction between victim and perpetrator becomes blurred. Each side is at the same time a victim of violence as well as a propagator of it. Within this dynamic, each side justifies its violation of the Other as a legitimate response to an unfair attack. Thus neither Col. van der Merwe nor I believed that our activities to advance our cause had been wrong, and we each had sustained our conflict narratives to justify this.

How did we then come to the point of reconciliation? Interestingly, each of us was able to acknowledge that our actions up to that point had had unseen consequences for the other. This realization had required us each to enter the other person's worldview, to understand how the other's narrative had been constructed, and ultimately, to admit that if our roles had been reversed, we would have behaved in a very similar fashion. In this process, I experienced a profound sense of being acknowledged as a human being who had made legitimate choices in response to an illegitimate situation. There was a fine line involved in taking responsibility for my actions, even while not releasing the sense that they had been correct within that context.

To acknowledge responsibility was different from believing that either one of us was wrong. To see myself as wrong would negate my life and make my existence up to that point meaningless or at best completely misguided. To believe this of Col. van der Merwe would turn him into a pathetic human being to be pitied, rather than a person of strong conviction who had had the courage to back his beliefs with action. The commonality was that we both had been prepared to lay down our life for something we believed in. I could respect him for this, and he could respect me.

Lesson: The outcome of deep engagement with the Other does not have to be a common narrative. Rather, this engagement can be understood as a co-creative process in which the individuals are challenged to extend their notions of self beyond the boundary of their existing narrative. With acknowledgement from the Other, and by seeing yourself in the Other, apologies become unnecessary. This positive engagement with the Other forms the basis for recasting individual and ultimately group narratives.

Rehumanizing the Other

Both Col. van der Merwe and I had been "soldiers" fighting on behalf of a cause. In delving deeply into the reasons that we each took this active stance, it emerged that we both felt a strong sense of allegiance to the land. This common loyalty or commitment to the country allowed me to realize that the sides we took became a question of history and place and the resulting perception of what the right solution was. With the transition to a new South Africa, we each realized the time had come to coexist on the same land, and it was our common love for the country that required us to reconcile.

In a strange way, soldiers share a code of honor and loyalty that binds them together, even as they perpetuate violence for their cause. This sense of loyalty and honor was something that I recognized in Col. van der Merwe, and it allowed me to see myself in the Other. Had he not believed completely in what he did, it would have been very difficult to accept the senselessness of it.

Even though I was suspicious of his motivations, from our first meeting I appreciated Col. van der Merwe's honesty, which gave me a sense of the type of person with whom I was dealing. His consistent honesty over time was what allowed me to take the risk in confronting him about the past. His willingness and ability to describe his experience sufficiently for me to understand it proved critical to my own ability to remain nondefensive in an interpersonal dynamic that allowed a friendship to grow between us. The elements of honesty, confrontation, and willingness to take risks were critical to our ability to share sufficient information for the narrative restructuring to take place.

Lesson: Reconciliation is made easier when the parties can identify a shared sense of motive. This shared sense of motive humanizes choices made by the Other, even though one vigorously disagrees with those choices.

Integration

The interaction with Col. van der Merwe resulted in a profound personal transformation that was mirrored in the restructuring of my narrative of self. I was changed in deep and meaningful ways, and this then required work to reintegrate myself into my primary identity group in a way that incorporated this new narrative. I could not have forgiven Col. van der Merwe for his actions if the cost had been exile from my community. The goal therefore became having members of my identity group accept, if even in a limited way, that this changed narrative was real for me.

Lesson: Integration of restructured narratives needs to occur on an individual and group level.

CONCLUSION

At the time of this experience with Col. van der Merwe, I had not yet explored a social constructionist reading of conflict nor experimented with positive approaches to conflict resolution. Using these approaches now to reflect on both my personal and professional experience, I am confronted by several interesting questions.

A common critique of the social constructionist reading of conflict is that it tends towards moral relativism in its interpretation of relationships and events. The social constructionist approach is seen as ignoring existing structures and institutional systems that are by nature unjust and immoral, and therefore as negating any responsibility that individuals hold for creating and sustaining these systems. This critique speaks directly to the question of power and how the unequal distribution of power impacts both the notions of reality that are constructed and by whom.

Layered onto this concern is a question about the role of positive approaches to conflict resolution. It is easy to interpret the notion of *positive* as advocating for the avoidance of the negative, or a request that people only focus on those aspects of their experience that are considered "good." This leads, it is feared, to a disregard for the pain and trauma that people in conflict have suffered, and with that disregard comes a negation of self. At its core, this is a concern about justice and the recognition that conflict often is caused by gross inequities and violations of human rights that need to be acknowledged and confronted directly.

When considering the process of reconciliation between former adversaries, these concerns become amplified because of the extreme nature of past relationships. One response to this critique is to take the discourse out of the realm of individual actors and into the realm of the relational nature of conflict. Reconciliation is at its core about the healing and renewal of relationships that have been damaged through conflict. This happens at a variety of levels: the relationship of the individual to self, the individual to the group, groups to other groups, and ultimately the relationship between people and social structures and systems.

To heal relationships requires an authentic and passionate engagement with lived experience, which cannot happen by ignoring important experiences or by simply agreeing to disagree. It also requires that participants move away from the roles of victim-perpetrator and power-powerless into that of co-creator. This shift is fraught with difficulties that come from external circumstance as well as internal consciousness. The conflict resolution practitioner plays only a limited role in this shift. Ultimately, it is the participants themselves who will walk this journey and determine its outcome, and it is in this regard that there is an important contribution for a social constructionist world view and for positive approaches.

Returning to my own lived experience, I grew up in Apartheid South Africa, which was a very sophisticated set of social, judicial, and political systems. These systems worked to construct my reality, and there was no effective way to ignore them or marginalize their power over my life. These systems and the people who perpetuated them invaded every aspect of my daily living and structured my opportunities in the world. The challenge became, what would be my relationship to these larger social and political constraints? As a community we believed in a very specific vision that was of a different reality than the one within which we lived. We made the choice to live as though that vision were already the reality and to accept the consequences of that decision, without being swayed in our commitment.

This has shaped my view of power. Power is real and it comes in many forms. The greatest source of power to which I have direct access is my own choices and how I manifest them in my relationship to events and people around me. Thus when confronted with Col. van der Merwe, I was challenged at the deepest level to live my own positive vision of the future by engaging and transforming my relationship to my past and to his role in that.

This leads me to the second discovery that enabled the reconciliation and healing to occur. Our history is not static; we continuously write and rewrite the story of events to create a narrative that makes sense in the present circumstances and gives meaning to our lives. Reconciliation offers the opportunity to revisit one's history in the presence of the Other, to release both parties from its negative repercussions, and to make both whole again. The act of forgiveness enables each person, victim and perpetrator, to break through to a future free of the cycle of violence and revenge, and it does this by (re)humanizing "the enemy" and reclaiming one's own humanity. Central to this humanization process is the rewriting of one's perception of the Other as evil. This is more possible when a positive impulse informs the new narrative. In the case of Col. Van der Merwe and myself, this positive impulse was the desire to see a future for South Africa as a whole and our identity groups specifically.

Where is the place of justice in all of this? There are many conceptions of justice. For me justice is about the future, which requires a healing of the past injustice, fueled by the belief in a better tomorrow. A just world is one in which relationships are realigned and we act in ways that construct a world in which each person can be fully human. This is a conception of justice rooted in the African concept of *ubuntu*—"people are people because of other people." To live with ubuntu challenges each of us to re-create our relationship with others and to generate social, political, and economic structures that are just. Justice is therefore less about punishment and more about responsibility; less about retribution and more about reconciliation; less reactive and more proactive. Justice is a co-creation born out of the everyday lives and choices that each one of us grapples with, in integrity and courage, to have a future worthy of our aspiration.

My own response to critiques of social constructionist theory and positive approaches to conflict resolution is epitomized in the words of Carl Jung:

> All the greatest and most important problems of life are fundamentally insoluble. . . . They can never be solved, but only outgrown. . . . Some higher or wider interest appeared on the patient's horizon, and through this broadening of his outlook the insoluble problem lost its urgency. It was not solved logically in its own terms, but faded out when confronted with a new and stronger life urge. (1938, as quoted in Storr 1999, 533)

This "outgrowing," said Jung, requires a new level of consciousness.

In one view, my story might be understood as simply a relatively interesting story of two individuals in a much larger picture. In that view, its lessons would apply only to situations with clearly similar dynamics, for example, in which the conflict has reached a point of resolution, or conflict parties are willing to engage one another, or there is a common project being pursued, or some other fairly particularistic factor.

Or, one might view my story as revealing a larger, more generic insight into how hope and healing are enabled through authentic and positive engagement with the Other. For me, the larger invitation is to understand that reconciliation and healing are a real possibility, regardless of the specific circumstances and history. This invitation is made more poignant by the realities of structural and relational inequalities that exist all over the globe. And it is made more necessary as options for the pursuit of war continue to multiply.

REFERENCES

Cobb, Sara. 2002. Abstract of "Talking Transformation: Narrative Evolution in Conflict Processes." Paper presented at a meeting at the University Of Arizona Department Of Psychology (April), Tucson, Arizona.

Jung, Carl G. 1938. "Commentary on 'The Secret of the Golden Flower'." CW 13, paras 18 and 70.

Lederach, John Paul. 1995. *Preparing for Peace: Conflict Transformation Across Cultures*. Syracuse, N.Y.: Syracuse University Press.

Storr, Anthony. 1999. "Is analytical psychology a religion? Jung's search for a substitute for lost faith." *Journal of Analytical Psychology* 44, pp. 531–537.

The real voyage of discovery consists not in seeking new landscapes but in having new eyes.

MARCEL PROUST

CHAPTER SIXTEEN

TRANSCENDENCE:
DISCOVERING RESOURCES FOR
POSTTRAUMATIC HEALING AND GROWTH

Nancy Good Sider

Appreciative interviews with peacebuilders who have survived trauma provide the context for this exploration of posttraumatic healing and growth. The author presents an adapted appreciative interview approach that balances the need to acknowledge traumatic experiences with the equally important need to identify the sources of resilience and resources for growth needed to transcend trauma. The chapter sets the interview findings in a broader context by looking at shifts toward positive, strengths-based approaches emerging in several related fields, and describes applications of positive-growth approaches in trauma work, known as "posttraumatic growth." It then explores the peacebuilders' interviews for insights into the processes and resources for transcending trauma. In so doing, it shows appreciative interviewing to be an essential discovery tool for retrieving such stories of transcendence, expanding the language of hope, and enhancing the pursuit of posttraumatic healing and growth for both survivors and caregivers.

❧

ecently I met Sumita Ghose from India, a mother of two teenagers whose husband was abducted by a militant group. As I interviewed her five years after the abduction, even though she still does not know the fate of her husband, Sumita is carrying out the vision for peacebuilding and development that they shared for twelve years. Looking back on the trauma of her husband's disappearance, Sumita realizes that the resources for growth and healing uncovered by the tragedy have allowed her to continue in this work.

Another peacebuilder, Sam Gbaydee Doe, has been threatened to the extent of having to hide and then flee from his home country of Liberia. Sam chooses to live into what he calls "compassionate anger" and to see his "enemy" as a man who loves his children rather than as a man who killed many other children of Africa. As I interviewed both

Sam and Sumita, I discovered stories with the same theme: In the very midst of trauma and its aftermath, people possess and can access resources for healing and growth.

Sam and Sumita exemplify many peacebuilders who directly experience trauma in their own lives and then, through their peacebuilding work as caregivers, possibly experience secondary traumatization through hearing the stories of others. Yet they nonetheless find a way to transcend trauma. How is this possible? How does Sam resist violent retaliation against those who threaten his life? How does he keep going back into the thick of violent conflicts in an effort to transform them? Why does Sumita refuse to stay secure in the victim narrative of her story and instead of seeking revenge, continue to assist the community where her husband was abducted? How did she break out of the victim cycle and refuse to become an offender herself? These two peacebuilders chose another way.

These are the kinds of questions that motivated my research and impelled my interviews with Sumita, Sam, and others like them. Why not strike back or simply give up? What do they do with the often all-consuming grief and rage that we know to be a normal reaction to the abnormal experience of the trauma they have endured? How do they go forward living lives overflowing with compassion, not just surviving the trauma but transcending it? Why do they then choose a vocation of peacebuilding in violent conflicts and expose themselves to secondary traumatization and compassion fatigue?[1]

Psychiatrist Viktor Frankl, a survivor of years in Nazi concentration camps, would often ask his clients in therapy: "Why do you not commit suicide?" This may sound like a crude and harsh question to put to a person swarming in traumatic pain and loss. But Frankl used the question to find a theme for his therapeutic work. He believed that if survivors could find some meaning in their suffering and misery, they could survive and move on. To explain his approach, Frankl often quoted the German philosopher Frederich Nietzsche: "He who has a *why* to live can bear with almost any *how*" (Frankl [1959] 1992, 7–9).

In search of the *why* as well as the *how,* I used an appreciative interview format to interview ten peacebuilders who have endured both primary and secondary traumatization. Through the interviews, their stories of tragedy revealed the resources that peacebuilders and caregivers can develop and rely on to grow beyond trauma. This chapter approaches these stories and discoveries within a broader context by, first, taking a brief look at shifts toward the "positive" happening in several related fields and, second, looking at emerging applications of the "positive" to what is called "posttraumatic growth." It then takes an in-depth look at the stories of four peacebuilders for insight into the processes and resources for transcending trauma, as well as vivid examples of the kinds of meaningful insight that the appreciative interview process can yield.

STRATEGIES FOR POSITIVE GROWTH: A CONVERGENCE OF FIELDS

Until recently, clinical psychologists have focused the majority of their attention on the diagnosis and treatment of pathologies, and in the quest for "fixes," have paid scant attention to the nature of psychological health. Practitioners of social cognitive psychology have devoted vast attention to the biases, delusions, illusions, foibles, and errors of human beings. To be sure, this emphasis on the problem has been an important step in identifying social and psychological difficulties and has generated a variety of tools and treatments for analyzing and solving the problem. It is becoming increasingly clear, however, that the normal functioning of human beings cannot be accounted for within purely negative, problem focused frames of reference.

In recent decades, a variety of disciplines have begun to emphasize the importance of positive, life-giving systems in healing and resolving life's conflicts. This convergence on positive, strengths-based approaches appears across fields as diverse as psychology, criminal justice, and social work. Practitioners in these disciplines have begun to realize their work has generally focused on diagnosing problems in the individual and/or social system. According to psychologists Kennon Sheldon and Laura King, however, problem-focused strategies tend to be negative and backward looking, and overlook the basic creative impulses of human nature. They argue that psychologists have been trained to view positivity with suspicion and suggest that "such skepticism, taken too far, may itself constitute a negativity bias that prevents a clear understanding of reality" (Sheldon and King 2001, 216–217). In fact, a majority of people achieve a state of thriving, rating themselves as happy and satisfied with their lives (Meyers 2000).

Concerned about the risks of problem-based approaches, increasing numbers of practitioners and theorists have begun to reorient their respective fields to focus on positive, creative, and forward-looking strategies. A brief survey of some leading examples follows.

Strengths-based Practice in Social Work

Many changes in human services have occurred since the mid-1990s. One innovation in the social work profession is the development of a strengths perspective and model of practice. Social work practitioner and educator Dennis Saleeby notes that this perspective, together with the literature on resilience, suggests that "social workers may learn from those people who survive and in some cases flourish in the face of oppression, illness, demoralization, and abuse. Social workers need to know what steps these natural survivors have taken, what processes they have adopted, and what resources they have used" (2000, 127–136).

Originally limited to work with severe, persistent mental illness, the strengths-based approach is now in use with the elderly in long-term care, emotionally disturbed youth and their families, people with substance abuse problems, and protective services for adults. The field of corrections has also seen initial applications. In addition, the strengths perspective is beginning to inform fields beyond direct practice such as community organization, social administration, and policy analysis. Training materials and curricula have been developed for practitioners, while scholars have moved toward the development of a theory of strengths (Saleeby 1997).

Positive Psychology

During the last decade, the field of psychology has slowly expanded its focus on dysfunction to include some curiosity about health, growth, and positivity. Although Sheldon and King decry how relatively little psychologists know about human thriving and how to encourage it (2001, 216–217), Dana Dunn, in reviewing the 2002 publication *Handbook of Positive Psychology,* sees marked progress toward an appreciative perspective. "What is clearly not up for debate," she writes, "is that publication of the *Handbook* establishes human strengths and resilience as a mainstream topic. . . ." (2002, 581).

In the *Handbook,* Martin Seligman, the researcher credited with coining the term *positive psychology,* explains:

> Psychology is not just the study of disease, weakness, and damage; it also is the study of strength and virtue. Treatment is not just fixing what is wrong; it is also building what is right. Psychology is not just about illness or health; it is also about work, education, insight, love, growth, and play. (Dunn 2002, 580)

Restorative Justice

Significant advances in some sectors of the criminal justice field have shifted the focus from retribution against offenders to restoration of individuals and the community. Psychiatrist James Gilligan has documented that the traditional "treatment" of offenders through punishment "does not prevent violence, it causes it, in addition to being a form of it" (2001, 18). In recent decades, many scholars and practitioners have begun to look at crime and violence through a new lens, a lens that focuses attention on the harm caused by crime to individuals, communities, and relationships and identifies the strengths and assets possessed by individuals and communities for redressing that harm, including meeting the needs of the victims and community. "Rather than defining justice as retribution, we will define justice as restoration. If crime is injury, justice will repair injuries and promote healing" (Zehr 1995, 186; see also Achilles and Zehr 2001).

POSITIVE GROWTH AFTER TRAUMA

Frankl wrote that optimism in the face of tragedy can turn suffering into a human achievement, an ability he called "tragic optimism." In the concentration camp, every circumstance conspired to make the prisoner lose his hold. All the familiar goals in life were snatched away. What alone remained was "the last of human freedoms"—the ability to "choose one's attitude in a given set of circumstances" ([1959] 1992, 9). This allows for the possibility of positive growth, even in the most tragic of circumstances.

In this section we look at recent applications of positive growth vocabularies and approaches in trauma work, whether dealing with primary or secondary traumatization.

Solution-based Therapy

Solution-based therapy is one specific therapeutic modality born out of this positive focus on strengths and what people are doing that works. Bill O'Hanlon, an originator of this approach, in his book *Do One Thing Different* (1999), encourages therapists and caregivers to help clients vision into the future by asking the "miracle question"—"if a miracle were to happen in your life and this problem were to disappear, what would you do differently and how would you be different?" This therapy encourages clients to shift their attention from what is happening to what they desire and to break problem patterns by doing one thing differently.

Positive Growth in Crisis Intervention

Many crisis practitioners see crisis as both an occurrence of injury and trauma and also a juncture in which growth and opportunity are probabilities. People resolve crises by connecting with others, making positive meaning of the experience, and taking action. Many people in crisis prove to be resilient and are able to develop a deeper appreciation of life through their crisis (Echterling et al. 2003, 3). In fact, it begins to appear that resilience is the rule rather than the exception for many facing traumatic events, regardless of their age.

Positive Illusions

Shelley Taylor looks at how people can have positive appraisals after threatening events. In her book *Positive Illusions* (1989), Taylor describes the ability of the healthy human mind to stave off negative information in trauma, allowing the mind to create what she calls positive illusions to help people cope.

Posttraumatic Growth

Growth outcomes are reported even in the aftermath of the most traumatic of circumstances, showing that posttraumatic stress (PTS) and posttraumatic growth (PTG), which might be seen as antithetical, actually coexist. Citing "a variety of aspects about which we have some reliable data," Lawrence Calhoun and Richard Tedeschi write: "It is clear that individuals who have faced a wide array of negative life challenges report that their struggle with those difficulties have, paradoxically, had positive effects on their lives. It is the personal struggle precipitated by the environmental demands, rather than the events themselves, that sets into motion the cluster of changes that we call posttraumatic growth" (1998, 215). Calhoun and Tedeschi challenge clinicians and scholars working in the area of traumatic stress "to revise their assumptions, so that they systematically attend to the possibility of PTG, even for the majority of persons who are more distressed than before the trauma's occurrence" (1998, 234–235; see also Tedeschi and Calhoun 1995).

THE APPRECIATIVE INTERVIEW: A METHODOLOGY AND RATIONALE

In this chapter I present the stories of four individuals that particularly illuminate the questions being explored here: "What is the path to transcendence after trauma?" and "How can caregivers assist individuals in transforming trauma through interviews that highlight personal resilience and growth?" Central to this exploration has been an adapted appreciative interview process that, resembling the developments in related fields, balances the need to acknowledge traumatic experiences with the equally important need to identify the resources to transcend trauma.

The *What*: Expanding the Questions

To elicit these stories of trauma and transcendence, I needed to expand the set of questions that those of us who work in the trauma field are accustomed to asking. I needed to develop questions that would uncover the resources for growth and healing that are inherent in the individual, even while the injury is raw and potentially life threatening; questions that would reveal strengths and hope in the midst of apparent weakness and helplessness; and questions that would elicit appreciation for what remains and what has been gained, even as the losses are being surveyed.

This need to expand my frame of reference is illustrated by the plight of a man who pulls off the side of the road after dark. A police officer arrives and finds this man crawling around talking to himself under a streetlight. The officer asks the man what he is doing, and the man answers in a troubled voice, "I dropped the keys to my house." The officer helps him look around, but after fifteen minutes, with still no sign of the keys, suggests, "Let's retrace your steps. Where was the last place you remember having your keys?" "Oh that's easy," replies the man, "I dropped them across the street." "You did!" cries the astonished cop. "Well, then why are we looking over here?" "There's more light over here," replies the man (O'Hanlon 1999, 1).

In many of the helping fields, we often look at the problem where the light is already focused rather than redirecting the light to illuminate other critical places. Analyzing and explaining why we have a problem doesn't necessarily offer many concrete ways to creatively and effectively move forward in life.

The *Why*: Why use the Appreciative Interview?

In the field of trauma healing and recovery, the appreciative interview—the Discovery Phase of Appreciative Inquiry (AI)—can awaken and uncover positive healing forces. Appreciative interviewing involves the art and science of asking questions that strengthen people's capacities to tap into and heighten their positive potential (Cooperrider et al. 2000). If people move in the direction of the questions they ask and where they consistently focus attention, then crafting questions with a vocabulary of pain, negativity, and loss may promote a downward spiral rather than upward movement toward growth and healing. Questions employing a vocabulary of hope, on the other hand, can redirect attention to the possibilities for healing and growth that exist in the midst of loss. This type of questioning begins to shine light on—to uncover or reveal—positive and restorative processes that exist but might not otherwise be seen.

Psychologist Barbara Fredrickson suggests that intervention strategies that cultivate positive emotions are particularly suited for preventing and treating problems rooted in negative emotions. Her broaden-and-build model of positive emotions provides the foundation for this application (2002). According to this model, the form and function of positive and negative emotions are distinct and complementary:

> Negative emotions (e.g., fear, anger, and sadness) narrow an individual's momentary thought-action repertoire toward specific actions that served the ancestral function of promoting survival. By contrast, positive emotions (e.g., joy, interest, and contentment) broaden an individual's momentary thought-action repertoire, which in turn can build that individual's enduring personal resources. . . . (2000)

James Ludema identifies the suitability of the appreciative interview for positive healing. Ludema proposes that the "purpose of social and organizational inquiry ought to be to create textured vocabularies of hope—that serve as catalysts for positive social and organizational transformation by providing humanity with new guiding images of relational possibility" (2000, 266). Understanding that the questions we ask determine what we find, AI emphasizes the importance of finding the right topics of inquiry. There is a need to balance a problem-focused vocabulary with a vocabulary that evokes vision and hope and leads to the discovery of resources for healing and growth.

The *How:* Rationale for Adapting the Appreciative Interview

In exploring how to promote growth after trauma, it is still important for the survivor to have the opportunity to tell and re-tell the painful story. Judith Herman reminds us that those who suffer trauma must be urged to speak the unspeakable as an important first step on their path to recovery.

TRAUMA RECOVERY IS A JOURNEY. Movement toward growth may differ dramatically among individuals and circumstances. For some, given the depth and devastation of the trauma, just staying alive is courageous enough. Caregivers must avoid setting rigid time expectations or "shoulds" for growth following trauma. Survivors often have to contend with their own internal finger pointing, let alone facing a host of external demands from caregivers who want to hurry the healing along. We should not presume that every person should be at the same "hopeful" place within the same predetermined time. The process of recovering is a journey, a long one perhaps, with no definite end in sight (Sider 2001).

Nonetheless, *transformation,* or posttraumtic growth, implies that while the trauma journey is ongoing, it offers many important choices and opportunities for change along the way. And *transcendence* implies the possibility of escaping from the victim trap and reaching an entirely new level of experience. In the past few years, as noted above, additional strategies for trauma recovery have begun to include discovery of resources for growth beyond the tragedy.

A "BOTH-AND" APPROACH. Henri Nouwen talks of moving "from hostility to hospitality" in describing the need to make space for change to take place in adverse situations. "Hospitality," he writes, "is not to change people, but rather to offer them space where change can take place" (1975, 71).

As peacebuilders working in the aftermath of trauma, our aim should be to widen the space so that people can explore both the losses and possible benefits of trauma—to create the space for transformational change to occur.

We do this by asking open questions that invite a full spectrum of options for choice and possible commitment as the person determines the journey.

In advocating for appreciative interviews in trauma cases, I am therefore calling for a "both-and" approach, not limiting the inquiry and storytelling to only the positive. As the adage says, "Life is best understood looking backwards and best lived looking forward." In the midst of pain, survivors can speak about what is lost and appears hopeless and also explore the present and the future so that the past does not limit their choices. The goal of the appreciative interview is to hold out hope for the survivor's future, offering the growth perspective without minimizing the negative effects of the trauma.

To understand better how to provide the space for growth choices and opportunities, I have used the appreciative interview to explore how and why some individuals grow in the aftermath of trauma. These appreciative interviews with peacebuilders who have experienced primary and secondary traumatization have revealed their capacities to transcend trauma. These peacebuilders have broken free of the victim cycle in personal and professional trauma and have chosen not to offend back, but rather to journey toward transformation and positive growth. (See appendix for the full interview guide used for the interviews.)

A GLIMPSE AT THE INTERVIEWS

To understand this crucial balance, I selected peacebuilders to interview who have attended to the injury of their trauma and have also appreciated their sources for transcending trauma. For purposes of this chapter, I use four of the interviews and focus on those parts of the interviews most relevant to our discussion here. For each I will give a brief introduction to the interviewee and then, in the following section, I highlight the key resources that allowed their journeys of transcendence over trauma.

José "Chencho" Alas

For many years, beginning in 1961, José "Chencho" Alas served as a Catholic priest in his native country of El Salvador. In 1968 he became a parish priest in the Suchitoto region, with a parish of forty-five thousand people living in poor and isolated villages. While there, Chencho participated in land reforms organized to raise the local people's awareness of the injustices that they suffered at the hands of the government. His purpose was to bring dignity and justice to the lives of the poor.

On January 8, 1970, a paramilitary group kidnapped Chencho and took him to the mountains, drugged and tortured him, and left him naked and close to death. Chencho survived after a fifteen-day recovery. He subsequently accepted an invitation from the International Association of Teachers to speak publicly about his ordeal. Despite death threats and attacks, Chencho continued his pastoral mission in Suchitoto until 1977, when he went into hiding at the request of Archbishop Oscar Romero. During a fifteen-year exile, Chencho continued working on behalf of the poor of Central America through a variety of different institutions. He received numerous awards, among them the 1991 Courage of Conscience Award given by Peace Abbey (other recipients include Mother Teresa and the Dalai Lama) (Alas 2002a; 2002b).

Chencho, now married, is the founder and executive director of the Foundation for Self-Sufficiency in Central America. A nonprofit organization founded in 1996, the Foundation strives to be a partner for social justice and peace in Central America by providing local people the tools needed to build a sustainable future for themselves and their children (Alas 2002b; see also chapter five of this volume).

In talking about the traumas he suffered, Chencho said that he had realized the potential for fear to paralyze him. "This fear is in yourself," he told me. "It is in your body, especially the vegetative fear that is blind. You react without thinking." At the time, to avoid being "captured" by the fears, Chencho recalled the counsel of his flight trainer when he was learning to fly small planes. "He was telling me always, if there is an accident and you are alive, you must control your fear immediately. Go to look for another small plane and start flying immediately. Otherwise, you will be unable to fly again because the fears will take you." So, Chencho said, "I applied the same thing to my kidnapping" (Alas 2002a).

Sumita Ghose

Soon after receiving her Master's degree in economics, Sumita Ghose gave up her plans to do business advertising in the big city and left with her new husband, Sanjoy, for eight years of development and activist work in rural Rajasthan, India. She could not put to rest the disturbance she felt inside, seeing the injustices and inequities around her—"the pavement people, the violence of poverty, and injustice of how differently women were treated" (Ghose 2002).

In 1996, Sumita and Sanjoy went next, with their two children and a small team of development workers, to live and work on the river island of Assam. The rationale for their work in this violent, conflict-ridden region was that if people could find expression in constructive development work, there would be a better chance for peace and progress. A little more than a year after the work began, militants abducted her husband. Five years later (at the time of this writing), Sanjoy remains missing.

For a while, Sumita's work came to a standstill. In recent years, after a period of searching, she has resumed her development and advocacy work. She has written several essays and a book, entitled *Sanjoy's Assam* (Ghose 1998b). She currently works as a senior program coordinator for The Hunger Project in India. Her work involves strengthening the leadership of Indian women who have been elected to village councils.

About surviving the trauma, Sumita says that her world literally came crashing down with Sanjoy's abduction. "For a year, I felt like I was on an emotional trapeze. The terrorists sadistically or maybe out of ignorance kept giving us contradictory news. My world was turned upside down in several ways—personally, the pain, of course, the pain of not knowing what has happened to a loved one, [and] the pain of separation" (Ghose 2002).

Sumita stresses again and again the importance and great challenge of moving out of the victim syndrome. "It prevents us from growing and living," she said, "but [it] can also lead to further deterioration of the situation and of ourselves" (Ghose 1998a). Sumita sees the victim mentality as often a major cause in perpetuating a cycle of violence.

Sam Gbaydee Doe

Sam Gbaydee Doe left Liberia for Sierre Leone while still in his mother's womb. His mother had gone to live with her brother in Sierra Leone after a divorce from his father. At seven, Sam returned to Liberia with his mother and eventually studied business administration at the University of Liberia. Then civil war broke out in the country. In 1993 Sam's village was destroyed. His uncles and other relatives were killed during the attack on their village. Sam had to flee Liberia in 1996, and again in 2002 because of threats on his life by the Anti-Terrorist Unit of the Liberian government. In the interim, he studied and received a Master's in Conflict Transformation at Eastern Mennonite University in the United States. Today he is the founding executive director of the West Africa Network for Peacebuilding (WANEP), based in Accra, Ghana. WANEP provides coordination and training among more than 125 peace and justice organizations in fourteen West African countries (Doe 2002; see also chapter eight of this volume).

Reflecting on the atrocities he has seen and endured in Liberia and also as a peacebuilder in other war-ravaged countries, Sam said that he had realized the danger of being trapped in fear, a fear that would keep him a victim and motivate him to seek revenge. "Yes I can be victimized," Sam said, "but it is clear to me that I cannot be a victim. Victimhood is a place of helplessness. Recognizing that someone has victimized me, I try to think about how I can move on." The devastation of the war shifted Sam's focus from being a student of economics and finance to a "student of human science, understanding who we are as people and what our potentials are in building relationship and community. So that's the path I have been discovering for the past twelve years" (Doe 2002).

Susan Russell

Even as a baby, Susan Russell experienced the trauma of being given up for adoption at six months of age and subsequently living in a foster home until age five. In 1992, as an adult living in Vermont, Sue was abducted by a man she didn't know. He assaulted and raped her and then abandoned her to die in a remote wilderness area. Trained as an emergency medical technician, Sue realized she needed immediate attention. She counts it a miracle that upon awakening, she stumbled upon teenagers camping nearby who called an ambulance. Ten years later, Sue emphasizes that not only did she survive the trauma of the attempted murder, but she also survived the criminal justice system. "My sense of hopelessness came when the system failed to meet these [the victim's] needs and when society continues to blame the victim. Violence escalates and there is no end in sight" (Russell 2002a).

Since that year, Sue has been working as a victim advocate and is currently a criminal justice and victim-services consultant based in Warren, Vermont. She has often been invited to speak on the subjects of survivorship, victims' rights, restorative justice, and offender reentry. Sue emphasizes that since the trauma she experienced, her passion for making sure that victims' voices are heard and included has remained constant. Having others, especially those who work with offenders, learn and appreciate the effect that violence has had in the lives of victims is the main focus of her advocacy work. It is her dream that these same criminal justice professionals begin to "recognize that crime victims are the experts when it comes to the field of victims' rights and services. They know what is best" (2002a).

DISCOVERIES AND INSIGHTS FROM THE INTERVIEWS

Now, looking more deeply into these interviews, a number of themes stand out that shed light on the resources and processes of posttraumatic healing and growth.

Making of Meaning

These peacebuilders all decided that simply surviving the trauma was not enough. Each developed a determination to find meaning and purpose out of their traumatic experience. In each case, that meaning resulted from the urge to help others. Their deliberate and persistent altruism motivated them to keep taking the next step forward. These individuals confirmed Frankl's assertion that suffering is in some way no longer suffering when it finds altruistic meaning ([1959] 1992, 105–107). Herman supports the importance of the making of meaning in transcending trauma: "While there is no way to compensate for an atrocity, there is a way to transcend it, by making it a gift to others. The trauma is redeemed only when it becomes the source of a survivor mission" (1992, 38). Each person interviewed has discovered a life's vocation in working for peace and justice out of the trauma they experienced.

Centrality of Choice

These courageous peacebuilders did not get to choose how trauma entered their lives or what type or how often. That is the nature of trauma. What happens afterwards, however, requires choices all along the road. Using the analogy of a lethal snakebite, a person can choose to run after the snake, expending lots of precious energy and time trying to fight back, or one can choose to first tend the wounds and then later decide what to do about the snake. If at some point the person does go after the snake, it must be decided how to approach it in such a way as to protect oneself and minimize the harm to others.

Similarly, many choices are present in the aftermath of traumatic conflict. An awareness of choice provided these peacebuilders with the initial clues that they were entering a recovering and transcending path, beyond the status of victim and survivor. Sam chose to creatively nurture compassionate anger whenever he thought about those who threatened or violated him and his people. Chencho chose to accept the invitation to speak out nationally, using the platform that the kidnapping "gave" him for some good purpose. Sue said she chose to evict the offender from her head since he wasn't "paying rent" and to find a more responsible tenant (Russell 2002a). Sumita chose to not do violence to herself by feeding the victim mentality and nursing bitterness.

The centrality of choice after calamity is depicted in the story of a Native American grandfather who was discussing a tragedy in his life with his grandson. The grandfather said: "It just seems as though I have two wolves fighting for my heart, one wolf that is vengeful and full of rage and the other wolf that is compassionate and merciful." "Which wolf do you think is going to win the fight for your heart?" the grandson asked. "I guess it's the one that I feed," replied the grandfather.

The lesson for me in this story and those of the individuals I interviewed is that both wolves may at some point need to be tended (or at least tamed), and yet over time, we do have choices as to which wolf we ultimately choose to nurture. At many points these peacebuilders encountered a fork in the road and had to answer questions of choice: "Am I being defeated by this trauma or growing beyond it?" "Is my energy compounding the violence in myself and the world or advancing the values of peacebuilding and justice?"

Facing Fear and Transforming Pain

When reading transcripts of the other interviews, Sue noted that each person named fear as a part of the trauma journey. Sue said that she now sees fear as her companion, as something that coexists with her, but it no longer controls her: "I acknowledge fear and try to work with it as a companion" (Russell 2003). Chencho warned, metaphorically, that fear will freeze and immobilize you, "if you don't get back in the plane and fly that same day after an accident" (Alas 2002a). In other words, if you don't deal with fear, fear will deal with you. For Sumita, the fear and pain caused her to explore deeper spiritual roots than she had ever needed to do before the trauma. It was on an inward healing journey that she faced and mastered the fear (Ghose 2002).

But what is a person to do with this burning pain and suffering within? Rather than running from the pain or being frozen in grief, Sumita found a way to transform them. Reading from an unpublished essay she had written, Sumita said:

> It is five years now since then. The pain is still there. The difference is that I no longer suffer because of it. Looking back, I realize that acknowledging the pain, being with it and suffering it instead of blocking it out or trying to escape it has been a healing process. Gradually the searing pain transformed itself to something quieter—instead of burning, it had a melting effect. (Ghose 2002)

Sumita resisted reacting to the terrorists and saw "no need for me to hit out at them in any way. I was not going to be a victim of pain hitting out with the same weapons and means as the terrorists. I would have to rise above the situation and respond with a higher force" (Ghose 1998a).

Rejecting the Victim Identity

Sumita stated emphatically that the way we deal with traumatic crises—whether we progress or deteriorate into pain and suffering—depends to a large extent upon our attitude. It is critical, she declared, to help trauma survivors "give up the victim self image and build up one's self image and self respect, maybe discover one's hidden potential, and to channel energy into constructive action." What helped her move out of victimhood was "the realization of the fact that by remaining a victim I was unconsciously admitting that the militant group had power over me. But I knew that this was not true—and that the power of the gun, of terror, can never be really strong. My inner power was definitely stronger! It was liberating to realize that" (Ghose 2002).

Sam's faith helped him resist victimhood. He referred to the loss of his family at the hands of another ethnic group in the Liberian conflict:

But I won't begin to hate that ethnic group who did that. Maybe it's through God's grace that I'm not able to do that. I'm not able to become a victim. . . . I have learned not to be defeated by anything. Anything that comes to me, I take as a challenge that must be overcome and . . . as an opportunity in which I can learn something new—something that makes me a better person. God is constantly creating, and we are co-creators. Every time one encounters a challenge (you may call it evil), it provides an opportunity for one to really be at work in creation. (Doe 2002)

As Sue sees it, "You can become a victim [of crime], but how you respond in the aftermath will determine if you can move from victim to survivor" (Russell 2002b). "Most definitely, becoming a crime victim, experiencing the violence up-close and personal, as well as experiencing the criminal justice system firsthand is what propelled me into doing all I can to end violence in our world today and to work towards building a peaceful and sustainable world" (2002a).

One certain indication for Sue that she was moving from a victim to a survivor identity and looking beyond was discovering, as she put it, that "[the offender] was renting space in my head! And he hasn't been paying the rent." She found a way to say, essentially, "Out of here! You're evicted!" Sue discovered she was the landlady and had the power to control what occupies her mental space (2002a).

The Power of Faith to Transform

As the interviewees spoke their stories of tragedy and pain, I wondered what internal and external growth resources had helped them transform and ultimately transcend the trauma. Sam described these resources as "four corners of a pillow" where he finds refuge, sustenance, and renewal in difficult times. The four corners are faith, family, coworkers, and his belief in the essential goodness of people (Doe 2002). Remarkably, Sam's four corners shared much in common with the resources that contributed to the other interviewees' healing and growth.

FAITH THAT GIVES LIFE. Chencho's Catholic faith reminded him that his life went beyond this tragedy. "The body can die," he said, "but not me as a person. I will not die. Life is not only here in this earth, on this planet…in this geography where I live now. Life is forever. So that continuity of life in a different way was always a big support for my work" (Alas 2000a). Chencho also talked about how his faith instructed him not to condemn his captors, but to go to them to see if he could help to regenerate their lives.

FAITH THAT GIVES PURPOSE. Likewise, Sam noted that one corner of his resting pillow is his Christian faith commitment. He readily admitted that he was not doing this work alone or with the attitude that it is just another job. Otherwise, he would have continued in the study of finance:

> But [peacebuilding] is a vocation, a call. It does not belong to me. I'm just
> one of those instruments that the Creator needs to use for this purpose.
> What it does is keep my ego out of the way. . . . Like [recently] I was going
> to Liberia, and I knew it was dangerous. I simply said a little prayer that I
> have to be there because this job has to be done. Whether I live or die, it's
> not my business. This is [God's]. I can't claim that I'm the only one here
> that can to do it. There are six billion of us. One way or another, if it has to
> be done, the Superordinate Being will still find someone, even if I'm not
> around. And while I'm around, and I've been convinced that I should do
> part of it, I have to go. And then it is God's responsibility, too, to provide the
> protection. "I do my part, You do Your part." That's a negotiation I have
> with God. I remain faithful with my part. You have to be faithful with Your
> part. (Doe 2002)

For Sue, faith provided the context for seeking God's plan for her life:
". . . faith plays a big part in my life, the belief that a Greater Power does
exist and perhaps has greater plans for me. There were some really definite
miracles there for me—like with the kids being camped so close to me. All
of those things I think about and think of the fact that I was meant to survive. I wasn't meant to pass out of this world. And that's just been a real help
for me" (Russell 2002a).

FAITH THAT GIVES INNER STRENGTH. Sumita underwent a powerful inner
transformation:

> Refusing to believe the lies and somehow just knowing that the truth was
> otherwise, I learned to look within myself. This happened partly as a sur-
> vival instinct . . . and partly as a result of help from friends who introduced
> to me a whole new world of peace within. Although I have always believed
> in a Divine Power, I had never been religiously or spiritually inclined. I had
> been living my life at a mental-emotional-physical plane, without having felt
> the need to explore other realms of my being. And when I turned within
> myself for answers, for peace, I found that I had been a stranger to my real
> self. I started getting drawn more and more towards this self. And in the
> process I found glimpses of what I was searching for—peace and the truth.
> However misleading and cruel the world outside may be, my inner being
> does not fail me. It gives me the strength not only to continue and cope, but
> also [to] take a fresh look at life, separating the lies from the truth. (Ghose
> 1998a)

Relationships That Support and Sustain

The ability of these peacebuilders to graciously acknowledge and rely upon family, friends, and community members who offered care, trust, and love in the face of suffering was vital to their transcendence. The interviewees consistently recalled individuals who had generously held up a positive-reflecting mirror for them as they picked up pieces and gathered strength. These external supports—people who elicited newly reconstructed beliefs about self, others, and the world, and who reflected positive images back to the survivors—assisted greatly on the transcending journey.

FAMILY. Continuing with the next corner of his resting pillow, Sam said: "Another place of refuge is my family, and they are a reminder that you just can't take reckless risks. You have a family to live for. That helps a lot as well in the decisions I make and the place I run to. . . . My kids inspire my life. They remind me of my childhood and the obligation of all adults to keep children happy. My kids give me comfort" (Doe 2002).

For Sue: "I relish my good fortune in having been married for almost twenty years to someone who has stood by my side through many traumatic events. All I need to do is reach out when I need that support (Russell 2002a).

COWORKERS. Sam's third corner are the people with whom he works: "We all are taking this risk together. We are all convinced of what we are doing together. We have a close bond because we share the same faith, we pray about the same things. We use that time to also share our fears, our anger, our frustration with the work and talk about it and then move on. That support network is a place that sustains me in the workplace" (Doe 2002).

COMMUNITY. Chencho described the importance of relying on supportive people as essential to his growth. "Once you are hurt, the only way to recuperate yourself is to go back to your people, the family, and the people in the place you work—what I would call 'to be nursed in the people'. . . . Instead of becoming isolated or instead of trying to ruminate, to be thinking and thinking and thinking about what's happening like, 'Why me, why that,' go to the people and be with them and work with them, smile or be with the people. That really heals" (Alas 2002a).

Sue has found great support from the people in her life:

> At the time of my kidnapping, sexual assault, and attempted murder, my community was shocked and angered at the idea that violent crime could occur in our rural valley. They sprang into action, providing an outpouring of support and commitment, helping me and my family to recover from this trauma. (Russell 2002a)

CHILDREN. Sue also remembered with great joy, as if it had happened yesterday, how about a year after the assault, a woman friend (also a survivor of sexual assault) asked Sue to care for her five-year-old son for two days a week. "I got to tell you, that little boy, he just did so much for me in those early days. I took that boy everywhere. We went skiing, hiking, we went biking, we went walking. I shared with him everything I knew about the woods, and he in turn gave me joy and happiness, a vision of life again." Sue speaks fondly of how both this little boy and his mother were such an inspiration for her (Russell 2002a).

Appreciating the Good

THE ESSENTIAL HUMAN GOODNESS. When Sam is asked how he is able to love his enemies rather than wishing them harm, he attributes it to grace.

> Because of grace I am able to use my difficult time as an opportunity for learning and to appreciate the world. . . . My belief in humanity goes beyond everything that happens to a person. The human person is essentially good and aspires towards goodness. Every evil person cries out for goodness, craves for something good. . . . A lot of the people I have worked with are seen to be the evil people in my region of the world. I have worked closely with them and seen their personal lives, seen them loving their children, wanting good for their children, for people they care about. It tells me something more than just the surface, which [appears to be] essentially an evil person. (Doe 2002)

Sam gives the example of Foday Sankoh, the Sierra Leonean rebel leader with a terrible history of committing evil acts, who is now awaiting trial as an international criminal:

> This leader of the Sierra Leone rebellion caused all the atrocities we are talking about. *And I know he has kids and I know that he loves them.* How is he able to express love at the same time when he does all that he did? Where do I want to see him? Is it when he looks at his kids' picture, and he smiles and talks about them? Is that what I want to know, or do I want to know about him on the battlefield, beheading many other children like his children? . . . That's how I envision him; that is how I have tried to see him, as a loving father of his kids. (2002)

This conviction of the essential goodness of humans allows Sam to develop what he calls "compassionate anger": "Compassionate anger comes from grace. It says to the evil doer you are a wonderful person, [but] you have refused to let the eternal goodness that wells up in you express itself. . . . Compassionate anger is not the type of anger that leads one to destroy the enemy. It is one that impels the one who is angry to seek the redemption of the one with whom he or she is angry" (2002).

ⓆＰ

THE GOOD GIFTS OF LIFE. Sumita summed up the transformative effect the healing of anger and pain has had on her life as she recognized how she is stronger in the broken places:

> Suffering the pain, the darkness, helped me to appreciate and experience more fully the other side—the calm, the joy, the bliss of existence, of life. It has helped me become more aware in many ways—the sunrise, the sound of birds, the fresh smell of the leaves, flowers, the air we breathe, smiles and compassion in the eyes of people, a thoughtful word, and so many other things, which I had begun to take for granted earlier, and therefore did not get any energy from. (Ghose 2002)

Sue, too, found she appreciated the little things life had to offer and was grateful for being alive. "I recall after coming home from the hospital after a man nearly killed me, how I spent hours watching the squirrels run around collecting nuts and storing them in their nest. This simple obser-vance helped me to reflect on the simple things in life and to be happy and thankful for every day and cherish the days we have here on Earth." Laughing at one point, Sue said, "I'm just listening to myself here and I think, 'God I've come a long way!'" (Russell 2002a).

DOING GOOD WORK. In spite of the great progress she's made, Sue is now approaching another critical stage in her life, ten years after the assault—the impending release of the offender. Drawing on resources discovered over the past decade, Sue organized "Come Unite," a public event to heighten her local community's awareness on the subject of violent sex offenders and their release and reentry into society. Her vision and determination expand-ing, Sue declared, "It's a shame that we do not live in a safe and trusting world. But we can mobilize, we can work together, we can educate our youth, we can form partnerships with law enforcement, with the Department of Corrections, with local businesses. We can create positive change. . . ." Sue continues to seek creative ways to work with her community and beyond to build a safety net for all of its survivors (2002b).

For Chencho, the speaking invitation from the International Association of Teachers opened up a whole new opportunity to work for good. "When I heard the opportunity . . . to start speaking immediately, I did it. And for me that was something very positive because at the same time, I thought, now I am a nationally known personality because my case has been in the papers, in the media, radio, the TV. There is admiration for my courage, so this is the time to continue. So that was something very positive. . . ." (Alas 2002b).

For Sumita, the answer was to continue being a part of and encouraging the forces of progressive, constructive action in society. "For no amount of retreating from life and getting away from action will make us immune to pain and suffering. Ultimately, we are all interconnected, and the pain and suffering of others will ultimately affect us as we are all interconnected in this human family (Ghose 2002)."

If, as the literature suggests, there is "learned helplessness" when trauma hits—when hope and trust in self and others is depleted (Janoff-Bulman 1992)—these interviews revealed the importance of what might be termed "learned resourcefulness" in transcending trauma. Such resourcefulness draws upon both internal and external supports. Like treating wounds in the physical body, trauma healing requires tending the injury itself, while also fortifying the surrounding healthy environment to compensate in some degree for the injury.

CONCLUSION

These stories of transcending trauma elicited by appreciative interviews must certainly have a moving and motivating effect on all who encounter them. In the same way that devastating accounts of trauma take my breath away, I found these stories about the transformation of trauma breathtaking. As the interviewer, I listened to the taped interviews many times, yet felt each time as if it were the first. These stories inspire me to live my life more fully, pursue my peacebuilding work with renewed hope and passion, and to ponder what the four corners of my resting pillow are, to use Sam's metaphor.

Each of the interviewees told me there were new insights for them also, either during the interview or in reading the transcript afterwards. Several recommitted to writing a book or article about their experience so that other survivors might be encouraged to grow beyond trauma. Some expressed amazement at their own courage and progress and marveled at the growth that had come in just one year or five or ten. Recognizing this progress was not a reason to rest, feeling they had performed their duty on behalf of trauma healing. Rather, reflecting on how far they had come helped them re-clarify their mission and recommit to their vocational call. Sue said she drew strength and courage from reading the other three interviews, noticing how creative each person was and how similar their areas of growth were, even though the precipitating traumatic experiences were very different.

It is my hope that as peacebuilders and caregivers we would become more courageous in our practice, routinely highlighting strengths and eliciting stories of posttraumatic growth, just as we have been trained to be attentive to pain and grief. To do this we need to be clear about our purpose, adopt a vocabulary of hope, and expand our tools for this practice of transcending trauma. In conclusion, I highlight three strategies for moving forward.

Opening Spaces for Hope and Resilient Growth

In order to not only survive trauma or endure compassion fatigue, but to hold open the prospect of transcendence, individuals and groups must find space to think positively and draw on hopeful energy, rather than withdraw into hopelessness and become entrapped by fears. Chencho urges us to metaphorically fly the plane again as soon as possible, so that the fears do not set in and take root. As a caregiver or friend, I am not doing harm in inquiring into what keeps survivors alive and how their views of the offender or enemy have evolved over time. In fact, I would assert, I am hurting— or at least not helping, perhaps, by a sin of omission—when I lack the courage to ask some positive, life-giving, growth-eliciting questions. The commitment must be, however, to ask the questions in a welcoming, helpful, "hospitable" way that nudges toward a hopeful future, yet also understands that answers may not now be available.

We have a responsibility as peacebuilders and caregivers to widen the space that we offer so that posttraumatic transformational possibilities may be seen and realized. This is not to shift directions entirely, but rather to become adept at doing both kinds of inquiry and listening and learning—to shine a light on posttraumatic joy as well as pain, on gains and gifts as well as losses, on blessings as well as curses. Without this dual approach, trauma care might move a person from victim to survivor, but there is little foundation for moving beyond mere survival to transformation and transcendence.

Caring for those on the transcending journey requires the agility to deal with paradoxes such as:

- To claim a future, we need to make peace with the past.
- Companioning with our fears unfreezes us for creative thinking and action.
- Trauma deprives us of choice, but choice taken back lights the path to transcendence over trauma.

Keeping the Movement Going

Now that various fields have begun to shine the light on positive inquiry and posttraumatic growth and thriving, more streetlights are needed to find more of the keys to transcendence. I share the sense of urgency of trauma specialist Sandra Bloom, who emphasizes the need to continue this "exciting and largely unexplored area of the social transformation of trauma":

> We know that unmetabolized, untransformed trauma interferes with healthy adaptation at an individual level. The individual adapts to a hostile environment and then proceeds to recreate a similar environment in order to make the best use of these adaptations. If groups—communities and even

nations—respond in a similar way, then we are dealing with a dangerous and volatile situation. (1998, 208)

To continue the momentum, we must expand the vocabulary of hope beyond the now-familiar terms of tragic optimism, resilience, broaden and build, and posttraumatic growth. This new language should be cultivated throughout the helping professions, beyond the few fields mentioned in this chapter. Caregivers and scholars working in the field of trauma healing and transcendence need to rigorously employ a balanced practice of healing traumatic pain and nurturing posttraumatic growth.

Recognizing "Everyday Gandhis"

Finally, we need to gather more stories of people like Sue, Sam, Chencho, and Sumita—ordinary people who in transcending trauma and giving new meaning to their lives have become "everyday gandhis" (Travis n.d. [2002]). Appreciative interviewing is an essential discovery tool for retrieving these stories, expanding the language of hope, and enhancing our pursuit of posttraumatic healing and growth.

ENDNOTE

1. An increasing amount of research has been done in the past five years on compassion fatigue, also referred to as secondary or vicarious traumatization. Peacebuilders and other caregivers working in trauma situations are vulnerable to secondary trauma, with symptoms similar to those of direct trauma victims. Dr. Charles Figley (1995), a psychologist who has written the most on this topic, calls compassion fatigue an "occupational hazard of caring service providers," with the more empathic caregivers being the more susceptible. There is also growing evidence to support the transgenerational and societal transmission of compassion fatigue.

REFERENCES

Achilles, Mary, and Howard Zehr. 2001. "Restorative Justice for Crime Victims: The Promises, The Challenges." In *Restorative Community Justice.* Gordon Bazemore and Mara Schiff, eds. Cincinnati, Ohio: Anderson Publishing.

Alas, José Chencho. 2002a. Personal interview, Harrisonburg, Virginia; telephone conversations; and email communications with the author (June-December).

———. 2002b. "Foundation for Self-Sufficiency in Central America." http://fssca.net/.

Bloom, Sandra L. 1998. "By the crowd they have been broken, by the crowd they shall be healed: The social transformation of trauma." In *Posttraumatic Growth: Positive Changes in the Aftermath of Crisis.* Richard G. Tedeschi, Crystal L. Park, and Lawrence G. Calhoun, eds. Mahwah, N.J.: Lawrence Erlbaum Associates.

Calhoun, Lawrence G., and Richard G. Tedeschi. 1998. "Posttraumatic Growth: Future Directions." In *Posttraumatic Growth: Positive Changes in the Aftrermath of Crisis*. Richard G. Tedeschi, Crystal L. Park, and Lawrence G. Calhoun, eds. Mahwah, N.J.: Lawrence Erlbaum.

Cooperrider, David L., Peter Sorensen, Jr., Diana Whitney, and Therese F. Yaeger. 2000. *Appreciative Inquiry: Rethinking human organization toward a positive theory of change*. Champaign, Ill.: Stipes Publishing.

Doe, Sam Gbaydee. 2002. Personal interview, Harrisonburg, Virginia, and email communications with the author (October-December).

Dunn, Dana. 2002. "Charting New Courses, Generating Positive Momentum: A Handbook For Positive Psychology." *Journal of Social and Clinical Psychology* 21:5, pp. 580–582.

Echterling, Lennis G., Jack Presbury, and J. Edson McKee. 2003. *Crisis Intervention: A resolution-focused approach*. Upper Saddle River, N.J.: Merrill/Prentice Hall. Forthcoming.

Figley, Charles. 1995. *Compassion Fatigue: Coping with secondary traumatic stress disorder in those who treat the traumatized*. Florence, Ky.: Brunner/Mazel Psychosocial Stress Series.

Frankl, Viktor E. 1992 [1959]. *Man's search for meaning: An introduction to logotherapy*. Boston: Beacon Press.

Fredrickson, Barbara L. 2000. "Cultivating Positive Emotions to Optimize Health and Well-Being." *Prevention & Trauma* 3, article 0001a (posted March 7). www.journals.apa.org/prevention/volume3/pre0030001a.html.

———. 2002. "The Role of Positive Emotions in Positive Psychology: The Broaden-and-Build Theory of Positive Emotions." *The American Psychologist* 56:3, pp. 218–226.

Ghose, Sumita. 1998a. "Dealing with conflict and violence: The power of attitude." In *The Awakening Ray*. New Delhi: Gnostic Centre.

———. 1998b. *Sanjoy's Assam: Diaries and Writings of Sanjoy Ghose*. New Delhi: Penguin Books.

———. 2002. Personal interview, Harrisonburg, Virginia, and telephone conversations with the author (August-December).

Gilligan, James. 2001. *Preventing Violence*. New York: Thames and Hudson.

Herman, Judith Lewis. 1992. *Trauma and Recovery*. New York: Basic Books.

Janoff-Bulman, Ronnie. 1992. *Shattered assumptions: Towards a new psychology of trauma*. New York: The Free Press.

Ludema, James. 2000. "From deficit discourse to vocabularies of hope." In *Appreciative Inquiry: Rethinking human organization toward a positive theory of change*. David L. Cooperrider, Peter F. Sorensen, Jr., Diana Whitney, and Therese F. Yaeger, eds. Champaign, Ill.: Stipes Publishing.

Meyers, David G. 2000. "The Funds, Friends, and Faith of Happy People." *The American Psychologist* 55:1, pp. 55–67.

Nouwen, Henri J. M. 1975. *Reaching out: The three movements of the spiritual life*. New York: Doubleday.

O'Hanlon, Bill. 1999. *Do One Thing Different: Ten simple ways to change your life*. New York: First Quill.

Russell, Susan. 2001. "I fell into this deep, dark hole with no steps." In *Transcending: Reflections of Crime Victims*. Portraits and interviews by Howard Zehr. Intercourse, Pa.: Good Books.

———. 2002a. Personal interview, Montpelier, Vermont, and telephone conversations with the author (October-December).

———. 2002b. "Community Awareness: A New Approach to Offender Re-Entry." *The Crime Victims Report* 6:4, pp. 49–60.

———. 2003. Email message to the author (February 1).

Saleeby, Dennis. 1997. *The Strengths Perspective in Social Work*. New York: Longman.

———. 2000. "Power to the People: Strengths and Hope." *Advances in Social Work* 1:2 (fall), pp. 127–136.

Sheldon, Kennon, and M. Laura King. 2001. "Why positive psychology is necessary." *The American Psychologist* 56:3, pp. 216–217.

Sider, Nancy Good. 2001. "Fork in the Road." *Conciliation Quarterly* 20:2 (spring), pp. 7–11. Also at http://www.emu/etp/bse-forkinroad.html.

Taylor, Shelley. 1989. *Positive Illusions*. New York: Basis Books.

Tedeschi, Richard, and Lawrence G. Calhoun. 1995. *Trauma and Transformation: Growing in the aftermath of suffering*. Thousand Oaks, Calif.: Sage Publications.

Travis, Cynthia. n.d. [2002]. *"everyday gandhis" Website*. www.everydaygandhis.com.

Zehr, Howard. 1995. *Changing Lenses: a new focus for crime and justice*. Scottdale, Pa.: Herald Press.

Appendix
APPRECIATIVE INTERVIEW GUIDE:
Discovering Resources for
Posttraumatic Healing and Growth

MOTIVATION OR "CALLING" IN PEACEBUILDING

- What was it that originally attracted you to peacebuilding work? What gave you the belief that this is critical work for you to do, that made you think that you could contribute in this way?
- Without being too modest, what are your own greatest strengths in this work? What values, qualities, and skills contribute to your capacities for peacebuilding?

Rationale: This begins the conversation by giving the peacebuilder an opportunity to revisit why s/he chose this work and remembering it in an affirmative way. It helps to recall the dreams and expectations that led to accepting the challenge or call. It may also provide a moment for reevaluation and recommitment.

SUPPORT BASE FOR YOUR WORK

- What are the most valuable forms of support for you in your peace-building or trauma-healing work? Who or what inspires and motivates you? What are the core factors that give life and resilience to you in your work?
- To use a metaphor, if your work is a trampoline, who and what are the supports that enable you to bounce back? Thinking perhaps of your family, organization, or community, what are the outer sources of strength for you in your work?

Rationale: Reflecting on one's support base reminds a person that this work is not done alone but in the context of a support community. This awareness offsets the isolation and hopelessness that can take root in traumatic conflict. Appreciating oneself models a healthy practice of self-care, which is one critical way of sustaining the peacebuilder or caregiver.

LIFE EXPERIENCES THAT GIVE HOPE

- What is the story of an experience in your life that gives you hope? During challenging times, what factors sustain your hope and commitment in peacebuilding work?

Rationale: Describing a peak experience gives the person a chance to draw from any number of life experiences. This question does not assume the trauma or trauma work is the main identity story to be told here. It may be helpful to recall other life stories that are also central to one's core identity, perhaps invigorating stories that haven't been told for some time.

STRENGTH IN COPING WITH TRAUMA

- Often in the face of trauma, people get stuck in the victim role or seek revenge, feeling justified in striking back. I'm interested in how you've found a way out of either of these roles, neither staying frozen in victimhood nor offending. What did you do to break free? How or why did you move on? How did you cope and find resilience? Tell the story of how you came through one experience.

Rationale: The focus here is not only on the trauma story, although this is a critical time to hear fully all that the speaker has to say. Space is created to also focus on the person's coping strengths. It may be helpful for the interviewee to identify the chapters of his/her life that followed the trauma chapter.

METAPHOR TO CAPTURE THE TRAUMA SHIFT

- Is there a metaphor that is meaningful for you that describes the shift from either the victim or offender cycle? How would you complete the sentence, "Moving on was like _____?"

Rationale: Metaphors drawn from a person's own experience give words for the next stepping stones along the path of healing and growth. Metaphors give insight and help reinforce the ongoing challenging work of transcending and the dreaming and living into a new future.

LESSONS LEARNED FROM TRAUMA-HEALING JOURNEY

- What lessons did you learn from your own trauma-healing journey or from your work with others? How did these lessons change how you see yourself? What was most helpful to you early on in your healing journey? Do you have one or two words of wisdom for others who see that you are miles ahead of them?

Rationale: Seeing that one has something to offer others shines light on the possibility that something good may come out of this painful, all-consuming journey. Many times survivors will say, "If I can help someone else by _____, then this experience will not be in vain." The last question may help the person recognize the significant movement that has already been made. This movement highlights posttraumatic growth in the midst of posttraumatic stress disorder.

DISCOVERING LIGHTNESS, HOPE, AND MEANING OUT OF THE ASHES

- Where or how do you find lightness and hope in the midst of pain and destruction? How are you able to keep a playful part of your being alive? How do you tap into your resilience and sustain it?

Rationale: In the midst of very challenging and difficult situations, some people say it's important to find some meaning out of the pain. Victor Frankl talks about surviving the World War II concentration camps and that some people always seemed to find a way to create lightness and hope. These can be expressed in many ways—as spirituality, humor, drama, prayer.

INFLUENCE OF LIFE EXPERIENCES ON WORK WITH PEOPLE

- I believe that our own self-awareness and growth shape our ability to help others. Learning from our own experiences opens avenues for us to reach out to others. So I'm curious to know how your own life experiences influence the way you work with other people. Tell a story that gives an example of this.

Rationale: This is a reflective-practitioner question that, among other things, helps a person to understand that our own life experiences do inform the work we do. It might also bring to the person's awareness that the healing journey has many paths and that others might seek forms of assistance that are different from those that helped us and gave us hope.

DREAMING THE IDEAL TRAUMA-HEALING PROCESS

* If you could create a process for peacebuilders that would help them heal their own life traumas so that they might help other people along the transcending path, what would that look like? Where would it happen? Who would be leading it? Where do you see yourself in that picture? Describe the process in as much detail as you can, whether a small or a large vision.

Rationale: An invitation to dream often opens up unexplored territory and new inventions. It frees a person from rigidity, shoulds, and unrealistic expectations that can be weighty and stifling. In a dream anything is possible! Asking where you see yourself in this dream assists interviewees in discovering their resourcefulness, seeing themselves as central to this work.

RESPONSE AND REACTIONS TO THIS INTERVIEW

* Think about the interview we've just had. What aspect of this interview process was most meaningful for you? Were there any new insights about your life, your work, or your healing journey? In what ways might you see yourself using an interview process like this in your work? In other settings? For what purpose(s)?

Rationale: The purposes here are to give feedback to the interviewer, to encourage further self-reflection for the interviewee, and to encourage interviewees to consider incorporating posttraumatic-growth inquiry in their own practice.

A spiritual teacher once asked his pupils how they could tell when the night had ended and the day was on its way back.

"Could it be," asked one student, "when you can see an animal in the distance and tell whether it is a sheep or a dog?"

"No," answered the teacher.

"Could it be," asked another, "when you can look at a tree in the distance and tell whether it is a fig tree or a peach tree?"

"No," said the teacher.

"Well then, when is it?" his pupils demanded.

"It is when you can look on the face of any woman or man and see that she or he is your sister or brother. Because if you cannot do this, then no matter what time it is, it is still night."

ANONYMOUS

CHAPTER SEVENTEEN

THE POSITIVE POWER OF VOICE IN PEACEBUILDING

Paula Green and Tamra Pearson d'Estrée

Narrative serves as a connecting thread in the long process of recovery in war-shattered communities. To recount suffering and survival, and to have adversity and small triumphs witnessed by those involved on all sides of the conflict, extends the possibility of healing and prepares the way for restoration of community. This chapter describes an infusion of two interethnic dialogue groups—one from the Bosnian war, the other from the Holocaust—and the value of voice for the combined participants. Appreciative Inquiry is discussed as an intervention tool in intercommunal dialogue, as a method for framing positive questions that uncover what gives life to survivors and their descendants, and for discovering what queries and narratives enable participants to move from victim to visionary. Other structures that employ narrative for the intention of communal healing are also explored briefly, such as truth commissions and documentation of rescuer stories.

❧

*H*uman relations are based on stories and memories, both our chosen traumas and our chosen glories (Volkan 1997). Each individual, each community weaves a narrative composed of myth, vision, triumph, and tragedy. Stories build bridges of understanding between people. Stories also wound, insult, and destroy the web of relations that bind us as humans. The narrative to which we give life may determine our history.

A Native American grandfather was talking to his grandson about how he felt. The grandfather said, "I feel as if I have two wolves fighting in my heart. One wolf is the vengeful, angry, violent one. The other wolf is the loving, compassionate one. "The grandson asked him, "Which wolf will win the fight in your heart?" The grandfather answered, "The one I feed."

APPRECIATIVE INQUIRY AND CONFLICT RESOLUTION

Sampson (2002, 2) inquires: "How can we find inspiration and hope in the midst of destruction and despair? How can we rise from division to envision and define together the kind of future we want to create together?" We would submit that dialogue is a "positive-change method," although the questions framed by a facilitator may be more oriented to encouraging narrative and acknowledgement for the sake of restoring life, rather than to lift up the positive-core theme. Intercommunal dialogue aspires to give voice as well as to restore and connect. Transformative moments in intercommunal dialogue breathe heart and life into peacebuilding, offering inspiration, hope, and the seeds of a new future. Its greatest gift lies in the fact that participants may move away from the cycle of victim-to-victimizer, to a new cycle where victims and victimizers alike become visionaries.

Appreciative Inquiry (AI) invites us to call forth the high road of our personal and collective narratives, finding the positive core, that which gives life (Sampson 2002). AI informs us that the questions we ask may also determine our history. In most conflict resolution methods, on the other hand, parties are guided to focus on the problem—the conflict and/or troubled relationship—and are more often asked about what is wrong than about what is right. If we follow the spirit of Appreciative Inquiry, which suggests that whatever we focus on will tend to increase, we may conclude that the more traditional conflict resolution approach could increase some dimensions of conflict—possibly the most destructive dimensions—even as it attempts to resolve the conflict. In the spirit of Appreciative Inquiry, we are thus challenged to consider what it might be like to focus on "life-giving" questions in our work with communities in conflict.

Admittedly, our initial reaction to AI was that an exclusive focus on the "positive" side of conflict resolution could be inappropriate and even dangerous. Conflicts are perpetuated by real grievances, injustices, and denials of oppressive and violent behavior. To avoid facing these realities during peacebuilding processes could unrealistically gloss over the core issues that encourage conflicts to rage, or at least to fester. In the context of war zones, starting with "appreciation" may seem naive, silencing, and violating to aggrieved parties. If we encourage premature appreciation, it may appear as if we as facilitators are collaborating with the lies, serving as partners in the denial of injury. Fridman (2002) convincingly suggests that to focus on "good news" in such contexts allows the stronger group to avoid hard questions of responsibility and yet feel as if they have contributed to making peace purely through their participation. Cooperrider and Whitney (1999) have, however, clarified that the driving question in AI is not necessarily "what is positive or good" but rather "what gives life." In conflict resolution, we submit that one crucial life-giving quality is narrative: finding the voice to tell the lived story. Accounts of peacebuilding reveal the life-giving quality for participants of sharing their own stories and narratives—their truths.

Reflecting its roots in organizational development, AI has traditionally been used as a change-management tool, in environments strikingly different from refugee camps, ravaged postwar zones, and other settings where intercommunal dialogue might be staged. AI has been largely a workplace technology, most ideally used in conditions where the structure may support and encourage participation in systemic change. We are challenged now to apply this technology to the craft of conflict resolution, where the parties are emotionally damaged, trust is nil, and leadership structures to embrace change are nonexistent. In these settings, how do we harness AI's appreciative questions to "liberate the human spirit and consciously construct a better future?" (Cooperrider and Whitney 1999, 10).

We are especially interested in the relevance of AI for intercommunal dialogue. How can positive approaches to peacebuilding be utilized in situations where histories of profound violation and distrust exist between group members? Is AI an entry-level intervention, or the reward for completing the painful tasks of uncovering the layers of grime from the picture of intercommunal conflict? As facilitators, we acknowledge the positive, life-affirming, and courageous behavior of participation in intercommunal dialogue with the identified *Other,* which is risky at best and downright dangerous in many postwar communities. Perhaps presence at dialogue itself, with its promise of relationship and healing, makes an appreciative statement: Maybe we can talk to each other. Maybe we can build a future together.

A CASE STUDY OF VOICE IN DIALOGUE

Finding voice for the pain to be spoken and acknowledged on both sides may be life giving although not classically "appreciative." Voice validates identity, shifts power, and restores one's humanness. It is also not just the voice of the speaker as victim that is critical to successful dialogue, but the recognition, acknowledgement, and validation of that victimhood by the listener, especially when that listener is part of the perpetrating community. In the example to follow, the repentant tears of a German minister validated the voices of Bosnian Muslim dialogue participants, a recognition longed for but withheld by their Serb counterparts. Story and acknowledgement form the core of the dialogue. In a point and counterpoint process, the voices of victims and the voices of members of perpetrating communities create collective meaning from their separate narratives, slowly building trust, understanding, and rapprochement. In the following case study of intercommunal dialogue, one of us (Paula Green) was a co-facilitator and will recount the story.

The importance of voice and recognition in intercommunal dialogue is well illustrated by a transformative meeting of two dialogue groups: one from the Holocaust of the 1940s and another from the Bosnian war of the 1990s. Members of these two groups were brought together in Bosnia to explore the healing potential of narratives, and to learn from one another's suffering and processes of healing. In this unusual, highly charged, and successful experiment in dialogue "infusion," a group of Muslim and Serb educators who participate in interethnic dialogue met for four days with members of a German and Jewish second-generation Holocaust dialogue group.

The Bosnian dialogue group, the Project for Dialogue and Community Building (Project DiaCom) consists of educators from the cities of Sanski Most in the Bosnian Federation and Prijedor in the Serb Republic, the two entities currently comprising Bosnia. The post-Holocaust group, One by One, meets in the United States and Germany and includes members whose families were directly affected by the Holocaust.

I initiated the Bosnian dialogue project four years ago at the request of Serb and Muslim educators whose previously intertwined lives have been split asunder by the violence that destroyed Bosnia. They wished to explore relations and to prepare their schools for the arduous tasks of repatriation and restoration of community. I also facilitated advanced dialogues for the post-Holocaust One by One group for members to deepen their relationships. Through years of persistent and difficult dialogues, members of this German-Jewish group have bonded deeply, brought together by the particular circumstances of their family histories.

Four selected members of One by One were invited to join the trip to Bosnia, where they could use their experiences as "wounded healers" to help Bosnians in their process of recovering from war. This proved to be a deep gift for all four groups: German Protestants, American Jews, Bosnian Muslims, and Bosnian Orthodox Serbs.

We met in a hotel in Sanski Most, a war-ravaged and "ethnically cleansed" city now the home to Bosnian Muslim (Bosniak) refugees and returnees. Our week together included public presentations by One by One in both Sanski Most and the adjacent and also "ethnically cleansed" Bosnian Serb city of Prijedor. The heart of our work, however, was a powerful and passionate four-day dialogue between our Bosnian Muslim and Serb training group and the German and Jewish members of One by One.

A U.S. participant named Mary from One by One, her mother a Romanian Jewish survivor of Auschwitz, wrote this observation of the first session:

> There is a feeling of woundedness in the room, and I register a shock to my system as I am staring right in the face of the aftermath of war. Time rolls backwards and I see my mother five years after the war. The Bosnians on the other hand look forward, and in us see their children fifty years after the war. We are two generations of genocide, facing each other across time. The ghosts in the room are louder than the living, and I feel overwhelmed in the face of so much unexpressed anguish. They sit in silence and the room is riddled with images. Nobody sheds a tear, frozen by the brutality of his or her recent pain.

In a closed session that included the ten Bosnian dialogue leaders-in-training, the four One by One members, and the facilitation and translation team, we worked steadily at exploring relations. A One by One member from Germany, a retired Lutheran minister who had been a member of the Hitler Youth, unexpectedly began his presentation in tears, setting a norm for emotional presence, authentic voice, and acknowledgement. Gottfried apologized to the Serbs for German aggression in World War II and to the Muslims for Germany's and the world's complicity in standing by and thus allowing the destruction of Bosnia. Ilona, the other German One by One presenter, spoke of her love for her father and the utter betrayal she experienced when she learned of his Nazi past. She mentioned the shame and the silence of bystanders and offered her concern for the next generation. "The younger generation will carry the guilt of their parents, if the parents do not deal with their own guilt."

Because of her early experiences and memories of Romania, Mary felt vulnerable in this former-communist Eastern Europe setting. She brought tears to everyone's eyes with her description of her mother's inability to recover from the concentration camps and the consequent effect on her own life. As she spoke, Mohammed, one of the Muslim participants, took an enormous emotional risk by noting with great anguish that the Serbs showed more concern for Mary, whom they had just met, than they did for his recently revealed suffering, although he is a long-term group member. "Our group shows more compassion for the Jews of One by One than for victims here—our stories are no less touching than theirs."

Watching the Serbs turn away from Mohammed's pain-filled eyes, we intervened as facilitators to encourage the group to pay attention to Mohammed and to their own responses. We saw that for the Serbs, listening to Mohammed's voice meant owning the truth about their Prijedor, their home and a city with its own camps and war-crime history. Mohammed, their colleague and group member for many years, was giving voice at that moment to his long-silenced anger at the Serb group members, his face a map of grief. To let in his story apparently stimulated anguish, shame, guilt, and their powerlessness as bystanders to stop the downward spiral of violence and pain against their former neighbors and friends. To accept Mary's Holocaust narrative, on the other hand, required nothing personal from the Serb participants.

A turning point had been reached in the group, one of many that occurred during One by One's presence. An emotional voice had surfaced that would shape relationships among all the Bosnians represented in the dialogue. We sensed there were more narratives from the Bosnian Muslim or Bosniak participants, but it was only after One by One departed that the most heart-rending story emerged.

After the One by One members left, we had one more day with the Bosnian trainees, the group with whom we have devoted the most energy in the past three years. Vera, whose real name must be withheld, told a story she had never before uttered, a story of unbelievable trauma and fear that remains in her body, sending her into periodic episodes of despair and shock. As she poured out her anguish, another young Bosniak participant held her and cried with her, mourning her experience and the thirty-six members of his own immediate family lost in the war. My heart reeled with the intensity of what I was hearing, while my mind remained watchful of the participants. The Serbs, all five of whom were women, were avoiding eye contact. One of them buried her face by taking notes.

My co-trainer and I knew we had reached a critical moment for intervention. The ground under us seemed to shake with the power of voice and the terror of listening. One by One, no longer physically present, remained with us as invisible witnesses. If the group could not respond to this outpouring of agony, if the Serb group members remained frozen in their fear and divided loyalties, we feared that the group would not move forward as a group of potential facilitators. If the group could not go through this pivotal incident together, we saw that the Muslim and Serb members might remain separated in alienation and despair, unable to join each other at this moment in their history, powerless to create a shared future based on the truth.

By an act of grace we found the words to comfort and steady Vera and simultaneously to help the Serb women find release from their shame and helplessness so they could reach out to Vera. A strong and capable Serb woman, Nada, bravely rose and crossed the room to embrace Vera and said as she held her: "What my parents suffered in World War II was terrible, but not as tragic as your experience." In this critical moment of their interethnic dialogue process, Nada acknowledged that Vera's story was true and also that she had been comparing this ethnic cleansing with that of her parents' experience as victims fifty years earlier. Milka, the Serb educator in the group closest to her feelings, through a burst of tears asked her Muslim colleagues for forgiveness and reconciliation. Here again we intervened, to make sure everyone registered this significant moment of asking for forgiveness, a first among this committed and struggling group. From this crescendo of emotion, the group members transitioned to a time of quiet reflection.

In the closing circle that followed, Faik, a male math teacher from Sanski Most, said: "One by One gave me the courage to tell my story. Our listening guidelines are the core of our work; we must listen to each other." Nada, who thought she had survived the war more or less intact, articulated the shattering of myths and constructs that must emerge for a new, hopefully more honest reality to break through: "I feel upset, maybe some dilemmas in myself. My head is chaotic. I thought I was really happy—a good husband, two kids, good work, everything okay. Now I feel broken and I must be with my new feelings to find out what has happened to me. I don't know whether my happiness was a real happiness."

Faik was not the only one to comment upon the powerful impact of this infusion dialogue. Returning to the United States, Mary wrote eloquently:

> Had I not gone to Sanski Most and Prijedor, I could have still maintained some of my innocence. But I was there and I cannot unlearn what I know and that is that genocide is still possible fifty years after Auschwitz, and the Holocaust is over only in as much as each of us has learned its lessons. There is a great risk in our ignoring what is happening and allowing the evil of genocide to seep even deeper into our souls. In a world plagued by people who are willing to set aside their humanity and slaughter their neighbor, we are all being called to action.

REFLECTIONS ON CASE STUDY OF GIVING VOICE

In assembling this mix of dialogue groups, several questions interested me. Observing the skills of the One by One group in the dialogue process and the intimacy many of them have achieved across seemingly impossible barriers, I wondered what they could model and teach to the Bosnians about speaking truth to the Other. Most of the German and Jewish members of One by One are second-generation survivors of the Holocaust or people whose parents were part of the Third Reich. Very few members of One by One are first generation, or those who experienced the Holocaust directly themselves. The Bosnians, on the other hand, are all immediate victims, members of bystander or perpetrator families, or perpetrators themselves. Despite these critical differences between the Holocaust descendants and the Bosnian survivors, in both instances the struggle to give voice and to witness remains strong.

From Witness to a Future of Service to Others

Prior to the episode recounted here, in an informal discussion about Bosnia after a One by One dialogue meeting, a Jewish group member had remarked that he wished healing and peacebuilding efforts had existed for his parents after World War II. My colleague did not envision his parents in dialogue with Germans but wished there had been some care and attention for their devastated emotions after the dehumanization and unrelenting violence of the concentration camps. "Had my parents received psychological support during these years," he commented, "I might have had a childhood less damaged by the Holocaust."

His remarks encouraged my thinking that One by One might have experiences useful to the Project DiaCom Bosnian participants, who struggle so bravely to speak to each other. I sensed that the Jewish and

German group could bear witness to the importance of giving voice to truth in the first generation, to the legacy of unprocessed trauma, and to the betrayals caused by silence, family secrets, lies, and distorted histories. It was on this basis that I invited One by One to select delegates to accompany me to Bosnia. An unexpected benefit was the effect that the Bosnians would have on the One by One group, illuminating the relevance of their experiences in dialogue for others suffering from the legacies of war and thus opening a way to a future for them of service to others.

When is it Time to Face the Truth of History?

Another question that concerns peacebuilders is the influence of the passage of time on voice, dialogue, and the healing process. The Bosnian war ended five years ago. In Bosnia, memories are immediate, the destruction visible, and the wounds palpable. For the Germans and Jews, whose dialogue participants are descendants of victims and perpetrators, more than fifty years have passed. What is the right time to begin interethnic dialogue after war? When is it too soon? What factors of time and readiness need to be considered for the emerging of voices besides the request of the participants and the need for safety? And from the AI standpoint, what kinds of questions will lift up the "life-giving forces that are present and active"?

One by One taught me something of the depth of perpetrator groups' suffering. I see how much anguish German members carry about the behavior of their family members and their nation. I know they long to heal these wounds and to experience themselves as good people, not through denial but through facing history. Their message to the Bosnians confirms that the path to forgiveness and restoration of dignity and community unfolds through voice, acknowledgement, and atonement. Children must learn the truth of violence committed by their elders and the truth of victimhood endured by the family. Repressed family and communal history, both among victim and victimizer families, reenacts itself, generation after generation. Traumas are transmitted. Ghosts emerge, demanding revenge. Only the truth can set us free. Who could be better qualified to give this message than descendants of the Holocaust and the Third Reich? From an AI perspective, the testimony of One by One would say: "what gives life is truth."

Yearning to Have Their Voice Recognized

For the Bosnian educators involved as future trainers in Project DiaCom, observing the closeness between Jewish and German dialogue partners touched them deeply. Currently the Muslim and Serb educators, formerly colleagues, neighbors, and some of them even relatives, still feel quite estranged from one another. They live in separate cities in different political entities, and carry dissimilar traumas from the same war: the trauma of victimization and profound loss and the trauma of involuntary membership in the perpetrating ethnic group. Our Muslim members yearn to have their voice recognized and to receive acknowledgement of wrongdoing by Serbs, at the very least within the confines of the group, whereas the Serb members continue to deny the atrocities and the extent of Serbian perpetration in this region of Bosnia. We had hoped that the great risks of honesty taken by One by One members and their commitment to dialogue and to each other would inspire the Bosnians, as indeed they did, profoundly.

Cultural Differences in Dialogue

In many ways, the situations of the two dialogue groups are not comparable. Factors of culture, isolation, economic and social devastation, political pressure, repatriation, and international intervention, among other issues, all influence the process of dialogue. Second-generation Germans and U.S. Jews live in cultural environments very different from Bosnia. The second generation Jewish and German One by One members frequently develop their dialogue skills through a process of psychotherapy, group work, and the norms of subcultures comfortable with self-disclosure and emotional expression. The Bosnians come from extended family clans, fifty years of communism, and limited experience with structured group process. As the Serb educator Milka reminded me, "We were taught not to interfere with public policies, express our emotions, or talk about our problems outside the confines of the family."

Political Dimensions of Dialogue

The political and economic environment in which dialogue is embedded clearly affects the process and outcome. Unlike Holocaust descendants, Bosnians must create a shared future as neighbors. Adding to their burdens, Bosnians face struggles with a stagnant economy, shattered infrastructure, and a demoralized, unemployed population. In this region of northern Bosnia, citizens of the two entities remain estranged and distant. Interethnic dialogue stands outside the prevailing social norms from even before the war. In such a bleak environment, how do dialogue participants heal themselves and rebuild community? What makes it possible for them to find their voice and what happens as a result?

Empathy and compassion, hopeful fruits of the dialogue process, do not flow easily in times of deprivation and struggle. Furthermore, dialogue partners frequently experience family and community pressure not to cooperate with the perceived enemy, and politicians protecting their own lives or interests can threaten dialogue members with loss of jobs or worse. Split loyalties that ripped apart mixed Bosnian families during the war now tug at families around issues of interethnic relationship building, an issue also familiar to One by One. In the best of circumstances, dialogue would be supported and augmented by public rituals of peacebuilding such as days of mourning, memorials, truth commissions, and trials for war criminals. This is not the case in Bosnia, at least not in the present moment. Few signs of economic restoration or life-giving, community-building processes exist to nurture the vision of a united Bosnia.

Facilitating Infusion of Dialogue

As a facilitator of this astounding combination of brave and wounded beings, I saw my task as that of container-builder, creating an environment sacred and safe enough for truth to be present, where the lived stories could have voice, and where acknowledgement could help to heal the pain. What made it possible for voices to emerge in this infusion of dialogues was the very careful and choreographed bringing together of these two groups, both of whom knew and trusted the facilitator, and all of whom were experienced group members. Each day we met in plenary and smaller sharing circles, working through structured questions and spontaneous emotions, sharing personal narratives and collective wisdom. We had present in the room five religions, two genocides, many cultures, and the complexity of using transla-tors. Yet much was positive here. Presence and voice, intention, courage and commitment, the will to heal and rebuild. These constitute a positive core.

In this experiment in multi-level dialogue infused with the history of two genocides, the members of One by One discovered the relevance of their arduous journey for others recovering from war and betrayal. The Project DiaCom members experienced a degree of intimacy among former enemies and their descendants previously unimaginable to them, and participated in acknowledging their own tragic past as a bridge to Bosnian healing and com-munity restoration. We as facilitators stood in awe of all the participants, Muslims, Serbs, Jews, and Germans, as they wove a new story from their intertwined histories, this one committed to honesty, introspection, civic responsibility, and compassion. We deeply felt the value of respecting all the parties in the dialogue, remembering that there is no life without suffering, especially in war, and that the journey to healing may begin with a single phrase: "Yes, this tragedy happened. I hear your voice. I acknowledge your experience. I accept your truth."

In our dialogues we do not use the language of forgiveness and reconcil-iation, but rather select more present-oriented words such as narrative, rela-tionship, community building, collaboration, and healing. We sense that for-giveness and reconciliation, if they develop, grow out of this larger journey of finding voice, rebuilding trust, and restoring relations. We believe that we cannot wait fifty years for the second generation to undertake the healing process, and indeed postponing the public narrative process is a betrayal of the second generation. Wounds pile upon wounds and the cleansing becomes even more difficult. We believe we need public rituals to bind the community, as well as private events like dialogue to strengthen collegial bonds and encourage collaborative development. It is difficult but not impossible to interrupt the cycle of blame, hatred, and revenge, and to balance out the needs for punishment and compassion. Our commitment to interethnic dialogue rests in the hope that transformation will emerge through the power of voice to build connection and caring and to unfreeze powerlessness produced by silence. Not a panacea, dialogue is but one significant element in the process of facing history, nurturing trust, and restoring intercommunal relations.

OTHER STRUCTURES FOR GIVING VOICE

If voice is considered to be the nutrient that "gives life" to conflict resolution, let us also consider other examples of structured processes, in addition to dialogue, that might increase voice. These include sharing stories around common themes or problems, organizing voices into collective empowerment, witnessing and testifying, collecting rescue narratives, and memorializing. In addition to these, every culture offers opportunities for stories and witness, which run the gamut from psychotherapy to coffee klatches to religious and cultural rituals to the writing of history, the latter which more often than necessary becomes the narrative of the victor.

Sharing: Telling Stories in Groups

A powerful technique for giving voice to experiences of suffering, marginalization, and oppression is the sharing of stories in groups of those with similar experiences. Groups that grew out of the women's movement, for example, or Alcoholics Anonymous and Alanon meetings, provide structures for others to witness one's story, frequently reducing the sense of isolation and stigma. Because structural violence so often creates a lack of recognition of one's own oppression (Curle 1971), finding common cause within a group may instruct, awaken, and release the silenced voices of the oppressed. In Chile during the years of dictatorship, for example, facilitated groups focused on the problems of fear, which helped to free the participants from the binding fear that prevented action against the regime.

We have, however, met cultures where even a closed, confidential group may still not be "safe enough," and is thus culturally inappropriate. In some settings, revealing experiences of injustice and injury in a group may risk further isolation, retribution, or even abuse. In these cases, victims may require another way to share the unexpressed narrative in personal conversations with a trusted other.

In the close and interrelated extended family systems in some traditional societies, where women are invariably related to the husbands of other women, no secret is considered safe, even among women. Their voices are silenced by family loyalty, tradition, fear, and the oppressions under which they live. In this type of setting, the threat of retribution for breaking silence outweighs the women's need to share their narrative within their community. In situations documented by one of the authors, women expressed their loneliness and their desire to share their difficult lives with peers, but anxiety over retribution ruled their lives and silenced their voices.

Organizing: The Provocative Voice

Sometimes raising a story to light may not be adequate to address a given concern, particularly if there are those who question its truth, have an interest in continuing the silence, or who merely maintain that "other priorities exist." Such is often the case with women's stories in times of war. In a refugee camp in Rwanda, for example, a female participant in a conflict resolution training group made a powerful appeal for the group to address the topic of rape committed by fellow refugees within the camps and quietly condoned by camp authorities. The group became silent, eyes averted and bodies squirming anxiously. The men, who were by far the majority in the room, protested both the lack of evidence of rape and the irrelevance of this topic in light of the urgency for repatriation. The woman held her ground. With the support of facilitators, the topic of rape in the refugee camps became central to the investigation of methods for organizing communities to meet needs and respond to violent behavior without further destructive aggression.

As facilitators we need to provide structures that challenge silencing and that uphold the concerns of disempowered and marginalized groups. Less privileged people are furthermore often told to wait for a more appropriate moment that may never arrive. In such cases, efforts must be made to strengthen individual voices and experiences through a public forum whereby multiple voices on the same theme are heard.

Witnessing and Testifying: The Public Voice

The South African Truth and Reconciliation Commission (TRC) provided the world with a groundbreaking model of speaking unspeakable truths in a very public forum for the purpose of witness, healing, and reconciliation. While there are both plaudits and criticisms of the TRC, most participants and observers agree that South Africa has offered the world a new model for testimony as a vehicle for healing the past that falls "between Nuremberg and national amnesia" (Tutu 1999, 10).

Anglican Archbishop and TRC Chair Desmond Tutu (1999) recalls that TRC commissioners worried that people who had been so brutalized by the decades of apartheid might not come forward. Those who had abused them might have intimidated them; they might refuse to be regarded as victims since they believed themselves to have been combatants in a struggle; or they might be disillusioned, not believing any longer that anything worthwhile could be expected from those who were forever making promises and being so painfully slow on delivery.

The commissioners need not have worried. People definitely did want to tell their stories. They had been silenced for so long, sidelined for decades, made invisible and anonymous by a vicious system of injustice and oppression. Many had bottled their feelings up for too long and when the chance came for them to tell their stories, the floodgates were opened.

The TRC provided a stunning and groundbreaking form of national healing and binding of the nation's wounds, whatever its shortcomings. While the journey of reconciliation requires a long arc of time and a multiplicity of processes, South Africa has approached it through the healing power of voice, so that this tragic history could be fully acknowledged and gradually transformed.

Remembering: The Rescuer's Voice

In several postwar societies, researchers have collected the narratives of those who defied oppressive regimes to rescue their friends and neighbors. Holocaust rescuers are now elderly, and those who wish to remember and honor their heroic acts are seeking out the rescuers to detail their stories. One of them, Eva Fogelman (1994), wrote: "the act of rescue was an expression of the values and beliefs of the innermost core of a person." Many had never told their stories, and Fogelman noted that ". . . they paid a terrible price for this silence. A vital part of their inner self was muffled, and it left some of them psychically wounded." After the Yugoslav wars of the 1990s, medical doctor Svetlana Broz, granddaughter of former Yugoslav President Marshal Tito, collected rescue stories among former friends and neighbors ensnared in those tragic events. These narratives will be published in English in the coming years.

For the rescued and the rescuer, and for the majority who stand by during times of war and oppression, these stories lift up honorable human behavior in its most positive aspect. Appreciative Inquiry suggests "creating opportunities for sharing good news stories" (Cooperrider and Whitney 1999, 9). What better news than to pay homage to those who ennoble human life?

Memorializing: The Silent Voice

Sometimes what needs to happen is not just the uttering of the story, but the validating of the stories in "bricks and mortar" museums and monuments that increase assurance that time will not erase their memory. Passing the memory to the next generation can either perpetuate the conflict and separation or create a shared understanding of the price of violent conflict. Creating a memorial also declares that silence will not triumph—the injury of denial of voice that accompanies the victim of violence will not repeat itself in the next generation.

Living memorials such as concentration camps, gravesites, and killing fields stand in mute testimony to our history. Museums, monuments, and hallowed ground complement the testimonies and endure to tell the story when the last human survivor is gone. In West Africa, dungeons for captured slaves awaiting shipment across the Atlantic remind the visitor of a profoundly tragic past. A school in Phnom Penh records the genocide of the Pol Pot regime in Cambodia; churches used for human slaughter remain in Rwanda; native populations in Guatemala tend sacred ground. One must be careful that these sites do not become stimulation for revenge, as occurred in Kosovo at the Field of Blackbirds, where Milosevic promised revenge for a battle lost by the Serbs in 1389. Our memorials and monuments must stand alongside the human narrative as reminders of past egregious behavior and as testimony to a shared commitment to achieve our ". . . dream for humanity, when we will know that we are indeed members of one family, bound together in a delicate network of interdependence" (Tutu 1999, 222).

CONCLUSION

In our work as facilitators and professors in conflict resolution, we are often confronted with the question of what heals and prevents the recurrence of violence conflict. Using Appreciative Inquiry as a reflective frame encouraged us to focus our attention differently. An AI frame encourages us to focus on "what gives life" and on what behaviors, realizations, and changes we would like to see increased. Speaking truths, finding voice, allows new futures to grow. Many conflict resolution processes can be focused or refocused on nurturing the expression of narratives that will support growth and life.

We have seen how dialogue between former adversaries, appropriately facilitated, can give voice and life. Creating a safe space, a sturdy container, provides the safety needed to name horrors and hurt. The occurrence of the dialogue itself can also give hope, demonstrating that "we can at least talk together." In particular, we have seen the value of immersion dialogue:

 immersing one successful dialogue into the midst of another. Such dialogues not only change the dynamics to nurture increases in finding voice and expressing truths, but also change roles of classic victims to ones where they help and lead. What allows this "dialogue within a dialogue" to be such a powerful process for giving voice?

First, the mere modeling of expressing one's voice can allow others who have been silent to find their voices and speak up. Such expression, and attentiveness by the group, validates the worth of both the truth and the telling. The powerful stories and reflections that were shared by the experienced Jewish and German One by One members when visiting in Bosnia modeled and validated a type of expression that otherwise might have been silenced by the Bosnian participants' larger communities. Alternative norms of voicing were enacted, allowing others to consider sharing their stories as well.

Second, there exists among those who have lived through such trauma a kind of knowledge of each others' experiences—anguish, fear, loss, betrayal, hopelessness, grief, tentativeness in happiness—with which only those with similar experiences can truly empathize. These others also have a credibility with those coming out of a recent trauma that few outsiders would have. Thus their testimony for sharing truths and witnessing others' truths—and for the possibility of positive futures—is more likely to entice the skeptic.

Third, meaning is created socially. In other words, humans create meaning in their worlds by sorting things out with others, particularly in situations where things are ambiguous and stressful, as Schachter first demonstrated early on (1959). As recent conflict survivors struggle to understand and make meaning of their experiences, the historical vantage of past conflict survivors can add wisdom and perspective.

Fourth, witnessing the One by One dialogue group allowed those within the Bosnian dialogue group to consider alternative possible futures. As revealed in Mary's quote above, by listening to the stories of the descendents of traumatized survivors, the recently wounded could see how their current tragedy potentially could live into future generations. They were given the gift of a window onto the future, to consider how their current choices might best mold a positive climate for future relations. They could choose which narrative, which "wolf in the heart," they would feed. Voice became a vehicle for expanding options and empowering choices.

Finally, the models of the Jewish-German partners in healing allowed the Bosnian participants to experience evidence of mended relationships and a more hopeful future. Amidst profound violation and distrust, participants witnessed those from another setting of profound violation who had begun to forge a future in which at least interpersonal trust and relationships were possible.

We acknowledge that this process of "wounded witnesses" from past traumatic situations helping those in more recent crises to make constructive meaning is not a new phenomenon. Support groups, religious settings, twelve-step programs, all build on these processes for healing through giving voice and modeling safe changes. More recently, we have seen the trend of survivors traveling to be present for those newly traumatized, as in the case of Oklahoma City bombing survivors working with survivors of the bombings in Nairobi and New York City.

As facilitators, we challenge fellow practitioners to be brave enough to give voice, and to be creative enough to find the positive uses of voice. Rather than fear the destructive future that narratives can create, or squelch the voice that then breeds future hatred of self and others, we should foster conditions that give voice and provide ways to narrate more positive futures. Giving voice and validity to victims and victimizers allows hope to grow, visions to be shared, and life to begin anew.

REFERENCES

Cooperrider, David, and Diana Whitney. 1999. *Appreciative Inquiry.* San Francisco: Berrett-Koehler.

Curle, Adam. 1971. *Making Peace.* London: Tavistock Press.

Fogelman, Eva. 1994. *Conscience and Courage: Rescuers of Jews During the Holocaust.* New York: Anchor Books.

Fridman, Orli. 2002. "An Appreciative Critique." *Conciliation Quarterly* 21:1 (winter), pp. 14–16.

Sampson, Cynthia. 2002. "What Do We Choose to Learn From? *Conciliation Quarterly* 21:1 (winter), pp. 2–3.

Schacter, Stanley. 1959. *The psychology of affiliation.* Stanford, Calif.: Stanford University Press.

Tutu, Desmond. 1999. *No Future Without Forgiveness.* London: Random House.

Volkan, Vamik. 1997. *Blood Lines: From Ethnic Pride to Ethnic Terrorism.* New York: Farrar, Straus and Giroux.

A beautiful word is like a tree, its roots are deep in the ground, its branches rise up to the sky.

SURA 14, 24, QUR'AN

CHAPTER EIGHTEEN

JOURNEY OF HEALING

Amela and Randy Puljek-Shank

Drawing from interviews with peacebuilding practitioners and the personal experiences of the authors, this chapter explores the healing of trauma as part of the positive core of peacebuilding. By examining examples of healing moments, rituals, metaphors, and conceptual models it attempts to answer the question, "How does healing take place?" An unanticipated theme that emerges is the contribution of nonverbal forms of understanding (symbols, images, and ritual acts) to the conditions that foster healing. The chapter concludes by using the five principles of Appreciative Inquiry to examine its relevance for understanding and strengthening the conditions under which healing takes place.

❧

Several paths converged for us in deciding to write about the process of healing. One of these paths is our personal experience of the war in Bosnia-Herzegovina. Amela survived that war and experienced some of its darkest times, ultimately fleeing her hometown. During the war she worked with people of different ethnic and religious backgrounds to deliver humanitarian relief and help the return of refugees. An important component of this work was opening a space for people to tell their stories, even in the midst of ongoing violence, and this provided an introduction into the process of trauma healing and recovery. After the war she moved to the United States, where she pursued studies in psychology and conflict transformation. During these studies she realized the degree of her own trauma and began a counseling process in which Randy, an American and frontline witness of the war, has been closely involved. In this process and in her subsequent work as a facilitator and mediator, Amela has found Olga Botcharova's model of forgiveness helpful in understanding the process of trauma recovery. This model emphasizes the importance of mourning and accepting loss in order to create a common history for the parties in a conflict and break the cycle of violence and revenge (2001).

Another path that led us to this interest came from Randy's exposure to Appreciative Inquiry in the organizational development field (Cooperrider and Srivastva 1987). Appreciative Inquiry (AI) is a whole-system change methodology, which builds on the power of positive stories and dreaming that is rooted in those stories. An early proposal for what later became the "Positive Approaches to Peacebuilding Conference" (held September 2001 in Washington, D.C.) spurred him to explore the possibilities of a project using AI on a community basis in Bosnia-Herzegovina. Numerous times in discussions in the United States and Bosnia-Herzegovina he heard, "People in conflict are not ready to discuss positives, they need to tell their stories and be heard first." His asking about "positive approaches" was understood as an endeavor to whitewash significant conflicts and hurt that had occurred. While considering these objections, Randy attended a training workshop on Appreciative Inquiry at which he began to value the insight that before beginning a change process, it is a good idea to ask ourselves, "What is it that we want to create more of?"

One answer certainly is, in a situation with hurt on many sides, we want to create more healing. Healing is a process that begins from being wounded but involves the creation of a new wholeness. Healing from psychological, social, spiritual, and emotional hurts taps into a rich experience to which we all can relate from the healing of our physical selves. We believe that healing is a powerful concept that invokes a spirit of newness and renewal, which is necessary for working in conflict situations. Using the medical metaphor, we mean healing in its deepest sense, not in a band-aid or snake-oil sense.

This is the point where our interests converged around the question, "How does healing take place?" Discussing the Botcharova model and the AI model, we began to see them as complementary and not exclusive of each other. The guiding question, "How does healing take place?" seemed to fit as a beginning place for this exploration because healing is a word with positive power and yet is rooted in real and difficult experiences. The strongest objections to using AI in conflict settings actually have mainly to do with what the starting point should be in a trauma healing process: Should it begin with the telling of painful stories and grieving losses (Botcharova and others) or should it begin with the retrieval of positive stories (AI)? If the question is, "Where do we start?" the two approaches seem to be in opposition. Yet to focus on healing is to focus rather on the question, "Where do we want to go?" To answer this question, we are interested in mapping out some possible complementary areas.

The last path that brought us to this inquiry led through learning in the Conflict Transformation Program of Eastern Mennonite University, as well as from Amela's colleagues as a facilitator with Seeds of Peace, a program that works with youth from conflict areas around the world. We wanted to acknowledge the work of these programs in many conflict settings and to strengthen our understanding of that work. To this end, we interviewed thirteen peacebuilding practitioners with experience in situations of deep conflict about their experiences of healing.[1] We asked about when they themselves had experienced healing, when they had witnessed moments of healing, and when they had seen positive questions or images contribute to healing. These interviews are the source of the quotes and many of the examples included in this chapter.

There are many examples of healing in peacebuilding work. We do not see ourselves as discovering something new here, but rather are seeking to illuminate the conditions that in our own and other practitioners' experience have helped to make healing possible, and ultimately to strengthen those conditions. Some of the interviewees commented on how few and precious have been the times they have witnessed true healing. Our hope is that the stories we have gathered will prove illustrative of the process of healing. We also saw how these examples were powerfully imprinted in the hearts of the practitioners and hope that recounting them here will serve to be a source of hope and motivation for others on this same journey.

We have two purposes in this chapter. The first is to be truthful to the stories of healing that were shared with us. The second is to explore the new impulses that Appreciative Inquiry might offer for healing practice. We discovered some tensions between these two purposes, on the one hand, honoring what was in the stories and, on the other, expanding our understanding of healing. We consider this an open exploration and hope that readers will join us in this same spirit of inquiry.

In pursuit of the first purpose, we will use three approaches to answer the question "How does healing take place?" The first is to recount specific stories of moments of healing from the interviews. One of the strong themes that came through was the importance of rituals in healing. The second approach is to explore the language and metaphors of healing that came out in the interviews. We also asked the practitioners about models of healing that they found helpful themselves and that parties in search of healing have found helpful. Our third approach, then, is to look at these models. Out of these approaches we draw together four characteristics of healing. In the final section of the chapter we then move to our second purpose and examine healing in light of the principles of Appreciative Inquiry.

STORIES OF HEALING

One peacebuilder told of a workshop of several weeks with youths from the Middle East. The group started their first day by telling about the family members with whom they felt the most comfortable. A Palestinian youth talked emotionally about his brother, who was partially paralyzed as the only survivor of a car wreck. This brother had had ten surgeries to help him increase his mobility. After the Palestinian youth had spoken, an

Israeli youth said that he understood what the Palestinian was talking about because his own father had died the previous year. With these two stories being told at the beginning of the group's time together, it brought the whole group into deeper conversations, which surprised the facilitators. Other group members started telling about their difficulties and pains. This common experience of pain brought the group members from different sides together and lessened the divisions within the group. They were able to connect on a human level. Three days later, the youths were able to be brutally honest with one another about their feelings about the conflict, including critical feelings about their own group. Although this honesty was difficult for the participants and for the facilitator we interviewed, naming the reality of these feelings seemed to help in letting go of the divisions. When the group came together again after that difficult session, the Israeli and Palestinian youths showed a closeness from which the facilitator we interviewed felt a life-giving energy.

Another practitioner described an extremely divisive conflict among three congregations over a pastor who had been fired after serving all three congregations at the same time. The facilitator suggested a process whereby each group would have one evening to tell the events from that group's perspective. Before beginning he made it clear that, "You need to know it will not be easy. It will be intense, and it may take some time, and it may feel strange, but I'll do it if you want. So they said yes." For each matter that a congregation was angry about, they would select one person from one of the other two groups to be a designated listener and to repeat back in the person's own words the events that had been told. A moment of healing came in the third evening: "There was such a sense that 'we are ready to move on'. . . . They got up and one by one said remarkable things of apology and confession, and each statement would bring a response from others. So it was one of those moments where it was very intense in a good and positive way, and you could just feel things rolling off."

During Amela's healing process, she had discounted the possibility that the Serbs from her hometown who had left the town, shelled the remaining residents, and eventually caused them to become refugees would take responsibility for those actions. Not knowing if this would ever happen, she had nonetheless made significant progress in healing from those disruptions. She was then caught by surprise when several Serbs acknowledged the wrong that Serbs had done in Bosnia and apologized for the harm that had been caused. The degree to which those statements opened up the possibility of a much deeper sense of healing on her part was unexpected. Apology created a new reality in which forgiveness was a possibility. The degree to which those Serbs took responsibility for the actions of their own group also

 called forth Amela's sense of responsibility for her healing and for creating the basis for new life together.

These three stories introduce some of the characteristics that were repeated during our inquiry into "How does healing take place?" Moments of healing took place during encounters with those who had caused harm or representatives of the same group. We will discuss below examples where this was not the case. The timing of these moments of healing shows that although there were specific moments and actions that were healing moments, these were the culmination of a longer process.

HEALING RITUALS

As we inquired into the circumstances that surrounded times of healing, we heard many examples of rituals of healing. Our understanding of what makes a ritual is that it involves the use of symbols within a public or private event (Romanoff and Terenzio 1998). The frequent presence of symbolic and ritual elements in the stories of healing—which for us was unexpected—suggest to us that this is an important aspect of healing itself.

One example comes from a week-long workshop conducted in Liberia following that country's civil war. One participant, a Christian pastor, had seen his parents killed before his eyes. He began the workshop by saying he "had the right to kill anyone from the other ethnic group, and he meant kill." He expressed great anger and said that all he could think about was revenge, while others were telling him that he should forgive. In the first day, the facilitators told him that it was normal to feel angry, and asked him if he also felt guilty and depressed, to which he answered yes. He then had a chance to tell his story. After this came a ritual where all of the participants were invited to name their dead, meaning those who were significant to them. This was important because people in that culture, as in many cultures, consider it to be essential to bury their dead, which is impossible if they cannot locate the remains of their loved ones. Naming the dead is understood to release the spirit of the dead from continuing to walk the earth. In this ritual people were invited to bring symbols, scripture readings, pictures, or whatever would evoke the memory of their loved ones.

After a week of working together in the group to understand the effects of trauma, another ritual was used in which the participants could write on pieces of paper things they wished to be free of, say them out loud if they wished, and then burn them. By this time, the pastor said that he was not yet able to forgive, but thought that he would be able to in several years. The moment of healing was in creating that possibility. This did not mean that the pastor's healing process was complete. In some ways the impulse to seek revenge was easier to comprehend than the complex issues that were raised by the loss of his parents and the guilt of being a witness without having stopped it from happening.

Another ritual of healing involved families of bomb victims in the town of Omagh, Northern Ireland. Shortly after the bombing, some residents of the town of Enniskillen who had themselves experienced the effects of a bombing traveled for a dinner with the Omagh family members. Later, the many flowers that had been left or sent from around the world in memory of the victims finally needed to be disposed of. At the suggestion of an area artist, a series of workshops was held in which local people created artwork from the flowers. They made the stems into paper and then decorated the paper with the petals. The surviving victims from both sides presented these creations as memorials to the families of each of the thirty who had died in the bombing. The practitioner who related this story was struck by the important role of creativity in assisting healing.

One practitioner talked about the importance of identity healing, which was explained in the context that ". . . in many conflicts our identities get wounded or attacked, as men, as women, as white people, whatever we are. Healing has a lot to do with self-esteem and feeling good about ourselves and confident in who we are." The practitioner described an example of identity healing that happened on the island of Fiji during a ritual of drinking kava together. It came in the evening during a national reconciliation workshop involving representatives of two ethnic groups, Indians and indigenous Fijians. These two groups, as well as other smaller ethnic groups, have significant cultural differences in how they act in the world, how they conceive of politics, and what they want for the future of their country. In the native Fijian ritual, everyone sits in a circle and shares in drinking the kava. Those who participate also talk about who they are and where they come from. For the Indians it was a new experience to participate in drinking kava. Afterwards, the Indians performed their dances and taught some dancing to the Fijians. In practicing the culture of the other group, people made mistakes and could laugh at their own and each other's attempts. Emphasizing aspects of their cultural identities that were different from those that divided them also contributed to healing.

As the importance of ritual in healing emerged, we wondered where the healing power in ritual comes from. There are moments of naming losses, as in naming the dead, and having losses acknowledged by others, as with the Omagh families. Typically for rituals, these involved both artifacts and a sequence of actions. The artifacts were the papers to be burned, the memorials made from memorial flowers, the cups of kava; and the actions were writing and then burning the papers, creating and presenting the books, and drinking kava and dancing together. Surely one aspect of the power of ritual is its engagement of our noncognitive selves, namely, our senses and feelings.

The rituals we heard about were ones that were shared. Shared acknowledgement of difficult experiences has a particular power. Lisa Schirch notes that communication via ritual is particularly powerful because it is symbolic and that ritual both assists and symbolically signifies the process of transformation (2001). In life, rituals are also ways that significant rites of passage are delineated. We see that in conflict settings, rituals have the power to mark and spur transitions from one phase to another, including towards healing. We believe that one aspect of the power of ritual in healing is that it nonverbally touches experiences and feelings that are difficult to name.

METAPHORS

In our peacebuilding work and in our own journey of healing, we are learning to pay attention to metaphors, in other words, the use of an object or idea with one literal meaning in place of another object or idea to suggest a likeness or analogy. We pay attention to all the images or pictures that come to mind when thinking about trauma and about healing. The metaphors that people use are often maps that reveal where they are in their thinking and feelings and what may lie around the next bend.

According to one of the practitioners interviewed, "moving from woundedness to health is a matter of changing metaphors. What we need to do is to help people identify what the governing metaphors are and find new metaphors . . . that will guide where they want to go." This attention to metaphors fits with our own experience in which various metaphors have helped explain what we sensed intuitively was going on with Amela's healing process.

One is that of a ball of thread, which represents the tangle of emotions inside that can slowly and steadily be unraveled, getting closer and closer to the core experiences and pain. Another is a scab on a wound, which draws attention—who can leave a scab alone?—and which either through action or inaction eventually reveals fresh skin underneath that for a time is overly sensitive to the surrounding environment. The ongoing pains of healing have seemed to us like a snake shedding its old skin, revealing something new, but only after struggling with the old. In a similar vein, we think of the internal work that is required for healing as the invisible transformation of a cocoon before the butterfly emerges.

Another metaphor that we have heard other people use to understand their own trauma is that of a volcano. A volcano is boiling inside and erupts after some time. When this happens, the hot lava destroys everything in its path. All the ground is burnt. But after some years, life slowly returns, drawing on the minerals that were contained in the lava. This metaphor illuminates the internal process (boiling), which is not visible from the surface. The lava represents the strong emotions (anger, pain, fears) that may erupt in a way that is destructive. After some period of recovery and a passage of time, there is the possibility that new life may emerge based on the integration of the traumatic events.

One practitioner used a metaphor to contrast the way that moments of healing happen early with how they might happen at a later stage. At first, water is flowing but is regulated by concrete waterways into constrained moments of healing. In the ideal future, whirlpools naturally emerge in the stream of water, not planned but spontaneous and recognized as opportunities for healing. Another spoke of trauma as a window into many different perceptions and desires that people in a conflict setting experience. A window reveals what is inside and also provides an opening for light to shine through. Or, trauma can be seen as a magnifying glass, amplifying both needs and biases.

Another practitioner introduced a story that uses a metaphor for both the healing process and the role of somebody who assists in this journey. Imagine that you have fallen into a well. A clergyman passes by, and you call to him to throw you a line. He looks in the well, says, "You're down in some kind of hole," and continues on his way. Next you see a doctor passing by, and you shout to him, "Can you get me out of this well?" He looks down at you and says, "Wow, that's a tough hole," before walking off. A friend comes by, and when you call to her, she jumps down in the well with you. Furious, you berate her for not throwing you a line so you could both escape. "It's okay," she says, "I've been in this well before, and I know the way out."

The role of the friend who accompanies a person through the healing process is revealing. The process may not be quick. It requires both commitment and action. The action, however, is not one that anticipates a quick fix, but rather one of steady accompaniment and joint effort. It is recognizing some of the markers along the way.

As before with rituals, this time we are also led to ask what it is about metaphors that contributes to healing. One characteristic of many of the metaphors that we ourselves have used is that they encompass a dimension of change and growth. Like rituals, metaphors are both descriptive and predictive, both describing what is already happening and alerting us to what is coming next. Like rituals, metaphors can make it easier to express something too complex or difficult or painful to put into words. They use some familiar image or activity to describe the process of healing, which can be a journey into the unknown.

MODELS OF HEALING

In developing our own understanding of healing, three models have been helpful. Each of these was also mentioned by at least several of the practitioners interviewed as influencing their understanding and practice related to healing. These models refer to healing, respectively, in the contexts of restoration of an existing relationship, therapy with survivors of violence, and intergroup dialogue. The models differ in the contexts with which they deal and the people who are involved in a healing process. The importance of encounter between the different groups also varies among the models.

One model of healing that we have found helpful comes from Ron Kraybill (see Figure 1). Kraybill writes from a perspective of hurt that occurs in the context of an interpersonal relationship. He distinguishes between two dimensions of reconciliation—that of the "head" and that of the "heart." Even when people think that they ought to be reconciled or want to be reconciled, this does not necessarily bring reconciliation of the heart. "[People] respond in ways that strengthen the 'head' message but ignore or disparage the cries of the heart" (Kraybill 1988, 2). After some form of injury has occurred in a relationship, there is often a period of physical and emotional withdrawal. Sometimes during withdrawal people think (in their head) that they should forgive each other, forcing or willing themselves into reconciliation, without being fully ready (in their heart). Self-awareness and acceptance of emotions and deeper vulnerabilities that may be touched by the conflict are often necessary to reach reconciliation of the heart. It is also important to be aware of one's own contributions to and power in the conflict. This self-awareness allows the choice of whether to enter a process of deeper reconciliation. Entering this process means taking risks that are necessary in any open relationship.

Figure 1
CYCLE OF RECONCILIATION

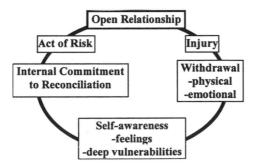

SOURCE: Kraybill (1988, 3). Reprinted by permission of the publisher.

Judith Herman (1997) writes from her experience as a therapist with victims of sexual abuse, child abuse, and war. For her, the key to healing is empowerment of the survivor. The process follows three steps, although they are not always distinct and may overlap. The first stage is the establishment of safety, in which it is important to name the problem and restore control of the body and the environment by the survivor. The second stage, remembrance and mourning, involves reconstructing the story, transforming traumatic memory, and mourning traumatic loss. Reconstructing and telling the story helps traumatic memory to be integrated into the survivor's life story. "Having come to terms with the traumatic past, the survivor faces the task of creating a future. She has mourned the old self that the trauma destroyed; now she must develop a new self" (1997, 196). The main task of the final stage is reconnection with ordinary life. This means learning to fight (a conscious choice to face danger), reconciling with oneself and with others, and finding a survivor mission.

Olga Botcharova (2001) has developed a model of reconciliation based on her work in areas of prolonged conflict and trauma. In her experience, lack of attention to the deep need for healing from victimization on the part of the parties in violent conflict is a major contributing factor to the failure of international peace initiatives. In her model (see Figure 2), forgiveness is the culmination of the healing process, which makes it possible for conflict parties to move toward reconciliation. One of the most powerful tools in her workshops was sharing stories from opposite sides of the conflict. These stories helped to establish empathy and begin a process of rebuilding trust. Botcharova's model contains an inner circle of the "seven steps toward revenge." This cycle is self-reinforcing, so that injury can lead to anger and a desire for justice and revenge and eventually an act of "justified" aggression against the offending party. The transition from this cycle to an outer spiral of reconciliation is the choice to grieve and accept the loss that has occurred. Also important along the spiral of reconciliation is the choice to forgive and the commitment to take risks. "Forgiveness is seen as evolving and mysterious and as something that cannot be simply taught, indoctrinated, or imposed. It can, however, be fostered through thoughtful, sensitive, facilitated dialogue among the parties to a conflict" (Botcharova 2001, 293).

The three healing models present differing stages and sequences through which healing occurs. We have seen the Botcharova model prove especially helpful for parties in providing a sense of the "big picture" and the larger process, which may span years or perhaps a lifetime. Our interviews and our own experience, however, have revealed that these models are not engraved in stone. In actuality, the healing process is often a jumble of contrasting feelings, experiences, and needs. One step does not flow into the next with clearly delineated signposts, but rather several stages may be combined or appear out of sequence. An important part of empowerment

Figure 2
SEVEN STEPS TOWARD RECONCILIATION

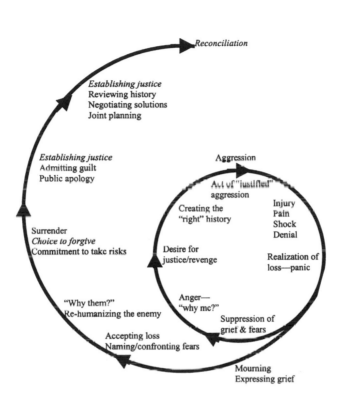

SOURCE: Botcharova (2001). Reprinted by permission of the publisher.

in the healing process is naming one's own needs and process and creating an individualized model.

Which elements of positive approaches are contained in these three models of healing? Although Appreciative Inquiry does not start with telling painful experiences, there is a common element of telling and acknowledging experiences. Acknowledgement, in other words, giving space to talk about experiences and validating them, has power in both cases. Another common element in the models is that of choice—the power of people who have been hurt to choose their own response and their own relationship with those that hurt them. The inclusion of choice in the models is a hopeful one, even an act of faith, spoken into situations in which choice is often not recognized. Daring to walk with a person who has been hurt because you see a potential for healing is a positive, affirmative act given the reality and understanding of that person at the beginning of such a process. Lastly, we can see positive approaches in the models in that choice opens up a creative process, the creation of a new identity and a new relationship.

CHARACTERISTICS OF MOMENTS OF HEALING

In looking across the stories of healing, including rituals and metaphors, and the models of healing, we see several characteristics in common. They are: (1) telling the story of what happened in a supportive and safe environment; (2) naming the injury; (3) the importance of encounter; (4) the significance of nonverbal forms of experiencing and communicating; and (5) allowing the choices of healing behaviors, time, and sequence to be determined by the survivor.

Telling the Story in a Safe Environment

In the examples recounted, healing occurred when stories of suffering and difficult times were told in an environment that was validating, or what has been described as an environment of prophetic listening. Elise Boulding has defined *prophetic listening* as "listening to others in such a way that we draw out of them the seeds of their own highest understanding, of their own obedience, of their own vision, that they themselves may not have known were there" (1980, 74). One practitioner we interviewed also described this as *bearing witness,* accompanying a victim along the path of healing. Stories often need to be told and retold, until the wronged party feels that the time is right to move to another stage in healing. This aspect was present in the church conflict over the fired pastor and with the Liberian pastor who had witnessed his parents' killing.

This emphasis on the kind of listening and environment into which difficult stories are told suggests that what is healing in telling goes beyond just the telling. What is also important for healing is the acknowledgement of that reality by those who are listening. Acknowledgement is an affirmation that truth has been told. Paula Green and Tamra Pearson d'Estrée have come to the conclusion that giving voice gives life to peacebuilding (see chapter sixteen). The person who acknowledges a painful story that has been told becomes an indirect witness and even a participant. While the models of healing emphasize the safe environment, they do not highlight the importance of the role of listener and of acknowledgement to the healing process. In our experience, acknowledgement often comes from others who have themselves been wounded.

Part of storytelling is giving a name to what happened that reflects the reality of that person's experience. This naming has tremendous power, especially if it is in the context of a wound that has not been named before. One practitioner labeled this power of naming as the strongest power that parties in conflict have.

Throughout the stories of healing, we heard of the importance of choice. In storytelling and in determining when the time for next steps has come, it is important that the survivor be empowered to choose the right time according to the person's needs. In our own experience, there have been moments of choosing to go into a difficult experience. For Randy as a companion in the healing process, this awareness developed when it became clear that his own tendency was to turn—to run—away from or to repress Amela's expressions of anger and fear. Self-awareness of these tendencies allows the choice to stay present with difficult feelings. In this process, it has also been helpful for Randy to realize that fixing the hurt is not required (and indeed not possible).

In the stories of healing, choices were made to enter into a reliving or reminding of unpleasant and painful experiences. A phrase we heard often was "staying in the process," meaning staying with the feelings, feeling them deeply, and allowing body, mind, and soul to digest them. Digesting of the feelings and actions needs to take place in order for the process of healing to start. It might start in small steps, but the important part in this is the acceptance of the trauma that took place. Very often survivors feel as if all that happened was a bad dream that will go away once they wake up. Upon waking up they realize the reality, and there is a constant struggle between living in the past and in the present. Digesting feelings helps in accepting the past, which in turn helps in living in the present, and finally, in creating a new future.

Many of the moments of healing came about through encounters between one who had been injured and the person who committed the injury or someone from that person's same group. Often healing did occur through such encounters as, for example, in a workshop in South Africa between black activists and white policemen who had interrogated and tortured them; or in a courtroom in the United States between family members of a murder victim and the perpetrator; or in a community meeting in Nicaragua between former combatants from different sides in that country's civil war. In stories of healing, the importance of encountering the former adversary or *the Other* can, however, be easily misunderstood or misused. It does not mean that an encounter alone will necessarily lead to healing, nor that an encounter is essential to healing. Encounter is not always possible, as when a survivor is unwilling to meet the attacker or feels unsafe in doing so; or when the perpetrator or a surrogate from the perpetrator's group is unavailable or not open to such a meeting. In our discussion of healing rituals, we noted the examples of the Liberian pastor and the families of bombing victims in Omagh where healing rituals took place that were powerful despite the absence of this kind of encounter.

SPIRITUAL DIMENSION OF HEALING

We have come to understand healing as not only a psychological and physiological process but a spiritual process as well. This spiritual struggle is embodied in the fundamental question "Why?" This is a question for which there are no easy answers. Amela had been engaged in her healing process for many years when she realized that the way she initially imagined healing was reconstructing the identity she had before the war. This identity included the country of which she was a citizen (Bosnia-Herzegovina), the place where she grew up (Jajce), and her place in her family and culture. Many of those elements had been destroyed or completely changed in the war. Treasuring these identities was instrumental in staying sane and not giving up during the war. What she realized, however, was that healing not only means rebuilding old identities but also requires discovering new ones. Healing must go beyond a process of reconstructing the self that existed before, which no longer corresponds to the new situation.

In Herman's model one of the latter stages of healing is "identifying a survivor mission." This is not a complete answer to why these difficult experiences happened, but Amela has experienced it as rediscovering reasons for living and reaffirming the sanctity of life. This spiritual process starts at the point when "enough" healing has happened on the psychological and physiological levels. What is enough healing cannot be clearly stated and measured. There is a time, however, when one feels that something has changed: One feels lighter, more joyful, less angry, and not hurting anymore. This change helps move the healing process into an even deeper stage. The spiritual healing process means discovering in a new way the essence that one is made of, the *essence* of one's own existence, and realizing that the essence of life has not been destroyed by violence. On the contrary, it seems that essence of life has been put away into the far corners of our soul for the mere purpose of protection. Once the danger to one's life is gone, this essence comes back and reminds the survivor of the presence of life and its sacredness. This is the moment when the spirit makes love with the soul in a gentle and caring way. It renews one's sense of life and reclaims one's right to live and breathe. This is a very sacred and special process that occurs at its own time and in its own way. Amela saw it as a gift from God that was helping her to reclaim her own humanity and right to live, hope, and create.

The concept of *integration* is a powerful one at this stage. This means integration of a difficult experience into the understanding of one's identity. This may require changing some aspects of a previous identity because they no longer fit. It means recognizing that life has a different meaning in the light of that experience. It is also a process of recognizing anew the preciousness of life and finding a space deep within the soul that is filled with peace.

Although healing happens according to the survivor's readiness to take each step and not by following a set sequence, the common elements we have seen in the stories and models of healing may provide some markers along the way. They include: finding a safe environment, telling the story, becoming aware of rage or a desire for revenge, grieving losses, noticing that the loss becomes easier, and integrating the experience. Even one's self-perception as wounded or as healing is an important distinction. The myriad ways that the healing process can unfold go beyond what any one model can capture. The adage "time heals all wounds" certainly does not seem to be true, however. For every story of healing there are countless other stories of hurts that are carried for years or even lifetimes. In our experience, the passage of time is significant, but does not alone open possibilities for healing without the choice being made (again and again) to enter upon the journey of healing.

APPRECIATIVE INQUIRY AND HEALING

So far in this chapter we have explored the question, "How does healing take place?" We now turn to considering what new impulses Appreciative Inquiry might offer for healing. We hope to illuminate both areas where AI and existing models of healing may be complementary, as well as areas where they differ.

To begin, we count stories of healing as among the best examples of peacebuilding work. Healing impacts the lives of the parties in profound, powerful, and positive ways. Healing is about the journey from injury to wholeness. It is about affirming life and hope for the future. If the conflicts around our world and the daily pain and injury they cause are like a raging forest fire, healing is the new tree sprout that rises from the scorched earth. Healing also inspires and sustains peacebuilders and gives life to the larger peacebuilding endeavor.

In examining the relevance of Appreciative Inquiry to healing, a good place to start is with the five fundamental principles on which it is based (Cooperrider and Whitney 2001; see also chapter three of this volume). We will consider each of these in turn.

The *constructionist principle* states that new language and dialogue can create a new social reality. This principle is consistent with peacebuilding practice in general, which consistently strives to get people talking or talking together in new ways, including reframing of issues to open up new possibilities for agreement on solutions. Moreover, the importance of language is demonstrated time and again in healing. Just as it may be important, for example, to use the term *victim* at one point in a healing process, in acknowledging the reality of what happened, it can also be important to talk about being a *survivor* and no longer merely the recipient of another's action, but rather empowered to redefine oneself in new ways. This process of redefinition can also arrive at a stage of *thriving*, having fully integrated the traumatic experience. These distinctions are important, because the language we use reflects and affects our understanding. The role in healing of storytelling and listening also support this principle. Talking about traumatic events in a supportive and empowering environment, speaking about the "unspeakable," can create a new reality about what happened. The events and the hurt have not changed, but the meaning can shift from being an event of disempowerment to one of giving life.

There were many examples of the *positive principle*—the power of the positive—in the stories of healing, such as sharing from the best of different cultures; sharing positive memories; or telling about people who are important in your life. Positive approaches, in other words, are not new to peacebuilding, and are often used because they are energizing and build empathy and rapport.

The *poetic principle* addresses the power of images and imagination. We are familiar with a number of powerful visioning exercises used in peacebuilding that draw on or generate positive images of the future. The story of Omagh in Northern Ireland shows the power of creativity in healing, in this case pictures made from flowers of condolence. This principle is supported in the importance of nonverbal forms of experience in the symbols and rituals used in promoting healing. Also compelling is the idea that healing involves helping people discover their governing metaphors and then find new ones that can help guide them to a better place. A continuing question for us is to understand how the poetic principle already occurs in healing practice and how can it be strengthened in healing and other peacebuilding work. The importance of the poetic principle as a component of Appreciative Inquiry might mean that peacebuilders would benefit from paying more attention to and learning from the AI change process.

The *principle of simultaneity* asserts that change begins with the first questions we ask. We saw in the workshop for Middle Eastern youth, it was a positive question that helped to create a dynamic of empathy among the participants. The empathy allowed the entire group to experience some healing, even though there were still significant differences and difficult interactions in their time together. Together with other practitioners who follow the models discussed above, we have not been inclined to see healing as about asking questions but rather about creating a safe atmosphere and facilitating the empowerment of the survivor's own process. From this encounter with

AI, we carry a new attention the questions we ask and how they affect the direction of a healing process.

Lastly is the *anticipatory principle*, a cornerstone of Appreciative Inquiry because it emphasizes that what we think and talk about affects what we become. As we have seen, telling stories of difficult times plays a key role in the healing process. Does an AI perspective imply that in talking about pain, we are strengthening that very pain? This gets to the heart of what is difficult for peacebuilders about Appreciative Inquiry. One important distinction is that AI is not about denying or not listening, but rather creating an environment in which people's stories are listened to most authentically. Still, could talking only about positives fully engage people who have been hurt? The importance placed on naming and talking about loss and hurt says to us that the answer is no. This is especially true if discussing positive topics is an imposition from the outside, violating the importance of empowerment, of allowing survivors to guide their own process.

We are interested, however, in the ways that Appreciative Inquiry or aspects of appreciative process can complement and extend the existing practice of healing. One application could be in the later phases of healing, what Herman calls "identifying a survivor mission" and which we consider to be the spiritual dimension. This is certainly a place where a trauma survivor might be fully engaged in an inquiry process about finding meaning in the midst of difficult experiences. Identifying that which was deeply meaningful from their earlier lives, as well as experiences of courage, resilience, selflessness, caring, and compassion in the face of great adversity, could be a natural way to affirm in themselves the best of what has been and yet begin to build a new identity. And, this is a process that can benefit from sharing experiences and learning from others in a similar position.

We know of dialogue groups in Bosnia that began by bringing different groups from the conflict together. After some time they discovered that it was helpful to work individually with the groups first, to help them clarify their own sense of identity before encountering that of the other groups. This single-identity work has proven to be important groundwork for coming together, including developing the ability to look critically at the actions of one's own group. We can imagine that an appreciative process that retrieved stories of the best experiences of being Muslim among a group of Muslims or being Serb among Serbs would be a safe place to begin. This might also be a starting point for those who are not ready to start by talking about their difficult experiences of being Muslim or Serb. To emphasize again, we do not see that appreciative process calls us to deny what is shared if that is difficult, but rather to pay attention to what questions we ask and continue to call forth the best.

We noted above that peacebuilders do not always emphasize the healing effects of listening to and acknowledging stories of loss. If acknowledgement has power to heal, we might understand AI's power in healing in a new light. AI is about telling stories to an interview partner and then having those stories shared by that partner along with the stories of others as the foundation stones for a change process. This means that there is both individual and group acknowledgement of stories, plus further affirmation as insights and themes drawn from them become the pathway to defining new visions for the future. Such an inquiry, for example, might be about the ways in which people transcended difficult conditions or even about funny moments in the midst of tragedy. Bosnians are full of such stories; even people who have experienced significant trauma talk about them readily amidst the many discussions of current and past difficulties. What has not been tested is the effect of telling these positive stories and having them acknowledged.

These are surely just some of the ways that Appreciative Inquiry and other positive approaches might be integrated into what is known and will be learned about healing. We hold onto the unexplored possibilities that AI may offer at various points in the healing process.

ENDNOTE

1. Interviews were conducted with Olga Botcharova, Jayne Docherty, Orli Fridman, Barry Hart, Vernon Jantzi, Ron Kraybill, Tammy Krause, Sonja Kuftinec, John Paul Lederach, Lisa Schirch, Nancy Good Sider, Marieke van Woerkom, and Howard Zehr, between December 2001 and February 2002. Many thanks to them for sharing their time and wisdom!

REFERENCES

Botcharova, Olga. 2001. "Implementation of Track Two Diplomacy: Developing a Model for Forgiveness." In *Forgiveness and Reconciliation: Religion, Public Policy, and Conflict Transformation*. Raymond G. Helmick, S.J., and Rodney L. Peterson, eds. Philadelphia: Templeton Foundation Press.

Boulding, Elise. 1980. Talk given at New Call to Peacemaking Conference. In *Mediation and Facilitation Training Manual* (4th edition). Akron, Pa.: Mennonite Conciliation Service.

Cooperrider, David, and Suresh Srivastva. 1987. "Appreciative Inquiry in Organizational Life." In *Research on Organizational Change and Development*, Vol. 1. Richard W. Woodman and William A. Passmore, eds. Greenwich, Conn.: JAI Press.

Cooperrider, David L., and Diana K. Whitney, eds. 2001. *Appreciative Inquiry: A Constructive Approach to Organizational Development and Social Change*. Taos, N.M.: Corporation for Positive Change.

Herman, Judith Lewis. 1997. *Trauma and Recovery.* New York: Basic Books.

Kraybill, Ron. 1988. "From Head to Heart: The Cycle of Reconciliation." *Conciliation Quarterly* 7:4 (fall), pp. 2–3, 8.

Romanoff, Bronna D., and Marion Terenzio. 1998. "Rituals and the Grieving Process." *Death Studies* 22:8, pp. 697–711.

Schirch, Lisa. 2001. "Ritual, Reconciliation, and Transformation." Harrisonburg, Va.: Conflict Transformation Program.

PART VI:

DESIGNING ORGANIZATIONS FOR PEACEBUILDING

The world is waiting . . . for new saints, ecstatic men and women who are so deeply rooted in the love of God that they are free to imagine a new international order.

HENRI NOUWEN

CHAPTER NINETEEN

THE UNITED RELIGIONS INITIATIVE AND APPRECIATIVE INQUIRY:
AN EVOLVING PARTNERSHIP

Charles Gibbs and Barbara Hartford

The United Religions Initiative (URI) has developed an innovative and positive approach to interfaith peacebuilding through its unique partnership with Appreciative Inquiry. This chapter documents that partnership since its inception in 1997. It was framed by a series of global and regional summits, which were all designed and conducted using Appreciative Inquiry (AI) and which created a global community schooled in the practice of AI. That practice has been marked by a suppleness that allowed AI to be adapted to the ever more focused work of completing the URI charter and establishing an organization designed to create enduring, daily interfaith cooperation. A current major URI focus is the development of a peacebuilding program, including training for grassroots leaders, locally contextualized projects, development of an interfaith peacebuilding curriculum, and a global inquiry to forge new visions and strategies for peace among religions for the twenty first century.

❧

"*W*e, people of diverse religions, spiritual expressions and indigenous traditions throughout the world, hereby establish the United Religions Initiative to promote enduring, daily interfaith cooperation, to end religiously motivated violence and to create cultures of peace, justice and healing for the Earth and all living beings" (URI 2000).

These words, representing thousands of voices around the world, launch the preamble to the charter of the United Religions Initiative. They are the hard-won fruit of a four-year journey to create a global network dedicated to interfaith cooperation for the good of all life. At the heart of this journey is an evolving partnership between the United Religions Initiative (URI) and Appreciative Inquiry (AI). This partnership led not only to the creation a new organization, it also forged a promising positive approach to interfaith peacebuilding. Together, the organization and its innovative approach to peacebuilding are the means and a major tool for carrying this work into the future, with the hope of helping transform human history.

The vision of peacebuilding through interfaith cooperation has been central to URI since the seed that led to its development was planted in the winter of 1993. The United Nations invited the Episcopal Bishop of the Diocese of California, the Rt. Rev. William Swing, to host a one-hour inter-faith service at Grace Cathedral on June 25, 1995. The service was to be part of a week of activities commemorating the fiftieth anniversary of the signing of the U.N. charter in San Francisco. When the bishop expressed his delight at hosting this service, the U.N. representative informed him that 185 nations would share in this celebration. He was to bring the world's religions.

That night Bishop Swing found it difficult to sleep. He realized that he had received an invitation, on behalf of the religions of the world, to celebrate fifty years of unprecedented peacemaking. During that time the nations of the world, even when some of them were at war, had had the moral courage to meet on a daily basis at a permanent center to work for peace. During that same fifty years, even though they were often implicated in the violence that helped make the twentieth century one of the bloodiest in human history, the religions of the world had barely talked with one another.

From this realization arose the vision of a forum where leaders of the world's religions would work to recognize and realize a collective vocation to be peacemakers; where they would match the moral courage of the world's nations, meeting on a daily basis at a permanent center to work for global good. And so the seed that would grow into the United Religions Initiative was planted and took root in the heart of a sleepless bishop.

That seed would take root in the hearts of thousands more people before the URI's charter was completed—and in tens of thousands more as the global URI was launched at a charter signing in June 2000 and began to grow into its potential. In that journey, as the bishop's own vision evolved dramatically, URI ceased to be "the bishop's vision" and became a vision owned by twenty-five thousand plus URI members from over sixty faith tra-ditions in forty-seven countries around the world.

FROM DISCOVERY TO DESTINY: THE DESIGN OF AN ORGANIZATION

This evolution of the URI vision, its articulation in an innovative charter, and its ownership by people all over the world was made possible by the partnership between the United Religions Initiative and Appreciative Inquiry, a partnership that helped build a positive approach to organizing and, ulti-mately, to peacebuilding into URI's "genetic code."[1]

This partnership was initiated in the winter of 1997, a few

months before URI's first global summit, by Dr. David Cooperrider, considered to be "the father of Appreciative Inquiry." Cooperrider read an article about Bishop Swing's vision and immediately wrote a letter offering his support. This letter and a subsequent visit with the Rev. Charles Gibbs, URI's future founding executive director, marked the beginning of a relationship that would synergistically match the embryonic URI's intuitive way of working with a field-tested organizational development methodology: URI met Appreciative Inquiry.

URI brought to the partnership the quest to create an organization by which people of faith would stop killing one another in the name of the Divine and start learning to live together, and a belief that the organization must be created by the people from diverse faith traditions it intended to serve. Appreciative Inquiry brought an organizing methodology to help accomplish this goal. AI is founded on a belief that any organization grows in the direction of the questions it asks and that the most effective questions are those that elicit visions of a shared positive future, as well as the best practices of the past that can help create that future. AI cultivates a practice of sacred listening. Based on a belief that every voice matters, it asks that the whole system of affected parties be in the room when an organization goes through a process of Discovery, Dream, Design, and Destiny (the 4-D Cycle).

Appreciative Inquiry carries a belief that the gathered community contains sufficient wisdom, without the need of privileged "expert" voices, to create a vision and the plan and commitments necessary to realize that vision. An AI conference is not a passive gathering where a few people talk and the rest sit and listen. In general, there are not speeches. The conference is fully participatory, with participants often working in small groups, organized for maximum diversity.

"Time for Action": First Global Gathering

The first fruits of this partnership were URI's first global summit, held in San Francisco in June 1997 and attended by fifty-five men and women from diverse religions, vocations, and nations. The summit's title, "Time for Action: Discovering the Steps for a United Religions Charter," provided the core focus of imagining the steps necessary to begin writing a charter for the United Religions.[2]

An opening appreciative interview helped set the tone for the conference. One question engaged the participants in a process of discovering values to be drawn upon in giving birth to a United Religions by asking what values each individual brings, what positive qualities come from our faith communities, and what the global and local trends and changes are that bring hope for such a possibility. Another question asked participants to place themselves thirty years into the future and visualize both an effective United Religions type of entity and the kind of world they really wanted.

The one-on-one interviews that flowed from these questions marked the beginning of Discovery, a process that would include introductions in small groups and in the whole. In this safe space, the interviews brought out shared visions, experiences, and passions, which created relationships of trust. A joyful energy enlivened the room. By the time this work had been done, fifty-five diverse individuals had formed a community ready to work. The next project, still part of the Discovery Phase, involved the creation and interpretation of three timelines and a mind map, all designed to build a shared sense of the historical context and trends that might assist or challenge the creation of a United Religions. The timelines of world events, interfaith events, and religious/faith events became great wall murals created by the whole group, constituting a collective historical context for our work. The mind map was an exercise that mined these timelines for historical insights and trends that could support or hinder the URI effort. These were then discussed and ranked; the most significant were trends toward global solidarity, a growing recognition of common values among religions, and an observable increase in collaboration among religions.

The Dream Phase called participants, first individually and then in small groups, to imagine an ideal world and the role the United Religions would play in creating that world. In the process we imagined what the United Religions would look like, what would be its guiding values, who would be involved, and what it would do in the world. Each small group then presented its dream to the whole group, mostly as skits. They dreamed of religions coming together, a 'spiritual United Nations,' mutual understanding and respect, ongoing dialogue, a deep sense of others, inclusivity, breaking down of barriers, and of engagement with individuals all over the globe in creating a United Religions.

Building on these dreams, the Design Phase asked people to imagine the key actions necessary over the coming year to enable URI to begin writing a charter with two hundred women and men from diverse faiths from around the world. The plans created during a day of small-group working sessions included drafting a mission statement, hiring a staff and opening an office, creating materials that would enable groups independently to go through the 4-D Cycle that summit participants had shared, creating strategic partnerships, hosting similar summits in different regions of the world, and essentially, raising the money to allow all this to happen.

The culminating Destiny Phase saw all those who wished empowered to take whatever initiative seemed best to implement the plans created in the Design Phase. Indeed, this phase extended through the next twelve months as plans were realized—a staff was hired and an office opened, a workbook was created, strategic partnerships forged, three regional summits planned and produced, the second global summit planned, and a line of credit established and funds raised to enable the work to go forward.

Expanding the Vision

In discovering Appreciative Inquiry, the URI found a process for creating an organization that reflected the values we felt the organization should embody. At the center was a belief in the essential nature of interfaith cooperation that honors and celebrates diversity, while striving to discover common vision leading to shared action for a better world. This URI-AI partnership, which would ultimately involve many of Cooperrider's graduate students from Case Western Reserve University and professional colleagues, would be developed and refined over the next four years, through four global summits, more than ten regional summits, and countless consultations, and it would lead to the birth of a global URI and a unique, innovative approach to interfaith peacebuilding.

Each of these summits was planned using Appreciative Inquiry. Each followed the 4-D format. Each saw an opening appreciative interview and shared visions of a better world meld a group of diverse individuals, often individuals from faiths in conflict, into a community of allies committed to working together. Each yielded a Destiny Phase that moved the work of creating the United Religions forward, both regionally and between the yearly global summits. In the process, we created a global community schooled in the practice of AI, a practice that stressed local contextualization and a suppleness that would allow AI to be adapted to enable the ever more focused work that would lead to the completion of the URI charter and the birth of a new global organization.

Together, we created an organization consistent with the original vision, focused on enduring, daily interfaith cooperation, and grounded in prayer, meditation, and dialogue leading to cooperative action. But some aspects of the original vision changed. Our evolving, growing global community came to focus not on attracting the world's top religious leaders, but on building a vast global interfaith network from the grassroots up, with a strong emphasis on the equitable participation of women, as well as men. We expanded the original vision beyond the narrowly construed world of "religion" to include spiritual expressions and indigenous traditions, ensuring that anyone motivated by deep spiritual values was welcome to join the effort; and beyond the world of religious and interfaith activists to include people from all vocational areas, ensuring that the wisdom of business, the arts, education, peacebuilding, medicine, the media, science, etc., was part of URI's effort to help shape a more positive future for all life.

Locally Active, Globally Connected

We also worked to include the voices of those not often heard, particularly the voices of indigenous people around the world (see Gibbs 2002). Instead of a centralized power structure, we created an organization that was globally connected, but which recognized the right of its local groups—cooperation circles (CCs)—to organize in any manner, at any scale, in any area, and around any issue or activity that is relevant to and consistent with the preamble, purpose and principles of URI's charter. To ensure interfaith cooperation, each cooperation circle required a minimum of seven people and three different traditions.

All this work found fruit in URI's charter and in the creation of a core community of eighty-five founding cooperation circles dedicated to making the charter a living document. Even before it was signed, the charter came alive for three days at the turn of the millennium, December 31, 1999 to January 2, 2000, in the "72 Hours of Interfaith Peacebuilding" global project. In this project, we invited people of faith from around the world to mobilize their communities for peacebuilding. Suggested activities were to hold a peace vigil, engage in prayer or meditation for their spiritual neighbors, do a clear and tangible peacebuilding project in their local community, call on political leaders to lead in ceasing violence during these seventy-two hours, or support interfaith solidarity with those working for peace in zones of conflict. Two hundred projects in sixty countries resulted from this initiative, including interfaith prayer services all over the world; the dedication of a peace monument in Ethiopia; an interfaith peace pilgrimage from Karachi to the Khyber Pass in Pakistan; and interfaith peace meditation trainings in Sri Lanka. It provided a foretaste of how URI's appreciative approach could motivate people to cooperative action for peace.

ONGOING ITERATIONS: DESIGNING AND DELIVERING THE URI VISION

In one sense, URI's history since the charter signing in June 2000 has been an extended Delivery Phase—building on what we learned during the chartering process about bringing together diverse groups of people in a safe space where old animosities could be overcome and a new future imagined.

A striking example of this occurred in April 2002 at a URI regional assembly for Europe and the Middle East in Berlin, Germany. Nancy, a young Muslim woman from Jordan, sat down for the first time in her life with a Jewish person, named Elana. Nancy's fear, perhaps even hatred of the other melted as she heard how Elana's son had nearly died in a suicide bombing, and how, rather than being defeated by bitterness and hatred, Elana had committed herself to work for peace so that other mothers and sons would not have to suffer what she and her son had suffered. Potential enemies were turned into allies with a shared commitment to work to create a new future of peace, justice, and healing in their communities.

As URI moved into its post-chartering life, the question of how this network of self-organizing cooperation circles would make real the vision of the charter became foremost. In an effort to explore answers to this question, the URI peacebuilding program came into being in 2001, under the guidance of Barbara Hartford, global staff member. A product of the URI-AI partnership, in which we had discovered and dreamed that we would create cultures of peace and build safe places for conflict resolution, healing, and reconciliation, the peacebuilding program became a path to carry out the Design and Destiny phases of the AI process. Appropriately, we began to create this program by asking questions such as:

- How do we create "safe spaces" for people of diverse faiths to work at conflict resolution, healing, and reconciliation together?

- We can see fear and division not only *among* religions, but also *within* religious communities; how do we deepen both interfaith and *intra*-faith dialogue to begin to mend these rifts?

- As people of shared principles, how do we go about developing the sensibilities, tools, and skills for dealing with differences from an interfaith perspective?

- Respecting and valuing the diversity of our traditions and wisdom, how do we learn collectively and not hierarchically?

Guided by the answers to these and other questions, operating from our AI-sourced principles and purpose, and designing as much as possible from the 'global whole,' we began to build a peacebuilding program.

Peacebuilding Program Launched

The URI peacebuilding program was officially launched in summer 2002 with three sequenced events: First, in May–June 2002, six URI CC leaders received peacebuilding training at Eastern Mennonite University's Summer Peacebuilding Institute (SPI), an institute selected for its alignment with URI values and faith-based approach and the elicitive instruction, which places great value on the experience of the participants. They came to learn skills in conflict transformation and brought to that community the commitment of ongoing daily interfaith cooperation. They also brought AI to the SPI community by offering a weekend workshop in "Appreciative Inquiry for Peacebuilders," taught by Claudia Liebler, AI consultant and leadership coach.

As the CC leaders studied together during the day, they began designing the URI peacebuilding training program in the evenings with the help of Liebler and Mohammed Abu-Nimer, associate professor of international conflict resolution at American University. Bringing together experiences from their home communities and their new learning at SPI, and standing in the principles of URI, this core group began dreaming and designing a five-day course to present to their URI colleagues at URI's first Global Assembly, "Sharing the Sacred, Serving the World," in Rio de Janeiro, Brazil, in August 2002.

Second, during the week prior to the Global Assembly, URI sponsored a five-day interfaith peacebuilding course, "Skills for the Religious/Spiritual Peacebuilder." Taught by Abu-Nimer and Liebler, with assistance from the core group from SPI, the course was attended by twenty-seven men and women from the global URI community, who came from ten countries, ten religions, and ranged in age from nineteen to seventy-five years. This group became URI's peacebuilding team.

Third, the peacebuilding team with instructors Abu-Nimer and Liebler prepared and presented three half-day training sessions for the 320 people gathered from around the world for the URI Global Assembly. These three sessions highlighted the unique aspects of URI interfaith peacebuilding that emerged from the five-day course.

The appreciative approach of URI in group gatherings, beginning with appreciative interviews and using other appreciative processes, has been key to creating the safe space of trust and respect in which deep shared examination of our faiths can take place honestly and without defensiveness. A core exercise of the Global Assembly sessions was an interfaith exploration of how rituals, teachings, and practices from our respective religious and spiritual traditions have been or could be used to promote inclusion, tolerance, and peace, and also—a first at a URI Summit—how our respective traditions have been or could be used to promote exclusion, prejudice, or violence against the Other. This exercise generated lively self-examination and discussion, first with people who shared a religion and then in groups of religious diversity. "I'm much more tolerant of mistakes of other religions when I see the mistakes of my own through this analysis," said one of the participants.

URI's ongoing peacebuilding work is taking several forms, with locally relevant interfaith peacebuilding models being shared in home communities around the world. In the Philippines, for example, "Interfaith Dialogue for Nation Building," a three-day workshop, initiated a year-long program. In California, the Bridge CC held a collaborative workshop between URI and the Council for the Parliament of World Religions. URI peacebuilders in Brazil have designed a multi-media tool kit, "People Building Peace." In Zimbabwe, a multi-year program to encourage nonviolent and impartial media reporting has begun. In Uganda, a youth peace leadership workshop is in place.

Building on this strong foundation, the development of a URI peace-building training curriculum is a current major global project. The curriculum complements existing peacebuilding methodologies with a unique interfaith perspective that is grounded in appreciative process.

The unique character of the emerging URI approach to peacebuilding adds Spirit, or Soul, to the traditional work of Head (mind, inspiration, thoughts, communications), Heart (emotion, compassion), and Hands (action-oriented endeavors). We engage in deep personal reflection; we ground ourselves deeply in our own faith tradition; and we engage the particularly spiritual capacity for forgiveness and reconciliation as we develop our capacity to deal with differences. This work is leading us into more meaningful intra-faith as well as interfaith discussions. Our approach to peacebuilding together with our unique organization design—a grassroots focus with a global vision and our appreciative way of being in relationship—is our way of seeking to create a culture in which peace can flourish. The peacebuilding curriculum will be made available to the URI global grassroots network, as well as to community interfaith councils, international interfaith organizations, peacebuilding institutes and regional training centers, academic institutions, and other strategic partners.

Visions for Peace Among Religions

Another AI-inspired aspect of the URI peacebuilding program is a project that was conceived shortly after the charter was signed in June 2000. The "Twenty-first Century Visions for Peace Among Religions" (VPAR) inquiry was proposed as a global action that would combine the potential of Appreciative Inquiry and the unique niche of URI's international interfaith network. VPAR was designed to engage millions of people over a three-year period in appreciative interviews, to gather their experiences, hopes, and dreams for waging peace, seeking justice, and healing conflict among the world's religions.

Of central importance, VPAR is intended to generate positive, shared images of and strategies for peace among religions. Over the next three years, the synthesis of the best stories, hopes, dreams, and ideas will evolve into a proposed global standard for peace among religions, representing the collective wisdom and moral voice of everyone who has participated in the process. In addition, VPAR will nurture the growth of a global community committed to interfaith peacebuilding and spawn local peacebuilding projects around the world. Such projects might include social action projects, books, works of art, and educational curricula.

OFFERINGS TO THE WORLD: INSIGHTS, OPPORTUNITIES, AND CHALLENGES

As the United Religions Initiative has evolved over the years, our work with Appreciative Inquiry has led to some simple and obvious but remarkable insights. Being listened to in an authentic way about experiences and learnings of deep, positive, personal importance matters. Similarly, listening authentically to another about experiences and learnings of deep, positive, personal importance matters. Being listened to and listening creates the potential for positive change, especially when those doing the speaking and listening have previously encountered each other mainly as negative stereotypes and enemies.

Speaking and listening authentically lays the foundation for meaningful peacebuilding work. It builds relationships and trust and creates the confidence among people that they can change the destructive patterns of the past and the present—that they can be peacebuilders. Creating shared positive views of a future that people of faith would like to build together creates opportunities for positive change. It inspires resourcefulness, opens the door to sustained interaction, and impels peacebuilding.

Again and again, URI has experienced that the human yearning for a better way runs deep and that collective wisdom is a powerful change agent. In our experience, which remains to be tested in zones of active violent conflict, this yearning and wisdom can be activated and engaged fairly easily. Appreciative Inquiry is an extraordinary activator and engager.

The challenges come in sustaining what is activated and engaged, in translating vision into action. Though people are infinitely resourceful, a mismatch between an exalted vision and the resources available to realize that vision can lead to frustration. On the other hand, a vision that isn't exalted enough can fail to inspire the resourcefulness and willingness to sacrifice that are needed to make the impossible possible. Finding the right balance is a challenge and an art form. In this endeavor, URI is an infant. The years ahead will test our ability to help groups strike this balance appropriately and create sustainable change.

Another challenge is how to scale the transformative experience that AI enables from small groups to whole communities. It is relatively easy to imagine you are creating transformative yeast that can be injected into a system in conflict. It is much more challenging to create the conditions that will enable the yeast to help the system rise out of separateness and hostility into community and cooperation. Again, URI is an infant in this endeavor. The coming years will no doubt see us challenged to create the conditions for more large-scale transformation.

Finally, as alluded to, URI's work has yet to be tested in a systematic way in zones of active violent conflict. We can imagine how well this method will work in such situations, but we will need to put our imagination to the test as we move increasingly into deeply conflicted areas.

It is URI's success to date, the promise it holds, and the profound challenges it faces that propel us forward with a blend of idealism and pragmatism. URI's work in peacebuilding represents an innovative and positive approach to interfaith peacebuilding, which has emerged out of the unique partnership between URI and AI that began in 1997 and continues to flourish. While the overall enterprise is still in its infancy, the partnership and the work it has given rise to hold great promise for a more positive and peaceful future for all life.

ENDNOTES

1. For more on the birth of the United Religions Initiative and its partnership with Appreciative Inquiry, see Swing (1998) and Gibbs and Mahé (2003).
2. The original concept was for a United Religions, paralleling the United Nations. The United Religions Initiative was created to carry forward the chartering process and prepare the way for the formal founding of the United Religions with the signing of the charter. As the mission and purpose of the organization was transformed, however, in the course of drafting the charter and designing the organization, it was decided to retain the name United Religions Initiative as more representative of the true nature of the organization.

REFERENCES

Gibbs, Charles. 2002. "The United Religions Initiative at Work." In *Interfaith Dialogue and Peacebuilding*. David R. Smock, ed. Washington, D.C.: U.S. Institute of Peace Press.

Gibbs, Charles, and Sally Mahé. 2003. *Birth of a Global Community: Appreciative Inquiry as Midwife for the United Religions Initiative*. Cleveland, Ohio: Lakeshore Press. Forthcoming.

Swing, William E. 1998. *The Coming United Religions*. San Francisco: United Religions Initiative; Grand Rapids, Mich.: CoNexus Press.

United Religions Initiative. 2000. "United Religions Initiative Charter." www.uri.org.

Where there is no vision, the people perish.

PROVERBS 29:18

CHAPTER TWENTY

WORDS CREATE WORLDS:
ARTICULATING A VISION FOR PEACEBUILDING
IN CATHOLIC RELIEF SERVICES

Jaco Cilliers, Robin Gulick, and Meg Kinghorn

Articulating a clear guiding vision for peacebuilding based on a process of ongoing reflection is changing agency practice for Catholic Relief Services, an international development and relief agency celebrating its sixtieth anniversary in 2003. In recent years, Catholic Relief Services has reached deep into its Catholic identity, deep into the hopes and desires of staff and partners around the world, and deep into the experiences and lived reality of the people we serve, in order to better express and improve the agency's commitment to work for justice and peace. The process undertaken has been necessarily appreciative and has served to model the change we hope to achieve, for we believe that our words do in fact create the world in which we hope to live.

⚘

As an agency Catholic Relief Services (CRS) has a long history of involvement in justice and peace work. In the beginning, though, the agency focused primarily on poverty reduction through development and relief activities. A number of events since the mid-1990s influenced agency practice and eventually led CRS to make a renewed commitment to promoting justice, reconciliation, and peacebuilding efforts. This is the story of how CRS used a continuous process of learning and reflection to articulate a clear guiding vision for peacebuilding. It was an iterative process that went through several rounds of activity, with each round involving new or enlarged groups of participants.

TOWARDS A DREAM FOR JUSTICE

CRS' journey to peacebuilding started with a dream for a better way to effect change in the world. The Rwandan genocide, not simply a nightmare but a horrible reality that crushed the hopes and dreams of many who lived and worked in that country, caused deep soul searching for Catholic Relief Services. The organization had been doing relief and development projects in the country for decades. Suddenly all the gains from those projects were wiped out in a matter of months—erased without a trace. CRS was ill prepared for the violence that steamed from deep-seated divisions and differences and resulted in the loss of hundreds of thousands of lives. We realized that we had been treating the symptoms of the situation and not the causes of violence and continuing injustice.

This prompted a reexamination of CRS programming in Rwanda and around the globe. We did not go to sleep, but instead awoke to the dream before us. We dreamt of a world where there is peace and justice, where people live together in 'right relationship,' and where people share in and care for the bounty of the earth. To achieve our dream, we began to view CRS programming through a "justice lens" to ensure we were addressing the root causes of injustice and not just the symptoms.

Our Catholic identity gave us a good grounding to understand and articulate this dream. A body of thought and call to action known as Catholic Social Teaching[1] provided the agency with a compelling positive image of what a *just* world would look like and how we could work towards bringing this image into reality. Our guiding principles (see Figure 1), based on Catholic Social Teaching, call people everywhere, and of every faith, to work toward the elimination of poverty, to speak out against injustices, and to actively shape a more peaceful and just world. What was missing was a clear map to guide our journey.

LOOKING THROUGH THE JUSTICE LENS

Out of the dream came the necessity to discover how this dream looked and felt in practice. A first step was to have everyone in the agency reflect on their understanding of justice and what it means for the everyday life of CRS. How would we treat our coworkers? How would we partner with others? How would we draw upon the rich tradition of Catholic Social Teaching for our inspiration and guidance? In order to address these questions, each CRS staff member around the world went through a justice reflection workshop. Each year, as new staff came into the agency, the reflections continued.

Reflecting on justice, however, would not go far enough if no connection were made between CRS staff inspiration and actual programming. We knew we needed to apply the justice lens to programming and also discover how doing so changes agency practice. In order to see the issues involved more clearly, each region selected a program to use as a case study. By increasing attention to the contexts in which we worked, and increasing focus on the people we served, we could examine the challenges and opportunities that materialized.

The case studies were implemented through a process that took
 nearly two years. It culminated in a Justice Lens Workshop, held in

Figure 1
CATHOLIC RELIEF SERVICES
GUIDING PRINCIPLES

- **DIGNITY AND EQUALITY OF THE HUMAN PERSON.** All of humanity has been created in the image of God and possesses a basic dignity and equality that comes directly from our creation and not from any action on our own part.

- **RIGHTS AND RESPONSIBILITIES.** Every person has basic rights and responsibilities that flow from our human dignity and that belong to us as humans, regardless of any social or political structures.

- **SOCIAL NATURE.** Our full human potential isn't realized in solitude, but in community with others. How we organize our families, societies, and communities directly affects human dignity and our ability to achieve our full human potential.

- **THE COMMON GOOD.** In order for all of us to have an opportunity to grow and develop fully, a certain social fabric must exist within society. This is the common good.

- **SUBSIDIARITY.** In order to protect the basic rights of the individual, the government or any large, authoritative structure should not replace or destroy smaller communities and individual initiatives.

- **SOLIDARITY.** We are all part of one human family, regardless of our national, racial, religious, economic, or ideological differences. In an increasingly interconnected world, loving our neighbor has global dimensions.

- **PREFERENTIAL OPTION FOR THE POOR.** In every economic, political, and social decision, a weighted concern must be given to the needs of the poorest and most vulnerable. This strengthens the entire community, because the powerlessness of any member wounds the rest of society.

- **STEWARDSHIP.** There is an inherent integrity to all of creation, and this requires careful stewardship of all our resources, ensuring that we use and distribute them justly and equitably, as well as plan for future generations.

Baltimore, Maryland, in the spring of 2001. More than thirty-five participants came together in this workshop to elicit lessons from the nine regional case studies and from their own experiences in applying the justice lens to programming. Through three days of discovery, they explored strategies for promoting justice in overseas programming and how the most effective of these strategies could be further promoted and supported. They also identified the opportunities and challenges in doing so and synthesized the implications and policy issues that emerged (see Figure 2).

Figure 2
RECOMMENDATIONS FROM
JUSTICE LENS WORKSHOP

CRS programming should demonstrate:

- **CLARITY OF STRATEGY.** Justice requires a clear vision for how to connect local and systemic change processes.

- **IMPLEMENTATION OF A PROCESS FRAMEWORK FOR CHANGE.** CRS should shift from a project-driven to a just-change and process-oriented framework of strategic action.

- **AN UNDERSTANDING THAT TRANSFORMATION HAPPENS THROUGH RELATIONSHIPS.** Our capacity to affect structural change is enhanced through working in relationship with others who share our vision and commitment.

- **A HOLISTIC APPROACH TO ACTION.** As expressed in Catholic Social Teaching, CRS should incorporate solidarity, peace, and justice components into programming design.

Of the many lessons we learned through this discovery process, one of the most important lessons drives the underlying premise of this chapter: *Words create worlds.* In order to transform itself as an agency, CRS learned that it must develop and apply a clear vision of justice that relates the justice lens to solidarity and peacebuilding. Fostering understanding of the relationship between these concepts and using a shared language would allow staff and the partners with whom we work to be fully engaged and on board with new visionary directions. Truly becoming a justice-centered agency required that our staff and partners understand and articulate the vision and, consequently, be empowered to contribute to the justice and peace strategy. Furthermore, the relationships established between our staff and partners and with a larger audience of donors and community groups would create opportunities to express our vision and core values, ultimately encouraging true partnership and contributing to broader societal transformation and structural change.

TOWARDS A DREAM FOR PEACEBUILDING

The timing of the Justice Lens Workshop fed into a new agency-wide strategic planning process. This process would further redefine the mission of the agency and illustrate how momentum builds from initial ideas and infuses the entire life of an agency or community.

The new strategic planning process began in 2000 and led the drive to focus more specifically on peacebuilding within the agency. The world had changed dramatically in the decade of the 1990s, and our dream needed to respond. This time four thousand staff in more than eighty countries would be involved in crafting our vision and directions. Together we would address the questions: "What should CRS be doing in the new world?" "How should we realize our dream?"

Each country and headquarters department held a summit to determine the challenges they faced, their dream to address those challenges, and the possible transformation needed to achieve that dream. A highly appreciative and participatory process was used. Staff and partners were singing, drawing, and debating answers to these questions. A similar process then was undertaken at the regional level. During nine regional workshops, global trends and new opportunities for CRS programming were explored. No idea was too radical to be considered.

From the country and regional summits, common trends emerged. These became the focus of the World Summit held in Tampa, Florida, in October 2000. In addition to inputs from the country and regional meetings at the summit, background papers were written on specific topics, issues, and concerns that needed to be addressed if CRS wanted to honestly commit to embarking on this journey. They were also meant to spark the imaginations of all present at the summit. In one paper CRS staff members wrote:

> We argue that the overarching goal for CRS' work in violent conflicts should be to work for a just peace, and that a peacebuilding strategic framework offers a comprehensive approach that concentrates CRS and our partners' many strengths in the service of a shared vision for peace. . . . A peacebuilding approach requires sophisticated, multi-dimensional capacities. Organizationally, this implies that CRS must be structured in a way that both maximizes the agency's existing capacities and creates new capacities. . . . We believe that peacebuilding and ongoing efforts to improve our humanitarian action operations are fundamental to an agency whose

primary motivation is the promotion and protection of human dignity and human development in a world wracked by violent conflict. Let us move into the twenty-first century by enthusiastically taking a role that was tailor-made for us and responds to what is most desired by those we serve in conflict situations: the right to peace. (Reilly and Cilliers 2000, 1)

Out of the World Summit came a new vision statement and set of visionary directions (see Figure 3), as well as a framework for action that would move us in that direction.

Following the World Summit, the set of visionary directions was transformed into objectives to guide the agency in its new strategic plan. Through one objective, peacebuilding became officially recognized as something CRS does as an agency. The language captured in papers on peace, the words expressed by staff around the world, and the visions shared and expanded through small-group discussions created space in which a new direction—a new world—was born. This objective states,

By FY2007 . . . CRS, our partners, and the people we serve [will] demonstrate attitudes and behaviors that promote peace, tolerance, and reconciliation.

The concept of peace is directly related to the promotion of justice. True peace is not simply the absence of war or violence. Rather, it is the fruit of just and right relationships and can be achieved only through the establishment of right relationships among members of the human family and through the transformation of society and unjust structures. Catholic Relief Services will work toward establishing right relationships in all that we do—both internally and externally. (CRS 2001, 9)

CAPTURING THE DREAM

Now that the vision was becoming clearer, CRS staff and partners were eager to begin to capture our dream and make it a reality. Guided by the words in the visionary objective above, we discovered that there were already wonderful peacebuilding initiatives and examples within and outside CRS that we could build upon as we set out to design our peacebuilding framework. CRS uncovered and produced a list of over sixty projects in which we were involved that could be identified as peacebuilding. Among the leading examples were:

- *Philippines*. CRS/Philippines helped develop a widely used *Culture of Peace* manual with a number of partners in 1998, and continues to actively support conflict transformation trainings and a peacebuilders network in Mindanao.

Figure 3
RESULTS OF CRS WORLD SUMMIT

Vision Statement

Solidarity will transform the world to

- cherish and uphold the sacredness and dignity of every person;
- commit to and practice peace, justice, and reconciliation;
- celebrate and protect the integrity of all creation.

Visionary Directions

- PURSUING THE RIGHT TO PEACE. CRS will build a culture of peace throughout the world based on a foundation of justice and reconciliation.

- TRANSFORMING OUR RESPONSES TO POVERTY AND VULNERABILITY. CRS will commit to full human development by transforming the structures, systems, behaviors, and attitudes that perpetuate poverty and injustice.

- PROMOTING PARTICIPATORY AND RESPONSIVE GOVERNANCE. CRS will support the active engagement and building of government and civil society to promote good governance and active participation of all people in the promotion of just political, social, and economic relations among all economic actors, with special consideration for the poor and marginalized in their countries and the world.

- EXPANDING COMMUNITY. CRS will mobilize and be guided by an expanding global network of partners, based on subsidiarity and equality, in concert with a vibrant movement of people working for justice and peace.

- BECOMING AN AGILE, INNOVATIVE, AND RESPONSIVE ORGANIZATION. CRS will put people first through new and dynamic organizational models and a management culture that enables CRS to be focused, agile, innovative, and responsive.

- *Cambodia.* In 1999 CRS supported the *Dhammayietra* peace walks and other violence reduction campaigns, as well as a women's rights and democracy training program in Cambodia.

- *Colombia.* CRS/Colombia developed a multilevel strategy, known as "Colombian Solidarity," with particular emphasis on local, national, and international efforts to support peace initiatives in Colombia.

- *Pakistan.* CRS supports interreligious dialogue through workshops and seminars that examine the social teachings of Islam and Christianity which promote messages of forgiveness, peacebuilding, and reconciliation. This interreligious activity was encouraged by a millennial interfaith peace walk that CRS helped sponsor. CRS also supports an interfaith harmony project of the Christian Study Center, called "Weaving Communities of Hope."

Defining the starting line by capturing these initiatives, however, was insufficient to keep momentum strong. The dream needed details to keep us all traveling in the same direction. We had to develop a definition and design guiding principles in order to best articulate what we meant by peacebuilding. The first step of drafting a definition for the agency was taken by the Peacebuilding Working Group, consisting of staff from various departments in the CRS Baltimore headquarters. Looking at such areas as conflict prevention, resolution, transformation, reconciliation, and what each would mean for the practice of peacebuilding, they debated the relevance and implications for CRS. This process eventually resulted in a draft peacebuilding definition and vision for the agency.

Everyone on the Peacebuilding Working Group realized, though, that it was crucial to tap into the hearts and minds of staff and partners overseas. Certainly, it is they who drive CRS programming, and their thoughts, ideas, and input were paramount. Having a clear understanding of the practical challenges and opportunities that justice and peace programming presented, it was crucial that they lead the effort to design peacebuilding principles that were realistic and yet still raised the bar and called us to further action.

During the summer of 2001, nearly thirty CRS staff and partners came from all over the world to the small town of South Bend, Indiana, to take part in the first annual Summer Institute on Peacebuilding, held at the Joan B. Kroc Institute for International Peace Studies at the University of Notre Dame. Throughout the ten-day institute, they struggled with the complexities of undertaking peacebuilding initiatives, participated in simulations and trainings, grappled with developing the statement and principles on peacebuilding, and shared their experiences and tools for working in conflict. It was an intensive and exciting ten days.

During this time, participants drew upon CRS' experience with Appreciative Inquiry (in organizational and partnership development) to formulate peacebuilding principles. Participants *discovered* the best of what they had been doing, created a *dream* of what peacebuilding would look like for CRS, *designed* the details, and *delivered* the results to the rest of the agency.

Discovery

The participants' experience was impressive. They came from some of the "hottest" spots in the world—Colombia, Liberia, Nigeria, Yugoslavia, Kosovo, and the Philippines. They also came from "tepid" to "cooler" places like India, Pakistan, Haiti, Zambia, Malawi, Madagascar, and the United States. The discussions were rich as they uncovered what has worked, what we have learned, and of what we are proud. As we listened to stories and identified commonalities, we found that common themes emerged. These themes became the beginning of the Program Quality Statements for Peacebuilding, which gave that sector of the agency's work further definition, credibility, and recognition.

Dream

Energized from the process, the group was ready to dream a vision, definition, and defining principles for peacebuilding. Since our passion for the work made it hard to decide where the vision stopped and the definition began, in the end we decided to merge the vision and the definition into a statement of purpose. One group debated the wording of this, while the others turned the themes from the Discovery Phase into guiding principles. Round after round, discussion after debate, the product finally came clear. The group agreed that the statement of purpose and the guiding principles reflected their concept of peacebuilding. They were excited about how their dream was beginning to take shape and were anxious to explain it to others.

Design

Participants realized, however, that there were gaps between the vision and current CRS capacities and understandings. We needed concepts, tools, skills, and frameworks. Questions of planning and evaluation began to arise. Luckily, the Kroc Institute professors were there to provide assistance. Through a series of workshops and case-study presentations, they began to fill in the theoretical underpinnings for the experiences the group had been describing. The field and academic perspectives began to merge and make sense to each other. Program approaches became evident and new innovations appeared that could be tested.

Destiny

On the last day of the institute, we put it all together by creating a matrix for next steps and evaluation in both the short and long term. We identified steps that should take place in the next three to six months, in the next year, in three years, and in ten years. Through this exercise, it became apparent just how difficult it is to think concretely and strategically in both the short term and long term. There were many activities listed for the short term and very few that would take place in the next ten years. As peace-builders, we talk about "decade thinking," and yet it is clear that we must develop that capacity in ourselves first. Nonetheless, participants left the Summer Institute on Peacebuilding assured that they had taken the first step by putting together a statement of purpose and clear principles. They were confident that it would provide for agency guidelines for setting standards in peacebuilding, as well as the basis and premise for future peacebuilding practice.

Sharing the Vision

The final stage of the overall process was to get the statement and peace-building principles approved and to ensure buy-in from a wider audience of CRS practitioners and staff. Approval from the agency's Executive Management Team was needed to ensure the principles would officially become part of agency policy and guidelines. The Peacebuilding Working Group at headquarters was also called upon to offer feedback on the statement and principles developed by the summer institute participants (see Figure 4).

While it was important to have clear words that would guide the "peace-building world" at CRS, it was just as important to build capacity, provide training, and support ongoing peacebuilding efforts within the agency. The agency appointed regional advisers and program managers responsible for peacebuilding in many countries and regions. It also made a large financial commitment to support partners and other institutions involved in conflict transformation and peacebuilding work. A training process is currently underway to ensure peacebuilding training is available to staff and partners of Caritas Internationalis, including CRS.

The increased focus on peacebuilding within CRS has resulted in the need to ensure that programs and initiatives are kept to the highest standards and evaluation frameworks are developed to measure and show impact. The next phase of this ongoing learning process within CRS will be to develop these standards and frameworks based on the peacebuilding principles, as well as a clear strategy that will guide the future direction of peace-building in CRS.

Figure 4
CRS PEACEBUILDING

STATEMENT OF PURPOSE

Peacebuilding:

- is a process of changing unjust structures through right relationships.
- transforms the way people, communities, and societies live, heal, and structure their relationships to promote justice and peace.
- creates a space in which mutual trust, respect, and interdependence is fostered.

Within CRS, peacebuilding is:

- rooted in CRS guiding principles and engages the local church, religious institutions, organizations, and other actors in a mutual process of dialogue and transformation.
- is both a broad conceptual understanding that provides guidance for changing unjust systems and practices, as well as specific activities that change attitudes and behaviors to promote peace, tolerance, and reconciliation.
- essential for transforming the world through solidarity

PEACEBUILDING PRINCIPLES

Peacebuilding for CRS:

- responds to the root causes of violent conflict, including unjust relationships and structures, in addition to addressing its effects and symptoms.
- is based on long-term commitment.
- uses a comprehensive approach that focuses on the grassroots, while strategically engaging actors at middle range and top levels of leadership.
- requires an in-depth and participatory analysis.

(Continued on next page)

Figure 4, continued

- provides a methodology to achieve right relationships that should be integrated into all programming.

- strategically includes advocacy at local, national, and global levels to transform unjust structures and systems.

- builds upon indigenous nonviolent approaches to conflict transformation and reconciliation.

- is driven by community-defined needs and involves as many stakeholders as possible.

- is done through partners who represent the diversity of where we work and who share common values.

- strengthens and contributes to a vibrant civil society that promotes peace.

CONCLUSION

This story represents just a short segment of the CRS journey, which began in 1943, with the founding of the agency, and stretches into the future. This segment has shown us the need for clarity of vision as well as ongoing learning. Many people had invested a lot of time and energy to promote peacebuilding within the agency. It wasn't, however, until language describing peacebuilding was officially adopted at the World Summit that it became a programming reality. Since then, we have refined the vision by crafting principles and a statement of purpose. This has had a tremendous effect in harmonizing CRS' guiding vision throughout its ethnic and geographic diversity, and it has helped more people share in this vision.

Simultaneously, the vision has been continuously reshaped through experience and reflection. While CRS practice has been strongly influenced by its language (words create worlds), the language has been even more strongly influenced by our experience. It is a continuing learning cycle that is facilitated by storytelling and reflection. Hopefully the CRS story will be one of continuing to pursue the right to peace.

ENDNOTE

1. During the past one hundred years, papal statements, the Second Vatican Council, and conferences of bishops have addressed urgent issues that have both national and international reach, such as human rights, economic depression, development, political participation, and war and peace. These messages form the body of Catholic Social Teaching. They are not only church doctrine, but also provide individuals with a framework for action.

REFERENCES

Reilly, Annemarie, and Jaco Cilliers. 2000. "Champions for Peace: The Role of CRS in Times of Violent Conflict?" Discussion paper prepared for Catholic Relief Services World Summit, October 8–13, Tampa, Florida.

CRS. 2001. *Catholic Relief Services Strategic Framework FY 2002–FY 2006.* Catholic Relief Services, Baltimore, Maryland.

In reality, the decent multitudes, performing their ten thousand acts of kindness, vastly outnumber the very few depraved people in our midst. Thus, we have every reason to maintain our faith in human kindness and our hopes for the triumph of human potential, if only we can learn to harness this well-spring of unstinting goodness in nearly all of us.

STEPHEN J. GOULD

CONCLUSION:
THE PROMISE OF POSITIVE
APPROACHES TO PEACEBUILDING

Cynthia Sampson, Mohammed Abu-Nimer,
Claudia Liebler, and Diana Whitney

*T*here are few topics of study or practice as important in the twenty-first century as building peace. Few fields hold such significant promise for improving the quality of human life as does the peacebuilding field. As we acknowledge the importance of peacebuilding, we must also acknowledge the complexities and challenges. In our experience, there is no arena for learning and action that is more systemically multifaceted and globally entangled than that of peacebuilding.

As the chapters in this book show, the peacebuilding field is diverse beyond comparison. It ranges from social transformation and building cultures of peace, to conflict resolution among groups and nations, to healing and reconciliation among peoples, to designing organizations that live and do the work of peace. And the cultures in which it occurs range from indigenous to land-based agricultural to industrial to post-industrial technological. Peacebuilding spans ethnic identities, races, religions, nations, generations, and epochs in history, as well as the core values and deeply held beliefs of diverse groups and peoples. The contributions—or failings—of peacebuilders may be small, personal, and private, or broad, global, and glaringly public. Every aspect of human life is affected by the pursuit of peace or the absence of it.

Peacebuilding is also a high-risk endeavor. It is populated by people willing to put their lives, their identities, and their ways of life on the line in the service of equality, social justice, and peaceful coexistence. They are the authors of this book and people from whom we can learn much.

This book, their book, is a bold invitation. It challenges us all to reflect upon our work and to consider new approaches, positive approaches, to serving in some of the most complex human situations that exist. It is a call to rethink peacebuilding—what it is and how it is done—and to shift from focusing predominantly on the conflict, struggle, and suffering to also shining light on cooperation, coexistence, and visions for a better future. These chapters are full of ideas for making this shift, many of them grounded in experience, some grounded in theory—and most grounded in both. Building out from the foundational positive core, the building blocks of positive change, they suggest hopeful new possibilities for the practice of peacebuilding.

In these closing pages we begin by highlighting some of the most provocative innovations and insights found in this book. Next we share our conclusions on the most appropriate applications for positive approaches to peacebuilding and also the biggest challenges facing them, in both cases giving focused attention to Appreciative Inquiry. We move on to propose an agenda for further research and experimentation with positive approaches to peacebuilding, and we close with an invitation to the "freedoms" offered by positive approaches.

INSIGHTS INTO POSITIVE APPROACHES TO PEACEBUILDING

We are sometime truly going to see our life as positive, not negative, as made up of continuous willing, not of constraints and prohibition.

MARY PARKER FOLLETT

What are the leading discoveries, insights, and innovations revealed in these pages?

First, the surprises. We set out to present some new theoretical ideas and were surprised and delighted by all that we learned was already in play. We found many cases in which positive-core elements in conflict systems inspired and impelled constructive steps toward peace and new relationship; for example, how inspiring personal stories, exemplary role models, artistic productions, rituals, and even epochs in history have all provided positive images of healing, forgiveness, reconciliation, or coexistence to inspire the hope of others and motivate change.

We also saw how positive approaches to peacebuilding, often as integral to or an enhancement of other sound peacebuilding practices,

- create a safe environment in which people can claim a space and an identity through an equal opportunity to tell their stories and be heard and acknowledged;
- allow people to heal and grow and thrive after trauma and then to become a force in the healing of others;
- tap into internal sources of strength and give courage to move toward recognizing and knowing the adversary or *the Other;*
- create encounters that humanize the Other so that trust can be built and conflict narratives can be rewritten;
- reveal that an individual—each committed individual—can make a difference and has a vital role to play in realizing the justpeace ideal;

- give conflicting groups reason to hope and dream and believe that a different future is possible and that they have a role to play in realizing that future;

- discover new histories and tell new stories of humaneness, human connection, and cooperation for the common good;

- provide hospitality and compassionate caring for the individual who is struggling with some of life's greatest challenges and dilemmas;

- allow people to confront the limits of their faith and to stretch those limits based on new understandings;

- use artistic, symbolic, and metaphoric expression to bring about perceptual change and to reconcile and heal;

- foster an understanding of human interdependency, that even the smallest action can affect everyone;

- empower participants to be co-learners together and co-creators of a new kind of future.

APPLICABILITY OF POSITIVE APPROACHES IN PEACEBUILDING

Vision—it reaches beyond the thing that is, into the conception of what can be. Imagination gives you the picture. Vision gives you the impulse to make the picture your own.

ROBERT COLLIER

What have our case studies taught us about the applicability of positive approaches in peacebuilding—the where, when, and how of these approaches at their best? We come at the question of applicability here by steps, beginning with appreciative interviewing, the technique that appears most frequently in our case studies and with which there is the most experience in peacebuilding to date. We next look at the broader set of methods and techniques that we categorize together as appreciative processes. We conclude by looking at the applicability of Appreciative Inquiry as a full-fledged process, in other words, the 4-D Cycle used in its entirety.

Appreciative Interviewing

Appreciative interviewing is the practice of asking affirmative questions, whether one-on-one in a workshop or an Appreciative Inquiry Summit, by a team of interviewers fanning out across a community or a society, or in a cluster of villagers sitting under a tree—and whether or not it takes on the appearance of a formal "interview."

In our case studies, we've seen appreciative interviewing (though not always given that name) carried out in the strategic opportunities assessment of Guinea-Conakry; more than six-thousand-fold throughout Nagaland society; as part of the conflict transformation process of the United Methodist Church; proposed for the Chilean-Bolivian conflict both in the society at large and within the Appreciative Dialogue Workshop; in dialogue sessions with evangelical and gay Christians; with peacebuilders who have survived trauma; and at every major consultation and summit of the United Religions Initiative, as well as in its peacebuilding methodology and the global inquiry, Visions for Peace Among Religions.

In looking across these cases and reflecting particularly on the context of trauma healing, which is an arena of practice requiring the utmost sensitivity and care, it is our conclusion that appreciative interviewing can be integrated into conflict resolution and peacebuilding practices virtually anywhere, at any stage of the process, without risk of doing harm to people or the process. We share the caution of a number of our authors that imposing a *wholly* appreciative approach in a situation prematurely, when people and situations are still raw, would seem insensitive, silence voice, and undermine the healing effect of telling one's story; or, in the larger context of a conflict, might appear designed to—or have the effect of—pacifying opposition and locking in conflictual power dynamics. But provided there is no attempt to impose an exclusively positive approach or silence legitimate expression, almost any time is appropriate to help even—or perhaps especially—those people who are oppressed or whose lives are shattered to recognize their own strengths, resilience, courage, humanity, and will and capacity to survive. We concur with the conclusion reached by Nancy Good Sider in this volume:

> As a caregiver or friend, I am not doing harm in inquiring into what keeps survivors alive. . . . In fact, I would assert, I am hurting—or at least not helping, perhaps, by a sin of omission—when I lack the courage to ask some positive, life-giving, growth-eliciting questions. The commitment must be, however, to ask the questions in a welcoming, helpful, "hospitable" way that nudges toward a hopeful future, yet also understands that the answers may not yet be available. (page 307)

We would, in fact, urge that appreciative questioning be liberally integrated with other approaches as a means of counteracting discouragement, buoying hope, breathing life into difficult dialogue or negotiations, and consistently connecting parties with their own humanity and basic goodness, as well as the humanity and goodness of the Other. To do this requires only a simple yet powerful skill, that of asking affirmative questions and helping others to reframe their experience in a way that connects them to their hopes, dreams, and deepest longings beneath the problems, fear, distrust, and despair.

Other Forms of Appreciative Process

Our case studies have shown that, in addition to affirmative questioning, there are numerous other ways of accessing the positive-core elements in a conflict system, such as through scholarly research, dialogue processes, visioning exercises, rituals, and various forms of artistic expression. Examples from the cases include: Elise Boulding's methodology for visioning a nonviolent world; the storytelling project, "How a High School Changed the World"; a book documenting creative coexistence in Muslim Spain; the identification of individual strengths as part of an empowerment program in Zimbabwe; the sharing in each other's cultural rituals by indigenous and Indian Fijians, the personal storytelling and stage productions of Initiatives of Change; the dreams and action projects to be created out of the Visions for Peace Among Religions project; and aspects of training to be included in the forthcoming United Religions Initiative peacebuilding curriculum, including exercises for self-reflection.

As with appreciative interviewing, we believe that many of these types of appreciative process could easily be integrated with other conflict resolution and peacebuilding approaches at various stages along the way. Diverse ways of accessing the positive core, dreaming and visioning, practices for individual and group reflection, music and art, all may be used appropriately, judiciously, to help lift spirits and dispel discouragement, unleash creativity, foster a deeper level of human connection, invigorate dialogue or negotiations, heighten the sense of positive possibility, and/or orient thought and action toward a more hopeful future.

Appreciative Inquiry 4-D Cycle

We now consider the application in peacebuilding of Appreciative Inquiry (AI) in its entirety. Although as a field we are still in the earliest stages of experimenting with AI, it seems safe to say that the methodology has much to offer peacebuilding. The questions of the moment are how best and when to use it—and when, if ever, not to?

In chapter two we saw many examples of how the AI 4-D Cycle has been used in business, international development, and other kinds of social-change organizations. Our peacebuilding case studies in this book include four: Imagine Nagaland, which engaged stakeholders from across Naga society on topics related to socioeconomic development, peace, and good governance; the Appreciative Dialogue Workshop, an AI-based adaptation of the problem-solving workshop, proposed for the Chilean-Bolivian maritime conflict; and two organizational applications, the first involving global consensus building around organizational design and charter development for the United Religions Initiative, the second, as part of strategic planning for the Catholic Relief Services peacebuilding program.

In light of what we currently understand about how Appreciative Inquiry works, and in light of our authors' and our own cautions and concerns about applying AI in conflict situations that may be highly complex in substance and dynamics; internationalized, with numerous external actors exerting influences of various kinds; volatile or violent and potentially dangerous; traumatized; politically oppressive and unjust; and/or in which there are multiple ongoing peace and humanitarian initiatives, what are appropriate settings for which to consider the use of Appreciative Inquiry?

First, we firmly acknowledge that no one methodology or approach could possibly provide all that is necessary to transform destructive conflict and build a justpeace. The full panoply of diplomatic and unofficial, track-two efforts is needed to deal with the complex issues, dimensions, and dynamics that characterize many conflicts in today's globalized world. In putting forward some ideas about appropriate applications of Appreciative Inquiry (and other positive approaches), we do so with the recognition and expectation that these applications would virtually never be carried out as an exclusive response to conflict. Our purpose is to propose applications that appear most suitable for Appreciative Inquiry to make a contribution to progress toward peace as part of a larger array of initiatives in a given conflict situation.

That said, we believe Appreciative Inquiry has a contribution to make in the following types of settings:

As a process for building cultures of peace and practices of peaceful coexistence in communities or societies that have stabilized in a postconflict phase—or proactively, in societies of latent conflict, to prevent the outbreak of violence—and in which the conflict parties are ready to be in relationship and work together toward building a shared future. The case study in this volume of the Usulutan region of El Salvador, in which a different visioning methodology, that created by Elise Boulding, was used is an excellent example of this type of setting. The ability of Appreciative Inquiry to involve hundreds or thousands of people in Discovery Phase interviews and also in an AI Summit event or series of events particularly recommends it for this type of application. What Appreciative Inquiry adds to other visioning methodologies is the grounding of the future vision, through Discovery Phase interviews, in the reality of the lives and experiences of the people in the system who will be co-creating and living out that vision. This groundedness heightens the sense of positive possibility for the participants and energizes the process with the kind of excitement that comes from remembering and sharing stories of ourselves and our communities at their best.

To prime the pump of the peace process with the infusion of new energy and ideas, as in a pre-negotiation phase or at critical junctures in ongoing conflict resolution efforts. This, in effect, is the scenario we see in the Bolivia-Chile case study presented in this volume. The century-long conflict, still bitter, hostile, and far from resolved, but currently stalemated, seems ripe for the same type of infusion of creative new thinking that a problem-solving workshop would aspire to, only in this case drawing on a different set of energies and resources, namely, the positive-core elements in the two societies, in the interstate relationship, and in the lives of the participants. Particularly intriguing would be the scenario of moving from a workshop format of sixteen to twenty participants to a larger forum by way of an Appreciative Inquiry Summit, which might involve hundreds or even thousands of participants from the two governments and all major sectors of their civil societies.

To bring a positive-change focus and process to a selected aspect or phase of an ongoing peace process, possibly to deal with a topic that is relatively less politicized and therefore relatively more "safe." Here, several illustrations from our case studies are suggestive. An Appreciative Dialogue Workshop or an AI Summit (provided the safety of participants to gather in substantial numbers could be assured) might be employed, for example, to advance some specific aspect of the Bolivia-Chile relationship, such as educational, cultural, artistic, and/or athletic joint programs and exchanges. The hope would be that if progress were made in bringing the two societies into healthier and more productive interrelationship, over time this would bolster conflict resolution efforts at the diplomatic level.

In the case of Imagine Nagaland, we note that this project was not conceived as part of a peace process between Naga separatists and the Indian government nor among conflicting groups within the Naga society. It might more appropriately be described as a "development for peace" project, as its originating purpose was socioeconomic development with an emphasis on the welfare of children. As it turned out, however, the participants selected as affirmative topics for the AI Discovery, Dream, and Design phases: "unity, peace, and respect for all," "education and employment," "ecology and development," "equitable development," "respect for the rule of law," and "Nagaland of our future" (with the Delivery Phase contingent on locating necessary funding). So while peacebuilding was not the original intent of Imagine Nagaland, it might be expected that progress in these topic areas would also contribute to progress in the social and political conflicts in which the Naga people and their state have been embroiled for decades.[1]

To work in microcosm with a part of a larger conflict system, for example, in a particular locality or subregion. Here again, the purpose would be to use Appreciative Inquiry in a setting where there is a receptivity and willingness to do so—and also, perhaps, a higher degree of safety—in the hope of helping generate interest and momentum for engagement of the entire system at a later time, or at least to create a model that might be replicable at such time as a shift in the conflict dynamics made that possible.

To empower and develop individuals as peacebuilders, whether through counseling and coaching, training, or some type of small-group process. Appreciative Inquiry provides a systematic, structured process for significant self-discovery and personal transformation through connecting individuals with their own strengths and capacities; helping them recognize and value their past contributions and their future potential for contributing to the common good; instilling hope; building courage, confidence, and vision for becoming an agent of positive change; and through planning and initiating concrete actions within their communities or larger society. This process can be especially powerful and transformative for people who have endured suffering and victimhood through conflict.

In creating organizational designs and missions that are congruent with an organization's vision for peace and principles for peacebuilding. Of course, organizational development is the original home terrain of Appreciative Inquiry, and in our volume we have an exceptional example of this particular application. The United Religions Initiative (URI), using Appreciative Inquiry at every step of its development, established an institutional form and organizational culture that on a day-to-day basis lives the kinds of enduring daily interfaith cooperation and cultures of peace that the URI hopes to help create in the world. This is reflected in inclusive membership, shared leadership, whole-system participation, and local self-organization, all carried out within a framework of an agreed purpose and set of governing principles embodied in the URI charter.

We also saw how Appreciative Inquiry contributed to Catholic Relief Service's process of discernment and development of a peacebuilding purpose and principles that will help the agency more effectively work toward the vision of social justice and peace embodied in Catholic Social Teaching.

To work at communication and coordination across levels and sectors of peacebuilding practice and among different fields of practice. Because of its special capacity for accommodating and maximizing diverse participation, Appreciative Inquiry holds particular promise for facilitating communication and cooperation across levels, sectors, and fields of practice. The Discovery Phase would enable the sharing of assumptions, values, guiding principles, best practices, and success stories, with the remaining phases (Dream, Design, Delivery) serving as a continuum along which the participating groups or individuals could choose to move on a situational basis, depending upon the extent of their willingness and ability to translate their
increased communication and understanding into synergistic, cooper-

ative action within the opportunities and exigencies of any given on-the-ground situation.

CHALLENGES FACING POSITIVE APPROACHES IN PEACEBUILDING

Wanderer, there is no path. You lay a path in walking.

ANTONIO MACHADO

We focus mainly on Appreciative Inquiry in this section for several reasons. It is the most developed as a distinctive process of the positive approaches we have looked at in this volume, and it is the process with which there is the greatest body of experience, dating from the mid-1980s, in other sectors and around the globe. It is a whole-system approach and one that has been used in systems as large as communities and in complex organizational systems, sometimes spanning the globe. AI has a clearly defined set of assumptions and principles that can be examined for their relevance and validity in peacebuilding contexts.

In addition, the demands of appropriateness to context and of timing and participant willingness are higher with Appreciative Inquiry, for as we have already indicated, we believe that appreciative interviewing and other forms of appreciative process can be quite versatile as to how and when they are integrated into other conflict resolution and peacebuilding processes. To state it another way, while other appreciative processes can stand alone or augment other practices and approaches, the AI 4 D Cycle presumes a commitment to move through a phased process, and it also makes bigger claims for what it is intended to deliver, namely, whole-system change.

As we have touched on above, however, conflict systems are often far more complex and volatile than other human systems. They may be violent or have a history of violence; they may be structurally violent (i.e., unjust) and oppressive; populations may have suffered severe trauma and dislocation; and unless the conflict is localized in scope (e.g., within an organization, specific identity group, or small geographic locality), the stakeholders may include groups from across the society, plus other national, international, and/or transnational actors (e.g., neighboring countries, allies, and former colonial powers; regional and global multilateral organizations; multinational corporations; religious communities; terrorist networks; etc.). Gathering all the stakeholders together in a room might be daunting at best or otherwise unthinkable!

All of that said, the challenges facing Appreciative Inquiry, and positive approaches to peacebuilding more broadly, are not that much different from those facing peacebuilding practice in general, though perhaps taking on a slightly different coloration. Major challenges for all of peacebuilding include how to deal with social injustice, power disparities, and large-scale social transformation and systemic change. An associated challenge is that of transferring change from the individual or micro level to the macro or societal level. We know, for example, that participants of problem-solving workshops can face suspicion or even rejection upon returning to their identity groups following the workshop, a phenomenon known as the "reentry factor." The challenge for peacebuilding has often been how to accomplish meaningful, deep, authentic change on a larger scale within identity groups and involving larger segments of the society.

Many of the questions for Appreciative Inquiry are the same as they are for other system-wide interventions that might be used in peacebuilding: Can we get the right people in the room together? Do they represent all of the important stakeholders? Do we have the "critical yeast" among us—those people who can influence and leaven change in the larger society? Are the participants willing to speak to one another? How much is in their power to influence or control? Can plans and actions be developed that are truly implementable? How can others be brought on board?

We acknowledge all of these as significant challenges and have tried to think realistically in proposing applications for Appreciative Inquiry above, some of which seek to work with a manageable subset of the larger picture in a conflict system.

Other challenges facing positive approaches to peacebuilding, however, are closer to home. As in other fields where positive approaches have come into practice, there are biases in academic and professional circles and systems of funding toward focusing on pathology, pain, and human deficits. It is only recently that psychologists and other scholars and caregivers have begun to study factors and processes that lead to human health and well-being such as forgiveness, resilience, human strength and virtue, posttraumatic growth and thriving, altruism, and unlimited love. Donors are accustomed to funding programs based on needs assessment and conflict analysis, rather than the assessment of positive potential and possibility. There are also biases in the way many of us as individuals think and act on a daily basis. Our habits of looking for what is wrong or not working and responding accordingly may be deeply ingrained.

How we present these ideas is also a challenge in peacebuilding. Do Appreciative Inquiry and other positive approaches come across as naive, "feel good" methods or as approaches with potentially significant, even strategic, impact? Appreciative Inquiry is a method or approach to change, a means to an end, yet often we lead with talking about AI (the means) rather than with what we are trying to accomplish (the end). Whether we cast Appreciative Inquiry in a supporting role or give it central billing is also important. In most conflict situations it would be unrealistic and unwise to propose that Appreciative Inquiry alone could carry the day in transforming the conflict. In some circumstances the most effective AI work can be done without calling it a methodology and giving it a name. This is not for the purpose of deceiving, but to preserve the focus of the process on meeting the interests and needs of the group and not on a preoccupation with the technology for getting there.

This discussion of challenges naturally leads us to consider the kinds of research and experimentation that will help clarify the appropriate uses of positive approaches, as well as ways of innovating, adapting, and extending their applications.

AN AGENDA FOR RESEARCH AND EXPERIMENTATION

don't establish the
boundaries
first,
the squares, triangles,
boxes
of preconceived
possibility,
and then
pour
life into them, trimming
off left-over edges,
ending potential

A. R. AMMONS

There are many possible approaches that could be taken to take to research and experimentation with positive approaches to peacebuilding. We present but an initial set of ideas here and take as our point of departure some research conducted on appreciative approaches in the field with the most experience in using them, organizational development.

In work on organizational cultures, Frank Barrett (1996) has identified four competencies that are created by appreciative learning cultures: *affirmative competence,* which is the capacity to focus on what the group has done well in the past and is doing well in the present; *generative competence,* which is a capacity to allow group members to experience the impact of their contribution towards a higher purpose; *expansive competence,* which is the ability to go beyond familiar ways of thinking; and *collaborative competence,* which is the power of dialogue to transform systems. This set of competencies suggests action research into several possible ways of developing appreciative strategies for peacebuilding:

The first would be to carry out inquiry into these competencies as positive-core elements in a conflict system, in other words, to uncover parables, stories, songs, poems, rituals, and experiences that speak to the existence of these competencies as peace-promoting capacities in the system. Strategies would then be developed to mobilize these competencies more fully in the society as a contribution toward the development of cultures of peace. The inquiry data might be used as the foundation for completing a 4-D Cycle to envision, design, and implement system change; or training might be provided in appreciative learning and leadership that is contextualized to the local culture and meaning structure, among other possibilities.

Another possibility would be to develop indicators and mechanisms for identifying and assessing the practice of these competencies as a means of evaluating—for research purposes and for funders—both personnel and the impact and success of initiatives in positive approaches to peacebuilding. In other words, the efficacy of positive approaches would be assessed in part by their ability to develop appreciative competencies in the social system.

Turning now to some of the challenges to positive approaches to peacebuilding identified above, a number of questions will need to be addressed by scholars and practitioners to advance the understanding of when and where and how best to integrate positive approaches into peacebuilding. Two questions relate to the power dynamics in the conflict and asymmetric power relationships:

The first is, how to address the tension between seeking justice and managing the exploration of positive interaction between conflicting communities. How can a community with a historic sense of injustice adopt a positive lens in examining its relationship with the Other, when such a shift can be interpreted as cooptation or surrender? A related question is, how to prevent the common tendency of those in the more powerful position to use any affirmative expression in a conflict by the weaker party to secure or reestablish their domination or to argue for locking in status quo?

Another question noted above is how to construct large-scale initiatives to mobilize large segments of the population in a conflict area. Appreciative Inquiry has the capacity to engage large systems in a single project such as the AI Summit, but how can such a design best be implemented in a peacebuilding context to move the silent majority, which often allows radical minorities to dictate the political agenda and prevent peaceful resolution?

A third question is how positive approaches might be used to link levels and sectors and types of peacebuilding practice, such as linking grassroots and micro-level interventions with policy makers and vice versa, ensuring that progressive policies or agreements in the peace process are carried out at the grassroots level and among groups that are disconnected from power elites. Or, can wide social processes based on an AI framework be beneficial in making missing linkages in peacebuilding; for example, can they translate thousands of peacebuilding workshops conducted over a decade into policy or into a social movement for peace?

Both field-oriented research and on-the-ground innovation are needed to address these types of questions and advance the understanding and effectiveness of positive approaches to peacebuilding. Still further possibilities for scholarly or action research include:

- Research and document other examples of positive approaches to peacebuilding, particularly by those found in indigenous cultures and those carried out by local practitioners and NGOs, including the use of ritual, storytelling, music, and art.
- Create a compilation of affirmative questions for peacebuilding and try them out in various settings.
- Conduct systematic research into the most conducive conditions for Appreciative Inquiry to be effective in peacebuilding.
- Study the long-term impacts of Appreciative Inquiry applications in peacebuilding.
- Create a learning forum in which peacebuilders and development practitioners can come together to share their experiences with positive approaches.
- Create a set of pilot projects employing positive approaches as part of an action-learning program and facilitate exchange and learning among the implementers.
- Study the question of timing in the application of positive approaches in ongoing conflict resolution and peacebuilding processes.
- Pilot test a cross-generational inquiry, with children interviewing their elders about a time when they lived in peace.
- Pilot test inquiry carried out by pairs of interviewers coming from different sides in the conflict who interview people from all sides in the conflict.
- Study the styles and impact of appreciative leadership, including peacebuilders; collect and analyze stories of what they did, how they acted, and the results achieved.
- Use Appreciative Inquiry to create an approach to interfield collaboration and conduct in-country pilot projects.

AN INVITATION TO "FREEDOMS"

Instead of looking for safety in numbers,
and noting those who feel like allies or fellow travelers,
what might we create if we seek to discover
those insights that are most different from ours?
What if, at least occasionally, we came together
in order to change our minds?

MARGARET WHEATLEY

Practitioner-scholars in the organizational development field have identified six freedoms that participants in Appreciative Inquiry processes commonly associate with the liberation of power—or the journey from oppression to power—in organizations (Whitney and Trosten-Bloom 2003, 237–251). They are:

- the freedom to be known in relationship
- the freedom to be heard
- the freedom to dream in community
- the freedom to choose to contribute
- the freedom to act with support
- the freedom to be positive

It is too soon to know whether these same freedoms—or possibly new ones—will be experienced by participants in peacebuilding contexts. But they are powerfully evocative of the kinds of possibilities that may await the intrepid explorer in peacebuilding, along with the great challenges.

Let us close by sharing our hopes and dreams—for you, for us together, for our fields, and for the future of this work:

We hope that through this book, the spirit of experimentation and risk taking are *ignited!*

We hope this book will provoke peacebuilding practitioners and scholars to question their frameworks and adjust their methods—that they will integrate positive approaches in their work, that many new action-research projects will be spawned. We hope that positive approaches will become an integral part of peacebuilding training, practice, and research.

We hope that practitioners and scholars of Appreciative Inquiry, likewise, are touched and inspired by the possibilities of using AI in the peacebuilding arena, and that new theory-building and practice will be developed by peacebuilders and AI practitioners working together. We hope that assumptions will be challenged and new ones will emerge, with new theories coming out of our shared experience. We hope that mutual respect and joint learning are triggered by this cross-field collaboration and that many more such partnerships of scholarship and practice will emerge.

We hope this book will stimulate the next step of developing concrete guides on how to integrate positive approaches in the various processes of conflict resolution such as dialogue, mediation, arbitration, and problem solving.

We hope this book will encourage funders to create new categories for granting in positive approaches to peacebuilding.

We hope evaluators of peacebuilding projects will find ways to recognize, value, and assess the impact of processes that create hope, positive energy, a heightened sense of possibility, the courage and confidence to change, and the realization of the positive potential of people and groups locked in conflicts.

And now, our hopes reside in you—that you may find these ideas useful; that they will capture your imagination; that you will apply them and go far beyond them; that you will join these authors in realizing the promise of positive approaches to peacebuilding; that you will seek and find new freedoms in peacebuilding.

ENDNOTE

1. It bears noting, however, that Imagine Nagaland did not proceed entirely without controversy, having raised the suspicions of the Naga Peoples Movement for Human Rights, which charged inadequate consultation and representation of the Naga people, lack of transparency, and interference of outside parties. This controversy points up the considerable challenges facing AI applications in complex situations of social conflict in which it may be much more difficult to identify and win the trust and engagement of all stakeholder groups.

REFERENCES

Barrett, Frank J. 1996. "Creating Appreciative Learning Cultures." *Organizational Dynamics* 4 (autumn), pp. 36–44.

Whitney, Diana, and Amanda Trosten-Bloom. 2003. *The Power of Appreciative Inquiry: A Practical Guide to Positive Change.* San Francisco: Berrett-Koehler.

One of the most important roles we can play individually and collectively is to create an opening, or to "listen" to the implicate order unfolding, and then to create dreams, visions, and stories that we sense at our center want to happen—that, as Buber said, "want to be actualized ... with human spirit and human deed."

JOSEPH JAWORSKI

CONTRIBUTORS

MOHAMMED ABU-NIMER is associate professor of international peace and conflict resolution at American University, where he also directs the Summer Peacebuilding and Development Institute and the *Journal for Peacebuilding and Development*. An experienced conflict resolution practitioner, Dr. Abu-Nimer has conducted workshops on conflict resolution, interethnic and interreligious dialogue, diversity, and multiculturalism in the Middle East, United States, Europe, Africa, and Asia. His research focuses on interethnic and intercultural dialogue, religious and interreligious peacebuilding, and the Middle East. He has published many articles and several books, most recently *Nonviolence and Peacebuilding in Islam: Theory and Practice*. He holds a Ph.D. in conflict analysis and resolution from George Mason University.

ELISE BOULDING is professor emerita of sociology at Dartmouth College. A longtime activist in peace and global issues, she has served as secretary-general of the International Peace Research Association and as international chair of the Women's International League for Peace and Freedom. Among her many publications are *Building a Global Civic Culture: Education for an Interdependent World; Building Peace in the Middle East: Challenges for States and Civil Society;* and *Cultures of Peace: The Hidden Side of History*.

MARK CHUPP is program manager of the Civic Engagement Initiative at the Center for Neighborhood Development, Cleveland State University, where he is responsible for promoting civic engagement, conflict transformation, and community organizing. As a community organizer and action-research practitioner, he previously founded a mediation and violence prevention organization. Dr. Chupp has lived and consulted in numerous Latin American countries and served as the primary consultant in the development of a local zone of peace in El Salvador. He holds a master of social work degree from the University of Michigan and a Ph.D. in social welfare from Case Western Reserve University.

JACO CILLIERS, a South African, is deputy regional director for justice and solidarity for Catholic Relief Services in southern Africa. He worked for two years in Bosnia-Herzegovina as conflict resolution program manager for the United Methodist Committee on Relief. His publications include "Building Bridges for Interfaith Dialogue" and "Organizing Conflict Resolution Interventions in Situations of Rapid Change." Dr. Cilliers holds a bachelor of arts (cum laude) and a bachelor of arts honors (cum laude) from the University of Port Elizabeth, and a master of science and Ph.D. in conflict analysis and resolution from George Mason University.

DAVID COOPERRIDER is associate professor of organizational behavior and chair of the SIGMA Program for Human Cooperation and Global Action at the Weatherhead School of Management, Case Western Reserve University. He is past president of the National Academy of Management's Division of Organization Development and a cofounder of the Taos Institute. Dr. Cooperrider has served as a consultant to a wide variety of businesses and social-change organizations. He is a recipient of both the Innovation and Best Paper of the Year awards at the Academy of Management, and numerous of his clients have received awards for their work with Appreciative Inquiry. His most recent books include *Appreciative Inquiry* (with Diana Whitney); *No Limits to Cooperation: The Organization Dimensions of Global Change* (with Jane Dutton); and *Organizational Courage and Executive Wisdom* and *Appreciative Management and Leadership* (both with Suresh Srivastva).

PETER DELAHAYE is director of the Brussels office of the United Nations Children's Fund (UNICEF). He formerly served as UNICEF deputy director (operations) in India. He has spent twenty-three years serving the organization in different managerial positions, including five years in India. Mr. Delahaye is an experienced facilitator and teaches management excellence, risk and control self-assessment, team building, and group dynamics. He has used Appreciative Inquiry extensively within UNICEF. Mr. Delahaye can be reached at pdelahaye@unicef.org.

TAMRA PEARSON D'ESTRÉE is Henry R. Luce Professor of Conflict Resolution at the University of Denver. She has also held appointments at the Institute for Conflict Analysis and Resolution, George Mason University, and the Psychology Department, University of Arizona. Her research interests lie at the intersection of conflict resolution and social psychology, including work on social identity, intergroup relations, and conflict resolution processes, as well as on evaluation research. Dr. d'Estrée is author of *Braving the Currents: Evaluating Conflict Resolution in the River Basins of the American West*, as well as several chapters and articles in interdisciplinary journals. She has facilitated trainings and interactive problem-solving workshops in intercommunal contexts, including Israel-Palestine, Ethiopia, and in U.S. intertribal disputes, and she has directed projects aimed at conflict resolution capacity- and institution building in settings of ethnic conflict.

She holds a Ph.D. in social psychology from Harvard University.

SAM GBAYDEE DOE is executive director of the West Africa Network for Peacebuilding. He is also an instructor with the Caux Scholars Program in Switzerland and the Summer Peacebuilding Institute of Eastern Mennonite University. Mr. Doe is vice-chair of the Forum on Early Warning and Early Response, a global network of conflict prevention practitioners and academics, and a member of the International Council on Conflict Resolution of the Carter Center. In West Africa, Mr. Doe is a leader in the revival of indigenous conflict prevention systems, from which he is developing his proventive peacebuilding paradigm. He holds a master of arts in conflict transformation from Eastern Mennonite University.

SCOTT D. FISHER is a management consultant specializing in change management and organization development. He has used the Appreciative Inquiry methodology extensively within several Fortune 500 companies, nonprofit organizations, and international nongovernmental organizations to carry out large-scale transformation and economic development initiatives. Mr. Fisher is a graduate of Vanderbilt University with a degree in human and organization development.

CHARLES GIBBS is executive director of the United Religions Initiative. He formerly served as rector of the Episcopal Church of the Incarnation in San Francisco and as pastor and executive director of the San Rafael Canal Ministry, an interfaith, multicultural ministry for immigrants and refugees in San Rafael, California. Rev. Gibbs was a presenter and participant at the Parliament of the World's Religions in Cape Town, South Africa, in 1999; an invited guest at the World Millennium Peace Summit of Religious and Spiritual Leaders at the United Nations in 2000; and he served as a resource person for the 2001 Leadership Summit for the United States Navy. A recent publication is *Birth of a Global Community: Appreciative Inquiry as Midwife for the United Religions Initiative* (with Sally Mahé). Rev. Gibbs holds a master of divinity degree from the Church Divinity School of the Pacific and a master of arts from the University of Minnesota.

PAULA GREEN is founder-director of the Karuna Center for Peacebuilding, a U.S.-based organization active in international peacebuilding. She is also a professor of conflict transformation at the School for International Training, where she created and directs the CONTACT Program (Conflict Transformation Across Cultures), which includes a summer institute, distance-learning certificate programs, and annual seminars in Africa. Calling on her skills as a psychologist, Dr. Green teaches peacebuilding and facilitates intercommunal dialogue in war-threatened or war-recovering countries in the Middle East, Asia, Africa, and Eastern Europe. She is a coeditor of *Psychology and Social Responsibility: Facing Global Challenges* (with Sylvia Staub)

and has authored chapters and professional articles published in the United States and abroad. She holds an Ed.D. in counseling psychology from Boston University.

PEGGY GREEN, director of First Be Reconciled, has facilitated dialogue on issues of abortion, race and class, and homosexuality and biblical inerrancy. Through dialogue and storytelling, while training "enemies" in the art of co-facilitation, she helps traditional adversaries build trust, build leadership teams, and model peace. Ms. Green promotes the work of reconciliation as a writer, public speaker, and video producer. She holds a master of divinity degree from the Pacific School of Religion. Ms. Green can be reached at Peggy@FirstBeReconciled.org.

ROBIN GULICK is a peacebuilding specialist with Catholic Relief Services, where she has been a member of the Program Quality and Support Department for three years. Her interests include peacebuilding and development and the role of religious actors in peacebuilding. She holds a master of science in conflict analysis and resolution from George Mason University and a bachelor of arts in mass communication from James Madison University.

BARBARA HARTFORD is peacebuilding program manager with the United Religions Initiative. She formerly developed and led international group travel with Cross-Cultural Journeys for the Institute of Noetic Sciences; served as volunteer coordinator and public relations manager for Grace Cathedral in San Francisco; and served as financial manager and then human resources director for The Hunger Project. Ms. Hartford has a total of twenty-three years experience with California nonprofit management, including finance, operations management, public relations, human resources, publications, and in volunteer and intern recruitment and management. She has broad experience in events production and publications production and distribution. She holds a bachelor of arts from Tufts University; is trained in mediation and cross-cultural conflict resolution; and has received conflict transformation training from Eastern Mennonite University's Summer Peacebuilding Institute.

MICHAEL HENDERSON is an English journalist and broadcaster. He is the author of nine books including *Forgiveness: Breaking the Chain of Hate; The Forgiveness Factor;* and *All Her Paths Are Peace.* Mr. Henderson has worked in thirty countries and recently returned to Britain after twenty-two years in the United States. In Portland, he served as president of the English-Speaking Union and of the World Affairs Council of Oregon and on the board of the Oregon United Nations Association. He was also a founder member of Oregon Uniting, a coalition for racial understanding. He has for more than fifty years been associated with Initiatives of Change. Mr. Henderson can be reached at michaeldhenderson@compuserve.com (see also www.michaelhenderson.org.uk).

MEG KINGHORN was senior technical advisor for partnership, capacity building, and civil society at Catholic Relief Services from 1999 to 2002. She currently is director of the Impact Alliance, a global capacity-building network at Pact, in Washington, D.C. Her experience in program development and management and in capacity building comes from overseas posts in the Pacific, Eastern Europe, and the Middle East with the Peace Corps, Save the Children, and the United Nations Development Programme. She has also worked on policy advocacy and partnership with InterAction. She holds a master of arts in intercultural management from the School for International Training and a bachelor of science in social work from the Rochester Institute of Technology.

BHARAT KRISHNAN is an independent management adviser and facilitator based in New Delhi, India. With a background in engineering and a postgraduate degree in management, he has twenty-one years of experience consulting in the corporate and noncorporate sectors. He is currently working with the United Nations Children's Fund (UNICEF) in East Africa and India as a lead facilitator for developing in-house capacity for a human-rights approach to programming. He is also the lead facilitator for a major project in South Asia for Save the Children Alliance, introducing for the first time a child-rights programming approach for combating trafficking of children and women. He is an experienced team coach and facilitator and has applied Appreciative Inquiry extensively in the field of development.

JOHN PAUL LEDERACH is professor of international peacebuilding at the Joan B. Kroc Institute for International Peace Studies at the University of Notre Dame, and a distinguished scholar at the Conflict Transformation Program of Eastern Mennonite University. He works extensively as a practitioner in conciliation processes in Latin America, Africa, and Central Asia. Dr. Lederach is widely known for the development of elicitive approaches to conflict transformation and the design and implementation of integrative and strategic approaches to peacebuilding. He is author of twelve books, including *Building Peace: Sustainable Reconciliation in Divided Societies; Preparing for Peace: Conflict Transformation Across Cultures;* and *The Journey Toward Reconciliation.*

CLAUDIA LIEBLER has been involved with international development for thirty years, with experience in twenty-eight countries in

Europe, Africa, Asia, and Latin America. She is known as one of a small number of professionals in the world who specialize in innovative approaches to capacity building. She has worked with professionals from many disciplines including peacebuilding, education, health, community development, micro-enterprise, and agricultural extension. As the project director and co-founder of the Global Excellence in Management (GEM) Initiative, she was recently on the staff of Case Western Reserve University's Weatherhead School of Management in the doctoral department of organizational behavior. For seven years, the GEM Initiative provided capacity building for non-governmental organizations worldwide, using Appreciative Inquiry and other assets-based methodologies to promote individual, organizational, and community change.

MARK CONRAD MANCAO is director of administration of the JUSTPEACE Center for Mediation and Conflict Transformation. A Roman Catholic and a longtime friend of The United Methodist Church, he formerly worked with the denomination's agency for ecumenical and interreligious relationships. He began living and working in the "appreciative mode" while interning with the Banana Kelly Community Development Organization in South Bronx, New York City, where Appreciative Inquiry has had a significant positive impact. He formerly served as co-coordinator of the Focus Group on Religion and Spiritualities for the 1999 Hague Appeal for Peace Conference. Mr. Mancao holds master's degrees from Union Theological Seminary and the Columbia University School of Social Work, and he received training in mediation and collaborative negotiation from the International Center for Collaboration and Conflict Resolution at Columbia University Teachers College.

ERIN McCANDLESS is a scholar and practitioner specializing in peace-building and development and a founder and co-executive editor of the *Journal of Peacebuilding and Development*. She consults widely with civic and intergovernmental organizations in the areas of conflict prevention and transformation, human development, and democratization. A doctoral candidate at American University, Ms. McCandless currently resides in Zimbabwe where she is a research fellow at the Institute for Development Studies, University of Zimbabwe, and is conducting field research into the role and impact of social movements in social, political, and economic transformation. She was a Peace Scholar Fellow of the United States Institute of Peace in 2002–2003.

JOSEPH MONTVILLE is a senior associate and founder of the former preventive diplomacy program at the Center for Strategic and

International Studies in Washington, D.C. He did graduate work at Harvard University and Columbia University and spent twenty-three years as a diplomat in the Middle East, North Africa, and at the Department of State. He is editor of *Conflict and Peacemaking in Multiethnic Societies* and coeditor of *The Psychodynamics of International Relationships* (with Vamik Volkan and Demetrios Julius).

THOMAS W. PORTER, JR., is executive director of the JUSTPEACE Center for Mediation and Conflict Transformation. He is an ordained elder and served twenty-three years as chancellor of the New England Conference of The United Methodist Church. Mr. Porter was a founding partner of the trial firm of Melick & Porter LLP and has been a trial lawyer since 1974, representing religious institutions, universities, hospitals, professionals, nonprofit organizations, and others. He is a member of the Journal of Law and Religion, which he chaired from 1989 to 2001. Mr. Porter was a lecturer and trainer in conflict transformation theory and skills at Union Theological Seminary. He was educated at Yale University and also holds a master of divinity degree from Union Theological Seminary and J.D. degree from Boston University Law School. He studied mediation at Harvard Law School and Eastern Mennonite University.

AMELA PULJEK-SHANK is co-country representative with the Mennonite Central Committee doing peacebuilding work in Bosnia-Herzegovina. A native of Jajce, Bosnia-Herzegovina, she also worked with relief and peacebuilding projects in 1994–1996, during and immediately following the war in that country. She has worked as a facilitator and trainer with Seeds of Peace and with the STAR Project (Seminars on Trauma Awareness and Recovery) for religious leaders at Eastern Mennonite University. She holds a master of arts in conflict transformation from Eastern Mennonite University.

RANDY PULJEK-SHANK is co-country representative with the Mennonite Central Committee doing peacebuilding work in Bosnia-Herzegovina, where he also formerly worked in 1995–1996. Since 1999 he has taught classes in social movements and been a trainer and consultant to peacebuilding projects in Croatia, Serbia, and Bosnia-Herzegovina. He holds a master of arts in conflict transformation from Eastern Mennonite University.

MAURICIO RÍOS, a native of the Andean region of Bolivia, is a communications specialist with a focus on international affairs and conflict transformation. He is currently consulting for nongovernmental organizations and corporations in Washington D.C. Mr. Ríos is interested in the role of the media as an instrument for both conflict prevention and resolution, as well as in alternative processes of dialogue and reconciliation for intra- and inter-state conflicts. He has completed studies in journalism, diplomacy, and international relations, and he holds a master of arts in international peace and conflict resolution from American University.

CYNTHIA SAMPSON is president of Peace Discovery Initiatives, a nonprofit organization that works in religious and interreligious peacebuilding and positive approaches to peacebuilding. She is an author and coeditor of *From the Ground Up: Mennonite Contributions to International Peacebuilding* (with John Paul Lederach) and an author and coeditor of *Religion, The Missing Dimension of Statecraft* (with Douglas Johnston). Ms. Sampson formerly worked with the Conflict Transformation Program of Eastern Mennonite University, the World Conference on Religion and Peace, and as an editor on foreign affairs at the *Christian Science Monitor*. She holds a master of international affairs degree from Columbia University and a master of science in environmental communications from the University of Wisconsin.

MARY HOPE SCHWOEBEL has more than twenty years' experience in the fields of peacebuilding and development, with five years spent in South America and six years in Africa. She currently serves as technical director for the U.S. Agency for International Development's Greater Horn of Africa Peacebuilding project with Management Systems International. She also teaches in the Program for Justice and Peace at Georgetown University. She holds a master in international development degree from the University of California, Davis, and is a doctoral candidate in conflict analysis and resolution at George Mason University.

NANCY GOOD SIDER is an assistant professor in the Conflict Transformation Program at Eastern Mennonite University, where she teaches courses in trauma healing and recovery. A licensed clinical social worker, she is a founding partner of Newman Avenue Associates, where she works as a counselor, mediator, and organizational consultant. Ms. Sider has been a practitioner for more than twenty-five years of family and community-based practice, currently specializing in trauma recovery and race, gender, and diversity-based interventions. She has worked to develop trauma-healing strategies in the United States and in several international contexts. She holds a master of social work degree from Virginia Commonwealth University and is currently pursuing doctoral studies with The Union Institute and University.

HERM WEAVER is associate professor of psychology at Eastern Mennonite University, where his primary teaching areas are in counseling and developmental psychology. His most recent research efforts focus on examining the role of the creative arts in the experience of reconciliation. Dr.

Weaver proposes viewing the process of reconciliation as primarily a creative process that is not given to the guidelines or constraints of linear thinking and strategies. He also has extensive experience in construction and is a singer-songwriter who has been telling stories with his music to a wide range of audiences for several decades.

ANASTASIA WHITE grew up in the Wilgespruit Fellowship Centre, a faith-based community active in the anti-apartheid movement in South Africa. She has worked in conflict resolution and reconciliation in South Africa with the Institute for a Democratic Alternative for South Africa, the Independent Electoral Commission, and the Ministry of Safety and Security. She currently works as a consultant to the nonprofit and corporate sectors in organizational design and human-resource dynamics. Ms. White is a doctoral candidate in organizational behavior at Case Western Reserve University, where her focus of study is on developing new theories and approaches to resolving identity-based conflicts.

DIANA WHITNEY is president of the Corporation for Positive Change, a consulting firm dedicated to the creation of appreciative organizations capable of balancing and sustaining economic viability and social well-being. She is a founder and director of the Taos Institute, a nonprofit organization focused on furthering the theory and practice of social constructionism for the benefit of businesses, communities, and families around the globe. Dr. Whitney is an internationally recognized consultant, speaker, and thought leader on the subjects of Appreciative Inquiry, positive change, appreciative leadership, and spirituality at work. She teaches and consults with businesses, healthcare associations, and nongovernmental organizations in the Americas, Europe, and Asia. She is a coauthor and coeditor of nine books and numerous articles, most recently *The Power of Appreciative Inquiry* (with Amanda Trosten-Bloom). Dr. Whitney is a distinguished consulting faculty member at the Saybrook Graduate School and Research Center and a World Business Academy Fellow.

HEIDI PAULSON WINDER is the former program coordinator of the preventive diplomacy program at the Center for Strategic and International Studies. She holds a master of theological studies degree from Harvard Divinity School and a bachelor of arts in religion from Principia College.

If you want to build a ship, then don't drum up men to gather wood, give orders, and divide the work. Rather, teach them to yearn for the far and endless sea.

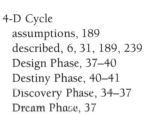

INDEX